Women Shaping Islam

Women Shaping Islam

Indonesian Women Reading the Qur'an

PIETERNELLA VAN DOORN-HARDER

University of Illinois Press

URBANA AND CHICAGO

♾ This book is printed on acid-free paper.

Library of Congress Cataloging-in-Publication Data
Doorn-Harder, Pieternella van, 1956–
Women shaping Islam: reading the Quran in Indonesia/ Pieternella
van Doorn-Harder.
    p.   cm.
Includes bibliographical references and index.
ISBN-13: 978-0-252-03077-2 (cloth: alk. paper)
ISBN-10: 0-252-03077-x (cloth: alk. paper)
ISBN-13: 978-0-252-07317-5 (pbk.: alk. paper)
ISBN-10: 0-252-07317-7 (pbk.: alk. paper)
1. Islam—Indonesia. 2. Women and religion—Indonesia.
3. Women in Islam—Indonesia. 4. Women—Religious life—Indonesia.
I. Title.
BP63.I5D66   2006
297.082'09598—dc22   2005035182

Let there arise out of you
A band of people
Inviting to all that is good,
Enjoining what is right,
And forbidding what is wrong

—Qur'an 3:104
    Adage of Muhammadiyah
    and Nahdlatul Ulama

Contents

Acknowledgments   ix

Introduction   1

PART 1: INDONESIAN ISLAMIC LANDSCAPES

1. Discussing Islam, Discussing Gender   27

2. Competing in Goodness: Muhammadiyah and Nahdlatul Ulama   50

PART 2: WOMEN OF MUHAMMADIYAH

3. 'Aisyiyah's Jihad   87

4. Nurturing the Future: Nasyiatul 'Aisyiyah   131

PART 3: WOMEN OF NAHDLATUL ULAMA

5. Tradition Revisited: The Pesantren   165

6. Tradition in Action: Muslimat NU   203

7. Post-Tradition: NU Activists   237

Conclusion   261

Notes   269

Glossary   293

Bibliography   297

Index   317

Acknowledgments

The list of people to thank is nearly endless, especially in Indonesia. Of course I am deeply grateful to all the women leaders involved in the organizations described. We met at seminars around the world and, over time, some of them became colleagues and friends. I am grateful to Mrs. Sinta Nuriyah Abdurrahman Wahid and her husband Abdurrahman Wahid for the interviews they granted me. In the 'Aisyiyah organization I thank Ibu Uswatun, Ibu Djazman, Dr. Suslianingsi, Prof. Chamamah Suratno, Prof. Shafi'i Ma'arif, and the many women and men who received me in their homes and mosques. I spent many hours discussing and visiting with NA members Rahmawati Husain, Siti Ruhaini, and Terias Setiyawati. Muslimat NU Lily Zakiyah Munir with her sister and mother introduced me to the world of the *pesantren;* I fondly remember the hospitality and generosity of *pesantren* leaders Ibu Siti and Ibu Fatma. Ibu Aisyah Hamid Baidlowi and Ibu Umroh Mahfudzoh took time from their busy duties in Parliament, while the energy and creativity of the now-retired Ibu Asmah Sjachruni and her younger counterpart Masrucha both made an indelible impression on me. Lies Marcoes-Natsir, Musda Muliah, Ciciek Farhah, and Noer Cholidah Badrus are just a few of the many women in whose debt I will remain. Without the patient help of Samsuri, Zainul Abbas, Siti Zaenab, and Saiful I would never have managed to gather the material.

Among the scholars with whom at various points I brainstormed about the book's content I can only mention a few: MaryJo DelVecchio Good, Amin Abdullah, Lance Castle, Greg Fealy, Nancy Smith-Hefner, Bob Hefner, John Bowen, Tore Lindholm, Dag Kaspersen, and Franz Magnis-Suseno, who commented on the entire manuscript. Sadly our dear colleague Herb Feith "met his maker on his bike" before the book was finished.

In the USA, I owe much thanks and gratitude to Constance Buchanan from the Ford Foundation, who generously awarded me a grant to work on the manuscript. Valparaiso University's travel funds allowed me to make several trips back to update the material, and a summer at the Institute for Human Rights Studies at Oslo University helped finish the book.

Kathleen Mullen carefully corrected my Dutch English; colleagues Kari Vogt, Marilynn Uehling, Ted Ludwig, and Ben Leese spent many hours commenting on the manuscript. My debt to them will never end. Ursula King and Rita Gross saw great promise in the topic and their encouragement helped finish this project.

Finally I thank Kerry Callahan and Rebecca Crist of the University of Illinois Press for their enthusiasm and support. The patient correction work of the anonymous editors was impressive.

My children Elizabeth and Hannah enjoyed and at times suffered through the many field trips, while my husband Paul graciously accepted the frequent absences.

Several topics discussed in the book have been published or are forthcoming in shorter articles.

Part of the material was read during scholarly meetings and some was used in articles. NU-related topics appeared in "Indonesian Muslim Women Creating Justice," *Nordic Journal of Human Rights* (Spring 2003). The published public lecture "Woorden Wegen, Vrouwelijke Schriftuitleggers van de Qur'an" (Weighing words, female interpreters of the Qur'an) (Amsterdam: Free University, 2004), and the article "Frauen Lesen den Koran" (Women reading the Qur'an) (in *Concilium, Internationale Zeitschrift für Theologie*, 12:5 [2005], 507–516) discussed the influence of women's interpretations on the Muslim holy texts. The book chapter "Re-considering Authority: Indonesian *Fiqh* Texts about Women" represents part of the discussion about new *fiqh* readings and will appear in R. Michael Feener and Mark Cammack's *Islamic Law in Modern Indonesia: Ideas and Institutions*, to be published by Harvard University Press.

My discussions about 'Aisyiyah were elaborated in "Mohammadiyah Ideologie: Maatschappelijke Hervorming via Goede Zeden" (The ideology of Muhammadiyah: social reform via outstanding morals), in *Theologisch Debat* 3:1 (2006); "Evil According to Muhammadiyah Ideologies" is forthcoming in Nelly van Doorn-Harder and Lourens Minnema, *Coping with Evil in Religion and Culture: Case Studies,* (Amsterdam: Rodopi, 2007). An article titled "The Ideal Muslim Family According to 'Aisyiyah Women" will appear in a book about Gender and Islam in Southeast Asia edited by Susan Schroeter of the University of Passau in Germany.

Because of their visible positions and professions, it was nearly impossible to conceal the identities of the women mentioned in the book. Only for the *pesantren* leaders Ibu Fatma and Ibu Siti have I used aliases to protect their identities.

Finally a note about the use of language: the material about 'Aisyiyah and NA covers the pre- and post-independence timeframes. Each had its own spelling. I use the modern spelling throughout the book and limit using the old version, when "u" was "oe" and "y" was "j," to titles of books and articles.

Introduction

> The Muslim voice most often heard is that of the law: highly authoritarian and patriarchal. But there is also an egalitarian voice in everyday life, seldom heard by outsiders or acknowledged by authorities. It is this voice that women are expressing, what we can call the voice of "Islamic feminism."
> —Ziba Mir-Hosseini, Iranian Islamic Feminist

When I asked Ibu Chamama Suratno in the summer of 2001 if she feared any negative consequences from the increasingly loud and visible extremist Islamic groups that had come to dominate the Indonesian press, she responded: "Never! We will never succumb to fundamentalist Islam. It has no place in Indonesia; it is a Middle Eastern import. And we will debate with those who preach it and teach them the true fundamentals of Islam." She is the national chair of 'Aisyiyah, one of the largest organizations for Muslim women. Since its inception in 1917 it has taught women the essentials of Islamic knowledge, helped improve their economic conditions, and advocated for their basic human rights. During the Suharto regime (1966–98), all dissenting religious, social, political, or economic opinions were muffled. One of the by-products of the more open, democratic climate after Suharto stepped down was the increased visibility of elements of extremist Islam. This is a potential worry for Muslim women because the ideologies of most of these groups, such as the Lashkar Jihad, have little space for women. When extremists get the upper hand, women are often the first victims, rendered voiceless and invisible. The example of Afghanistan under the Taliban testifies to this shocking reality. Such extreme groups have tried to justify violence against women and control their sexuality in the name of Islam. Many Indonesian scholars of Islam hold that the success of the Taliban and others hinges in part on the fact that throughout most of Islamic history women were not involved in the center of religion: in learning the Holy Scriptures, their interpretation, and their history. Extremist groups can oppress women by claiming to find certain rules as they mine the vast Islamic tradition. In most parts of the Muslim world, few women can speak back, as they lack the required religious knowledge that would authorize their challenge.

The Indonesian situation is different, nearly unique among Muslim countries. Indonesia has thousands of institutions where women can become specialists of Islam. For example, in Islamic boarding schools called *pesantren,* male and female students spend years studying the Islamic sources. These schools produce female preachers, intellectuals, and activists who are equipped with deep Islamic knowledge. Many of these women have focused for years on the heart of this knowledge, the law and its Jurisprudence (Shari'ah and Fiqh) and go on to become professors at Islamic universities. Not only can these women debate with extremist Muslim groups who propose a different interpretation of the holy texts concerning gender issues, they participate equally in the interpretation and reinterpretation of these texts.

Creating Islam for Women

Muslim women leaders arose from the vast networks of two central Muslim organizations, Muhammadiyah and Nahdlatul Ulama (NU). These groups have guided and influenced Indonesian Muslims since the beginning of the twentieth century. They have historically had branches for women, providing female members with opportunities to be active as preachers and teachers. Indonesian Islam is dominated by these two large Muslim organizations, the reformist or modernist Muhammadiyah (founded in 1912, with around twenty million followers) and the traditionalist Nahdlatul Ulama (founded in 1926, with around thirty million followers).

The main differences between the two organizations are reflected in their methods of interpreting the sources of Islam and in their tolerance for local culture. Reformists, much like Protestant Christians, promote direct reading of the holy texts of Qur'an and Hadith, the Tradition that contains the deeds and sayings of the Prophet Muhammad and his companions. Reformists allow the use of independent reasoning (*ijtihad*) in shaping opinions about these texts. Furthermore, they strive to cleanse Islam from all non-Islamic elements such as indigenous rituals and beliefs. Traditionalists accept expressions of local culture as long as they do not contradict Islamic teachings. In the interpretation of the Islamic teachings, Traditionalists rely on Qur'an, Hadith, and the entire body of Jurisprudence (Fiqh); in their deliberations they prefer to make use of the entire body of knowledge created since the time of the Prophet Muhammad. They argue that ignoring this vast body of knowledge developed during the first centuries after the birth of Islam and limiting one's reading to the basic texts of Qur'an and Hadith impoverishes the vast heritage of Islamic learning, embodied in the writings of all those scholars who spent a lifetime trying to understand the essence of God's will for humans as represented in those holy texts.[1] NU exercises *ijtihad* within the framework of the four legal schools (*mazhab;* Ar.: *madhhab*) accepted by Sunni Islam. Although they are free to refer to these schools, reformists are not obligated to use them.[2]

Indonesian Islam is Sunnite, Shi'ism being virtually nonexistent, and the Shafi'ite school is predominant. Each follows its own charter and philosophy, but both Muhammadiyah and NU promote a moderate version of Islam. Some of the extremist groups seek political power and want to impose Islamic law (Shari'ah) on Indonesian society by force. Muhammadiyah and NU strive to make Islam a force of change and development within society, not a tool to gain political power.

The leaders described in this study are active in the Muslim women's movements connected to reformist Muhammadiyah and traditionalist NU. Through their offices in all of Indonesia's provinces these organizations have created enormous networks that promote religious learning and social and political activism. Their educational facilities and networks have become venues for upward mobility available to all strata of society. Benefiting from formal or informal Qur'an education in combination with state-mandated schooling, a poor girl from the countryside can now graduate from the Islamic State Institute for Higher Learning (Institut Agama Islam Negeri [IAIN], or any other Islamic university) and end up as a successful politician.

Muhammadiyah's 'Aisyiyah was set up in 1917; the NU did not allow its women to start the Muslimat NU until 1946. Both organizations created branches for girls and young women to guarantee the continuation of their movements, Nasyiatul 'Aisyiyah (NA, 1919) and the Fatayat NU (1950). Muhammadiyah and NU are called Ormas (Organisasi Masa)—mass or grass-roots organizations—because they represent and cater to a large segment of Indonesia's population. Ormas are private organizations that do not depend on governmental support or funding from western organizations. They are technically nongovernmental organizations (NGOs), although in Indonesia, one must differentiate between Ormas and NGOs. NGOs are based on the model of the Ormas but tend to be smaller, often advocating a particular cause (such as health, environmental issues, or human rights). Their staff has regular salaries, often funded by the western sources. Ormas focus on a variety of causes. Their leaders are volunteers who often sacrifice part of their salaries earned in regular jobs.

At the time Muhammadiyah and NU came into being, they had to adapt to the influences of Dutch colonization and the ensuing struggle for an independent Indonesian nation. The Dutch brought in their wake Christian missionary activities that vied with the organizations to convert followers of the Indonesian indigenous religions. While expanding, Muhammadiyah especially was involved in the discussion of the role of women. Its interpretations were based on the holy sources of Islam and competed with the ideas about women promoted by the Dutch colonial government as well as preconceptions from the many local cultures.

In the twenty-first century, the organizations face an equally complex society that produces numerous new challenges, from large forces such as globalization and state control and from the abiding discussion about woman's position in Islam as it is embedded within interpretations of Islam that range from progressive to extremist. As many feminist theoreticians have observed, the discourse about gender is itself a complex, fluid construction, shaped by context, environment, and issues of power at the junctures of the vast domains of history, culture, family, class structures, civil society, and the nation.[3]

Thus the organizations operate where the development of women's expressions and their quest for equality and justice intersect with the many-leveled discourses about women and Islam. Throughout the Islamic world, since the beginning of the twentieth century, gender has remained one of the largest and most contested issues. No matter the countries or cultures, men and women disagree about what the sources of Islam teach concerning women's public or private roles.

Women leaders are deeply involved in shaping the complex Indonesian discourse on Muslim women. They advocate a range of causes while trying to overcome multiple obstacles women face in society and religion. In order to teach women, they had to study the Islamic sources. Purposefully or inadvertently, this knowledge gave them entrance into the conventionally masculine world of the interpretation of holy texts. The actions of these women speak for themselves: over the course of several decades, they have provided a female interpretation of Islam and thus helped shape Islam for Indonesian women. They have achieved what few Muslim women have done—they have appropriated the authority to interpret the holy text of Islam.

In *Speaking in God's Name: Islamic Law, Authority, and Women,* Khaled Abou El Fadl explains the dual sides of authority: one can be "in authority" or "an authority." When obeying "an authority," "a person surrenders private judgment in deference to the perceived special knowledge, wisdom, or insight of an authority."[4] While male leaders of Islam can be "in authority" (for example, when holding positions of power from which they enforce certain rules upon society in the name of Islam), women always remain "an authority," they never hold official positions of religious power. This subsidiary position requires that they use not only powerful persuasion but especially clear reasoning so that audiences will accept their interpretations.

Within the network of NU and Muhammadiyah, women have regularly managed to convince male leaders and their audiences to take women's issues seriously and sometimes to change religious opinions. Originally they did not accomplish this on men's terms, by sitting in a room filled with scholars or from academic platforms. Their contributions often arose from their experiences in the field and at the grassroots level. The fact that they operate on many levels and in different areas of society complicates any effort to name their role. I call them "leaders" because in many of their religious activities they lead, guide, are in charge, or exercise a degree of influence over those with whom they work.[5] In trying to define them, we need to keep in mind that their leadership roles are embedded within the organizational structures of Muhammadiyah and NU. Thus, in some instances we will not be able to find comparable roles for women in the West or in other Muslim countries.

Difficulties of Naming

Within the context of Indonesian Muslim women's organizations, the word "leader" has manifold meanings. Some of the women work as preachers (*muballighat*) who deliver religious messages to groups of women (and sometimes to mixed audiences) in mosques, private houses, or community buildings. Women are never allowed to preach during the ritual Friday sermon, the *khotbah*, even in Indonesia. Their sermons are called *pengajian*, from the verb *mengaji* (to learn; to recite the Qur'an). In Arabic these sermons would be called *wa'za*. Many *muballighat* also work as religious counselors and give religious advice to individuals or married couples. Other leaders teach and interpret the Qur'an, in formal or informal settings, such as a *pesantren*. The spectrum of activities, however, is not limited to the word only but stretches to include family counseling, education, care for orphans and the poor, social or economic development, and medical services. Some *muballighat* become *da'is*, or missionary preachers. They work in areas where many still follow indigenous beliefs.

To get an idea of how many women we are speaking about, we can study the membership of one of the five groups this book examines. In 2004, 'Aisyiyah counted 5,130 women preachers who preached and taught in 6,959 of its study groups, which met at least once a month. These activities have evolved continuously; at the beginning of the twentieth century they were limited to simple literacy classes for women, as they learned the basic Islamic prayers. Today their activities encompass the grassroots and academic levels, for some groups including advocacy for women's reproductive rights.

Since they do not hold officially recognized religious positions, most of these women do not earn money for their religious activities. They volunteer, thus cutting out expensive salary costs and contributing to the long-standing success of the Ormas. Many of the women preach and teach religious topics in their free time while working as housewives, civil servants, teachers in state schools, university professors, medical doctors, and politicians. Few refer to themselves as leaders; they consider themselves to be preachers, teachers of religion (*guru agama*), or specialists of Qur'an recitation (*mengaji*). Some are called "feminist" (*feminis*), although this is a contentious word; others prefer the term "activist" (*aktivis*) or simply "preacher" (*muballighat*). Throughout the book I refer to them as "leaders," "preachers," "women preachers," or "activists." I reserve the term "feminist" only for those who are widely known as such.

Judging from the sum of their activities, however, these *are* leaders of Muslim women. At the heart of their religious activities lies a quest to participate in the interpretation and reinterpretation of core Islamic teachings concerning the role and rights of women. Since the 1920s, these leaders have provided guidance in how to interpret the Qur'an and how to apply the teachings of Islam. Even while male scholars of Islam promote archaic opinions, women preachers teach alternative ideas to the women in their audience. These teachings have taken on various forms, from private (modeling a certain behavior) to public debates and publications. 'Aisyiyah women, for example, started wearing the veil during the 1920s as a sign of Muslim identity at a time when few Indonesian women wore it. On the surface they wielded little influence in the public reformist debates concerning polygyny and a woman's right to divorce. In private gatherings, however, women expressed their own interpretations of the holy texts concerning these matters, suggesting ways for women to convince their husbands not to take a second spouse, for example, by referring to certain verses of the Qur'an.[6] These texts, of course, were selected by the women leaders. Over time, 'Aisyiyah leaders have developed a comprehensive family program to protect women against the pains of polygyny. They could not ban the practice, as the father organization of Muhammadiyah did not forbid it; but they did work to make it more difficult for men and more bearable for women.

Muhammadiyah and NU women are all deeply committed to the teachings of Islam. They apply a range of strategies to improve the condition of women, but their work is always based in Islam. Since "a strong position for women in Islam" is generally considered an oxymoron, few consider the activities of these leaders to be feminist. So the question arises: Can their quest to liberate women within the framework of Islam be considered a feminist pursuit, or should we call it something else?

Islamic Feminism?

Because the women leaders of Muhammadiyah and NU operate in Indonesia, where the religious and ideological frameworks for women's rights differ vastly from those in the West, the prevailing attitudes cannot be compared to western liberal feminist ideas that stress individual agency. The concept of the "autonomous and self-reliant individual" in particular does not correspond to the Indonesian emphasis on community. In fact, the majority of Indonesian Muslim women leaders consider the good of the community to overrule their individual wishes. In the first chapter I will elaborate on what these leaders themselves consider to be an Indonesian feminist.

Whether conservative or progressive, these women are connected by their deep commitment to Islam. Their point of reference is the Qur'anic message that, according to their reading, brings "mercy for all creatures" (Q. 21:107) and frees human beings from any oppression and discrimination due to sex, race, and ethnicity (Q. 49:13). They consider their religion to be one of their strongest weapons in the fight to improve women's conditions, since in their interpretation it preaches justice for all and equality between men and women (Q. 33:35).[7]

These women are feminists in the sense that they want to liberate women from the shackles of religious and cultural injunctions, and they seek religious, social, economic, and political equality with men. Yet their goals and beliefs are not monolithic, and some of them hold ultraconservative positions. For example, many women of 'Aisyiyah stress that men and women complement each other with their own prescribed roles and duties.

The appropriate term to describe these women might be "Islamic feminists."[8] This term emerged during the 1990s in the writings of Muslims to describe a new gender paradigm; it is meant to draw a distinction between secular, Islamist, and Islamic feminists. "Secular feminism" is an amorphous term in the Muslim world, generally referring to those whose activism for women is not grounded in the Islamic tradition. To these feminists, Islam should be restricted to the private and spiritual domains.

Islamist feminism stresses male authority over women and complementarity rather than equality between men and women. It bases women's rights primarily on the Islamic law of Shari'ah and favors an Islamic state. Its ideology is not only religious but carries a strong political agenda as well. The two interpretations of secular and Islamist feminism are most predominant in the Middle East, but neither is as strong in Indonesia as Islamic feminism.[9]

Islamic feminism at the most general level encompasses the work of Muslim scholars and leaders for whom Islamic teachings form the frame of reference for their discussions about women's rights and role in Islam. They are not of one single view either: some see men and women in complementary roles, while others stress the teachings of the Qur'an that mandate gender equality and social justice for all. They reinterpret the Qur'an in a woman-centered fashion and combine the methodologies of *ijtihad* and *tafsir* (interpretation) with tools taken from nonreligious sciences such as social science, psychology, history, anthropology, and medicine. Most 'Aisyiyah women and many of the Muslimat NU teach that men and women complement each other, while those of the younger generation, NA and Fatayat NU women, see men and women as equal.

The women who speak in this book are seldom heard outside of Indonesia. Few of them have published books or articles in Indonesian, let alone in English. They carefully operate within the constraints of the Islamic teachings, local cultures, and local expectations about the role of women. Although they all strive to liberate women in the context of Islam, within their own ranks there are many disagreements as to how exactly women's dignity, morality, and rights should be protected. Yet when the rights of Muslim women are at stake, these leaders, each in their own way, will join public debates, fight back, and not allow the fruits of their efforts to be destroyed.

Women Interpreting Islamic Sources

While most Indonesians recognize that the women of Muhammadiyah and NU undertake all types of social, educational, and medical activities, the fact that many of them are also involved in rereading the holy texts of Islam has been largely overlooked. Especially since the 1990s this has become a formative activity for women who graduate from *pesantren*, or Islamic universities. When we try to find comparable activities in the Muslim world, we cannot simply look at women in other countries doing similar exercises; we also must distinguish their study according to their frame of reference, whether reformist or traditionalist.

Comparable material for reformist interpretations comes from male and female Muslim feminists in the United States, such as Aziza Al-Hibri, Amina Wadud, Riffat Hassan, and Asma Barlas. They have developed hermeneutics and rereadings of the Qur'an and Tradition that are liberating to women.[10] In principle, these Islamic feminists are reclaiming part of the authority of Islamic knowledge forbidden to women since the early centuries of Islam. Following the reformist methodology, they rely directly on the Qur'an and Tradition. The Egyptian Muslim scholar Muhammad 'Abduh (1849–1905) started to interpret those sources using the method of *ijtihad,* bypassing where necessary the teachings of the *madhhabs.* His "reformist" or "modernist" method of interpreting the holy sources was continued and elaborated by his student, Rashid Rida. Rida was more conservative than 'Abduh and eventually influenced the reformist movement in Indonesia more than his teacher. 'Abduh bypassed the traditional Fiqh sources and placed Qur'anic verses about women's comprehensive veiling, seclusion, polygyny, and unilateral divorce rights of the husband in their original social and cultural context. He argued that since those contexts had changed, the modern application of the texts had to be adapted as well. The men and women of Muhammadiyah used this reformist frame.

To gain knowledge of the Fiqh requires decades of deep study in special schools, few of which are open to female students. But because of the *pesantren* network connected to NU, Indonesia is one of the few countries where considerable numbers of women have this specific knowledge. Finding a comparative frame for the feminist interpretations of the traditionalist NU scholars was therefore a challenge when I started this research in the late 1990s. There were few studies in English discussing Islamic feminism from the traditionalist point of view. Ziba Mir-Hosseini's book on the Iranian religious debates concerning Shi'ite Islam and gender that appeared in 2000 was one of the first to describe the use of Fiqh sources in the reinterpretation of the Islamic texts on women.[11]

Khaled Abou El Fadl recognized that many patterns of Islamic patriarchal thinking are based on Fiqh texts created by local authorities during the formative centuries of Islam.[12] Some of these texts, according to scholars such as Brannon Wheeler, gained canonical authority, and Muslim believers came to regard them as immutable.[13] This was especially the case with texts concerning the role of women in Islam and led to instances where Muslim scholars bypassed Qur'anic injunctions that actually treat gender in egalitarian terms. Instead they gave preference to texts that assigned women a lower position than men. Continuing Abou El Fadl's line of reasoning, scholars such as Kecia Ali drew attention to the fact that to understand and reinterpret the Fiqh rules concerning the marriage contract, for example, one must understand the underlying mindset that shaped this contract analogously with that of the contract concerning slavery.[14]

Similar to traditionalist scholars in Indonesia, Ali concluded that the reformist work of Al Hibri, Wadud, Hassan, and Barlas highlights the egalitarian texts of the Qur'an and Hadith but ignores the cultural influences that shaped the Fiqh. Living in the United States, where these writers are protected by the legal system, they can afford to ignore the Fiqh. But the reality is that many women in Muslim countries continue to suffer injustices within their marriage because their husband's frame of reference about marriage adheres mainly to the Fiqh. When scholars who try to reread the Islamic texts on women ignore these Fiqh texts, they ultimately fail to address the legal system that has reproduced Islamic misogynist teachings on women. The result has been, according to critics of the reformist mode of interpretation, that its discourse about women often remained vague and apologetic. Chapters 2 and 3 discuss the discourse of Muhammadiyah that started during the 1920s; even now it remains vague about certain problematic issues for women.

Traditionalist Muslims connected to NU started to address problematic issues concerning women's status during the 1980s, but they always have included reference to the Fiqh texts. Often this has led to clear answers, even to the problems of the most misogynist texts. Chapters 5 and 6 refer to examples of this exercise.

It remains exceptional that in Indonesian Islam, reformist Muhammadiyah and traditionalist NU women are participating in reinterpreting women's lives and rights. Muhammadiyah women did this nearly from the start of their movement in 1917, gradually becoming well versed in Islamic learning. NU women started later, by the 1950s. Their quest for knowledge accelerated toward the end of the 1970s, when several NU scholars, led by visionaries such as Abdurrahman Wahid and Sahal Mahfudh, started a movement that aimed at shaping community frameworks based on Islamic principles and values.[15] In NU circles, these ethics and ideologies were applied to society via the teachings of the Fiqh. Hence the Fiqh texts, most urgently those that treat gender issues, needed to be reinterpreted in view of contemporary conditions. This new development resulted in the so-called Social Fiqh school.[16] The call for rereading arose at the same time from the grassroots level, where NU women had struggled to explain the biased texts to their female audiences. This development of the law from below, according to Muhammad Khalid Masud, Brinkley Messick, and David S. Powers, signifies a vital process whereby law is shaped in response to actual needs and requests from Muslims.[17]

In the early years of the twenty-first century, these developments have led to the interesting reality that NU interpretations concerning women have become more progressive than the reformist interpretations. These processes largely developed within the archipelago, seldom drawing the attention of Muslim and non-Muslim scholars from outside Indonesia. Another point of interest is that while the rest of the Muslim world reconsiders the merits of reformist or traditionalist interpretations, in Indonesia the two modes have come to borrow each other's methods. Traditionalists now include references to secular sources such as philosophy, sociology, and economics, while reformists are returning to a deeper study of the Fiqh sources.[18]

Authorities

'Aisyiyah was born in what has been called an age of motion, the time that Indonesians became aware of their potential as independent citizens. The atmosphere was filled with expectation that *kemadjoean* (progress) was within reach for native Indonesians and not the sole domain of the Dutch colonizers.[19] 'Aisyiyah saw supporting the *kemadjoean* of Indonesia's Muslim women as one of its primary tasks. Since they recognized education as the most powerful tool to bring about progress (studies have shown that a few years of schooling have an enormous impact on women's autonomy, including a decrease in the number of children[20]), 'Aisyiyah developed educational strategies that started with informal literacy and reading circles and grew into the extensive educational system it oversees today.

Through the educational system they guided women in their understanding and practice of the Islamic religion. Preaching in Islam is an activity that commands great respect and authority. Men and women who preach must prepare themselves by studying the holy texts and their interpretations. Because there is no ordained clergy in Islam, leaders earn respect and authority through the knowledge they display.[21]

Before Indonesia became independent in 1945, women preachers were informally educated. After independence, the Indonesian government opened state institutes for Islamic higher learning where men and women could study to become leaders of Islam. These forms of preaching and teaching by and for women give them formidable potential in transmitting and interpreting holy texts. Muhammadiyah and NU recognize the potential of women scholars of Islam, and during the 1990s both organizations allowed women to become members of their respective bodies that produce *fatwas* (religious opinions) and interpretations of the holy texts: Muhammadiyah's Majlis Tarjih and NU's Syuriah.

Ziba Mir-Hosseini's book provides an example of how this process developed within Iran. Authority in Iran is mostly in the hands of male scholars, because few women are prepared to assume the task.[22] Women's journals serve as the main site for the unofficial discourse.[23] This is still the case in most Muslim countries. Indonesia is exceptional in that it counts large numbers of women who officially or unofficially participate in the interpretation of the holy texts. This does not mean, however, that men have given over the fort without resistance. Women still struggle for a share of the Islamic discourse.[24] It is also important to realize that Indonesian women need the support of male scholars to move their interpretations of Islam into practice.

For example, when the Muhammadiyah scholar Amin Abdullah became president of the large IAIN in Yogyakarta in 2002, he started by examining the curricula followed at fourteen state institutes and found that most lacked attention to gender issues. Realizing that participation of women safeguards against misinterpretation and the continuation of myths about women's allegedly lesser capacities, he encouraged the professors at the Women's Study Center (Pusat Studi Wanita; PSW) of his school to develop it into one of Indonesia's most active Islamic research institutions on Islam and gender.

Women who are lifelong students of Islam will not remain silent when male scholars propose interpretations that are harmful or unfair to women; they can provide alternatives to misogynist readings of the holy texts. In fact, many scholars of Islam today claim that any interpretation proposed by human beings is fallible. While the word of the Qur'an is sacred, any interpretation is neccesarily influenced by the environment, culture, and society in which the interpreters operate. Abou El Fadl, for example, argues that the early scholars realized this and taught that their personal opinions could never be presented as the final and exclusive reading of a certain text. When interpretation is seen as absolute, religious authority becomes authoritarian.[25] Although dangerous in itself, such an authoritarian approach is even more dangerous for any group or individual being judged by such a standard.

Most of the time, the influence of Indonesian women on the process of religious consensus building has gone unnoticed, as the men's interpretations often overshadow those of the women. At times, the women's voices have been incorporated into the men's writings. Yet within the circles of classes and groups they teach, they present their own opinions and indirectly influence thousands of women. The discussion surrounding the use of birth control during the 1970s illustrates how this process develops. While the male scholars of Muhammadiyah and NU were debating for years whether or not birth control is allowed in Islam, several women preachers studied the texts and concluded that the Qur'an allows it. In their sermons they encouraged women to limit their number of pregnancies to improve the quality of life for their families. A decade later, male scholars of Muhammadiyah and NU produced official *fatwas* on the matter, allowing for birth control. Women's interpretations can attend to urgent grassroots needs and in this manner influence the construction of new legal opinions. The framework of the mass-based organizations made it possible: as women are actively involved in grassroots activities, they participate in formal and informal levels of textual interpretation.

What Is Emancipation?

When considering the activities of the women's groups, we should not assume that they share a common vision about how to improve the condition of Muslim women. In its early years, 'Aisyiyah regularly clashed with non-Muslim organizations over issues such as polygyny, and there was disagreement within its own ranks concerning formational ideas about gender. At the time 'Aisyiyah was set up, its leaders were not considered a great force of change; secular women's movements were considered more progressive. 'Aisyiyah's agenda was foremost religious and, according to Sally Jane White, "Pious Muslim women, except when they contributed to women's education and social welfare, were portrayed primarily as a liability or hindrance in the process of reform."[26] For 'Aisyiyah, "progress" meant a return to the teachings of the Qur'an. This return was expressed in antiwestern stances: for example, they opposed men and women socializing freely; they admonished women to wear the veil and urged them to comply gracefully with their husband's wish to take a second wife.

The divide between 'Aisyiyah members and women belonging to secular movements became public in 1928 during the First Indonesian Women's Congress in Yogyakarta. 'Aisyiyah's representative, Siti Moendjiah, spoke about "different" social rights for men and women and defended polygyny by arguing that the Qur'an allowed it, the Prophet had practiced it, and that it was preferable to extramarital relations.[27] This ideology was the cause of great disagreement with Christian and Chinese women's groups, who held that polygyny should be restricted or abolished altogether.[28] Privately, many Muhammadiyah women might have agreed with their opponents' views, but in public they espoused the official teachings of the male leadership. A similar difference of opinion surfaced during the debates concerning the marriage law of 1974, as Muslim women from Muhammadiyah and NU protested against drafts of the law that prohibited polygyny.

During the 1960s fierce disagreements erupted between Muhammadiyah and NU women (including NA and Fatayat NU) and Gerwani, the movement for Communist women. Gerwani was a large organization that fought for women's political rights and, like many other non-Muslim movements, opposed practices such as polygyny and child marriage. It greatly appealed to women of the lower classes, at its height numbering a million and a half members, but it was completely wiped out after Suharto's military takeover in 1965. Muslim and Christian women's organizations felt threatened by its power and were actively involved in its destruction.[29]

To protect their own agendas they were prepared to disregard the formative work of Gerwani to improve the condition of women. This was a black page in the history of Indonesia; the rights of tens of thousands of women suddenly no longer counted because they belonged to the wrong "confession." I seldom heard Muhammadiyah or NU women reflect on these events; sometimes they mentioned in passing how Gerwani had scared and even "persecuted" them. Only after Suharto stepped down did Indonesians dare to openly discuss the bloodbath of 1965.

During the past decade, opinion has been divided not so much between Muslim and other organizations but within the Muslim organizations for women themselves. Members of the Fatayat NU no longer agree with the methods of the Muslimat NU. Nasyiatul 'Aisyiyah women at times deliver harsh criticism of 'Aisyiyah projects and methods. Dedicated from its inception to changing the abysmal conditions of many Indonesian women, 'Aisyiyah consistently developed its work and ideologies in compliance with the male leadership of Muhammadiyah. 'Aisyiyah women mostly reorganized societal conditions, since these activities were condoned by the male leadership. As a result, they have had to cope with conflicting realities and ideals concerning the roles for women that they find in their grassroots activities and the ones sanctioned by the male leaders. In the early years before World War II, for example, Muhammadiyah teachings portrayed a woman simultaneously as a full partner in marriage and as an obedient servant.[30] In 1999, during the debate on the possibility of a woman president, 'Aisyiyah produced a document that concluded, "There is no objection to a woman becoming a leader" as long as she does not ignore her main duty "as housewife."[31]

Many younger NA women reject these dichotomies and instead try to find lasting solutions to such inconsistencies. For example, they seriously study gender theories, trying not only to familiarize women with analyses of gender but also to build awareness among Muhammadiyah men. As a result, younger generations of Muhammadiyah are developing new paradigms concerning the role of women.

Throughout this book I provide examples of intergenerational conflicts of opinion between the Muslimat NU and Fatayat NU, or between reformist and traditionalist interpretation. Disagreements develop at various paces between groups and generations; they are a natural phenomenon not limited to the Indonesian context. Once 'Aisyiyah women were considered paragons of progress among Muslim women; now they lag farthest behind. Hammed Shahidian describes similar conditions within Iranian women's movements.[32] He uses Alberto Melucci's model of "crisis-oriented" and "conflict-oriented" movements to distinguish between groups that aim to restructure society and those that do not. Movements that are conflict-oriented aim to fundamentally reorganize societal conditions, while those that are crisis-oriented try to remedy problems within the existing systems. Crisis, explains Melucci, points to a breakdown of the functional mechanisms of social relations; it denotes disintegration and imbalance among subsystems of society. Conflicts point to struggles between groups and actors who compete for available resources.[33] The contemporary crisis between and within the organizations is evident, for example, in the hesitation of the women of Muslimat NU to approach the contested issue of polygyny (see chapter 6). But when the Fatayat NU and members of the NU-related Yayasan Kesejahteraan Fatayat (YKF; Fatayat Welfare Foundation) openly started to attack those propagating it (see chapter 7), the Muslimat NU organized an open forum condemning the practice and reconfirming their support for the current legal restrictions.[34]

The Issues: Indonesia in the Muslim World

The agenda of Islamic feminists in many countries is often reactive and has been shaped by the most burning challenges presented by local law, social conventions, and culture. Considering these issues helps us to see how the position of Indonesian women differs from that of Muslim women in other areas such as the Middle East and its neighbor, Malaysia.

In many Middle Eastern and African countries, the energy of activists for women's rights is consumed by fighting against practices that are virtually unknown in Indonesia, such as honor killings and invasive and even debilitating female genital mutilation. Iranian women have recently started to demand the same amount in blood money (*diya*) as that paid for a man's life: the price for a woman's life is, by law, half that paid for a man's. The interpretation of the Islamic Personal Status Law that regulates the areas of marriage (including polygyny), divorce, child custody, and inheritance can cause women great suffering. While in many countries men have the right to unilateral divorce (*talaq*), women who want to leave an abusive marriage have no recourse if the husband refuses to allow them a divorce.[35] In some places, the husband can lock up a wife who applies for divorce, invoking the rules of *bayt al-ta'a* (house of obedience). During the 1990s Malaysia's Personal Status Law was amended to make divorce and polygyny easier for men and to reduce their financial responsibilities towards women. Less serious but still troubling is the ongoing discussion about women's freedom to travel and the requirement that they always be accompanied by their *mahram* (male guardian), without whom women in countries such as Saudi Arabia cannot go out.

In Egypt, the year 2000 began with a tornado created by a new law concerning the practice of *khul'*, a type of consensual divorce by which the wife gives her husband the monetary equivalent of the dowry or bride price in return for the freedom to leave the marriage. Although this practice was based on interpretations of the Qur'an (Al Baqara, 2:229) and Hadith, it had not been applied in Egypt, and the step to allow this type of divorce was considered revolutionary. The entire issue of *khul'* is pointless in Indonesia, since the marriage law allows both men and women to initiate a divorce. Also, the law recognizes the category of "marital property," which allows a spouse half of all property acquired during marriage upon its dissolution through death or divorce. This diminishes the importance of a dowry, which in many countries serves as collateral for the woman in case the marriage fails.[36]

In Indonesia, equality between women and men is enshrined in the 1945 constitution. In the same spirit, Indonesia ratified international conventions that guaranteed women equal pay for equal work and pledged to eliminate discrimination against women.[37] The marriage law of 1974 set a minimum age (nineteen for males, sixteen for females), required free consent of the partners, allowed women the same rights to initiate divorce as men, and forbade men to take a second wife without the consent of the first wife and judicial permission. Divorce cannot be unilateral but has to be carried out before a court of law.

On the books, this law treats women quite fairly; however, feminists have regularly pointed out that it is rife with ambiguity and patriarchal values. It considers the husband as head of the household; it promotes stereotypical roles for men and women and ultimately sees the woman as subordinate. Analyzing gender equality from the Islamic perspective, the former Fatayat and current Muslimat NU leader Siti Musdah Mulia concluded that a woman's role in Indonesian society is "subordinated."[38] According to her, religion greatly contributes to this subordination because "society knows and understands little about the religious values that explain the role and function of a woman, and . . . many religious interpretations are being taught that are harmful to the position and role of women."[39] The legal specialist Nursyabani Katjasungkana has added that the marriage law is not the only text carrying these stereotypes. She points out that the law regulating conditions of female workers and the entire bureaucracy that enforces them see women as "non-autonomous domestic creatures, weak and in need of protection."[40] This tendency to "domesticate" and marginalize women has strongly shaped Indonesian discourse about women. For example, the attempts of the state to control the size of families has brought attention to the topic of women's reproductive rights, including birth control, abortion, marital rape, and domestic violence. The latter two topics are still considered taboo, even for discussion, in most Muslim countries.

Issues are scrutinized on the basis of Islamic teachings, with NU scholars basing their reasoning on the teachings of Fiqh, and reformist scholars referring to the Qur'an and Hadith. For the Fiqh-oriented discussions, analysis of the text is the basis for new gender insights; how this analysis occurs will be discussed in chapters 5 and 6. Both modes of interpretation make use of modern sciences such as biology, psychology, and sociology. More recently, the discourse also has included theories of the construction of gender and sexuality. As will be mentioned in chapter 7, this opened the door to discussion about topics that in many parts of the Muslim world would cause hysteria: homosexuality, lesbianism, and those whose sexuality is exploited, such as prostitutes.[41] Some Indonesians, including many women of 'Aisyiyah, are not prepared to discuss contested issues such as homosexuality and marital rape. However, in their own way they have tried to design programs that allow women to have stronger positions within their marriage.

Several contested issues arise when men ignore the injunctions of the marriage law, including polygyny (some men simply marry without obeying the legal rules) and underage and forced marriage. In NU circles, all three practices occur regularly, which means that they are hotly debated, especially by its younger members. Marrying more than one spouse is considered prestigious in some *pesantren* circles, while families force girls to marry a son of a *kiai* (head of a *pesantren,* or religious leader) to strengthen bonds between two families.[42] The discussion about polygyny has also become front-page news, since in the post-Suharto era there is a call for the "full restoration of men's Islamic rights." Some men have started to promote the practice, unrestricted by the injunctions of the marriage law. Since 2000, several networks promoting women's rights have sprung into action to oppose these polygyny advocates with unyielding religious arguments.

Now that many young adults strive to be more faithful to Islamic injunctions, some new issues have arisen. Female circumcision was seldom considered a problem; most women in Java have been circumcised, but the procedure was ritualistic and noninvasive, nipping a piece of skin from the clitoris or putting a turmeric root between the baby's legs and cutting a piece of that. Since the invasive operation is practiced in several Muslim countries, some Muslims have started to consider it an "Islamic" procedure. Seeing economic advantage in this wish to be religiously correct, hospitals have started to offer packages at birth. Parents can have their baby girl's ears pierced and have her circumcised at the same time. This is potentially dangerous. When the procedure takes place in a medical facility it can be far more insidious than the benign ritual it usually is.[43]

Another heated debate concerns marriage practices not condoned by Sunni Islam: *mut'ah* (temporary marriage that is legal in Shi'ite Islam) and *kawin sirri* (secret marriage, where the bride's guardian or *wali* is not present and that is not officially registered as required by law). Both marriages are detrimental to the woman, since they are illegal according to Sunni Islamic teachings. A child from an unofficial union is considered illegitimate in Indonesia. But these "intermediate" types of marriage have started to gain in popularity, especially among university students who wish to date without committing the sin of *zina* (fornication).[44]

The women of Muhammadiyah and NU address these issues on various levels: some conceptualize analytical frames, while others simply sense that injustice has occurred and bring it forward through discussion. They are aware of most of the topics in the gender discussions and often have sufficient knowledge about them to answer questions. For example, they can explain to concerned parents whose daughter wants to enter into an illegal form of marriage what the consequences of this union will be. In the end, the women advocate issues that are closely connected to their own experiences. Although they cannot be active in all fields of discussion, their influence is especially prominent on two levels: they interpret and reinterpret the sacred texts that lend authority to certain points of view concerning women's rights, and they work at the level of the lived experiences of individuals and local communities. This is the level where even poor women can gain some measure of control over their own resources, opportunities, and roles.[45] But this is not the level where the centers of power are. As a result, these women leaders have remained largely invisible to the public eye, inside and outside Indonesia.

Invisible in Print

In spite of their importance for the development of Indonesian Islam, little has been written about the women of Muhammadiyah and NU, either in English or in Indonesian. Because of the lack of published material, this study is largely based on fieldwork, mostly done in Central Java while I taught at a university in Yogyakarta from 1994–99, with yearly follow-up visits after I left Indonesia. The material ranges from sermons, scholarly meetings, and publications to observations made during vaccination drives and rituals surrounding birth, death, and marriage. Much of my information comes from interviews with women and men from Muhammadiyah and NU. I started out trying to understand why these women's groups had survived so long and what their role was in transmitting religious ideas. I ended by looking more closely at how they actually have helped shape Islamic teachings and law from below.

Although Indonesia is one of the largest Muslim countries in the world, with over two hundred million Muslims (around 88 percent of the population), until the 1990s the focus of most scholars of Islam was the Middle East and South Asia. Studies by Robert W. Hefner and John Bowen were among the first to correct the odd reality that anthropological studies about Indonesia largely ignored the role of Islam.[46] The influence of Islam on gender in Java received even less attention as a serious topic of research.[47] More has been written on Muslim women in Sumatra, especially about the matrilineal Minangkabau.[48] Few of those taking Indonesian Islam seriously regard the role of women as a topic of interest. Possibly this reflects the fact that women have operated outside of the public eye. They were not among the visible faces in NU and Muhammadiyah, which already had prominent spokesmen such as Amien Rais and Abdurrahman Wahid; nor were they well-known public scholars of Islam, such as Nurcholish Madjid.

As the women in this book mostly operate in Java, the academic work on constructions of gender and the role of women—for example, in factories and the marketplace in Java—was crucial in understanding the underlying cultural constructs.[49] Most of these women are Javanese or have lived in Java for most of their adult lives.[50] This does not mean that they aim at creating something called "Javanese Islam." This would be impossible, as their organizations operate in the entire archipelago. Their efforts to reread Islam for women are not local but concern the entire nation. However, we cannot ignore Javanese culture, since it is in Java that the organizations began and grew. Scholarship on the colonial period testifies to the variety and complexity of this culture.[51] In Java, cultural and religious forces joined to create the so-called glass ceiling that women face. At the same time, Javanese culture undergirds the commitment of these women: they think relationally and perceive individuals within their family, community, and environment.[52] For the women leaders, how one handles this microcosm ultimately testifies to one's relationship with God. They see this as more important than seeking personal gain or stardom.

While women have helped shape Indonesia's Islamic landscape, they regularly have had to negotiate expectations about their *kodrat* (God-given innate nature). The Suharto regime especially promoted a state policy that stressed unequal relations between men and women. Its systematic bureaucratic attempts to keep women outside the centers of power and to perpetuate gender distinctions have received ample attention in research about Indonesian women.[53]

It is puzzling, but few Indonesian scholars have written about the women of NU and Muhammadiyah. Lies Marcoes-Natsir, an Islamic feminist who graduated from IAIN, is one of the few Indonesians who has analyzed the work of the women's movements.[54] Most of the information available about this topic has been published by the organizations themselves for their own members.

So this book tries to give the women a voice. The glue that binds them is their deep knowledge of Islamic traditions. Each of these women was shaped by her social, cultural, and religious milieu, as well as by her own particular experiences and histories.[55] Some operate in an urban, middle-class environment; others are based in a rural *pesantren*. Of various ages, they are all instrumental in shaping an evolving Islamic discourse based on women's experience, a form of Islam for women. The book moves from Ormas to NGOs; from the conservative to the highly progressive Muslim activist/feminist; from 'Aisyiyah to the Fatayat Welfare Foundation (YKF). I have tried to let the women speak for themselves, quoting them at length; if nothing else, this alone will make up for the paucity of material about them.

These women helped develop an authentic Indonesian Islamic identity for women, whether reformist or traditionalist, that remains true to the teachings of the Qur'an yet strives to be in harmony with its current context. They did not set out to be activists or feminists but wanted women to fulfill the status originally given to them by Islam: equal human beings in front of God. They have learned that equality for God does not automatically mean equality between men and women on earth. In their own particular ways, these women strive to protect women's dignity, morality, and integrity. They help shape the authority of Islamic teachings. Through their religious knowledge, they are uniquely prepared to protect authority against authoritarianism and against any development that attempts to undermine women's potential and empowerment. They feel that the struggle has barely begun, but compared to the condition of women in other Muslim countries, their influence on reinterpreting Islam for women continues to grow. And their voices grow louder daily.

A Short History

These Indonesian women must operate within the frame of Indonesia's complex history, which is sometimes dizzying in its speed of change. On the one hand, they helped shape it, while on the other hand, they were forced to adapt to its sometimes unpredictable events. To provide a frame of reference for those who are unfamiliar with Indonesia's history, I will end this introduction with a short overview of some of its main milestones.

In broad strokes, one can define four eras within Indonesia's history, based on religious, colonial, and political developments: 1) the era of Islamization (1500–1800); 2) the consolidation of the colonial state (1800–1910); 3) the birth of Indonesian nationalism (1900–45); and 4) independence (1945–present).[56]

Islam was first brought to Indonesia around the eighth century BCE by Arab Muslim traders. The process of society-wide Islamization did not start until the thirteenth century, with the kingdom of Aceh in northern Sumatra, situated at what used to be Indonesia's gateway to India and the Middle East. In the next hundred years, local communities of Muslims sprang up in port towns.

Between the fifteenth and the seventeenth centuries, Islamic kingdoms replaced the Hindu-Buddhist states, and Islam spread rapidly throughout the Malay world due to intense commercial activity. Islam was a religion and an ideology of rule. The Islam that was received was pluralistic and mostly tolerant of other religious traditions; cultural influences from the Hindu-Buddhist era were tolerated or incorporated into Islamic rituals. According to the tradition, nine saints, the *wali songgo*, were instrumental in shaping Indonesian Islam, using expressions of the local culture in their missionary activities. The most famous of these, Sunan Kalijaga, is credited with using Javanese art forms such as the shadow play and gamelan music in spreading Islam.

Island Southeast Asia was the major source of spices and other natural resources that Europeans sought to control. The Dutch started trade missions to Indonesia's Spice Islands in the seventeenth century, gradually colonizing Indonesia. They ignored Indonesian Islam and its deep societal roots, stressing local traditions and law instead. Under their rule, local customary law (*adat*) was made the basis of laws for the indigenous population. Personal matters normally regulated by Islamic Shari'ah law, such as marriage, divorce, inheritance, and almsgiving, were under the jurisdiction of *adat* laws. Recourse to Islamic law was only allowed when the rules overlapped the *adat*. As a countermovement, rural Islamic boarding schools, called *pesantren*, where students studied religious subjects combined with mystical practices, became the heart of orthodox Islam in Indonesia.

Around the beginning of the twentieth century, several developments changed the frame of reference of the Indonesian people. First, the educational level rose when the Dutch colonial rulers replaced their policy of exploitation with a program called the Ethical Policy, which allowed Indonesian children to attend Dutch schools. Second, Islamic awareness grew with the rapidly expanding print culture and increased contact with the heartlands of Islam in the Middle East after the Suez Canal opened in 1869. The growing number of pilgrims who made the Hajj to Mecca brought back deepened Islamic learning and reformist ideas that they believed would help Indonesians shed what they saw as the burden of superstition and backwardness.[57] Third, during the early decades of the twentieth century, in response to the colonial bureaucracies, voluntary organizations appeared throughout the archipelago, ranging from literary clubs to trade organizations, educational institutions, and religious movements. This led to the Islamic reformist movement in the nineteenth century in Sumatra, to the formation of Muhammadiyah, and later to the establishment of NU. These initiatives provided a new social space for personal action in the public sphere and eventually allowed for new educational developments.

Reformist ideas from the Middle East were spread by teachers of Islam and journals published in Singapore and Egypt. These ideas converted Islam into a rallying cry against (Christian) colonialism. In 1912, the Muhammadiyah movement was set up and became one of the vehicles for revitalizing Islam and spreading nationalist ideas. Apart from the religious movements, several nationalist groups sprang up. Together they brought about the dream of independence. The Sumpah Pemuda, or Youth Pledge, is considered the first occasion where cultural and political trends were translated into a plan of action toward Indonesian unity. It was taken during a Youth Congress in 1928 and professed the ideals of one fatherland, one nation, and a language of unity.[58] Indonesian was to replace Dutch and the myriad local languages.

The Japanese occupation of Indonesia during World War II (1942–45) was a watershed event that accelerated the destruction of the colonial state. The Japanese interned most of the Europeans in camps, banned the use of Dutch and English, and encouraged Indonesian nationalism. The occupation was ruthless, and Indonesians suffered greatly from suppression and lack of food. When Japan surrendered on August 15, 1945, Indonesia's leaders used the vacuum of power to declare independence on August 17, with Sukarno as the first president.

Sukarno and the other new leaders faced two enormous challenges: the Dutch tried to reconquer Indonesia during a guerilla war that lasted until the end of 1949, and the new government had to draft a preliminary constitution that allowed room for all ethnic groups and religions. This led to the Pancasila model, a "religiously neutral nationalism" based on five principles: belief in God, nationalism, humanitarianism, social justice, and democracy. Although the majority of its inhabitants are Muslim, Indonesia is thus neither an Islamic state nor a state based on secular principles. The ideology of Pancasila professes monotheism and freedom of religion for Muslims, Catholics, Protestants, Hindus, and Buddhists.[59] At the time the Constitution was written, conservative Muslim groups lobbied for the Jakarta Charter. This charter consisted of only seven words in Indonesian, but it would have added a significant element to the constitution: "Belief in one God, with the obligation for adherents of Islam to practice the Shari'ah"[60] These words come down to a semi-adoption of Islamic law in Indonesian society. Not only were Indonesia's Christians, Hindus, and Buddhists against it, but the "seven words" have remained a source of disagreement among Muslims.

The following years saw a spectacular growth of the Communist party. To the dismay of many Muslims, it gained 16.4 percent of the votes during the first democratic elections in 1955, while the Muslim parties combined had 39.3 percent. Muslim opposition to communism grew when Sukarno increased contacts with the Communist party and sealed an alliance with Beijing in 1965. At this point, with its political structures fragile, Indonesia was also on the brink of an economic meltdown. The situation escalated, and with a coup on September 30, 1965, Suharto took over. He ruled from 1966 until 1998.

Sukarno was placed under house arrest until his death in 1970. One of the bloodiest periods of Indonesian history began in 1965 with Muslims purging the country of communism by killing hundreds of thousands of its adherents. Suharto's regime was called the New Order (Orde Baru), and its power was based on controlling the population. The Suharto administration was pragmatic. In a series of five-year plans, its bureaucracy brought about sustained economic growth, universal elementary education, and a successful family-planning program. Yet the regime became increasingly oppressive over the years, silencing dissent while corruption became rampant throughout all the layers of the bureaucracy. When in 1997 an economic crisis hit part of Asia, Indonesia's economy came down like a house of cards.

In May 1998, after violent antigovernment riots spread through the country, Suharto stepped down and let his vice president, Bacharuddin Jusuf Habibie, take over. The time of Reformasi (reformation) had begun. June 1999 saw the first democratic elections since Suharto came to power. That October, Abdurrahman Wahid, the chair of the Nahdlatul Ulama and well known for his opposition to the regime, won the presidency. He soon found out that being an activist in opposition is very different from being in the seat of power. His presidency was a debacle. In July 2001, his vice president Megawati Sukarnoputri replaced him. In 2004, during its first democratic presidential elections, Susilo Bambang Yudhoyono became Indonesia's sixth president.

Chaos, rapid changes, great successes, and daunting challenges mark the past fifty years of Indonesian history. Many of the women leaders portrayed in this book have lived through much of that history. In those times of great adversity and heady success, Islam was their consolation, strength, and stability.

PART 1

Indonesian Islamic Landscapes

1 Discussing Islam, Discussing Gender

A process is going on within our society of creating gender awareness
and teaching alternative interpretations of the Qur'an that are inclusive
of women. This new knowledge cannot be stopped. It is slowly spreading among the youth of *pesantren* and among members of Muslim
organizations; eventually, it will trickle down into the high schools.
—Wardah Hafidz, Muslim activist for women and children's rights

The work of the women of 'Aisyiyah and Muslimat NU cannot be separated
from their environment; it sustains continual conversation with local cultures, with developments concerning women's position generated by the
state, and with trends within Islam. Islamic opinions concerning the status
of women are not static but are influenced by historical conditions and
recurring or newly emerging debates about gender. This chapter surveys
some of these constellations in places where they affect the activities of the
women leaders. It tries to provide a roadmap situating the women within
the forces they must respond to at all levels of work, grassroots and academic. These include influences from outside Indonesia, such as Middle Eastern
culture and ideas. Inside the archipelago, Javanese culture shaped misogynistic ideas about women, while the state during the time of the Suharto
regime reproduced a combination of Middle Eastern and Javanese culture
to engineer a comprehensive theory about women's roles and duties.

Discussing Islam

The Speech

"Indonesian Islam" is a complex and continuously developing concept that
encompasses various interpretations of the holy texts. In June 1998, Dr. Malik Fadjar, the Minister of Religious Affairs, gave a speech to the Muslimat
NU pointing out some of the challenges and changes facing Islam in Indonesia, especially where women were concerned. Not only was Fadjar the

Minister of Religious Affairs, he was also a famous Muhammadiyah leader and former president of one of its largest universities in Malang. In five points, Fadjar summed up what he considered the building blocks of Indonesian Islam at the end of the twentieth century:

1. We have to look at Islam's context, especially at its leaders, male and female, and at the leaders of its organizations. They come from over twenty provinces, each with his or her personal context and symbolism.

2. From the houses of worship we continuously hear the call to prayer. Even at the bus terminal there is a small prayer house, albeit dirty. Yet we cannot measure how much blessing it can bring.

3. Our Islamic educational institutions, beginning from the preschool [Bustanul Athfal] to kindergarten [Taman Kanak-Kanak], nowadays offer Islamic learning similar to that available at the mosques. Also the traditional Islamic boarding schools [*pesantren*] have become connected with the secular institutes for education. Even though 95 percent of the *pesantren* are private and independent, they now offer the public high school curriculum.

4. Our tradition can be witnessed when we celebrate feasts; these are the times when we hear Qur'an recital and preaching all around. Local delicacies for the feasts show how Islamic traditions are intertwined with local cultures.

5. In understanding our Islam, we also have to consider factors like economic growth, social mobility, and cultural expansion. Economic growth has given us things we never had before. It is global and can be witnessed everywhere. At the same time, Muslim women choose to wear a *jilbab* [full hair cover] instead of the traditional *kerudung* [scarf that is loosely draped over the head]. What is the significance of this trend? Social mobility brings youngsters from different Islamic backgrounds to the city. There they meet with others belonging to Muhammadiyah or NU; they worship together and forget about their differences. We now have cars and airplanes, which lead to cultural expansion. We become more efficient and practical. Even in the holy city of Mecca, coming out of the Al-Haram mosque, you walk into a McDonald's or a Kentucky Fried Chicken. Everything is now oriented towards efficiency and growth.

People discuss their faith and moral values. These cannot be taught at school only but also belong in the sphere of the family and society. We now see a gap between school, family, and society. The women's organizations continue to create new generations of religious leaders [who help bridge this gap]. My own children do not want to pursue further studies in religion. They want to study business and economics. We are facing growth, change, and renewal and constantly have to adapt our religious movements to the changing environment.[1]

In this speech, the minister covered the range of challenges that are shaping the Indonesian Islamic landscape. Technological advancements and influences from the West and Middle East that affect economic growth and communications are gradually changing ways of thinking and bringing large parts of Indonesian society into processes of transition called "moderniza-tion" and "globalization."[2] These complex and multifaceted processes are stimulated by, among other modern developments, the free education pro-vided by the Suharto government since the 1970s. Cities and communities have become an amalgam of different stages of thinking and experience: past and present, local and global are interwoven. In rural places removed from the centers of advanced growth and communication, traditional life goes on. But many Indonesians now live in a world where they can go on-line in the cyber-café in the afternoon and attend a traditional wedding ceremony at night.

The dingy prayer rooms the minister mentions are still evidence of a vi-brant faith. Since the 1980s, Islam in Indonesia has seen an unprecedented resurgence that is reflected in the increasing presence of mosques and prayer houses. Their number nearly doubled between 1973 and 1992.[3] Since 1998, Indonesia has seen an increase in groups that advocate extremist forms of Islam and are changing the Islamic landscape.

These transitions greatly influence the lives of the women leaders, as they must be agents of change in guiding women on religious, practical, philo-sophical, and strategic levels. They not only influence styles of women's personal piety but also guide them in matters concerning hygiene, nutri-tion, child rearing, politics, and economic development. In their sermons, they can introduce new ideas to the millions of women who listen to them via cassettes, at schools, or at the local mosque. Women leaders can reshape or reinvent rituals, working to make indigenous rituals that do not agree with the basic Islamic teachings into rituals acceptable to Islam.

Islamic schooling and the raising of children are among the most im-portant areas of work of the Muslim organizations. From its inception, the reformist Muhammadiyah created schools with a curriculum that com-bined nonreligious and Islamic knowledge in the cities, while in the rural *pesantren,* religious topics were mainly taught. According to Malik Fadjar, these two poles of learning have become interconnected: formal schools have incorporated more of the informal religious curriculum, while the *pesantren* have adopted the formal curriculum of nonreligious subjects.

Finally, the minister mentioned the teaching of *akhlak* (morals and eth-ics) and the importance of the family in preventing problems such as drug abuse among the younger generations. Many Muslims perceive the youth to be in a permanent state of "moral crisis" and even "moral panic," which in their view can only be remedied by proper moral teachings. Forming the moral and ethical attitudes of its members has always been one of the main goals of the Islamic organizations.

Generational differences also shape the new religious landscape. Students who grew up in a staunch NU or Muhammadiyah milieu meet on the neutral grounds of universities, where they join Muslim student organizations and get involved in discussion groups with students from different backgrounds. Modernization here can mean becoming a more fervent devotee of Islam and expressing this, for example, by joining an Islamist-minded group and wearing Arabic-inspired Muslim dress. Advanced education and the introduction of western ideas about gender roles have changed young women's perspectives concerning the role of women in society and the household. The right of personal choice has become an issue, as young women increasingly favor choosing their own future profession or marriage partner. Up until the late 1970s, parents decided what their children would study and whom they would marry. These changing paradigms have opened up room for personal choice in the religious field as well. Muslims can choose which authority to follow. The organizations are not the only ones guiding the believers with *fatwas* and moral advice, and their women leaders are not the only moral voice women will listen to.

What stands out in the minister's speech is that he envisions a moderate Islam, one that allows women to play important public roles. This attitude is unique to Indonesia; in most Islamic countries, especially those in the Middle East, Islamic resurgence often means reducing women's roles to the domestic sphere.

The Muslim women's organizations face the challenge of designing effective programs that suit Indonesian Islam in the twenty-first century. When they started over fifty years ago, their goals seemed simple: to spread Islam among Indonesian Muslim women and children, and promote development by designing simple self-help projects. At that time, the basic religious education of Muslim women and children was their main task. Now organizations such as the Muslimat NU must act not only in the face of rapid societal changes but in the many new venues those changes create. Ibu Sjachruni, the organization's chair from 1979 to 1995, expressed this predicament: "We are marking time [*jalan di tempat*]; we never seem to move forward; we have to address the urgent problems surrounding us before it is too late."[4]

The remark resonates with many active women leaders within Indonesian Islam. Society moves around them at a dizzying speed and sometimes with deplorable results. Since Suharto stepped down, Indonesia has witnessed many incidents of ethnic and religious violence. The economic crisis of the late 1990s caused grinding poverty in a nation that had lived in relative comfort for three decades. Indonesia's youth are overwhelmed with images from western TV programs that portray greed, infidelity, and free sex as the norm. Muslim leaders dread the use and abuse of drugs as a problem with the real potential to destroy Indonesia's youth. A growing array of Islamic discourses vie for young people's attention. In a vital effort to strengthen community, female religious leaders try to help women from different walks of life to come to terms with these new challenges for themselves and their families. At the same time, they try to help them discover how to be agents of change that can transform society for the good of women and men.

Women leaders are also involved in shaping the evolving debate about gender in Indonesia. Broadly speaking, the development of the discourse on gender and Islamic feminism in Indonesia took place in three stages. Grassroots movements focusing on illiteracy, basic education for women, and charity started in the early twentieth century. They produced the second stage of different types of women's activism that ranged from educational to human rights programs. The final stage is the development of an academic discourse on women's rights. This is shaped by women's studies programs in the state and Islamic universities and through writings of women activists, including writings about Islamic sources, especially Islamic law as applied through the Fiqh.

History: In the Footsteps of Kartini

The daughter of a Javanese regent, Raden Ajeng Kartini (1879–1904) is considered Indonesia's first female advocate for women's rights. She was among the first indigenous women to be allowed to attend the Dutch elementary school, and she briefly ran a small school for girls herself. In letters to Dutch and Indonesian friends, Kartini regularly mentioned the importance of education for girls and the predicament women faced because of the customs of polygyny and arranged child marriages. Kartini died very young in childbirth after her arranged marriage. Her letters became famous in 1911, a few years after her untimely death.[5] Around the same time, the Dutch colonial government, moved by increased awareness of the plight of the indigenous population, started to implement its so-called Ethical Policy that opened Dutch education to larger groups of the Indonesian population.

Railways were built at the beginning of the twentieth century. Along with faster transportation, the increased use of the printed word helped spread new ideas rapidly throughout the archipelago.[6] The number of girls attending school was rising, and separate schools for girls were opened.[7] Between 1913 and 1918, women's associations such as Putri Mardika (The Independent Woman) came into being and lobbied for education for girls and were concerned with issues such as child marriage, forced marriage, polygyny, trafficking in women and children, and prostitution. Most of the women active in these associations were of noble birth or from the upper classes.[8] At the same time, religious organizations such as the Sarikat Islam and Muhammadiyah created sections for women, among them 'Aisyiyah, that appealed to middle- and lower-middle-class Javanese women.

Although most of the women's activities were on the local level, during the first decades of the twentieth century the women's movement was divided into two currents: secular-nationalist and religious-nationalist. Both movements regarded women as a vital force for national and/or religious development and eventually for the independence struggle. National coordination started to become evident in 1928 when about six hundred women representing thirty women's associations gathered in Yogyakarta for the first Indonesian Women's Congress. The main points on the agenda were education and marriage. Differences between the religious agenda of 'Aisyiyah and the secular-nationalist agendas of the other associations stood out. A Dutch observer recorded that one of the ideals discussed was a united Indonesia in which men and women could freely socialize while honoring the limits of such socialization.[9] 'Aisyiyah had just begun its campaign against men and women freely mixing and dancing and considered such socializing to be amoral, contrary to Islamic teachings.[10] While the majority of the congress members lobbied against polygyny, Siti Moendjiah, one of the 'Aisyiyah representatives, defended the practice with great fervor, claiming that it prevented men from having extramarital affairs and women without a husband from falling into prostitution.[11]

Until the 1950s, women and men worked in close partnership in the struggle against the Dutch and in the quest for public and political rights. World War II ended with the Japanese defeat in 1945; Indonesia declared independence, and the Dutch started a vicious war to regain their territory. Women joined this struggle and volunteered as medical aids, couriers, or weapons smugglers.[12] Some women even took up arms. This was a period of great enthusiasm in Indonesia, during which a heightened Islamic consciousness became the motivating force for Muslim political involvement and devotion to the liberation movement.[13] However, after independence, men competed with women for jobs and political roles, pushing women away from prominent positions. By the 1970s, the Suharto government tried to confine women again to domestic roles by establishing its own women's organizations, Dharma Wanita (for female civil servants and the wives of civil servants, founded in 1974), patterned after Dharma Pertiwi (for the spouses of those serving in the police or military departments, founded in 1964). These developments greatly influenced the Indonesian discourse on gender.

Some of the main issues facing the women's movement between the time of independence and the 1980s included clashes with the Communist women's movement of Gerwani at the end of the Sukarno era, the marriage law, and the introduction of birth control.[14]

Marriage legislation had been a contentious issue since the 1920s and 1930s. Liberals wanted to ban polygyny and grant women the right to divorce if a husband took a second wife. 'Aisyiyah and other Muslim women's associations were vehemently opposed to such legislation, since in their opinion it ruled against the injunctions of the Qur'an. However, they did want to tighten the conditions under which polygyny was allowed. Because of this and other disagreements, the legislation did not materialize until 1974. The final version gave women the right to initiate divorce and required permission of the first wife before the husband could take a second wife. The marriage act also addressed the long discussion about child marriage, raising the minimum age for marriage to sixteen for girls and nineteen for boys. Family planning (with its obvious impact on women's health and the education of children) proved a decisive reason to press for delaying marriage.

Developing Islamic Feminism

The social-religious activism of the women's associations during the colonial time prepared for contemporary feminist-activist movements. 'Aisyiyah, the only one of the early associations that still exists, taught women from the lower and middle classes about the rights granted to them by the Qur'an. To improve the literacy of the Muslim population, it set up schools where children received religious and secular education. Expanding as the country's needs changed, it stressed women's self-esteem, designed small business projects to help women escape abject poverty, and honed their managerial and organizational skills.

Lies Marcoes-Natsir, a prominent Indonesian Muslim feminist, has commented on the uplifting aspects of these activities. She wrote about Ibu Darojah, a prominent member of 'Aisyiyah. Darojah grew up in the countryside, where she and her seven brothers and sisters used to play the same games, but when her brothers went to school, she and her sisters stayed home. Ibu Darojah felt "forced to rebel." When one of her brothers left for school after the summer holidays, she followed him: "Without a ticket, and with only the clothes she was wearing, she jumped on the train leaving for Yogya, ... shouting to her parents on the platform, 'I am going with Mas Samsi, I want to go to school.'"[15] In Yogyakarta, Ibu Darojah received free education in the 'Aisyiyah school (the Mu'allimat). She participated in political training programs, opened a small business, and became a local 'Aisyiyah leader. According to Marcoes-Natsir, this biographical detail shows how the ideology of 'Aisyiyah "stresses the role of a woman as both student and educator and helps her to become independent, economically and in making decisions."[16]

Not all women of Muhammadiyah and NU became activists or feminists, but the activities of their organizations helped create the foundation for contemporary women who advocate for women's rights from an Islamic frame of reference. Many Muslim activists and feminists have a background in Muhammadiyah or NU, where grassroots advocacy preceded theory. Women intellectuals, many of them professors and active members of the organizations, started to develop the intellectual framework to support these already existing activities. The results of their research can be directly applied in the classrooms at the Centers for Women's Studies at several Indonesian Islamic universities, where future male and female leaders of Islam receive their education.

From the start, Islamic women activists tackled questions that were related to women's position within the Islamic law and Jurisprudence. During the 1990s, several simultaneous developments intensified the Indonesian discussion about women, gender, and Islam: Islamic resurgence opened Muslim vistas to feminist writings in other Islamic countries, participation in global events, such as the Beijing conference on women in 1995, and a growing number of women and men whose educational level allowed them to understand the significance of these developments.

The revitalization of Islam also encouraged Indonesian Muslims to reconsider their place in society. NU set up NGOs that could develop new ways of thinking about topics such as Islam and democracy. One such NGO was the Perhimpunan Pengembangan Pesantren dan Masyarakat (Center for the Development of *Pesantren* and Society; P3M), which opened in 1983 and continues to strengthen Muslim knowledge and awareness about democracy, Islam, and the rights of women. Lies Marcoes-Natsir was a visible representative of the P3M who became a leading advocate for women's reproductive rights. Women followed this trend and initiated other agencies with a similar focus on women's issues. For example, Kalyanamitra was set up in Jakarta to advocate for women's rights, while Rifka Annisa in Yogyakarta focused on victims of domestic violence. By the end of the 1990s,

P3M's advocacy for reproductive rights continued through Rahima, led by Ciciek Farha Assegaf, but was forced to shift its focus to the Shari'ah debates and their impact on women.

On the academic level, schools such as the Islamic State Institutes for Higher Learning (IAINs) in Jakarta and Yogyakarta opened Centers for Women's Studies, which researched such diverse social issues as the lives of street children and the influence of the female preachers on their audiences. In 1991, the first women's studies graduate program was established at the University of Indonesia by Saparinah Sadli. Due to the paucity of local references, the scholars at this center started with translating and interpreting methodological frameworks from western feminist writings. At the same time, Muslim scholars—for example, women and men associated with the IAIN—obtained graduate degrees in gender studies from western universities.

One of the main goals of the Muslim scholars and activists was to translate feminist thinking into an Indonesian model acceptable to mainstream Muslim believers. In August 1992, Marcoes-Natsir gave the first workshop about gender and Islam in Indonesia. Organized in Jakarta by Kalynamitra, it provoked passionate reactions from Muslim religious leaders, underscoring the need for an Islamic-based foundation for the activities of Indonesian activists for women's rights.

To strengthen their understanding of Islamic gender discourse, activists started to read works of Muslim intellectuals from the Middle East, Pakistan, India, and Malaysia. Writings by Riffat Hassan, Fatima Mernissi, Ali Asghar Engineer, and the Sisters in Islam were translated into Indonesian. During the 1990s, early grassroots work fused with academic thinking about women and Islam. A form of Indonesian Muslim feminism was about to be born.

Discussing Islamic Feminism

Between 1995 and 2000, the theories and ideas developed by feminists and activists gradually became known outside of academic and NGO circles. In Yogyakarta, for example, seminars, conferences, and discussions held about the topic of gender and Islam mushroomed. The flurry of meetings increased so much that the term "seminar subscription holder" (*langganan seminar*) came into use, identifying those whose jobs required them to attend such events frequently. Many of these meetings revolved around the question of how to create an Indonesian form of Muslim feminism. Participants discussed the extent to which western feminist ideas were compatible with Islamic teachings about women's rights and duties. They wondered whether such a thing as "Muslim feminism" existed and investigated whether it was Javanese culture or Islamic teaching that assigned women a secondary status.

Men and women, many of them trained in the *pesantren,* discussed the traditional interpretations of Islam as represented in the classical Arabic texts written by men. They considered most texts that concern women to be misogynistic, espousing a discourse that represents women "as creatures whose only use lies in serving men in everything."[17] Discussing these teachings was a first step in the creation of gender awareness. In spite of the conservative views constructed and maintained by these texts, participants in these discussions agreed that women in Indonesia enjoy a high degree of freedom and can be active in the public life. After all, many of the women present had come by motorbike, had the freedom to study, and were never forced into a state of seclusion.

Feminists and Activists

These discussions about Islam, gender, and influences on them from various forces engaged a wide range of Indonesian Muslim society, with 'Aisyiyah, the Muslimat NU, and similar mass-based organizations (the Ormas) on the one side, and the NGOs (in Indonesia, the Lembaga Swadaya Masyarakat; LSM) on the other side. Many of the NGOs, inspired by western ideas about women's and human rights, do not necessarily have an Islamic agenda. They do not have large followings, but through publications and the causes they advocate, they greatly influence the discussion about women. These NGOs were initiated by a younger, highly educated generation (most of them only started during the 1990s), and they draw attention to urgent women's matters that are seldom discussed in public, including violence against women, domestic violence, women's position in the civil law, inequality in women's pay, and the rights of female workers and sex workers, including women working in domestic service in the Arab oil countries. The work of the Ormas and the NGOs are linked by the (mostly young) activists who participate in both. NGOs provide a platform for them to address issues that do not yet have a place in NU or Muhammadiyah. The NGO Yayasan Kesejahteraan Fatayat (Fatayat Welfare Association; YKF), for example, was started by NU women who felt that there was no place to address women's reproductive rights within their organization. Ormas and NGOs often build on each other's activities, creating beneficial and fluid relationships.

Younger women who are active in NGOs call themselves "feminists" or "activists." What exactly the term "feminist" means is not always clear. Many Indonesians and women of the older generation are not comfortable being called feminists—it calls up images of western supremacy, individualism, and selfishness. They believe that western feminism leads to immoral behavior such as free sex, that it wants to subdue men to give women power, and that it causes the breakdown of the nuclear family, which eventually leads to a total corrosion of society. Such beliefs embody fears hidden in the social fabric of Islamic Indonesian society, which highly values community and especially family. One of the prime teachings of Islam concerns chaste living. *Zina* (adultery or fornication) is considered the root of total destruction of Muslim life, since eventually it leads to families breaking up.

Against this negative stereotype, Indonesian Muslim feminists teach that woman's emancipation is fully compatible with the teachings of Islam. In their view, women can never degrade men, since many believe that the Qur'an assigns men a degree of responsibility over women. At the same time, the Qur'an teaches that men and women are each other's mates and protectors (Q. 16:72 and 9:71–72). They argue that erroneous interpretations of Qur'anic teachings have been used by male scholars to deny women their basic human rights. Making women aware of the rights given to them by the Qur'an, according to Indonesian Muslim feminists, eventually will result in the liberation of women and men.

The well-being of the community (*ummah*) is central to the Indonesian Islamic understanding of feminism. The smallest unit of the community, the nuclear family, must be protected to keep the community whole. In a logical step, Indonesian feminists are also concerned with other at-risk members of the community such as the poor and the elderly. In Indonesia, feminism and activism are a natural combination; Indonesian feminism is inclusive of religion, gender, and community. Indonesians use the terms "feminism" and "activism" to denote activities that work to improve the condition of women and men of all classes, strive for equality between sexes and classes, and engage in Islamic discourse with the goal of empowering women, men, and the suppressed.[18] Ibu Sinta Nuriyah Abdurrahman Wahid expressed this ideal as follows:

> "To be a feminist in the same sense as feminism in the West might also mean that I want to be a capitalist or a socialist. I am a feminist according to Indonesia's state ideology of Pancasila. That means that I base my actions on my belief as a Muslim, but also accept the other religions that are present in Indonesia. My goal is equality between men and women, because it says in the Qur'an that men and women are each other's helpers."[19]

Muslim feminists in Indonesia believe that a woman-oriented interpretation of classical Islamic texts eventually will lead to liberation of women and men. Still resisted by many men and women of the older and some of the younger generation, they disseminate their views in the schools where they teach and through seminars and publications. They can also spread their views through the Ormas they work for. These activities create an enormous network that helps carry an irreversible trend of new gender understandings.

Indonesia and the Middle East

Women's freedom to move is a prerequisite for all of these developments. Women connect, gain information, and form critical masses through their networks. They are accustomed to operating in an environment that tolerates diverse interpretations of Islamic teachings. Only at certain points in Indonesia's history have women faced extremist trends that intended to curtail their movements. Extremist movements started to emerge at university campuses in mild forms in the wake of the Islamic resurgence of the 1980s. Some of these groups demanded that women be secluded, not allowed to leave the house without their husband's permission. They belong to what the sociologist Kuntowijoyo called "Muslims without a mosque."[20] They prefer to stay within their peer group, they are not integrated into the rest of the Muslim community, and their religious learning is narrow and lacks the substance of contextual understanding.

After the collapse of the Suharto regime in 1998, several extremist groups came onto the Indonesian scene that mandate little space for women. When the Majles Mujahidin Indonesia (MMI) held a congress in Yogyakarta in August 2000, women were not even allowed into the building. This type of gender-segregated society is alien to Indonesian Islam; Indonesians maintain that it is "a Middle Eastern import," and many resent it as much as they resent "western materialism." These groups alarm the feminists/activists, however, especially when they try to transform their ideologies into law. In the post-Suharto era this has happened in Aceh, where Shari'ah law was established on March 15, 2002; several other areas are also considering such a move. With typical Indonesian attentiveness, several advocates for women's rights have started to research the immediate effects and larger consequences of these trends.[21]

Javanese and Middle Eastern influences

This freedom to move and resist suppressive forces is confirmed by studies of gender in Asia that generally stress that Southeast Asian women possess greater economic autonomy and physical mobility than women elsewhere in Asia or the Muslim world.[22] On the surface, relationships between Indonesian men and women seem to be quite equal. But examples from daily life indicate that one cannot presume gender equality too readily; rather, one must explore underlying cultures and contexts. "Gender is a fluid, contingent process characterized by contestation, ambivalence, and change," Aihwa Ong and Michael Peletz observe. In their book *Bewitching Women, Pious Men: Gender and Body Politics in Southeast Asia,* they detail some of the hidden modes of discrimination Southeast Asian women face. Being allowed to operate in public life does not necessarily yield respect or proper treatment for a woman; often it means that she bears the double burden of earning income and running the household.[23]

The question most frequently asked about Java is, Is it culture or religion that causes bias against women? Muslim women generally claim that it is the culture. Others blame Islam and, for example, assert that after Hinduism and Islam penetrated into Southeast Asia, their influence diminished women's position within marriage and public life.[24] These observations suggest that the question needs a larger framework: Is it Arab culture or Islam?[25] "Classic patriarchy," or what the Egyptian sociologist Nabil Abdel-Fattah calls "a dictatorship of machismo,"[26] is alien to Indonesian society, occurring more often in the Middle East, North Africa, and southern and eastern Asia (in particular India and China). In fact, many Javanese Muslims, women and men, consider Arab or Middle Eastern culture an undesirable influence on their own expression of Islam and culture. Of course, they respect the Islamic holy shrines in Mecca and the great Middle Eastern scholars of Islam, but many moderate Indonesian Muslims do not appreciate the extreme views that have emerged from the Middle East.

Comparisons: Indonesia and the Middle East

In spite of frequent, often negative references to the Middle East, direct contacts have only recently been established between the women's movement in Indonesia and those in other parts of the Muslim world with the goal of discussing gender issues. This network was encouraged by the Ford Foundation, among other sponsors, and mostly covered countries in Southeast Asia such as Malaysia and the Philippines. Because of geographical distance, lack of opportunities to learn English in Indonesia, and different agendas, there is hardly any contact with women's groups from the Middle East.

Furthermore, studies that present Islamic women's movements usually do not include Indonesia. Indonesian women have started to remedy this

neglect by organizing international meetings. In July 1999, the YKF, under
the sponsorship of the Ford Foundation, invited several activists from the
Middle East, North Africa, South Asia, and Southeast Asia for a meeting in
Yogyakarta on "The Role of Muslim Women's Organizations in the Eradi-
cation of All Forms of Discrimination, a Comparative Study between the
Middle East and Southeast Asia." This meeting was an eye-opener for the
Indonesian women because it helped them realize that they were ahead of
the rest of the Islamic world in shaping the Islamic discourse. The Indonesian activists also realized that two things make Indonesian feminism/ac-
tivism unique in the Muslim world: the extensive networks of the Muslim
women's organizations, and the fact that women can become specialists of
Islamic knowledge. They also saw that in spite of many constraints, they
have access to broader platforms for debate of contested issues, and they
can make their voices heard publicly.

Indonesia's form of Islamic feminism never remained only in the upper,
upper-middle, and middle classes and never expressed itself in westernized
and secularized language, as in Egypt, for example, where the indigenous
feminist discourse compatible with Islam is still quite limited.[27] Islamic
leaders in the Middle East do not support these western, secular ideas, and
they lack support among the majority of the population. Hence, feminists
in the Middle East are accused of being western agents; Indonesian activists
seldom hear such complaints.[28]

Azza Karam describes Egyptian Islamic feminists whose mindset is close
to that of the Indonesian women leaders.[29] According to Karam, they are a
handful among mostly secular feminists, but their activism involves textual
reinterpretation similar to what the Indonesian women leaders practice. In
Egypt, however, these activities are not regarded with great respect but result in frontal resistance from the conservative clergy. Azzam writes that
for women "to refer to traditional authoritative religious texts is permissible and encouraged, but to attempt to reread the meanings is not. Reinterpretation involves challenging the traditional, hierarchical, institutional,
and predominantly male religious power structures, a task which women
in general are not encouraged to do—*and especially not when these women
have not gone through the traditional religious institutional training.*"[30]

Yet some Egyptian women scholars continue to interpret the holy texts.
Amna Nosseir, a professor of Islamic philosophy at the women's section
of Al-Azhar University, is one of a small group of Egyptian women who
publicly advocate for the reinterpretation of the original texts of Islam. She
has received much praise and much criticism for her bold actions.[31] Furthermore, a growing number of women in Egypt preach to large groups of

women. Their frames of reference differ greatly from those of Indonesian women since, influenced by the intensified extremist opinions in Egypt, they aim primarily at "perpetuating a notion of religiosity that aims at self-perfection." To them, "feminism and emancipation from gender discrimination are irrelevant paradigms."[32]

In Indonesia, authority concerning the religious texts is not the prerogative of men only but is shared with women, all practicing *ijtihad* (independent judgment) when necessary. This shared authority necessarily changes their perceptions of gender, even though many are still uncomfortable with this new reality. Yet this is more than a simple struggle between the sexes: Javanese culture, state programs, and hierarchies of age greatly contribute to the complexity and vitality of Indonesian Islam.

Discussing Javanese Culture

One of the pressing questions for women activists to sort out is the one posed earlier: Is it Javanese culture or Islamic religion and the Middle Eastern culture it stems from that traditionally assign women to a secondary place? Muslims, women and men, unanimously answer "Javanese culture." But defining Javanese culture is not easy, and how this question is answered depends on who is speaking. Women tend to believe that Javanese culture places them in an inferior position to men. Many Muslims I interviewed, men and women, feel that it interferes with the originally egalitarian spirit of Islam. Yet, paradoxically, this same culture has allowed women to be active religious leaders and scholars of Islam.

Living in Java and studying the literature on this topic, I saw a mixed picture emerging, one that is further complicated by the fact that urbanized younger generations especially are rapidly leaving behind rituals and notions of Javanese culture. The picture is two-sided: one side conveys Javanese perceptions that consider women to be emotionally, spiritually, and rationally inferior to men; the other side speaks of "egalitarian structures," especially at the village level and among working classes.[33]

Although Islam is often singled out as the strongest force shaping a patriarchal culture, according to observers of Javanese culture, the idea of women's inferiority to men derives from the pre-Islamic Hindu culture that later fused with Islam. These ideas were elaborated by the royal courts of the sultans (*kraton*) and handed down in special essays on ethics and morals written for the sultan's spouses and concubines. One such essay is the *Serat Candrarini* (Book on the beauty of women). Although few in Java have actually read these texts, their stereotypical views linger on in society.[34]

The social class called the *priyayi* (the Javanese intellectual class of officials that later influenced the Suharto state bureaucrats) in particular took their gender ideologies from the royal courts.[35] Powerful stereotypes maintained that women are weak and submissive, the ones "serving in the back" (*konco wingking*). Furthermore, Javanese belief held that the salvation of a woman's soul depends on her husband's spirituality rather than her own piety (*swargo nunut neroko katut*). Some see the explanation for this condition in the Javanese perception of power and status. According to the Javanese worldview, spiritual power is enhanced or accumulated by practicing asceticism. Men are considered better practitioners of mysticism than women, whose concentration is lessened by mundane occupations like caring for children and the household.[36]

Current research on Indonesian literature and the media shows that the ideal of weak, submissive women still permeates religious, social, and cultural expressions. The world as presented in novels, news, and movies largely depends upon and reflects the male perspective.[37] The perfect wife as portrayed in the media excels in silent, selfless surrender to her husband, which in turn results in a harmonious household.[38] She takes responsibility for the man's weaknesses, blaming herself when things go wrong.[39] She is perfectly in tune with her *kodrat*, an elusive concept signifying her innate or essential "womanly" nature.

Popular culture depicts men as the ones in control of themselves and the world around them, while women are thought to lack self-control, to be less rational and less powerful spiritually than men. Similar ideas are found in the Arab literature about women's Fiqh found in the *pesantren*, and here Javanese culture coincides with Arab Islamic concepts of gender. In the Javanese and Middle Eastern contexts, the prejudice prevails that women have more "passion" (*nafsu*) than men and that women's rational capacities (*akal*; Arabic: *'aql*) are less than men's.[40] This polarization stems from the classical Middle Eastern patriarchal model in which men study and women are confined to the domestic sphere with limited access to knowledge.[41] A woman's presumed lack of self-control translated into the notion that women are less powerful not only mentally but spiritually and intellectually.

Social change and daily reality, now and in the past, are chipping away at this monolithic, imagined view of the ideal Javanese woman. Already in 1917 'Aisyiyah had started corrective teaching against this worldview, stressing the Qur'anic message of equality and preaching that a woman is responsible for her own religious merits (Q. 16:97). Ironically, the religion of Islam that is considered detrimental to a woman's position equally functions as her liberation.

Recent studies such as those by Suzanne Brenner about the marketplace show the other side of the picture.[42] She concludes that men are lustful creatures who never manage to hold on to their money. In real life, according to Brenner, men's *nafsu* runs more deeply and more quickly out of control than women's.[43]

Women manage their families, the flow of household money, small businesses, and are the majority of salespeople at the vegetable and fruit markets. On a national level, they participated in the struggle for independence, are active in politics (accounting for around 10 percent of the members of local and national parliaments), and serve as *hakim*, judges in Islamic courts (currently 14 percent of these judges are women). In 1999, a woman president was a problematic concept for certain Muslim leaders, but in the end those who were against Megawati Sukarnoputri had to give in to the popular voice that voted for her.

Men are aware of this reality just as much as women are. When I asked a ninety-five-year-old Muhammadiyah member what he remembers most of the role of women during the first decades of the movement, he referred to the volunteers who donated their time and money: "You know what was always interesting in the Kauman [the area where Muhammadiyah first became active in 1912]? Families would have their batik factories; the wife was in charge of the production, the husband of sales. When the husband died, the wife would continue the business. When the wife died it would disappear within a few years. Those men simply could not do it."[44]

Ironically, while they did much to promote the cause for women, Muhammadiyah consolidated its own hierarchical organizational structures in ways that denied women direct leadership. For decades its women's branch would remain subservient to the men's, closely following the Javanese models. In spite of this, throughout the years, 'Aisyiyah has continued to produce many strong women who defied the Javanese ideals of women's submission. Today they openly criticize ideals of male supremacy: as the chair of 'Aisyiyah, Dr. Chamamah Suratno, puts it, "People who say that women have less mental capacity [than men] are still living in the past."[45]

Discussing the State

Javanese gender ideals thus diverged significantly from social realities. Despite this fact, the Suharto government based its official state ideologies concerning women on a combination of Javanese and Islamic idealizations of the perfect wife. In an intentional effort to "mainstream" or "domesticate" women, the regime promoted gender differences. While this official policy was discarded when the regime ended, these deeply engrained ideas still hold a grip on society. The so-called housewifezation program of the Suharto regime has incurred the wrath of women activists inside and outside Indonesia. The program aimed at the consolidation of a patriarchal state as part of an overall policy to "functionalize" the entire population. In the name of economic growth and the country's stability the state introduced a technocracy-oriented ideology. Its apparatus relied on perfectly obedient civil servants to initiate economic and technocratic modernization. To curb resistance, "Every significant association in the fields of politics, business, labor, education, and the media was pressed into umbrella associations organized along 'functional' rather than interest group or ideological lines."[46] The regime's restrictive ideologies targeted women, "workers, farmers, academics, journalists, and bureaucrats, in service to social stability and comprehensive order."[47]

The state took several steps to control the activities of women's organizations. Kowani (Kongres Wanita Indonesia; the Indonesian Women's Congress, the federation for women's organizations) came under strict government control. It set up a special association for female civil servants and spouses of civil servants, Dharma Wanita, in 1974, which allowed direct control over men and women. Furthermore, seeking control over lower-class women in 1980, the state launched a program for the development of rural communities, the Pembinaan Kesejahteraan Keluarga (Family Guidance Welfare Program; PKK). Its hierarchical structures were similar to those of Dharma Wanita. The women's activist Julia Suryakusuma described Dharma Wanita as espousing "the ideology of 'State Ibuism' [domesticated spouses], which defines women as appendages of their husbands and casts female dependency as ideal."[48] In a top-down approach, the "five duties of women" (Panca Dharma Wanita) were emphasized: women were to be companions of their husbands, bearers of the nation's future generations, mothers and educators of children, managers of the household and contributors to the household income (that is, not the main source of income), and finally, good citizens. This state ideology of the modern Indonesian woman tried to squeeze all women into the mold of middle-class housewives and to co-opt the Indonesian family into its development programs, thus "domesticating the domestic sphere."[49]

In this process, the state had to compete with Muslim movements such as Muhammadiyah and NU, since these had a stake in the family as well. They were interested in raising a future generation of devout Muslims, and their leaders had the last word in allowing or forbidding practices such as birth control. The efforts of the Suharto regime to narrow the definition of women as wives and mothers found support among many Muslim groups. Muslim organizations equally extolled the virtues of good wives and mothers and foresaw the destruction of society when mothers stopped educating their children.

In chapter 3 I will discuss some of the rural development programs and family models developed by 'Aisyiyah that overlap at many points with those created by the Suharto government. This overlap has led to criticism that the Muslim women's organizations allowed themselves to be co-opted by the regime. This criticism is only partly valid. In many of its activities, 'Aisyiyah utilized meetings mandated by the government to spread its Islamic message. For example, at a PKK meeting for young mothers and children, an 'Aisyiyah preacher would give a short sermon about the expectations of motherhood in Islam. In the repressive climate of the Suharto regime, 'Aisyiyah and Muslimat NU had little room to move while remaining faithful to their own religious agenda and negotiating the government's tightly controlled development policies. The women did the same as many other suppressed groups: they obeyed to a certain extent in order to reach their own goals.[50]

In a peculiar complication for the women's organizations, the Suharto government forced their leaders to give up leadership positions when they held official positions in Dharma Wanita. Such positions were not optional; when husbands were promoted, women were assigned equal ranks in Dharma Wanita. These government tactics to undermine the mass organizations resulted in loss of leadership. Yet 'Aisyiyah and Muslimat NU were led by women who had shown great strength in the face of difficulties in earlier times, and the majority continued their work, although not "officially" on behalf of their organization. The price they paid was invisibility, but they resisted government domination, subtle or open.[51]

Their male counterparts, NU and Muhammadiyah, largely remained out of state control. Their chairs, Abdurrahman Wahid (NU) and Amien Rais (Muhammadiyah), were prominent critics of the government and transformed their organizations into forces of resistance. They used their grassroots involvement as a venue to create the basis for a stronger civil society.

The government model was heavily criticized by women activists, who perceived it as unrealistic and geared towards the middle class. It was not primarily inspired by Islamic teachings but by Javanese and Dutch colonial ideals.[52] While the government extolled the virtues of the housewife, many Indonesian women lived in dire poverty and were forced to work to provide for their families. In 1995, women comprised 40 percent of the workforce.[53]

These gender ideologies reflected imagined ideals of women, male fantasies; reality in Java superseded both models.[54] Breaking down this fantasy and exposing reality is one of the tasks of the Muslim women's organizations. They must rethink the gender paradigms they formerly tolerated. Creating awareness of the multiple influences that have shaped opinions concerning women is crucial as a first step in redefining their position in society and religion.

Hierarchy of Age: Generation Gaps

A point that keeps recurring in the relations between different groups of women leaders is the gap in generations. Javanese culture contributes to this gap; in the hierarchy of age, respect is due to the older person. During seminars, for example, younger members of the organizations are expected to serve tea, even if they have more knowledge of the issues discussed.

Some of their critics complain that the Muslimat NU and 'Aisyiyah are mostly run by women over fifty who are neither excited about changing their models of action nor aiming for radical change in societal conditions. Many are set in their ways, while change requires the reeducation of workers and the continuous overhaul of programs that have been developed over many decades. This is not easy. What used to be revolutionary has slowly become less dynamic, sometimes even obsolete. The paradigms concerning women's issues have changed rapidly over the past two decades, so women leaders must continually learn about a new wave of gender awareness to make their speeches relevant. They must modernize their methods of doing business for the sake of efficiency and study the religious texts anew to avoid repeating obsolete interpretations.

In the hierarchy of age, three generations of activists can be discerned: the young activists (aged twenty to forty-five), the generation in the middle (forty-five to sixty-five), and the older generation of women (now seventy and over) who fought for independence and struggled to spread Islam in an era when the religion was not considered a force to reckon with. The oldest generation has lived through wars, poverty, and deprivation and comes from a background where a teacher's certificate was the highest goal in a girl's schooling. Their (often arranged) marriages took place before their twentieth birthdays. They are the generation of Ibu Asmah Sjachruni, who only finished middle school and taught herself the knowledge she needed for her more than fifty-year career. This dynamic leader was the chair of Muslimat NU from 1979 to 1995 and a member of Parliament for several decades.

The generation in the middle came of age during the Suharto era. Better educated than the older women, many work as teachers, judges, or civil servants while doing volunteer work in 'Aisyiyah and Muslimat NU. They are financially better off than the older women, not only enjoying the fruits of better education themselves but celebrating their children's university degrees. As civil servants, however, they had to endure the suppressions of the Suharto regime for over three decades. This has made them a silent generation, shy to speak up or to show initiative openly. For them, the words of the poet W. S. Rendra resonate: "[I]nstitutions of public opinion / are covered in cobwebs / people speak in whispers / and self-expression is suppressed / into a 'Yes.'"[55] This generation, however, was never completely devoid of initiative; because they had little choice, the women kept a low profile to avoid undue government attention.

The younger generation of leaders, often from the university campus, did not shy away from criticizing the Suharto regime. Islam has become a natural part of their cultural identity, and they consider it a force for political and societal reform. They believe in equality between men and women, while many of the older generation still follow the model that believes that men and women each have their own God-given tasks and complement, rather than equal, each other. The younger women pursue graduate programs in and outside Indonesia, carry cellular phones, correspond via e-mail, and discuss their faith on the Internet. They have more individual choices than their mothers had, earn salaries, and hold strong bargaining positions in choosing marriage partners. In gender matters, they are more progressive than their mothers; they know their rights and can defend their positions. In Islamic expression, however, they are more conservative, some criticizing their mothers for not wearing a full veil.

These differences in age and education do not mean that only the young generation is interested in emancipation and change. 'Aisyiyah and Muslimat NU women are just as keen to improve the condition of women as their younger colleagues are. The differences between them lie in how they define empowerment of women and how they want to improve their condition. Many of the younger generation define "empowerment" as the ability to make individual choices, to participate in decision-making processes, and, if necessary, to challenge existing power structures. In contrast, many of the older women continue to teach women to be patient and rely on God to improve their conditions.[56] This difference in posture results in different programs and target groups. We can almost say that the oldest group used to be of the "conflict-oriented" model, the middle group became "crisis-oriented," and with the younger generation the pendulum is swinging back to women seeking a restructuring of the existing societal models.

Conclusion

The rapid societal changes that can be witnessed in intensified expressions of individual Muslim piety are only part of the many developments Indonesia is going through. Other aspects of Indonesian/Javanese society, such as the notions of hierarchy and ideologies created by the state and local culture, are similarly shifting. Relations between men and women are changing, as are those between parents and children. Old models of hierarchy are eroding, and nobody can foretell what the new ones will be.

Education and career now support women in finding a certain degree of independence from men. Men do feel threatened by this development. A middle-aged professor expressed this fear: "Nowadays women work all the time, they have their own income and no longer need the men. That is why we have so many divorces."[57] The fall of the Suharto regime in 1998 has intensified these trends; a time of motion seems to have returned. According to the social critic Bakhtiar Effendi, "Indonesia faces a multidimensional crisis. We have to redesign the nation and find new levels of social, religious, and political harmony."[58]

These trends directly influence the ideologies and activities of the women's organizations. Especially now that the straitjacket of governmental control is gone, competing paradigms have become visible within the organizations. These shifting landscapes also partly explain why some of the women's movements seem utterly conservative, while others are considered beacons of progress. Some have adopted new ideas from outside Indonesia concerning universal human rights and feminism, while others try to weather societal transitions by holding on to their familiar programs. For women of Muhammadiyah and NU, a particular challenge lies in being able to adjust to new developments while remaining faithful to their founding beliefs. The new force in this spectrum is Muslim women's activism, or Islamic feminism. A new generation of women and men are criticizing the traditional models of the organizations. They criticize some of them for perpetuating the gender gap with social activities that cater to women only.[59] In the newly opened climate, they criticize not only activities of their own but all the structures that perpetuate biases against women from the culture, the state, or religion.

If they realize how to use the new ideas and potential, women of Muhammadiyah and NU can greatly benefit from these criticisms. Since their contacts range from the highest to the lowest classes in society, from cosmopolitan Jakarta to the smallest hamlet, they can discuss new ideas on several grassroots levels and in cooperation with their audiences design new models of work. The hope is that a form of Islamic feminism will emerge that is indigenous to Indonesia as well as acceptable to a wide segment of the population. "'Would it not be possible that the right kind of Islam exists precisely in Indonesia?'" wondered the Nasyiatul 'Aisyiyah leader Terias Setiawati.[60]

The organizations serve as frameworks to guide believers in these processes of change. They guard the bond with society and protect against sectarianism. Their teaching about women's status in Islam guarantees a role for Muslim women, unlike the teachings of some groups that are influenced by Middle Eastern models. The organizations affirm that Indonesian Muslim women can operate within the mosque and be an active part of it. Progressive or conservative, they are deeply committed to improving the condition of women and attempt to change religious systems that hold women back. Change is in the air; a new phase has begun. That reality was underscored by the Indonesian public intellectual Franz Magnis Suseno, who stated that, "In Indonesia, especially the Muslim women's movement will have a big influence."[61]

2 Competing in Goodness: Muhammadiyah and Nahdlatul Ulama

> NU and Muhammadiyah are instrumental in providing guidance
> about how to understand Islam and how to guard the religion against
> misuse . . . with the help of *ulama*, intellectuals, and preachers they can
> redirect the rules of how to be a Muslim in present-day Indonesia. . . .
> NU and Muhammadiyah want to return to the position in the middle,
> of moderation, not move to that of violence and terrorism.
> —Kiai Hajji Hasyim Muzadi, national chair of NU

Indonesia is a vast country, and "Indonesian Islam" comprises a variety of interpretations concerning the role of Islamic law, methods of interpreting the holy sources, and opinions about religious pluralism and local cultures. This chapter looks at some of the main representations of Islam in Indonesia. It tries to locate the organizations of Muhammadiyah and Nahdlatul Ulama within this spectrum in order to understand how their religious propensities have contributed to their teachings on gender issues.

Trends of Indonesian Islam

There are continuing discussions about how to discern the different groupings within Islam.[1] Sharp definitions from the past are fading as new trends develop and individual Muslims have more options in defining their spiritual and devotional life. One way to discern the various trends is to look at the intensity and modes of Islamic religious practice in daily life. During the 1950s, Clifford Geertz identified Javanese Muslims who actively practice Islam and obey the core teachings of the Shari'ah concerning rituals and rules as *santri* (this term is also used for students at the *pesantren*). He referred to less-committed or nominal Muslims as *abangan*.[2] The *santri* do not form a clear-cut group but represent several groups of committed Muslims. Their commitment to Islam may lead them to follow mystical, normative, or Islamist interpretations and practices.

Another way to discern *santri* is to look at their modes of interpreting Islamic scriptures and their degree of accepting local culture. Following these lines, we may identify four groups: 1) traditionalists; 2) reformists or modernists; 3) renewalists, who combine traditionalist and reformist teachings; and 4) Islamists, also referred to in Indonesia as radicals, fundamentalists, literalists, and extremists.

Traditionalists represent the original Indonesian mode of Islam as it developed after Islam entered the archipelago. Next to the sources of Qur'an and Hadith, they consider Fiqh (Jurisprudence) as the basis of their interpretations of Islam. Traditionalist interpretation of the Qur'an honors and includes the interpretations of a chain of authoritative scholars extending from the seventh-century companions of the Prophet Muhammad. Traditionalism is in principle tolerant of local culture: it promotes versions of Islam that are adaptable to Indonesian conditions, and it looks favorably on the practice of Tasawwuf (Sufism, mysticism). Connected with NU, traditionalists used to be considered extremely traditional, even somewhat backward (*kolot*), as opposed to "modern" (*moderen*) Muhammadiyah members.

Modernists or reformists are so called because they study the original sources of Qur'an and Hadith in an independent way, using their own judgment rather than relying on the chain of scholars—a method called *ijtihad.* Their teachings are influenced by the reformist movement led by Jamal al Din al Afghani and Muhammad Abduh. Begun in the Middle East at the beginning of the twentieth century in resistance to western supremacy, it aimed at revitalizing Islam into an all-encompassing force in society. In Indonesia the movement developed an indigenous character but shared with the original reformists the goal of eradicating local practices and beliefs and replacing them with the original, pristine teachings of Islam. In principle, reformists frowned on the most popular expression of Islam at the beginning of the twentieth century, that of Tasawwuf. In their opinion, that practice involved idiosyncratic rules of particular Sufi groups and required not only total submission to a leader but also visiting his grave after his death. They also objected to Tasawwuf if it meant otherworldliness, aberrant behavior, and ignoring one's earthly duties; instead they advocated "original Sufism," a set of behaviors that aimed at purifying the soul and improving one's character.[3] Between these two modes of interpretation, the growing group of renewalists combine reformist and traditionalist approaches towards interpreting the holy texts of Islam.

The fourth group—radicals, Islamists, fundamentalists, or extremists—is more difficult to pinpoint. Their opinions about the role of women vary

greatly; some want to apply rules that forbid women from pursuing active public lives, while others encourage women to engage in public careers
as long as this does not hinder their role as mothers.[4] The radicalism of
these groups depends on the ideology that influenced their thinking. The
two most visible strains are the Egyptian Muslim Brotherhood created by
Hasan al-Banna in 1928 and the more conservative movement inspired by
Saudi Wahabi teachings that call for the return to the pristine rules of seventh-century Islam. Many but not all of them strive to introduce Islamic
law (Shari'ah) into society. Both types of radical Islam follow the modernist method of interpretation, independent reasoning based on Qur'an and
Hadith. The number of radical Muslims in Indonesia who are willing to
commit violence is relatively small. Yet some of them express their opinions
vocally and thus capture headlines and attention. Following the Indonesian
practice, I use the terms "radical" or "extremist" for groups that lobby to
enforce Shari'ah.

The actions of radical Muslims have called into being what could be
considered a new, fifth group: the liberal Muslims. This network, based in
Jakarta and led by Ulil Abshar Abdallah, consists mostly of young NU followers who try to counter the radical discourses with publications, radio
shows, and TV appearances.[5]

Across the spectrum, the group of nominal Muslims, the *abangan,* is still
the largest.[6] Until recently, these men and women performed their Islamic duties summarily; however, because of more intensive religious education in government schools and active propagation of the Islamic faith by
groups such as NU and Muhammadiyah, the younger generation is becoming more pious and observant.

This trend became visible in the 1980s as part of the Islamic revival that
is changing Indonesia's society. Its roots are manifold: a worldwide revival
of Islam that many believe to be connected with the 1978–79 Iranian revolution (which boosted Islamic confidence all over the Muslim world), increased numbers of students graduating from Islamic institutes, and the
repression of all forms of politicized Islam by the Suharto government from
1966 until 1998. In this era of repression, Muslims focused more on private
and public modes of worship and education than on the proscribed political activities.[7]

In the wake of this revival, mystical expressions of Islam (Tasawwuf)
have gained in popularity. At the same time, more radical groups called Islam Baru (New Islam) are on the rise among university students. All serve
as evidence of the search for an Islamic identity that is not only visible in
clothing and the use of Islamic greetings but includes a search for a deeper

spirituality that helps the believer face the many challenges of contemporary society.

These very different interpretations of Islam produce a variety of discourses about the role of women. Topics range from equality within the family to the application of the Qur'anic inheritance principle that a woman is entitled only to half a man's share. In interviews with twenty-three Muslim women, the French political scientist Andree Feillard tried to find some common denominator among the opinions concerning certain Islamic teachings; but her research showed only enormous diversity in the women's views about the Qur'anic rules and how to apply them.[8]

Discussions about the role of women are at the forefront of debates about Islam in contemporary society. What stands out in Indonesian Islam is the vibrancy of these debates and the number of Muslim scholars and intellectuals who participate in them. The organizations of NU and Muhammadiyah actively engage in these debates.[9] Unlike liberal thinkers in many other Islamic countries, Indonesian intellectuals are not silenced or forced into exile but allowed to express their ideas in a public chorus that comprises progressives, conservatives, and extremists. The newest voice on the block is extremist or radical Islam; many listeners do not understand this new voice, and they are unsure what the older voices in the chorus are claiming in today's discussions. A summary description may help sort them out.

Extremists and Radicals

During the past five years, extremist or radical interpretations of Islam have become an unexpected challenge for the women's organizations. Indonesian extremism comprises a diversity of interpretations and ideologies, ranging from intense personal expressions of piety and identity as expressed in wearing the full veil (*jilbab*) to political opinions concerning the role of Islam within the state, for example in the call for Shari'ah-based law.[10] Many turn to these groups out of disillusionment with corruption and social ills and assume that Islamic law will remedy the malaise of their country. Painting with a broad brush, we see movements emerging from isolated Qur'an schools, where students rally around a charismatic leader; other groups are inspired by puritanical teachings from Saudi Arabia. Radical groups created outside Indonesia, such as the Hizbu-ut-Tahrir, have set up branches at Indonesian universities.

During the Suharto era, political activities by students and Muslims were banned. This led to groups such as those under the umbrella of Islam Baru, venues to channel expressions of discontent through Islam. They organized Qur'anic study groups at public universities and aimed at wiping out vice and un-Islamic trends in society. According to Robert Hefner, they "rejected the scholastic arguments of traditionalist Islam and the exclusivism of Modernism. In order to Islamize the secular state universities, they adopted relaxed, democratic forms of dress and amusement, while encouraging strict adherence to Muslim devotional acts (*ibadah*), including daily prayers, the fast, and payments of alms (*zakat*) to the poor."[11] Women affiliated with these groups started to wear the veil; some even chose to cover their face as well.

Other more violent and radical groups, several of which aspired to political power, suddenly proliferated after the demise of the Suharto regime. The Laskar Jihad (Holy Warriors), for example, preached the need for *jihad* to "cleanse society of un-Islamic influences and to bring God's law into daily life."[12] They shocked the world with armed campaigns against Christians in the Malaccans (2000). Others sowed distress by bombing a disco in Bali (2002).

During the 1990s, the women's organizations regularly faced challenges from the Islam Baru groups. Young Muhammadiyah women from Nasyiatul 'Aisyiyah, for example, often were invited to meetings to find spouses for male members. When their friends thus found husbands, they were lost to the organization, as their husbands forbade them to leave the house unaccompanied. From these meetings, the women realized that Islam Baru followers did not possess a profound depth of Islamic knowledge. They lacked the solid background of those educated in Muhammadiyah or NU-related schools and often blindly followed the narrow Qur'anic interpretations of their leader.

Another challenge grew out of the fact that students of Islam Baru groups adopted practices such as the Shi'ite temporary marriage (*mut'a*) and the *nikah sirri* (the secret marriage that is conducted without the obligatory presence of the bride's guardian [*wali*]) in order to date while still being "proper Muslims." The *mut'a* marriage is technically not a marriage, although Shi'ite law allows it. It is an agreement with a time limit between a man and a woman under which the woman has none of the rights she would have in a legal marriage, such as the right to maintenance and inheritance from the husband; neither, however, does she owe her temporary husband obedience. Men from the rich Gulf countries, for example, draw up a contract of *mut'a* to live with a prostitute during the summer months when they escape from the heat of their country to cities such as Jakarta and Cairo. *Nikah sirri* is simply not a valid marriage contract because the bride's guardian must be present for it to be legal. Both are forbidden by

Sunni Islam, since they deprive the woman of her basic marital rights. In case of pregnancy in a *sirri* marriage, for example, the child is considered illegitimate, and the woman is left with the burden of responsibility. Women of 'Aisyiyah and Muslimat NU try to address this issue regularly.

These challenges are considered benign compared to those from radical groups that have started to vie for political power in the post-Suharto era. These groups strive for the formal adoption of Shari'ah law and are committed to enforcing confining religious rules concerning the status of women. They see their interpretation of Islam as a means to battle the moral demise of society. For instance, to prevent the sin of adultery, they advertise their support for early marriage and polygyny.

As Shari'ah now can be locally imposed by the decentralized governments of Indonesia's provinces, demands for its institution have arisen in several areas. Many see it as the answer to social ills, yet activists realize its serious implications for women, and several groups have started to teach women about what the application of Shari'ah would really mean.[13] Activist women also perceive these radical trends as culturally inauthentic, undesirable influences from the Middle East. Many adherents advocate that women are meant to occupy subservient roles and are deemed more emotional in comparison with "rational" men.[14] Azza Karam notes that the views of many radical groups differ little from those of conservative male religious leaders in Egypt, revealing the heavy influence of Middle Eastern culture.[15]

To see whether these radical groups truly resonate with Indonesian society and find new followers, it is useful to study the results of the 1999 and 2004 elections. The majority of Indonesian Muslims still prefer religious pluralism, but a growing number voted for parties that call for the application of Shari'ah. In 1999, 60 percent of the population voted for the Democratic party (PDI-P) and the religiously neutral governmental party, Golkar. Only 15 percent of the vote went to the purely Islamic parties, of which the most conservative gained only 3.6 percent. In 2004 the religious parties gained nearly 20 percent, but the Prosperous Justice Party (PKS), among the most conservative in the 1999 elections, in 2004 no longer called for the application of Islamic law. Its share of the votes went from 1.7 percent to 7.3 percent.[16] Around 20 percent of Indonesian voters chose a party with an Islamic basis. The attraction to these parties seems to have increased at a time of economic hardship and rampant corruption on all levels of society. For example, the PKS was considered a clean alternative, since its platform focused on providing medical facilities for the poor and fighting corruption. At the same time, learning from the 1999 elections, PKS no longer featured the call for Shari'ah in 2004. Although its leaders still see Shari'ah as the perfect law, Agus Purnomo, the head of its branch in Yogyakarta, said in 2004, "We realized that calling for Shari'ah at this time would be political suicide."[17]

The "Shari'ah mindset," however, is not the prerogative only of radical groups. Within Muhammadiyah and NU, some leaders have opinions that could be labeled as "extreme." In its desire to Islamize society and in its methods, Muhammadiyah is akin to the Muslim Brotherhood. Many young Muhammadiyah followers read translations of the works of radical Brotherhood thinkers such as Sayyid Qutb. He has gained immense popularity all over the Muslim world since the 1970s because his language is easily understandable, in contrast with the complicated Arabic of the traditional scholars. Zuli Qodir, a young Muhammadiyah member, speaking about a "regression" (*kemunduran*) in the religious ideas of his colleagues, states: "The religious thinking of the young Muhammadiyah generation is following very limited radical-fundamentalist strains that are far removed from religious tolerance."[18] However, the national leaders of both organizations have openly opposed the application of Shari'ah law in Indonesia.[19]

The various opinions about Shari'ah do not necessarily affect the freedom of Muhammadiyah or NU women to operate in the public arena. The former national chair of Muhammadiyah, Amien Rais, wants "the establishment of an Islamic society for Indonesia" but has never indicated that this would require women to withdraw from public life.[20] As far as NU is concerned, during the 1999 debate about the possibility of a woman president its leaders issued a *fatwa* allowing women to hold any public position, including the presidency (some added, as long as they did their housewifely duties).[21]

Competing in Goodness

One of the reasons that radical groups began to flourish after the fall of Suharto was that the fledgling democratic movement again allowed Muslims a place in the political arena after thirty years of forced inactivity. Since independence in 1945, Muhammadiyah and NU had actively participated in Indonesian politics, both were involved in the pan-Islamic Masyumi party (banned in 1960), and from 1952 to 1973 NU had its own political party. The Suharto regime systematically curbed Muslim voices in its political bodies out of fear of strong Islamic influence that could bring about a revolution similar to the one in Iran. This forced the Muslim organizations to withdraw from politics, and they directed their energies to societal activities instead, such as education and social activities. Their main slogan became:

"Up to now we used politics for religious propagation [*dakwah*], now we will use religious propagation [*dakwah*] for politics."[22]

At the same time, the state tried to control Islamic developments by introducing religious-study classes in state schools. It supported the building of new mosques and prayer houses and distributed religious literature that it approved of.[23] These governmental activities, combined with the work of the Islamic organizations, contributed to a new Islamic consciousness.

Since it was fruitless to aspire to political power in the political climate created by the Suharto regime, NU and Muhammadiyah moved into a "competition of goodness" (*fastabiqul khairat*). They decided that the propagation of Islam (*dakwah*) should be intensified through tangible actions of charity called *dakwah bil-hal*. Drawing the nominal Muslims to Islam—not only those living in remote areas such as Irian Jaya, but also the middle class and elite in the cities—became one of their pressing goals. The organizations started to design social development programs and established Islamic banks. After having worked as isolated units for centuries, NU *pesantren* developed strategies to raise the local quality of life.

Other new activities encouraged leaders of Islam to reconsider the holy texts with a view to changing social and political conditions. The role of women in Islam became one of the most prominent topics of debate. Renewal of Islam took place within a wide spectrum of social, economic, intellectual, and religious developments. Muhammadiyah and NU men and women became actively involved in creating a new Islamic discourse specific to Indonesia. They combined progressive, liberal convictions concerning the state and civil rights with solid Islamic learning. Each followed different methods of interpretation and proposed a Qur'anic exegesis that would be sensitive to the historical and cultural contexts within which these scriptures arose and would compare this context to contemporary society. These activities evolved among conservative and progressive thinkers within each organization, proving that Muhammadiyah is not strictly conservative, and NU is not strictly progressive. While following their specific methods of action and interpretation, however, they share the desire to save the souls of Indonesian Muslims by guiding them to the straight path of Islam.

The Soul to be Saved

Local culture and beliefs still permeate the religious life of many Javanese Muslims. The lives and work of two women, Dr. Yati, a pediatrician, and Ibu Utaryo, an activist for the poor, may serve as a brief illustration of how Javanese beliefs shape one's thoughts and actions.

Dr. Yati is a prominent pediatrician who teaches at the Gajah Mada University in Yogyakarta. Both of her parents were Muslim.[24] In 2000 she made the Hajj to Mecca for the first time, and since then she sometimes wears a loose veil over her hair. When reading the Qur'an and saying private prayers she uses the Javanese language, not Arabic. To Dr. Yati, Islam is vertical: a personal relation with God. On the horizontal level there is space for all that God meant to be good. Three of her husband's brothers and sisters are Christian, and the family celebrates the Christian and Muslim feasts together. Her father was a doctor at the Catholic Panti Rapih hospital. Dr. Yati values Javanese culture; during all of her three pregnancies she performed the seventh-month *mitoni* ritual that involves a *slametan,* a meal of reconciliation that is held to maintain or restore harmony. The *slametan* is considered the central ritual in Javanese society and is generally performed by NU members. According to Dr. Yati it is a meaningful ritual not only from a religious but also a medical point of view, since at seven months the baby is ready to be born, and the pregnancy requires special attention. Once a year, as a good Javanese should, she visits her parents' graves to pay her respect. She has little patience with her students who follow the Islam Baru trends, many of whom are found in the medical school where she teaches. Dr. Yati finds that they want to segregate the classroom and refuse to examine patients of the other sex. To her, this type of intolerance disturbs the harmony among the beings God created in a state of goodness and perfection.

Ibu Utaryo is a well-known activist for children and the poor. She set up Sayap Ibu, an orphanage for foundlings, and singlehandedly forced the Indonesian legislature to draft an adoption law. Her parents followed Javanese tradition but encouraged their fourteen children to choose the religion they were most comfortable with. Ibu Utaryo chose Islam; three of her siblings are Protestant, and four are Catholic. She became a devout Muslim and regularly attends Qur'anic studies in the mosque. She also made the pilgrimage to Mecca. Her family has remote ties with the Kraton, the sultan's palace. Like many Javanese, she believes that the Sultan has extraordinary powers. She also believes in the power of the *kris,* the Javanese traditional dagger. In her father's will, she—not her brothers—inherited a *kris* because he believed that "she was the only child strong enough to handle it." A special story is connected to this *kris.* She stored it away in the attic of an orphanage she ran in Jakarta, but not in a special place as it was supposed to be. One day, several orphans fell ill without obvious cause. Doctors were at a loss, especially when several children died of the mysterious disease. A *dukun* (a Javanese shaman or medicine man) located the problem in a neglected *kris.* Ibu Utaryo remembered the *kris* her father had given her and immediately performed the required rituals. After this the children were cured and stayed alive. Ibu Utaryo does not try to explain the extraordinary occurrence, nor does she try to bring it into accordance with her Islamic belief. She says it is simply part of what happens in this vast universe.

The worldviews of Dr. Yati and Ibu Utaryo center on a belief in the unity of being that must remain in a state of harmony (*kerukunan*). Unseen powers that affect the human condition are part of this universe. To reformists, this belief is not harmless syncretism but a genuine threat to Islamic teachings. Guiding Muslims away from all possible religious intermingling has become one of their major tasks. But at the same time, reformists are as keen on preserving harmony as Dr. Yati and Ibu Utaryo are. Reformists transformed this Javanese concept into one of their most cherished characteristics: *ikhlas,* or total dedication to God's will.

Muhammadiyah Spirit, NU Spirit

When Indonesian Muslims are asked whether they belong to NU or Muhammadiyah, many answer that they are "just Muslims." Yet most have some sort of affinity with reformist or traditionalist Islam as represented by Muhammadiyah and NU. Their allegiance becomes visible in matters of worship and in rituals surrounding birth, marriage, and death. This does not mean that all Indonesian Muslims are officially affiliated with Muhammadiyah or NU, although the two organizations are the largest in the archipelago. Combined, they represent over sixty million Muslims.[25] Outside Indonesia few are aware of their existence, since relatively little has been published about them in western languages. Several books and articles about Muhammadiyah appeared in the 1970s, written by Alfian, James Peacock, Howard Federspiel, and Mitsuo Nakamura.[26] Few subsequent studies have been dedicated to Muhammadiyah by scholars from outside Indonesia. With the Islamic resurgence in Indonesia, the organization became the focus of several Ph.D. theses, but mostly by Muhammadiyah members themselves.[27] This interest resulted in a steady stream of books in Indonesian. The first book in English about NU, a compilation of articles on NU-related topics by the scholars Greg Fealy, Greg Barton, Andree Feillard, Martin van Bruinessen, and Mitsuo Nakamura, appeared in 1996.[28] Some of these scholars have since published more books about NU in Indonesian, French, or English. NU members themselves have also begun to study the organization and to produce books and articles in Indonesian.[29] Because of the relative paucity of books on these organizations, I will elaborate on the specific traits that divide Muhammadiyah and NU to show how these have influenced the activities of their women's organizations.

Differences: Mystical NU versus Rational Muhammadiyah

The difference between Muhammadiyah and NU is rooted in what, according to Karen Armstrong, divides *mythos* from *logos.* Mythical thinking does not demand explanation for its rituals and ceremonies but considers them necessary because they invoke "a sense of sacred significance" and help "to apprehend the deeper currents of existence."[30] A similar comparison could be drawn between Protestants and Catholics: Protestants teach and learn their faith mostly through scripture, while Catholics learn through scripture and by participating in rituals such as daily Mass. Catholics have an awareness of and respect for the traditional teachings of their church that is rare in Protestant circles.

The logical approach looks forward; it is rational, pragmatic, and scientific. NU Islam stands out for its long sessions of chanting, repetition of mystical prayers, recurring celebration of rituals such as the *slametan,* and visiting the graves of saintly *kiai* and other ancestors. Muhammadiyah seeks to modernize Islam, to prove that it is a logical and rational religion. It does not tolerate local rituals such as visiting graves because they imply an irrationality contrary to Islam, the belief in spirits.

Muhammadiyah was founded in 1912; its main goal was to preach, teach, and explain Islam in accordance with the original sources and to purify the religion from non-Islamic elements. Like other reformist groups, it preached against many of the practices of traditionalist scholars of Islam, the *ulama,* who in the early twentieth century held total power over their followers, lived in remote villages far away from the centers of worldly power, and did not promote social development among their followers. The reformist message proved successful, especially in its emphasis on education. It was so successful that the NU was set up in 1926 as a countermovement to represent and defend traditionalist Islam.

Rituals followed by traditionalists are local, while reformists aim at globalizing the Muslim faith. This indirectly influenced the Muhammadiyah and NU stance on the role of women. When the male *kiai* set up NU, they did not consider women. They wanted to represent traditionalist Islam, not to reshape society. In contrast, reformists envisioned a moral rebirth of Islamic society that moved them to reinterpret Qur'anic teachings about women and strengthen women's rights within the family. As Barbara Stowasser remarked, "These interpretations, however, were put forth not for the benefit of women in and of themselves" but rather to benefit Islamic society.[31] Although they encouraged women to participate in the movement, Muhammadiyah also tried to restrain them by imposing rigid gender roles.

NU men did not try to control the women within the organization; at first they were simply kept outside. After they were accepted into the organization in 1946, women used their early omission to their benefit, as they could now have a larger voice in shaping traditionalist teachings about their rights and responsibilities.

That Muhammadiyah and NU emerged out of different sources affected their approaches to several central areas of Islamic religious life. They were distinguished by their methods of interpretation of religious texts and in several matters of worship and ritual. Their organizational and educational models also differ, and these variables influence the general way of thinking and behavior of respective Muhammadiyah or NU members. Woven through these differences are the Javanese-Islamic themes of stratified power structures, hierarchy, and spiritual authority.

Differences in the Interpretation of Texts

Muhammadiyah and NU have different modes of interpreting the holy sources of Islam. In principle, NU scholars rely on a larger body of texts and scholarship than Muhammadiyah scholars. According to Martin van Bruinessen, "tradition" in NU circles means Hadith, Sunnah, and Adat.[32] The Sunnah is recorded in the Hadith ("Hadis" in Indonesian), the tradition that reports what the Prophet said or did. Reformists and traditionalists have "different perspectives of the *sunnah,* rooted in different attitudes towards the *hadis.*"[33] In their interpretations of the Qur'an, traditionalists rely on the teachings of Jurisprudence, or Fiqh, and mostly use Hadith in a "processed form," as quoted in the Fiqh texts. These are taught in the *pesantren* that train the future generation of NU leaders.[34] Reformists want to refer directly to the texts of the Qur'an and Hadith.

NU follows the explanation of law and Fiqh according to the Al-Shafi'i school (*madzhab;* Ar.: *madhhab*), one of the four Muslim schools of law.[35] Following the authority of the *madzhab*'s founder is called *taqlid* and implies that one relies on the legal opinions of the *madzhab* rather than one's own independent interpretation (*ijtihad*). NU scholars believe that independent judgment can result in errors because few contemporary scholars of Islam have the vast knowledge required for this process. Only scholars who have mastered the science of independent reasoning are called *mujta-*

hid mutlak or *mujtahid bebas* (unconditional or free interpreters). Nowadays this designation is rare, since most scholars specialize in only one instead of the many fields of study required for this high level of authority.[36]

Independent reasoning, according to NU, is also considered disrespectful to the scholars who interpreted the religious sources at a time that was closer to the time of the Prophet Muhammad. That is why in making religious decisions NU scholars follow the principle of *ijma'*, in which the community of scholars must reach a consensus on a particular issue. This process does not preclude *ijtihad* or independent reasoning. Even when using the teachings of the *madzhab* and the explanations of centuries of Islamic scholars, NU scholars must follow their own line of reasoning to reach decisions. In the end, they decide which opinions to accept and which to ignore. Yet they stress the relevance of the *madzhab,* since it serves as an aid to Muslims who are not deeply familiar with the teachings of Islam to find the will of the Qur'an and the Hadith.[37]

Respect for the chain of great scholars who had the knowledge to interpret the holy texts is necessarily part of NU tradition. *Kiai,* the founders and leaders of *pesantren,* enjoy enormous respect from their students (*santri*), who continue to demonstrate their respect after the *kiai's* death by upholding his teachings and regularly visiting his grave. The *kiai* holds a spiritual authority that places him at the top of the spiritual hierarchy. This model is not only not practiced but is greatly detested by reformists.

Legal advice provided by NU takes a different form from that of Muhammadiyah. When an NU scholar is asked his legal opinion, the result, a *fatwa,* will be based on references to and quotations from the Qur'an and an authoritative text from the standard works of Al-Shafi'i Fiqh. The answer can be short, sometimes simply "yes" or "no." A Muhammadiyah *fatwa* is primarily based on verses from the Qur'an and Hadith. Reference to Fiqh sources is not excluded but is not mandatory. The Muhammadiyah *fatwa* reads like an essay; arguments are discussed, and conclusions are drawn in the end.[38] This method of interpretation refers to one of the first rules in Muhammadiyah, the rejection of *taqlid,* which they understand as "blind following." This rule is expressed in a phrase that is often heard in Muhammadiyah circles: "Do not rely blindly on the judgments of a *kiai,* but use your own brain."[39] Instead of following blindly, the believer can practice *ijtihad* to understand the Islamic sources.

Outsiders have erroneously understood that blindly following a *madzhab* means that traditionalist *ulama* are only capable of producing rigid opinions, devoid of personal or creative judgments.[40] Historically, the polyinterpretable character of the Fiqh has given *ulama* sufficient leeway to produce innovative legal answers. Tradition by itself is not an inflexible body but can be used as a tool of renewal and change, as the new NU interpretations concerning the position of women clearly show. Studies of ritual and social change have shown that tradition can be powerful in justifying new approaches or renewing old ones.[41] Many NU scholars are well versed in this process of interpretation and have used it to their advantage. Knowledge of the entire tradition leaves room for creativity. As a result, NU scholars are in the forefront of progressive trends of thinking about Islamic issues particular to Indonesia.

Differences in Rituals and Worship

Other differences between reformists and traditionalists are situated in ritual practices, especially those honoring the dead. NU followers continue to pay respect at the graves of their teachers, reciting *tahlilan* (repeating the confession of faith *la ilaha illa'llah* [there is no god but God]) and saying other prayers considered a gift to the deceased.[42] When someone dies, NU followers spend several hours before the burial reciting *tahlilan* and other religious texts. At the gravesite, the *talqin*, a set text, is read to prepare the deceased for questioning by the angels Mungkar and Nakir concerning the strength of their faith. Questions such as, "Who is your God?" (Allah) and, "Who is your prophet?" (Muhammad) must be answered correctly to prevent severe beating. The third and seventh day following death, meals of reconciliation derived from pre-Islamic Indonesia, called *slametan* or *kenduri,* are held at the home of the departed, while men and women take turns reciting the Qur'an. Traditionalist Muslims believe that the spirit benefits from the merits of the reciting and delights in the foods offered. They also hold *slametans* to commemorate the fortieth, hundredth, and thousandth day after a person's passing.[43] Based on the belief that the dead derive merit from prayers and enjoy the food offered by the living, NU followers regularly visit the graves of family members, as scores of other Indonesians do.

Reformists raise grave objections against all these practices. The thought that the dead can hear is ridiculous to them, based on the Qur'anic verse, "Truly thou canst not cause the dead to listen, nor canst thou cause the deaf to hear the call" (27:80). Reformists refute the practice of chanting for the dead, since there is no Hadith testifying that the Prophet ever chanted. Chanting, however, is a widespread practice all over the Muslim world.[44] My NU friends used to say that burying your loved ones without chanting praise is "burying them like a chicken: just dig a hole and get it over with." Muhammadiyah followers not only take issue with the spiritual practices surrounding death but also consider their social ramifications. They argue that to provide a steady stream of food weakens a bereaved family materially, which goes against the Muhammadiyah philosophy of moderation. Women play an especially important role here. They are at the forefront in times of economic hardship, since they are the ones who struggle to get food on the table. Teaching a message of moderation, advising people not to waste money on costly rituals, they argue, in the long run benefits the well-being of a family.

Some other visible differences between reformists and traditionalists especially concern worship. Traditionalists say out loud the *niyat* (Ar.: *niyyah*; also called *ushalli*, Ar.: *usalli*), the intent to worship, before saying their ritual prayers. They also like to add extra prayers to the morning ritual prayers (*nuqut*). Reformists teach that these are innovations not based on the tradition. The *niyat* should only be uttered "in the heart," and it is forbidden to add superfluous prayers to the ritually prescribed ones. During the fasting month of Ramadan, Muslims perform additional *taraweh* prayers at night. Like the five ritual prayers, these consist of a certain number of cycles called *rak'ah*. Traditionalists perform twenty-three cycles or *rak'ah*, while reformists hold that eleven is correct. The fixing of the date for the feast following Ramadan has been a point of contention between NU and Muhammadiyah as well. NU scholars wait for the appearance of the new moon to announce the end of the fast, while Muhammadiyah computes the phases of the moon through a system designed by Islamic astronomers. This can lead to great confusion among the population, since one group might start the feast a day before the other decides its time has come. At the time of the feast, the Eid ul-Fitri at the end of Ramadan, and also at the Eid ul-Adha at the end of the Hajj, Muhammadiyah people will hold the morning worship outside in the courtyard of a university or at a soccer field. NU followers will squeeze into a mosque.

Muhammadiyah followers are identified as urban and middle or upper-middle class who rely on the printed word. NU finds many of its members in lower-class rural Indonesia where cultures are still largely oral. As Dr. Malik Fadjar pointed out in his speech, these differences are slowly fading. NU members have become educated in secular matters, while Muhammadiyah tries to train leaders with better knowledge of the original sources of Islam and the Arabic language. Growing urbanization has drawn millions to the cities, and so the division between rural and urban is fading. Muhammadiyah and NU frequently cooperate for the common good. At times of national crisis, Muhammadiyah leaders have joined NU prayers of the kind Muhammadiyah abolished decades ago.

Muhammadiyah

Muhammadiyah Ideology

When Ahmad Dahlan (1868–1923) founded the Muhammadiyah movement in Yogyakarta in 1912, he was driven by several goals. He wanted to teach the proper modes of Islamic worship to syncretistic Javanese. He also spoke for Indonesian Muslims who felt ignored and overlooked by the colonial Dutch government, which gave preferential treatment to the *abangan*. At that time, according to estimates, only 10 percent of the population was actively practicing Islam in the *santri* way. These were mostly concentrated in the *pesantren* and the Kauman neighborhoods, the exclusively Muslim areas in large cities. *Abangan* were considered easier targets for conversion to Christianity, and only *abangan* of the higher classes had access to the Dutch educational network. *Santri* were educated at the rural *pesantren*, where over time they formed pockets of anticolonial resistance. Through their schools and hospitals, Dutch Christians monopolized the service systems in the archipelago. Muslims were acutely aware of this situation but felt helpless in the face of this overwhelming colonial power. Dahlan's struggle against ignorance and colonial suppression was inspired by reformist ideas from the Middle East, where Muslims had introduced new methods of Qur'anic interpretation and taught that Islam is fully compatible with modern life as represented by Europe.

Although it was set up in reaction against the Dutch colonial Christians, Muhammadiyah copied many Christian/colonial strategies for social work, education, and religious propagation. And while it rejected religious practices that were not accepted by Islam, it rarely condemned these outright, choosing instead to gently convince believers that rituals such as praying to ancestors are wrong.[45] This turned out to be an extremely successful approach, and the movement spread rapidly all over the archipelago.

Ahmad Dahlan's ideology and message were inspired by the Qur'anic verse that calls on believers to join "a band of people . . . enjoining what is right, and forbidding what is wrong" (*amar ma'ruf, nahi munkar*; Q. Imran 3:104). The most obvious wrongs to combat, in his view, were forces that prevented Islam from reaching its full potential. He called those forces TBC (the Dutch/Indonesian acronym for tuberculosis), and he identified them as *takhayyul* (imaginations), *bid'ah* (innovations, such as the introduction of beliefs that are forbidden by Islam), and *khorafat* (superstitions). TBC activities ranged from following mystical orders (Sufi) to participating in local rituals. The weapons to combat TBC were reason (*akl*), hard work (*kerja keras*), outstanding morals (*akhlak*), and sincerety (*ikhlas*).

Muhammadiyah members were to serve as impeccable models of and for Islamic believers by using their own minds and relying on direct interpretations of the Islamic sources. "Oneness of God," or "making God One" (*tauhid*), came first, then proper behavior (*akhlak*) had to be cultivated and ritual obligations conducted according to the original teachings of the Qur'an and the Prophet Muhammad. The Muslim who "made God One" did not practice non-Islamic rituals or rituals at odds with the original teachings of Islam; these constituted *bid'ah* (innovation). In Muhammadiyah interpretation of the Islamic faith, *abangan* Javanese and traditionalist Muslims practiced rituals that departed from the original teachings of Islam.

Independent use of reason became the basis of the Muhammadiyah philosophy.[46] Reason eliminates the need for *taqlid* (imitation), and through reason a person can discern good actions from bad. Members were encouraged to practice introspection into their soul, mind, and thoughts and retrospection at night to ponder wrongs committed that day, because this fostered awareness of sins and non-Islamic behavior.[47] Here they followed the Javanese ideals that promote harmonious relations between the believer and his or her environment through self-correction.[48]

Using one's mind also required learning, and Muhammadiyah stressed education. Learning was commendable, as it helped Muslims to understand Islam and to improve their socioeconomic condition.[49] Their philosophy maintained that an educated and well-fed person can change his or her environment. Change could be achieved through hard work (*kerja keras*), efficient use of time (*menghargai waktu*), and self-discipline (*disiplin tinggi*).[50] Laziness was considered lethal to the cause of progress. According to Muhammadiyah, it could lead to religious lethargy, such as simply chanting verses without actively trying to improve one's condition. (In other words, they implied that traditionalist Muslims spent their time in laziness.)[51] Of course, all these efforts would be fruitless if they were not undertaken in a state of perfect morals (*akhlak*) and sincerity in the sense that one did not strive after personal gain but performed the task purely for the sake of God (*ikhlas*). "*Akhlak* is the mirror of a person's belief," states 'Aisyiyah in the "Guidelines for a Muslim Woman's Personality."[52]

Thus a particular Islamic Muhammadiyah work ethic came into being that is similar to the Calvinist Protestant ethos. It continues to influence its members, who dedicate themselves to studying, preaching, or working on charitable causes. As with the Protestant Reformation, active membership in Muhammadiyah still requires "total belief and not a little self-sacrifice as well."[53]

Muhammadiyah members do not earn money to become wealthy but to dedicate their income to those in need. Ahmad Dahlan used to preach that serving God in words alone is not sufficient to alleviate the problems of the Muslim community. So the idea of *ibadah sosial,* worship in the form of service, developed. In 1923, a Muslim hospital was opened so that Muslims no longer had to use the Dutch Christian hospitals. Needless to say, this came at great financial sacrifice for Muhammadiyah members. Living out its philosophy, Muhammadiyah designed a holistic model of social mission that permeated every aspect of life and resulted in a network of schools, orphanages, hospitals, and clinics. In the 1980s, when Muslim organizations turned away from political involvement to social actions, the concept of *ibadah sosial* was redefined to *tauhid sosial*—preaching the Oneness of God through social activism.[54]

Preaching Islam for Muhammadiyah was based on learning and hard work. The results of one's labor were transformed into charitable activities. Activities that yielded visible results, such as working in hospitals, orphanages, and schools, were favored. This triad of activities became the model for *dakwah* (from the Arabic *da'wah*), the broad term for Islamic religious propagation. Muhammadiyah divided *dakwah* into three levels: *dakwah* through preaching (*bil-lisan;* language), teaching (*bil-ilm;* knowledge), and charitable activities (*bil-hal;* material goods).[55]

In the beginning, literacy courses provided the basics for the study of Islam. Qur'anic study groups were launched so that Muslims could read and discuss the Qur'an themselves instead of depending on religious specialists. *Mencari ilmu* (learning) became the battle cry for men and women. Joining Muhammadiyah meant becoming "modern." Not only did one's religious practices change; one's entire life was reordered by adapting costume, language, education, literature, and music. Men changed into western pants, which set them apart from traditionalist Muslims who were averse to wearing coats, pants, hats, ties, or other clothing that resembled Dutch attire.[56] Women dressed in what became their trademark outfits: the Javanese long skirt and a tight jacket. They also started to wear the veil at a time when this was still unusual in Indonesia.

Because Muhammadiyah started as a Javanese movement, its documents were originally written in Javanese and Dutch. But as its expansion coincided with growing national awareness for all Indonesians, in 1928 the Indonesian language was adopted and used in its schools, congresses, and publications. At that time, sermons in the mosque were in Arabic, a language understood by few. Muhammadiyah popularized Islamic knowledge, making it accessible to all. Up to then, a boy memorized the Qur'an as the word of God that he never understood. He had no idea that "if it were translated into his own native tongue, it might become something meaningful for his own life."[57] Muhammadiyah used the Indonesian language as a vehicle to initiate modernity and nationalism. In its religious services there was no religious chanting or meditation; instead, time was filled with Qur'anic recitation, lengthy sermons, and announcements. Its educational system offered a combined religious and secular curriculum. Many alumni of Muhammadiyah high schools went on to earn university degrees in various fields. Continuous reading was encouraged, and to provide its members with appropriate literature, Muhammadiyah set up its own publishing division that continues to publish the Muhammadiyah journals and a steady stream of books about religion, culture, and Islam. It also translated books from Arabic into Indonesian. Since Muhammadiyah advises against chanting religious texts, a tradition of singing songs developed. Each division has its own anthem, and at Muhammadiyah schools children as young as three are taught songs written by respected members of the organization.

An important aspect of the reformist movement was its inclusion of women. When Muhammadiyah started in 1912, Dahlan handpicked nine of the brightest girls in his neigborhood and educated them to be the leaders of a branch for women. They were still teenagers in 1917 when 'Aisyiyah officially started. Their task was to spread the Islamic core message of the Unity of God who created human beings that they may serve Him (Q. 47:19 and 51:56). Active belief in God would result in a prosperous society (*sejahtera*). Men and women were called to participate based on the Qur'anic verse, "Whoever works righteousness, man or woman, and has Faith, verily, to him will We give a new Life, and life that is good and pure, and We will bestow on such their reward according to the best of their actions"(Q. 16:97).[58]

Documents from this time of great change exude a spirit of enthusiasm and vitality. Women gathered to pray and study together; they were eager to send their girls to school. A prayer house for women (*musholla*) opened in the Kauman on October 16, 1923; women would gather there in the middle of the night for extra prayers in 1933. In the same year, an Islamic boarding schools for girls, the Mu'allimat, opened in Yogyakarta. In Padang Panjang, Sumatra, the now-famous Diniyyah Puteri had started a few years earlier. Many of the schools' graduates rose to high positions in Indonesian society.

The Javanese-Islamic Core of Muhammadiyah Being

In its formative years, Muhammadiyah had to build an Islamic counterculture that resisted traditionalist Islam, later embodied in NU, and the surrounding Javanese culture. At the same time, it had to adapt to the culture it was attempting to change. It did not agree with the "mindless" memorization of the Qur'an and Fiqh, and these two core elements of traditionalist Islamic experience were abolished. Muhammadiyah stressed instead that its followers live virtuous moral and ethical lives (*akhlak*) and demonstrate pure dedication to their work (*ikhlas*). These two characteristics did not arise out of a vacuum but were embedded in Javanese culture and were also part of Islamic teachings. To change the religious practices, Muhammadiyah reconstructed virtues from the surrounding culture as Islamic virtues.

To familiarize all the members with these teachings, they were enshrined in twelve steps or rules and published in 1939. These steps became the basis for Muhammadiyah life. They are:

1. Grow in the Islamic faith.
2. Increase in religious knowledge.
3. Improve one's moral behavior [*budi pekerti*].
4. Practice criticism/introspection [*intiqad*].
5. Strengthen the unity of the organization.
6. Stress justice.
7. Exercise wisdom.
8. Hold a national meeting [*majlis tanwir*].
9. Hold regular branch conferences.
10. Discuss decisions in a democratic way.
11. Spread the movement.
12. Entertain relationships with other similar organizations in Indonesia.[59]

The first seven steps are directly based on the teachings and ideology of Ahmad Dahlan. The five that address organizational matters were added by Haji Mas Mansoer, chair of Muhammadiyah from 1936 to 1942. Learning (step 2) enhanced Islamic knowledge and led to good conduct (*akhlak*, step 3), the result of the proper understanding of Qur'anic teachings. Thus, reformists replaced the traditionalist comprehensive knowledge of Fiqh with the ethical Islamic/Javanese system. Ethics yielded social action, but the core and motivating force of real action was the moral quality of *ikhlas*.[60] *Ikhlas* moved the members to sacrifice time (hard work) and wealth so that the movement could grow.

The steps first link personal beliefs and behavior and then transpose them onto the organizational model. Step 4 moves from personal introspection to keeping proper minutes at meetings, since these are a tool used to check what was decided upon and what could be improved.[61] Preserving the unity of Muhammadiyah (step 5) purposely took precedence over the application of justice and wisdom because the leaders understood that "kingdoms, movements fell ... because they were not united."[62] Unity in spirit and organization is the expression of a state of harmony. Success of the moral, ethical, and organizational system depended on preserving harmony in one's environment, similar to the harmony Dr. Yati and Ibu Utaryo were striving for.

What emerges is a culture that is thoroughly new and yet deeply embedded in its Javanese origins. Dahlan focused the new Muslim life on virtues that were both Islamic and Javanese. Javanese virtues became internalized forces of religious motivation, *and* they were incorporated into the organizational structure of Muhammadiyah. This reflects the Javanese duality in existence of the inward and the outward (*batin* and *lahir*). Inwardly, the Muhammadiyah Muslim fosters the virtue of *ikhlas,* while outwardly he or she preserves the harmony (*rukun*) of the social environment.

Franz Magnis-Suseno explains that in the Javanese worldview "an inward attitude of resignation" spares a person "much avoidable frustration."[63] This attitude is part of the outward *rukun* (harmony) principle, the avoidance of any type of open conflict that might upset the social harmony.[64] Unity and order should be preserved at all times. Ahmad Dahlan imbued the Javanese concept of *ikhlas* with an active, Islamic, transformational dimension where accepting one's fate meant to take action—not for oneself, but for the sake of God.[65] The Javanese ideal of a well-ordered, harmonious society requires a person to know his or her place and to pay the proper forms of respect to those around him or her.[66] Knowing one's proper place in society is strengthened by a correct inner attitude and correct action.[67] Step 3 of the Muhammadiyah code concerns this correct inner attitude (*akhlak*). The Muhammadiyah definition extends to "keeping one's promise," "being truthful," and "being kind to other Muslims."[68] To differentiate this behavior from that of the average Javanese (or *abangan*), Muhammadiyah taught that these qualities cannot develop in a person who does not live in the "fear of God."[69] Step 5, preserving the organization's unity, ultimately concerns the ideal of harmony. To realize this ideal, Muhammadiyah members must help each other, pay respects by visiting other members, and discuss all decisions that affect the organization.[70] These teachings also replace the popular ritual of *slametan* that originally aimed at restoring good relationships among society and with the world of the spirits. Instead of performing the *slametan*, Muhammadiyah members created harmonious relationships through polite, virtuous, and honest behavior. Following the different steps and guidelines carefully, the reformist theology was translated into a religious, action-oriented ethos.[71]

Thus, a new reformist tradition was invented by a process that Eric Hobsbawm describes as inculcating "certain values and norms of behaviour by repetition, which automatically continues continuity with the past."[72] Originally this was a creative process, but, as Hobsbawm has pointed out, by repeating the same message over and over again, a process of formalization and ritualization becomes inevitable.[73] Muhammadiyah members developed a ritualized set of activities, behaviors, and speech that reflected the characteristics of their belief. Unity of the movement's goals and teachings, enshrined in the maxim "one vision, one mission," helped focus this behavior.

The goal of the organization was to Islamize society through the inculcation of Islamic virtues infused with Javanese virtues. Muhammadiyah published scores of books to detail and spread its vision and mission. The essentials of these teachings were further transmitted through booklets studied in Muhammadiyah elementary, middle, and high schools, where students memorize "Kemuhammadiyaan" (facts about the organization). Important decisions made at meetings are printed in pocket-size booklets and sent to all Muhammadiyah branches throughout the archipelago.[74] Over time, however, and despite its energetic beginnings, this emphasis on regulation led to stagnation in Muhammadiyah religious thought. While during its formative years (1912–42) reformist Islam was hailed as the force that could revive Islam and provide answers to contemporary problems, formalizing the rules and teachings into a set Muhammadiyah tradition turned it into a form of "neoconservatism" that stressed a "legal-formalistic" attitude.[75]

At the beginning of the twenty-first century, according to Martin van Bruinessen, "traditionalist *ulama* often appear more flexible than the spokesmen for reformist Islam."[76] NU members learn to breathe their tradition rather than memorize it. For example, although they do exist, it is hard to find booklets that help students memorize "KeNUan" (facts about NU). When issuing legal opinions (*fatwas*), NU leaders have the freedom to mine the entire Islamic heritage rather than only that section promoted by the early Muhammadiyah leaders. The traditionalist heritage is not uniform; it contains mutually opposing pronouncements and allows NU scholars a large freedom of choice.

Muhammadiyah is aware of its loss of flexibility and has devoted countless meetings to discussing the situation. In 1985, it identified its main shortcomings: leadership and cadre, the organizational model, a loss of clear vision, and invisibility in the national press.[77] But finding well-educated new leaders who are willing to devote as much time to Muhammadiyah as the older generation remains problematic. This is equally true of 'Aisyiyah, which is run essentially by an aging group of women who take on multiple tasks. The younger generation of Nasiyatul 'Aisyiyah are far better educated and have full-time, demanding careers, and they face different questions concerning their role in society and at home. In short, *ikhlas* alone can no longer carry the burden of work. Developing a clear vision means that the Muhammadiyah tradition, the teachings of its early leaders, must be reinterpreted. One of the most significant steps to facilitate this process was taken by Amin Abdullah. In 1995 the Majlis Tarjih, the Muhammadiyah council that rules on religious matters, was redefined into a body that would study not only Islamic law but also social, economic, and gender issues. Three women of 'Aisyiyah were invited to join the council for the first time in Muhammadiyah history. Many call it "opening Muhammadiyah to the world outside," in the hope that fresh and new ideas will help to recapture the original spirit of vibrancy and change.

Muhammadiyah: The Organization

Muhammadiyah defines itself as "a missionary movement that dedicates its activities to the service . . . of human life and society"; its stated goal is "to uphold and to uplift the religion of Islam to create the true Islamic society."[78] Governed in a bureaucratic, hierarchical fashion and headquartered in Yogyakarta, it has "subordinated autonomous organizations" for married women ('Aisyiyah), unmarried women (Nashiyatul 'Aisyiyah), students (Mahasiswa Muhammadiyah Indonesia; MMI), male youth (Remaja Muhammadiyah Indonesia; RMI), and young men (Pemuda Muhammadiyah). All of these, including 'Aisyiyah and Nasiyatul 'Aisyiyah, follow the Muhammadiyah organizational model. They each have their own hierarchy and hold their own meetings. They can design their own programs but are also expected to implement Muhammadiyah decisions in order to strengthen the "one vision, one mission" ideology. Ibu Baroroh Baried, chair of 'Aisyiyah from 1965 to 1985, once expressed her frustration with the system: "'They [Muhammadiyah] can also fire members of the 'Aisyiyah board, which they have done in the past. We cannot fire members of their board, and we don't have a veto in their organization. You see, it is rather like a husband-wife relationship.'"[79]

The highest Muhammadiyah body is the Central Board (Pimpinan Pusat; PP) in Yogyakarta; at lower levels each province (*wilayah*) and district (*daerah*) has its own local board, the lowest level being the neighborhood (*ranting*). These boards are divided into departments or councils, each of which has a specific focus: preaching (Majlis Tabligh), social welfare, education,

Islamic Jurisprudence (Majlis Tarjih), higher education, economics, library and publishing, and *wakaf* (religious endowments) and property. Each department acts according to official guidelines that are typically drawn up at the top, announced, discussed at national conferences, and disseminated through Muhammadiyah publications such as the journals *Suara Muhammadiyah* (Voice of Muhammadiyah) and *Suara 'Aisyiyah* (Voice of 'Aisyiyah). The goal remains to create and uphold "one vision and one mission." To sustain this goal, in 1927 the Majlis Tarjih was created to exercise *ijtihad* collectively to preserve unity of opinion within Muhammadiyah.[80]

Muhammadiyah represents around 10 percent of Indonesian Muslims, around twenty to twenty-five million people who consider themselves to be "Muhammadiyah-minded." The actual number of official members is not as large (around eight hundred thousand in 1998). Most people attend its religious meetings and other activities without ever becoming active within the movement. Called *simpatisan* (sympathizers), they follow Muhammadiyah modes of worship and living and regularly attend gatherings organized by Muhammadiyah but do not become leaders.

'Aisyiyah is thought to be among the largest organizations for Muslim women in the country. It counts around two million sympathizers, of whom over six thousand women are active members. Becoming an official member means becoming an active missionary. Because there is no official hierarchy of clergy in Islam, every believer who possesses the required knowledge has the potential to be recognized as a religious leader. Most active members, those who hold official membership cards, belong to this group of leaders.

Because membership is voluntary, the only disciplinary action against those who step out of line is withdrawal of membership. This is considered a traumatic experience. So being Muhammadiyah-oriented also means being part of a subculture and a vast network from which friends and spouses are chosen. For example, a young Muhammadiyah leader found that in the town of Pekanjangan where Muhammadiyah established its first chapter in 1922, 85 percent of its new leaders, women and men, are chosen from among the prominent, old-time Muhammadiyah families.[81] Starting at the preschool level, children are taught Ke-Muhammadiyan, knowledge about Muhammadiyah history, its great leaders, and the main points of reformist religious understanding. Moderation is expressed by simple living with regards to clothing, housing, and food. Muhammadiyah members bond together by sharing resources via frequent and generous giving (*zakat* [tithing] and *sadaqah* [charity]). They try to be conscientious about their use of time, not wasting it in inactivity. Muhammadiyah members are upset when events do not start on time and seem to have "an obsession with schedules and plans."[82]

Moderation in behavior is highly valued, while being eccentric or standing out is discouraged. Muhammadiyah tries to follow a sort of middle way, religiously, socially, and politically. From the beginning it tried never to antagonize the Dutch or Indonesian governments. As an organization it stayed away for most of its history from setting up political parties, while enthusiastically serving as the main drive behind Masyumi and preparing many future leaders for Islamic political involvement. It has a long history of proximity to politics without direct involvement. After many years of nonpolitical activity, in the post-Suharto era many of its members have taken key positions in the government and in parties associated with Muhammadiyah. However, true to its charter, it has not initiated a party itself; in fact, Muhammadiyah asked Amien Rais to step down as its chairman when he became the head of the PAN party.

Nahdlatul Ulama

Nahdlatul Ulama Ideology

Nahdlatul Ulama (the Awakening of the Religious Scholars) was formed in 1926 by traditionalist religious scholars from East Java. The most famous among them were Hasyim Asy'ari and Abdul Wahab Chasbullah. Hasyim Asy'ari was the most prestigious *kiai* of East Java, and many of his descendants, among them his grandson Abdurrahman Wahid, became prominent leaders in Indonesian Islam and politics. Most of those present at the founding meeting in 1926 were *kiai,* religious leaders who had their own *pesantren* and could count on large local followings.

NU was set up to counter two movements that the *ulama* perceived as a threat to traditionalist Islam: the reformists, whose criticism of traditionalist Islam was mounting, and political Islamic groups such as the Sarekat Islam party that had become heavily influenced by Marxist ideologies.[83] Most of all, traditionalists needed an official body to identify with, so that invitations—for example, to international meetings—would not only go to Muhammadiyah.

NU has its headquarters in Jakarta. It has autonomous branches for women (Muslimat NU), young women (Fatayat), young men (Gerakan Pemuda Ansor [GP Ansor]), male students (Ikatan Putera NU [IPNU]), female students (Ikatan Puteri-Puteri NU [IPPNU]), and several professional networks.

Its original constitution voices goals similar to those of Muhammadi-yah: to promote educational and social growth. Its essential approach is similarly grounded in moderation, tolerance, and the preservation of harmony. NU *dakwah* takes the form of sermons and activities such as chanting, rituals, and social and educational activities. Its membership is based in the *pesantren*, the mostly rural, independent Islamic boarding schools. *Pesantren* range from the elementary to university level, and the Muslimat NU runs a vast network of kindergartens. NU is the largest Ormas in Indonesia, counting between thirty to forty million followers.

Unlike Muhammadiyah, NU has been actively involved in politics from the time of independence. NU originally took an accommodative position toward the Dutch government, but this changed when the Japanese trained *kiai* to be officers in its independence army during the occupation of Indonesia from 1942 to 1945. At the end of World War II, Indonesia declared independence, and these *kiai* became involved in the struggle against the Dutch. After the war, NU leaders became active in politics. At first they joined the pan-Islamic Masyumi party but felt pushed out by its Muhammadiyah majority. This led to the creation of their own separate party, which in 1973 was forced to merge with three other Islamic parties into the United Development Party (PPP). Seeing its interests neglected by PPP leadership, NU held a historic congress in 1984 and decided to "return to the charter of 1926" (*kembali ke khittah*). This choice led to their withdrawal from politics and a total refocusing on education (*ma'arif*), social development (*mabarrat*), mission (*dakwah*), and economic activities (*mu'amalah*). Until 1984, NU women mostly had carried out these activities. The same congress elected the liberal intellectual and theologian Abdurrahman Wahid as NU's new chairman. Known for his unconventional ideas and openness towards non-Muslims, he became the younger generation's leader of choice who would reform and modernize NU. Under his leadership NU also became a strong civilian oppositional force against the Suharto regime.

As with Muhammadiyah, moderation is among NU's goals, but it is not the highest. Many *kiai* are known and respected for their odd behavior. Abdurrahman Wahid even published a book about the "eccentric *kiai*" within NU, showing that they "have a logic and rationality all their own, even though it differs from that based upon modern thought."[84] For example, Kiai Mbah Liem (Grandpa Liem) lives near Yogyakarta in his "Pancasila Pesantren," a name that indicates his firm support of the Pancasila principle and the government. A steady stream of government officials, journalists, and ordinary people with problems visit Mbah Liem daily to benefit from his spiritual powers. He is regularly featured in newspaper articles about thorny political questions but seldom provides outright answers. His behavior seems fully erratic. One day I visited him, taking along my daughter, who was a baby at the time. He took her in his arms and for the next hour danced around the room holding her, singing "baby, baby." All those present were awed by this intense attention. At the end of the visit Mbah Liem handed out holy water to those in need, mumbled some prayers, and indicated that the meeting was over. Although the visitors had been largely ignored, given a few seconds to relay their requests, all present seemed satisfied and strengthened by this visit.

Since NU represents Islam that was indigenous to Indonesia, originally it did not train its members to become active bearers of *dakwah*. Students graduating from the *pesantren* were automatically destined for careers as local or national religious leaders. *Dakwah* was not tightly defined, since for traditionalist Muslims practicing the daily rituals and hearing the chants of Qur'an and the praises for the Prophet Muhammad is believed to be a powerful draw to the faith. By repeating the holy chants for hours on end, they believe, the environment becomes sanctified. NU never developed a set of strict ideas concerning the moral and social behavior of its members, but it is led by the belief that when Muslims become more intense in their religious lives, oneness with God will become visible in superior moral behavior.

Akhlak (ethics or morals) is important to NU members and considered the basis for a proper Muslim life along with *ikhlas* (sincerity). But to NU they need no elaboration, since they are a given, based on Qur'anic teachings.[85] When, for example, I asked NU women to reflect on the concept of *ikhlas,* their first reaction was, "But it is just part of being a Muslim." The extent to which this attitude is engrained seems clear; without a specifically spelled-out work ethic, NU people still work hard for the cause of Islam.

Many women members of NU work as Qur'an reciters and teachers or are graduates from institutes for advanced Islamic studies. Unlike the reformists, NU initially did not actively support women's education. That some women became respected scholars was due to the initiative of their male family members. Only later did women demand that NU allow them to set up the women's branches.

NU rejects the "one vision, one mission" ideal, allowing for wide ranges of opinions to congregate under its umbrella. Of course, shaping NU ideologies takes work and endless discussion. These, however, can remain openended. The process and sincerity to find the truth is what matters, since, in NU reasoning, in the end only God knows best.[86]

Nahdlatul Ulama: The Organization

The NU organizational model is entirely different from Muhammadiyah's; it is based on the independence of the local *kiai*. Its critics have long connected this basis with sloppy administration and ineffective central organs.[87] Actually, benefits and drawbacks both have to do with the role and spiritual authority ascribed to the *kiai* or *ulama* (Ar.: *'ulamā*, singular: *'ālim'*). The *ulama* are regarded as links in an unbroken chain that goes back to the Prophet Muhammad, the bearers of tradition and guides for the faithful. NU considers *ulama* "the primary pillar [*tiang utama*] of the community of the faithful."[88] The community of Muslims as a whole accredits respect and authority to an *ulama* based on personal charisma and learning. Most *ulama* are men, but the erudition of a handful of women has gained them the same degree. For example, Hasyim Asy'ari's sister Ibu Choiriya studied in Mecca for many years and upon her return to Java gathered a following of male students, several of whom have become *kiai* of *pesantren*.

Although it also includes members who are not *ulama*, NU is essentially a collegial alliance of *ulama*, united in a horizontal model. The majority of NU members, women and men, come from *pesantren* backgrounds. Its organization runs along religious councils (*syuriah*) and executive councils (*tanfidziah*). The division of levels runs similar to that of Muhammadiyah: national, province, district, and neighborhood. From the central to local levels these two tiers of councils are present. The religious councils consist exclusively of *ulama*, while the lay members are part of the daily administration in the executive councils. Because each *ulama* is autonomous, a decision made in a higher council is not binding for lower-level councils or for individual *ulama*.[89]

This autonomous structure conveyed to its critics the impression of a disorganized body filled with bickering *ulama*. Most western observers of Islam ignored NU, under the impression that NU traditionalist leaders were not equipped for the task of modernizing Indonesia and assuming that the reformists were the hope for the future. This may explain why the first book about NU in English was published only in 1996.[90]

I fully realized the implications of the different organizational models of NU and Muhammadiyah and the importance of personal authority within the NU structure when in 1998 I attended the national meetings of the Muslimat NU and 'Aisyiyah. My presence at the Muslimat NU was spontaneous, after speaking with Ibu Umroh Mahfudzoh, one of its vice presidents and a granddaughter of Wahab Chasbullah. A verbal invitation from her side and the announcement that I would be present opened all doors dur-

ing the meeting. For 'Aisyiyah, I and another researcher studying the movement had to file a formal request by July to attend the meeting in November. After discussing the requests during the board meeting, we were given
permission to be at the official opening ceremony on the second day and at
the presentation I was asked to give on the first day.

Woman's Space

The role of women belonging to Muhammadiyah or NU is necessarily defined by the organizational systems, the ethical teachings, and the modes
of interpretation of the Islamic sources practiced by these organizations.
Following Javanese society and Islamic teachings, the women define themselves in relation with and subordinate to men. Many of the male leaders
have little awareness of or concern for the profound gender differences that
run through their organizations, just as it runs through Javanese culture—
and, for that matter, the rest of Indonesian society.

Women of Muhammadiyah

Because of the organization's structure and its reformist stance, Muhammadiyah women face a different situation than that of NU women. Islamizing society by including the women, not true emancipation of women, was
the original goal of the Middle Eastern reformists. Because 'Aisyiyah women
started their preaching activities during the 1920s, long before NU women
could, many Muhammadiyah leaders now seem to have the impression that
their organization has sufficiently dealt with gender issues. This provides an
excuse to ignore fundamental gender issues and to seldom question models
that portray a woman's role as submissive and secondary to a man's. These
same models were propagated by the Suharto regime. It is symptomatic
that few Muhammadiyah men ever attend serious discussions about gender
organized by Muhammadiyah women. Their involvement is mostly limited
to studying religious questions concerning women. In the twenty-first century, this unconcern risks confining Muhammadiyah women to the gender
ideologies formulated before the 1950s.

'Aisyiyah was set up in 1917, but it became an official branch of Muhammadiyah only in 1924. When Muhammadiyah had to formulate rules concerning women's role, they enacted a multilayered process, considering
decisions made during the annual Muhammadiyah congresses, opinions
issued by the Majlis Tarjih, publications by 'Aisyiyah (such as articles in
Suara 'Aisyiyah), and responses to practical needs. The first official booklet

about the status and role of women, *Isteri Islam Jang Berarti* (The Muslim spouse who matters), appeared only in 1939, long after Muhammadiyah ideology had been fully formed.

Women who joined Muhammadiyah during the early years lived in a contradictory state of being. In the areas where women's discourse and work are most prominent, they experienced tension between the level of religious teachings and women's daily reality. For example, traveling was neither common for women at the time nor sanctioned by Qur'anic teachings. The prevailing attitude was that women should not enter a mosque, lest it become polluted.[91] Yet female preachers formed the backbone of the movement to recruit women members. They had to travel to reach potential believers, and they needed to meet for Qur'an studies, often held in mosques. In some tension with Muhammadiyah male leaders, both presented studying and preaching as a woman's duty.[92]

In 1932, Muhammadiyah's Majlis Tarjih made two decisions concerning women: women would be allowed to teach men as well as women, and they could go out but only during the day and never alone.[93] That women could teach men was considered a revolutionary step; however, at the same time, women's movement was restricted, as they had to be back by nightfall. Although it never openly attacked the decision that its preachers could only go out during the day, 'Aisyiyah insisted that women were under the obligation to go out and preach if they had the competence to do so. Its journal held that there should be no obstacles for female preachers and that husbands should gladly allow their wives to pursue these activities, since "preaching is better than gossiping."[94] To circumvent the problem of meeting in the mosque, women started building their own prayer houses (*mush-olla*). In 1933 those living around the Kauman organized a drive to gather for midnight prayers (*tahajjud*). The unimaginable happened: two hundred women came in the middle of the night to the first gathering.[95]

In spite of directives fired at them by Muhammadiyah, the women themselves often decided what activities to pursue and dared to use *Suara 'Aisy-iyah* as a platform to debate controversial issues. Only in 1972 did the Majlis Tarjih issue an official statement allowing women to go out by themselves, provided the husband had given them permission to do so.[96] This seemed less a necessity then a gesture to show that Muhammadiyah was still in tune with modern times. Yet the tension continued within the organization. By that time, 'Aisyiyah women were traveling by themselves all over Indonesia, while they had defined women's self-restraint in accord with reformist writings from the Middle East, such as those by the Egyptian Muslim Brotherhood.

The Egyptian Muslim Brotherhood stressed that education is as important to women as it is to men, especially in view of their future role as wives
and mothers. It also commended the virtues of gainful employment for
women to help the family thrive, and it frowned on polygyny, since the
practice contradicted other teachings of the Qur'an, such as to show love,
kindness, and mercy in the context of marriage.[97] But, at the same time, the
brotherhood taught, "'The woman's natural place is in the home, but if she
finds that after doing her duty in the home she has time, she can use part
of it in the service of society, on condition that this is done within the legal
limits which preserve her dignity and morality.'"[98]

The language of this last condition contradicts the reality of women leaders who are continually busy working for 'Aisyiyah, but ironically it keeps
recurring in their statements concerning women's role. For example, in
1999, the 'Aisyiyah office, addressing the question of women's leadership
in Islam, concluded that "there is no objection for a woman to become a
leader, from the level of the household to the level of head of the country,
as long as she possesses the capacities to complete her task in a faithful way,
using her knowledge, while at the same time not ignoring her main duty,
that is as a housewife."[99] This statement implies that the household is a
woman's primary duty; only when that is in order can she move on to other
positions in society.

In retrospect, it is evident that 'Aisyiyah women always accommodated
their ideology, work, and propagation to the directions of Muhammadiyah
men. Originally these were fresh and innovative, opening new vistas for
women who now could learn, pray together, teach, and preach. They meant
the fulfillment of the Qur'anic teachings that promise great rewards to men
and women who practice their religion sincerely, a return to the true, egalitarian, and liberating spirit of the Qur'an.[100] But true liberation on the
social level could not be achieved, and 'Aisyiyah women had to accommo-
date themselves to the structures of society as constructed by culture, the
Muhammadiyah men whose ideas are akin to those of the Muslim Brotherhood, and later, the Indonesian state. At this point of disjunction, the
innovative and fresh spirit of reorganizing religion gave way to repetition
and accommodation. Initially, 'Aisyiyah brought about a fundamental reorganization of women's religious life, but with time its approach changed
into providing remedial solutions while avoiding some of the most pressing
issues facing women. On the nonreligious level, 'Aisyiyah women soared to
great heights: deans, politicians, medical doctors, Islamic judges, lawyers,
and professors, many of whom educated by 'Aisyiyah, number among the
membership. But on the religious level, women had to perpetuate the ide-

ology that considers them not fully equal to men. Not that their preaching and teaching activities became futile: these continued as ever, even when they disagreed with the men's opinions. While Muhammadiyah directives came in from above, at the grassroots level the preachers provided their own interpretations of the Islamic injunctions. In theory they complied; in practice they might do otherwise.

It remained problematic for 'Aisyiyah to translate the reformist gender philosophy into authentic and realistic action. This translation has become one of the biggest problems it faces today. Somewhere along the road its original spirit of innovation and enthusiasm was replaced by a bureaucratic and protectionist machinery. Filing reports packed with tables, rules, names, and dates and holding repetitive meetings gained precedence over innovative ideas. In the end, 'Aisyiyah was, as one observer saw, "At risk of being eaten by its own structure."[101] Whether such cannibalism will occur remains to be seen.

Women of NU

NU women had their own struggles with the NU *kiai* and with gender prejudices in society. Paradoxically, the lack of unity in vision and mission, combined with the fact that no women were part of the early NU, allowed them more space to find their own direction. First of all, they were careful to know what was going on in the male section of NU. While 'Aisyiyah held its national meetings at the same time as the Muhammadiyah meetings, NU women decided to meet on separate dates so they could attend the male gatherings. NU answers questions concerning women's role through *fatwas* issued during its national meetings or, as needed, by regional boards. NU women often press for official advice to clarify certain discussions. In 1957, NU issued a *fatwa* that allowed women to become members of legislative bodies, and in 1961 it allowed a woman to hold the position of village head (*kepala desa*).[102]

NU has never officially stated that women cannot be members of its highest boards. In principle, any woman who has the knowledge of the *ulama* can compete for a seat. During the 1950s and 1960s, three women reached this position: Nyai Choiriyah Hasyim (the sister of Hasyim Asy'ari), Nyai Fatimah, and Nyai Mahmudah Mawardi. But a gap developed during the 1960s, when women benefited from the educational opportunities offered by the government and studied secular topics instead of pursuing religious studies. For the next forty years, until 2000, only two women, Mursyidah Thohir and Huzaemah Yanggo, were elected into the highest NU religious council, the Syuriah. Although they are not yet allowed to vote, their presence is a sign of the upcoming generation of women who can assume the task.

The 1997 Lombok conference decision about women's political leadership was a watershed event. After extensive discussions, the council of NU *ulama* decided that "women can hold positions in the public sphere, provided they are capable [or have the right qualifications for holding these positions]." Basically, this meant that in the national arena, no limits were placed on what women can do, including becoming the president.[103] Not all NU religious scholars agreed on this point, however, and some later interpreted this decision as allowing a woman to go as high as the vice presidency only.[104] They based their interpretation on the reasoning that a woman could never hold the highest state authority, since in worship the man should lead.[105]

The same issue provided a telling example of the divided opinions within NU. Prior to the presidential elections of 2004, fifteen *kiai* issued a *fatwa* stating that a woman could not be head of state. This opinion was not only directed against Megawati's candidacy, it was also a criticism against her vice presidential candidate, Kiai Hashim Muzadi, NU's national chair at the time.

Conclusion

During the 1990s, two new developments changed the paradigms of Indonesian Islam: the religious awareness, knowledge, and practice of Muslim believers intensified, while new ideas about gender emerged. The intensified religious practices were for NU and Muhammadiyah partly the fruits of their programs to propagate the faith. At the same time, they brought in challenges to the organizations, such as some students' preference for the simplified language and expectations of Islam Baru groups over the cumbersome practice and demands of the established organizations. These groups also spurred reactions within the organizations: Muhammadiyah youth became more conservative, while within NU a new development stressed the liberal sides of Islamic teachings.

Both trends yielded myriad studies and discussions, influencing the ideas of Muhammadiyah and NU women. The challenge for both groups was to incorporate the new gender ideas into their respective ideologies. This did not mean accepting all the new ideas that came in, only to discuss them and provide rationales for their rejection or approval.

Women of 'Aisyiyah faced the toughest challenge with these new ideas, having to fuse them with the Muhammadiyah gender ideologies. Since these proved to be as ambiguous as those of Indonesia's government, women faced tough choices as to where to lead their movement. While the older generation focused its energies on streamlining and bureaucratizing their activities, younger NA members studied the new gender ideas and tried to transmit them to the research focus groups on local levels. Looking back at the twelve steps of Muhammadiyah teaching, NA members stressed the practice of justice and wisdom, while 'Aisyiyah women tried to maintain the organization's unity. This inevitably led to a collision of ideas that will be described in the next two chapters.

In many ways, NU women faced the same ambiguity about gender notions, not so much in NU's organizational structure as in the diverse personalities of the *kiai*. Even within one *pesantren* this diversity of opinions might be evident. In one of the large *pesantren* in Yogyakarta, I observed the woman leader of one of its branches for women teaching a Fiqh text to refute its ideas, while her female colleague in the branch next to hers with great fervor tried to convince her students of its deep truths. On the level of NU gender ideology as produced by the *fatwas,* women can take for granted the NU stance about, for example, woman's leadership, although not all *kiai* will agree. The absence of strong unity within the organization also allows some NU members to study and discuss issues such as homosexuality, while this topic is still being considered taboo by many *kiai*.

In trying to understand the position of Muhammadiyah and NU in the Indonesian Islamic landscape, it becomes clear that the terms "reformism" and "traditionalism" do not connote black-and-white versions of Islam. The reality is far more complex. Liberal and extremist members flourish in their midst. Muhammadiyah has adopted many aspects of the Indonesian culture and has developed a new identity in comparison with the original, puritanical reformist movement that came from the Middle East. NU's continual modernizing has produced some of the most innovative leaders of Indonesian Islam in the twenty-first century. At the same time, distinct differences remain between the two modes of interpreting Islam, differences that can never be completely abolished.

The women who try to bring about change in gender ideologies about women know that in the Indonesian context patience (*sabar*) is the ultimate key to success. Many explain it as one of the main pillars of *ikhlas*. Seasoned by experience, the women hold that "evolution, not revolution," is most effective in bringing about change.

PART 2

Women of Muhammadiyah

3 'Aisyiyah's Jihad

> When we die only three things remain: the blessing of the alms
> we gave, our knowledge, and our good children [*anak shaleh*]
> who continue to pray for us.
> —Ibu Sulistyowati, 'Aisyiyah leader

Ibu Uswatun

In May 1998, Ibu Uswatun gave a passionate speech to an enthusiastic audience. Standing on a platform facing the mosque of the Kraton, the palace of the sultan of Yogyakarta, she called for the end of corruption and the end of the Suharto regime:

> All Mbak Tutut [the president's daughter, who was the minister of social affairs at the time] does to heal the wounds of our nation is hand out bags of rice. We Muhammadiyah women can do that. We do not need to be in the ministry for that. We have handed out food to the poor for nearly one century!

Ibu Uswatun's hand was raised in a fist, and many of the thousands of listeners returned the gesture with fervor. As a preacher of 'Aisyiyah, she was used to addressing large audiences, but not in her wildest dreams had she expected to air her political opinions in front of such a large crowd. In spite of the fact that she was a well-known preacher, her work had mostly been confined to mosques, schools, and peoples' homes. As a preacher with a vast knowledge of Islam, she also had to be acutely aware of political and economic developments. These developments drove her and many of her colleagues into the limelight of this defining moment just before the end of the Suharto regime. Through her sermons she had helped women cope with the regime, but now she had to guide them through the transition as a massive economic crisis was suffocating daily life.

The place where Ibu Uswatun stood embodied the dichotomies of Javanese Islam, especially for someone belonging to a reformist group. Behind her was the sultan's palace that embodied the syncretistic version of Islam in Muslim-Javanese Kraton culture. In front of her was the Kauman, the neighborhood where in 1912 the Muhammadiyah organization had been born.

'Aisyiyah had assigned Ibu Uswatun to guide me in my research about the organization. Of all the women I worked with, I came to know her best. In this chapter I will follow her and her colleagues in the 'Aisyiyah activities at the heart of its mission: preaching, education, and guiding family life. In these areas new members are formed, women who can, in Muhammadiyah parlance, "make Islam the spirit of civilization in a time of globalization." This ideal can especially be realized, in 'Aisyiyah's view, by instilling the right virtues into the next generation: hard work, a zest for learning, and forbearance (*ikhlas*). 'Aisyiyah tries to cast its net wide, bringing Islam from the confinement of the Kauman neighborhood to the whole nation. Expanding in ever larger circles, its mission reaches the individual through formal and nonformal education, to the family (*keluarga sakinah*), and to the village (*qoryah thoyyibah*; ideally a place inhabited by Muhammadiyah-minded people, all members of harmonious families and involved in village development). In a perfect world, the next level would be the whole country, but that is a complicated move in contemporary Indonesia. The circle originally expanded from the Kauman, the neighborhood that is still the symbolic heart of reformist Islam.

From Kauman to the Nation

The Kauman

Ibu Uswatun's and Muhammadiyah's place of birth is the Kauman in the heart of Yogyakarta, an area that has traditionally been reserved to Muslim inhabitants. At the beginning of the twentieth century, most of its inhabitants were the families of preachers from the sultan's mosque. Walled off and accessible only on foot, it is a maze of narrow, winding alleys that recalls the medieval quarter in a Middle Eastern city. There are few gardens. The houses are built right on the street, so close together that, when the windows are open, inhabitants can converse with each other as if they were in the same room. Often the sound of Qur'an recital drifts through the alleys, and at the Islamic prayer time many of the Kauman people hurry through them to the mosque.

Ibu Uswatun's father belonged to the Muhammadiyah members of the first hour, and she received her Islamic education from him. He worked as the director of the Muhammadiyah teacher-training college (Mu'allimat) and later became the head of the Pengadilan Agama (religious court). He spoke Indonesian, Dutch, and Arabic in addition to his mother tongue, Javanese. He taught all his children Arabic and the principles of Islam. Her mother was the first head of Nasyiat ul-'Aisyiyah, the Muhammadiyah organization for girls and young women, and later became an active leader and preacher of 'Aisyiyah. Ibu Uswatun has eight brothers and one sister, all of whom became active members of Muhammadiyah.

She was born in the 1930s, a time when a girl was expected to marry before the age of twenty, and often with the man of her parents' choice. Because that pattern left no time to pursue further studies, a girl had to graduate by the age of sixteen. Many of Ibu Uswatun's generation hold teaching certificates based on only a few years of high school work. Still, this was a step up from most of the other Kauman residents, who usually earned their income by producing batik. Ahmad Dahlan, the founder of Muhammadiyah, had supplemented his income as a Kraton preacher by trading batik in Java. During his business trips, Dahlan became acquainted with new ideas to reform Islam that came trickling in through Sumatra from distant places in the Middle East such as Mecca, Medina, and Cairo.

Women were economically powerful in those days, the main producers of batik, and often families relied on their income. Naturally, Ahmad Dahlan included them in the struggle to transform Indonesian Islam from personal practices of piety into a force for social change. Since few women had sufficient religious knowledge, he had to create a cadre first, so he encouraged bright young daughters of his friends and family to finish high school to become leaders and teachers of Muslim women. In 1917, the organization called 'Aisyiyah was born. Its goal was the same as that of Muhammadiyah, but with a "mission to women to seek the good work and leave the bad."[1]

The name 'Aisyiyah was carefully chosen; it was meant to be symbolic of its future members. 'Aisyiyah had been the Prophet's favorite wife, marrying him at the age of nine. Economically independent and not shy about expressing her opinions, she had been his closest companion, and after his death she became a religious authority herself.[2] At the same time, she was fully obedient to her husband.

In the 1930s, when Ibu Uswatun was born, many Indonesian women earned their own income, but the majority were illiterate.[3] Only a few Javanese Muslim women had any knowledge of their religion. Most believed in one God, prayed some Muslim prayers, and often fasted during Ramadan. They complemented these beliefs and practices with Javanese practices (*kejawen*) such as placing small offerings around their homes and at the graves of their dead ancestors. At the time 'Aisyiyah was set up, formal religious knowledge simply was not for women, because in Java women were not considered responsible for their own salvation.

Over time, the Kauman became the symbolic center for Muhammadiyah Islam. All of its winding alleys lead to some Muhammadiyah building of importance. Within walking distance are the former headquarters of Muhammadiyah, those of 'Aisyiyah, NA, and several other organizations related to them, the boarding school for girls (Mu'allimat), the first Muhammadiyah hospital, and the bookstore. It is a place where, according to Ibu Uswatun, people are honest; you can leave your door open without fear of theft, and the street vendors will never overcharge you for their wares. It remains a pure place, while the rest of the country is rife with corruption. However, outside the Kauman is another demographic reality. Today, according to the statistics of the local office for religious affairs (Kantor Urusan Agama; KUA) the larger neighborhood around the Kauman is not entirely Islamic but has a substantial Christian population.[4] A few steps removed from the Kauman is a large church for ethnic Chinese. And the Kauman lies within the area connected to the Kraton, where tenacious Javanese beliefs and practices hold sway.

Ibu Uswatun's house embodies the fusion of Muhammadiyah and local cultures: outwardly Javanese, on the inside Islamic. Its front door opens into the room where Indonesians customarily receive guests (*kamar tamu*). Its decor is a mix of Islamic, Javanese, and western art: texts of the Qur'an, pictures of landscapes definitely not in Indonesia, and a wedding picture of the family's only son. In the picture, the family is not dressed in Islamic dress but in traditional Javanese costume with tight skirts and jackets in colorful batik. Ibu Uswatun often dresses in the traditional Javanese outfit, but the jacket is not as tight as that of the Javanese version. The guestroom of the house leads into the family room, where most of the space is taken by an elevated platform that serves Ibu Uswatun and her husband as a sanctuary to perform their ritual prayers. Here they can move inwardly, from the world back to what the real Kauman signifies, the Kauman of the heart where the spirit of Islam reigns.

'Aisyiyah

A Life for 'Aisyiyah: Invisibly Visible

Ibu Uswatun lives in semi-retirement. For many years she was a member of the national board of 'Aisyiyah and now serves as an advising member. She still faithfully attends the weekly meetings, a discipline she is accustomed to, since she has been active in Muhammadiyah from the age of twelve, first as a leader in divisions of Nasyiat ul-'Aisyiyah and after her marriage in 'Aisyiyah. Her husband is retired from his work and remains active on the local level of Muhammadiyah. Ibu Uswatan still teaches Islam at the Muhammadiyah academy for nurses. Her week is packed with activities, most of them religious and in the service of 'Aisyiyah. Several mornings a week she leads the early morning prayers in the Kauman prayer house (*musholla*) for women. After the prayers she gives a short sermon called *kultum*, *kuliyah tujuh minit*, a seven-minute "lecture." On Mondays she organizes a Qur'an study after the early morning prayers (around 4:30 A.M.), a meeting her mother started several decades ago. Monday and Thursday afternoons at four she organizes another Qur'an study that ends before the call to the Maghrib prayers in the early evening. Thursday morning she leads an advanced Qur'an study that has been going on since the Second World War. Twice a month she spends a morning counseling Muslim couples for marriage preparation at the local Office for Religious Affairs. Apart from her activities as a teacher and at 'Aisyiyah's national board, she is the editor of *Suara 'Aisyiyah*.

Following the Muhammadiyah slogan that human beings should "use their brain and always learn," Ibu Uswatun is a voracious reader and continuously studies books on Islamic religion. Most of these books are published by Muhammadiyah and contain detailed information about Islamic life. From its inception, 'Aisyiyah encouraged women to read, even if they were at risk of getting "smarter than their husbands."[5]

In spite of her busy schedule, Ibu Uswatun always performs the five daily ritual prayers on time. If possible, she adds to that the Sunnah (not obligatory but recommended) midday prayer at 10:00 A.M. and the midnight prayer at 3:00 A.M. To the obligatory fast of the month of Ramadan, she adds the Sunnah fasting, called the Fast of David, two days a week, on Monday and Thursday.

Such an intense level of activities is common for 'Aisyiyah members; it is their form of *jihad*: "They struggle for Islam via 'Aisyiyah."[6] Sanctifying life, not only by worship but also through work, results in schedules packed with meetings, study gatherings, publications, and speeches. Frequent meetings and publications help 'Aisyiyah aspire toward the organizational goal of preserving a unified vision and mission.

The oath pronounced as the membership card is handed to a new member conveys 'Aisyiyah's expectations of its members:

> I declare that there is no God but God and that Muhammad is His Prophet.
> I am prepared to accept Allah as my God, Islam as my religion, and Muhammad as my Prophet. As a member of 'Aisyiyah, God willing, I will remain

faithful to the organization. I will protect its good name and submit myself to its rules. I will join the activities of the organization, support its work, pay my monthly dues, and apply the teachings of Islam in the right way so that it may please God. Amen, oh Ruler of the Worlds.[7]

The sense of their high calling so overwhelms women that it often brings tears to their eyes.

Ibu Uswatun is a missionary, and her foremost goal in life is to liberate women through Islam. All in 'Aisyiyah agree that this goal is not yet fully realized. Negative attitudes toward women are tenacious within Javanese society, and a steady stream of Indonesian men, upon returning from study in the Middle East, try to enforce extreme ideas that deny women public space. The former national chair of 'Aisyiyah, Ibu Baroroh Baried, expressed her frustration about this never-ending struggle: "Women here are not yet respected. Even in modern families one finds a negative attitude towards women. Worse, nowadays there are men with graduate degrees who forbid their wives to work, even if she has a college degree."[8]

The struggle is social on the outside and spiritual on the inside. 'Aisyiyah women dedicate their lives to the cause of Islam. Their Javanese/Islamic virtues compel them to remain invisible in this struggle because of a self-image that hinges on modesty and self-control. "Glamour" is a sin of the world, equal to the vice of consumerism.[9] Yet their attitude of docility is complicated by their recognition of the power of their work. These manifold works have visible results but stay in a woman's world; few men, even within Muhammadiyah, pay much attention to them.

The 'Aisyiyah Works

'Aisyiyah has aimed to make "Islamic society a reality for women" and to "reviv[e] the Indonesian spirit of Islam"[10] through performing "all types of work that are suitable [pantas] and profitable [bergoena] for women."[11] By combining religious, educational, social, and health work, it developed into an organization that took care of women, children, and the elderly. Through its educational and social projects, it molded and modeled the ideal of how to be a "virtuous Muslim woman." Its programs comprise kindergartens, clinics for mothers and children, orphanages, academies for nurses and midwives, health programs for elderly women, and savings and loans projects for women's businesses. This broad range of activities is the result of a transformation from mission through preaching and teaching to mission through services, designed to encompass every aspect of life.

'Aisyiyah's focus is the most central unit of society, the family; its care, ideally, surrounds one from cradle to grave. The moment a baby is born in an 'Aisyiyah clinic, the appropriate Muslim phrase is whispered in her ear, since "every baby is born a Muslim obedient to God." It was essential to have 'Aisyiyah midwives, since the traditional midwives (*dukun bayi*) transmitted also the magical formula and prayers accompanying the birth of a child and performed the folk rituals before and after birth. Setting up birth clinics was a means to eradicate this strong influence of indigenous culture.[12] Care ends at death, when they see to it that a woman's body is properly prepared for burial by another woman, not by a man, and that all rituals are performed according to Muhammadiyah teaching, with no forbidden elements slipping in, such as "prompting" (*talqin*) the dead.[13]

As 'Aisyiyah runs many programs, one person cannot possibly cover them all. Yet Ibu Uswatun's work includes several of its core activities: formal and nonformal education (preaching), counseling, and the family program called Keluarga Sakinah (the harmonious family). Ibu Uswatun is among the creators of the family model and transmits its ideals especially through her work as marriage counselor. Her vast knowledge of 'Aisyiyah's history, ideology, and rules resulted in her position as editor of *Suara 'Aisyiyah*. All 'Aisyiyah work demands a lot from its volunteers, but this work is especially demanding. Expecting financial rewards is forbidden; Ahmad Dahlan exhorted his followers to "bring Muhammadiyah to life, but never look for a living in Muhammadiyah."[14]

Informal Education

Teaching and Preaching the Faith

'Aisyiyah's first focus was teaching literacy courses so women could read the Qur'an and follow religious lessons. In 1923, a prayer house for women opened in the Kauman—the same one where Ibu Uswatun still regularly leads the prayers. It gave women a place to study and practice Islam away from home, where many had their batik businesses.

During the first years the focus was on preaching and teaching the correct Islamic rituals; according to 'Aisyiyah, performing them would bring women great blessings. In combination with the rules of appropriate behavior, women had to learn the text of ritual prayers. Ibu Uswatun remembers, "Some women were well-to-do batik merchants and dressed up to come to the mosque. Their long necklaces jingle-jangled during the prayers and disturbed the worship." At that time, "Many cheated during the fast of Ramadan by drinking water while taking a bath," rendering the fast invalid.[15]

'Aisyiyah stressed that completing the fast successfully yields uncountable blessings and merits (*pahala*) that could serve as a reservoir throughout the year.[16] In other words, it was important to show women that merit was not only for men but within easy reach for them as well, simply by forgoing a few drops of water.

Women also had to learn the Islamic Jurisprudence (Fiqh) concerning women's impurity (such as during menstruation and after childbirth), at which times they were not allowed to enter a mosque and could not participate in ritual fasting. Their knowledge thus prevented the women from inadvertently annulling their merit.

Practicing the Islamic rules correctly was connected with possible economic gain. 'Aisyiyah preachers stressed the fact that Islam and the Qur'an give women certain rights and then connected this knowledge with practical advice, such as to abolish the indigenous ceremonies for a pregnant woman held at the fifth, seventh, and ninth months. They emphasized the high costs involved rather than telling the women that those cherished ancient traditions were considered *shirk* (polytheism). Women often did the same work as men, so instead of preaching women's right to work, 'Aisyiyah preachers taught that women had the right to rest and refuse work that was too heavy "while the husband sits at home doing nothing."[17] Sally Jane White's research about the formative years of Muhammadiyah (1900–42) shows that women constructed their right to worship as well, since that had been mostly the prerogative of men.[18]

At a time when Islamic dress was not common in Indonesia, 'Aisyiyah encouraged women to express their Islamic identity by creating a Javanese Islamic uniform: the *kain* (wraparound skirt) and the *kebaya* (traditional Javanese jacket buttoned in the front), to which a *kerudung* (a veil loosely draped around the head) was added.[19] This dress became the marker of a changed religious identity. 'Aisyiyah women like Ibu Uswatun still wear it and encourage those who wear the veil only incidentally with compliments such as: "It makes you look years younger," or, "The veil highlights a woman's prettiness." These comments, while masking the religious purpose, encourage women to follow the virtuous practice.

Finally, learning (*mencari ilmu*) became fundamental in Muhammadiyah teaching. It was not only the road to religious correctness; it conferred powerful social and economic benefits. Based on the Qur'anic statement that "religion is logic, or understanding" (*Ad-din akal*), reformist thinking assumed that those who "use their understanding are able to accept religion" (*yang menggunakan akal bisa menerima agama*).[20] Teaching women to read helped them become active in religion and inspired them to study religious texts more deeply. Their accomplishment would help them value education for their children and might move them toward economic independence. According to 'Aisyiyah, this increased religious knowledge automatically resulted in intensified worship, which encouraged virtuous behavior, which in turn would lead to increased participation in 'Aisyiyah activities. On the public level, this active involvement in the community could inspire women to become role models and eventually missionaries. The visible proof and symbol of this religious, social, and cultural transformation for 'Aisyiyah was the construction of a kindergarten to transmit the Muhammadiyah principles of Islam.

Teaching children Islamic values became one of 'Aisyiyah's main activities. In 1919, the first Indonesian Muslim preschool opened in the Kauman. To provide teachers for the different educational activities, a teachers' training college (Mu'allimat) was set up in 1922 (it remains active). The primary goal was to create a generation that knew the proper rules of Islam and could continue teaching religion. Creating a new cadre for Muhammadiyah later became the second goal. A booklet for middle-school students states, "The function of the Muhammadiyah educational institutes is to be tools and channels of mission [*dakwah*] and to serve as an incubator for future charity workers for Muhammadiyah and society."[21] After the Suharto regime ended and Muslim organizations could be active in politics again, another goal was added: to groom future political leaders.[22] In the Muhammadiyah structure, 'Aisyiyah is assigned to teach the three-to-six-year-olds and to prepare female students for positions traditionally filled by women, such as teachers of small children, nurses, and midwives. Today, Muhammadiyah runs elementary, middle, and high schools; in 1998 it ran 128 universities and professional schools.[23]

Muballighat and Pengajian: Preachers and Qur'an Studies

Preaching to women forms the core of 'Aisyiyah work and originally was the main tool to spread the message of reformist Islam. When Ibu Uswatun improves her intellectual and spiritual capacities daily, she not only gains merit (*pahala*) but also qualifies as a female preacher, a *muballighat*. *Muballighat* preach and teach in Qur'an gatherings (*pengajian*). Many of them specialize in certain aspects of 'Aisyiyah mission: the harmonious family, preparing for the Hajj, preaching to factory workers, transmigrants, the sick, or nurses. *Pengajian* sessions are among the most popular social-religious events in Indonesia and reflect the reality that large populations in Indonesia still do not rely on the printed word but transmit knowledge orally.

Sessions are held weekly, monthly, or on other schedules, and their level can vary from simple Qur'an recitation to high-level *pengajian* for the preachers themselves or academic lectures for teachers at Muhammadiyah universities. Women preachers tend to cater to women's groups but also speak to mixed audiences. The content is always a religious message, sometimes combined with a discussion about health, birth control, or social problems such as prostitution or drug abuse.

Pengajian are held at set times according to a set pattern, in a private house, a community building, or at a mosque. The women attending are of mixed ages; some bring their children, all dress in their prettiest outfits. Members of 'Aisyiyah organize the study session and take turns serving snacks and drinks. The session starts with greetings, upon which all present recite the Fatihah. The preacher then recites in Arabic the text that will be discussed during the study meeting.

In the 'Aisyiyah model of teaching Islam, setting up a *pengajian rutin* group is considered the heart of its mission and organizational life. How often it meets is not as important as the fact that it meets routinely at regular intervals. The smallest unit, the *ranting* (at least five persons), starts out by organizing a weekly *pengajian* to transmit "the [reformist] Muhammadiyah spirit and its core teachings" and to increase its visibility in society.[24] These courses were the original venue to train new preachers, starting from the elementary level. Many active members became gifted speakers and were successful in Indonesian society as politicians, teachers, professors, and civil leaders. As the *muballighat* became better educated, *pengajian* also became a means to "Islamize the Muslims."[25]

Pengajian can be a series that discusses parts or topics of the Qur'an, faith, and dogma, or it can follow the annual cycle of Muslim feasts. During a feast, *pengajian* are held to discuss and explain what the particular celebration commemorates. Some 'Aisyiyah preachers teach a "package" for women: a series of lessons that covers the basics of Islamic theological, moral, ethical, and legal teachings and includes memorization of prayers and verses from the Qur'an in Arabic. There are *pengajian* for widows, mothers of young children, women in prison, the poor, and the elderly. All of these study groups provide occasion to discuss the problems of the day in light of Islam.

Sometimes *pengajian* are combined with another cherished Indonesian activity, the *arisan*, a savings and loan club. At each meeting, members give a fixed amount of money. Lots are drawn during the meeting to decide which of the participants will get the entire amount. For many poor Indonesians, this is the only way they can afford to buy a refrigerator or fix up their homes. Muhammadiyah also has created charitable *pengajian-arisans,* for example the *pengajian semen* (cement study group), which saves money to build houses for the poor.

The decision to become a preacher is not made lightly. Most women preachers prefer not to be called *muballighat*, since they feel incapable of living up to the high demands of this calling. Perhaps because of these demands, Muhammadiyah suffers a chronic shortage of qualified preachers, female and male. 'Aisyiyah preachers model good behavior and ethics (*akhlak*), know the Islamic Jurisprudence, and have learned substantial parts of the Qur'an by heart. A woman preacher's knowledge earns her a high level of respect, and with her discourse she exercises a certain amount of authority and power.[26] As with male preachers, it takes many years of study to reach this level. A *muballighat* can also serve as a female *imam* and lead women-only prayers. Some give sermons via the radio, cassettes, or even TV. Local government rulers in Indonesia make sure they are not at odds with the preachers and often seek their help in times of social unrest or when important events such as parliamentary elections are at stake.

'Aisyiyah preachers are mostly from middle-class backgrounds and hold at least a high school degree. Few have official religious training but have reached their position by a lifelong habit of studying, participating in Muhammadiyah events, and following directives from workshops. Their preaching of official directives is especially important for the less-educated rural audiences who must learn by oral transmission.

Preaching is one of 'Aisyiyah's main weapons against what it considers vice in society. *Muballighat* address social ills and encourage women to equip themselves with the spiritual, educational, or economic tools to face adversity. Preachers help their hearers cope with issues such as unruly children, drug abuse, globalization, and secularization. Of course, the theme that people should not participate in rituals that are not Islamic recurs throughout reformist preaching. For 'Aisyiyah, a solid knowledge of Islamic teachings safeguards a person from many evils and creates a life of "truth, peace, tranquility, and well-being."[27]

Ibu Uswatun belongs among 'Aisyiyah's best preachers, especially because of her religious knowledge. When she preaches, it seems that her personality changes: no longer just an average person, she becomes a charismatic advocate for true Islamic living. Whether she speaks to women only or to a mixed audience, all want to hear what she has to say. In Indonesia it is easy to see which preachers are considered interesting: the listeners do not chit-chat among themselves when he or she speaks but give their full attention. The language is most often Javanese, but if people from outside Java such as myself are present, the *pengajian* is held in Indonesian.[28]

The Message

To keep its message unified, the 'Aisyiyah central office in Yogyakarta regularly issues documents that advise preachers how to tackle certain topics. For example, during the economic crisis in 1998, 'Aisyiyah preachers were urged to preach about how to cope with the decrease in family income. Women all over Indonesia, including those in overcrowded, urban Jakarta, were urged to grow their own vegetables. Women were also called to practice patience (*sabar*) and to give thanks for what they had instead of thinking of what they could not afford. This, promised 'Aisyiyah, would yield great *pahala* and help them get through the crisis.[29]

During Ramadan in 1998, I attended several *pengajian* by Ibu Uswatun and other preachers. That year, unfortunately, provided numerous examples of the role of preachers in times of adversity. The economic crisis was one of the foremost topics. Ibu Uswatun's listeners were in shock and distress; she could do little more than stress the spiritual aspects of life. On January 11, at four in the morning, she preached, "There are several vehicles to guard against the current crisis: patience, thanksgiving, and worship [*sabar, syukur, ibadah*]." She continued to tell the audience that secularism and corruption were the cause of the disaster: "Secularism is one of humanity's worst enemies," Ibu Uswatun said, quoting Qur'an 2:204: "[T]he type of man whose speech about this world's life may dazzle thee." She elaborated that this verse alludes to "egocentrism" and "ruining our world." She also blamed the government and its cronies, but, of course, her language was veiled; the Suharto regime was still firmly in place, so open criticism was not possible. Later, at an 8:00 A.M. session, she picked up the theme of secularism again and connected it with globalization. "Globalization is a direct threat to good morals, creating people who only look for material values and forget the teachings of religion." Globalization, according to Ibu Uswatun, introduces values opposite to Kauman mentality:

> Nowadays, women can just get any man; in Jakarta there are rich women who overwhelm men with their possessions. . . . The poor boys . . . start to think that money is good for everything. This is the way of thinking of people from the era of globalization . . . they do not care about morals any longer . . . they go to the local hospital to "buy sperm." . . . They see no objections in drinking alcohol, one beer, two beers, three beers, what arises is a spirit of beer [not of religion]. . . . Mothers of Indonesia, we have to strengthen our faith, there is no other answer. . . . Fast on Mondays and Thursdays . . . increase your prayers . . . and keep an eye out for the signs of addiction to alcohol such as lack of appetite.[30]

That year the economic crisis intensified, and whatever the text of the day, preachers spent most of their time giving advice to desperate listeners. During a meeting preceded by a health checkup for mothers and children, Ibu Uswatun discussed the Jurisprudence concerning cleanliness, spicing it up with advice about women's health.

> Let us clean and sanctify our clothes. Our clothes, body, and the utensils we use to eat and drink have to be ritually clean. ... If the water is clean and sanctified we can drink it, but if we are not sure whether the sugar [for tea] was a product of corruption, it is not clean, not *halal* [permissible according to Shari'ah law]. ... According to our religion there is outward and inward cleanliness. ... By performing the ablution five times a day, our faces are always clean. ... On Fridays we clean our house, since we live in a place where mosquitoes carry dengue fever. ... Women should also stay healthy by not ignoring their body. ... Eat and drink, but not too much, since God does not like overeating.

Her niece, Ibu Ismiyatun, a prize-winning preacher, continued this lesson with a song:

> For sure cleanliness comes from faith.
> It is my duty.
> God the most Holy, Source of Sanctity,
> Likes cleanliness.
> Your cleanliness is the measure of your faith.
> Remember to be clean.

The message was that women should take care of themselves and not fall back on old models where women had to do with the leftovers after the men and children had eaten their fill. Women had to preserve their health to survive.

Ibu Ismiyatun is famous for her songs, which, in Muhammadiyah circles, make up for the absence of chanting. During another meeting she tried to lift the spirits of those present by spelling out what they did have and trying to take their minds off of what was taken away by the crisis. After praising God that there was still food to eat, she sang:

> Fried soybean cakes, praise the Lord
> For lunch this afternoon.
> If we do not have them, never mind,
> Marinated soy cakes [*tahu baceman*] taste just as delicious.

She continued to elaborate on each reason for thankfulness:

Thank God for a whole body, thank God for sanity, for the things we already possess, for our food that we can fry in oil, for opportunities to learn and for free time, for the world around us, and thank God for our culture that encourages us to help each other.

She stressed that a sound brain is a person's most precious possession:

What is this sanity? At this time, praise the Lord, we still have a sound brain. Are there people who do not have that? Very many . . . you should visit the asylum in Pakem and see those whose brain is not sound. There are no medicines for that condition. Maybe their mother fell during pregnancy. . . . There are also those whose soul is sick. Nowadays many have that condition because they never thank God for his beneficence. . . . Thank God, all of you are healthy of mind and spirit so that you will not fall victim to "Ahmad stress" [stress] but remain a friend of "Muhammad patience" [remain patient].

Several themes appear in this short impression of sermons: the economic crisis and how to react to it, secularism, globalization, and how to stay within the rules of Islamic teaching. According to 'Aisyiyah, outside influences—from the West, the East, and from globalization—are among the most dangerous distractions. The view stems from the Muhammadiyah teaching to guard the heart by staying close to reformist teachings. Vice came from Jakarta, the seat of government that ignored the valuable teachings of Islam and flirted with the West, a dangerous alliance that could lead to a total breakdown of society. Other evils emerged from places like the Middle East and Malaysia, where extremist sects attracted scores of adolescents. In the face of these seemingly overwhelming forces, Ibu Uswatun reminded her audience, women are not powerless. Women could save the faith, increasing their spiritual exercises to start a counterattack. She stressed the power of the individual: one individual can corrupt society as one rotten apple in a full basket does, but the reverse can be achieved by replacing it with a good one.

Examples of this type of preaching, typical for 'Aisyiyah, can be found as early as 1930. By spelling out possible onslaughts on Islam, preachers encouraged believers to guard themselves and their community. In the 1930s the dangers were "women who imitate the West by dancing, playing tennis, and having bobbed hair."[31] In the 1940s, "music, dancing the rumba, wearing certain types of fashion, and men without religion" were identified as great dangers to Muslim society, especially its women.[32]

Ibu Ismiyatun's message also illustrates how individual preachers convey the Central Office guidelines and encourage their practice. She positioned the lack of wealth and even food against the worst that could happen to a human in the Muhammadiyah worldview: losing the capacity to think. She stressed the virtues of patience and thankfulness in the face of adversity and urged women not to lose courage. The solace and the challenge at the core of her songs was to remember that there might always be someone worse off than you. Ibu Uswatun and her colleagues tried to keep their message on a level the audience could understand, even here and there adding a sniff of criticism. Being nearly invisible proved useful in this respect, as nobody reported her to the police.

The question that arises when looking at some of the topics discussed in the sermons is straightforward: Do they affect and/or empower women? Little overt gender-awareness building takes place, yet the preachers' references apply to the daily lives of most women. It is the only level on which their empowerment can work if all other structures fail them. Maila Stivens argues that politics and resistance are made not only on the high level of parliamentary chambers but also "in the kitchens, living rooms, bedrooms, workplaces."[33] In a complex, multilayered reality, the preachers use what Michel Foucault calls "spaces of dissension."[34] Within the spectrum of their own interpretations, women preachers develop a range of discourses that must be placed in the women's context. The religious message not only encourages women directly but also helps subvert local structures and customs that harm them. The bottom line for many women at the grassroots level is to take care of themselves; in many cases, this means that they should eat well and not reserve the good food for the men in the household only. A male preacher might have reversed the message; he might have urged the women to give more food to the men of the house and disregard their own health, extolling some sort of misplaced martyr syndrome.

Most *pengajian* take place on the grassroots level. As women become better educated, they can begin to read and interpret the religious text of the Qur'an themselves. When they reach this stage, 'Aisyiyah provides more advanced Qur'an lessons, as the following examples illustrate.

The Qur'an Lesson of Outside Boundaries

One advanced study group has met weekly since 1943. The participants are a mix of older and younger women, all of whom have reading knowledge of Arabic. Ibu Uswatun is one of its three leaders.[35] The group sometimes organizes charitable events, and as its members grow older, it has started to coordinate the work of women's burial. The group teaches the exact rules concerning rituals (Fiqh) and dogmas. Women discuss the text of the Qur'an and other religious texts intensely, using their own insights and judgments (*ijtihad*).

I attended several sessions during September 1998. One of these started with a close reading of Surah 24:21–22. Focusing on the first verse—"You that are true believers, do not walk in Satan's footsteps"—the group discussed how to react when someone in the family converts from Islam to another religion, especially Christianity. After that they studied the rules concerning worship in the mosque. Who is qualified to lead the prayers, and who is not? Both themes led to a vivid discussion that included syncretism, incorrect behavior, and matters of worship concerning women. "Never ever can someone who adds unlawful elements to the prayer [ahli bid'ah] become the leader," said Ibu Uswatun. "Those who say qunut [supererogatory prayers], or speak the intention [niyat] out loud can never lead the prayers." This saying was a dig against traditionalist practices and implied that reformists cannot join prayers led by a traditionalist. In the same context, Ibu Uswatun stressed the importance that women know their rights and status in Islam. Believing that women harm themselves when they lack knowledge of the Islamic teachings, she provided the following example to stress her point:

> Once I went to a mosque in Sulawesi, and several women were waiting to perform their prayers. I wondered why they did not go ahead. Suddenly a man walked in, and the prayers started. It hurt my feelings to see that this group obviously believed that a woman cannot lead prayers for women. Yet the Prophet once said that women leaders are preferable.

This particular lesson covered a range of topics related to women and the reformist ideology: women's responsibilities, the importance of their knowledge, the goal to Islamize society, and how to apply this knowledge in an ever-changing society. Obeying the rules was considered a sure way to guarantee women's rights. It is 'Aisyiyah's philosophy that women's liberation will happen once they secure their proper rights in Islam. At the same time, its leaders acknowledge that although the Qur'an teaches women's equality in religious matters, the social and cultural reality remains that "as long as we can remember, men have colonized women."[36]

The other topic, conversion from Islam to another religion, remains problematic. Islamic law forbids it, but the Indonesian legal system allows it. In many Muslim countries, those who convert to another religion are put in jail or punished by death, but not in Indonesia. This inconsistency between law of the land and law of religion has been among the reformists' greatest concerns since the beginning of the twentieth century. For Muhammadiyah, even the lawful marriage between a Muslim man and a Christian woman is, in principle, undesirable, since the mother is a child's first teacher of religion. Thus, preventing family members from conversion to Christianity or another religion has always been a crucial strategy. Such a conversion, or even a mixed marriage, most serious for the one who chooses it, is no less fraught with danger for mothers, for they hold the responsibility for bringing up their children to keep true to Islam. Mothers whose children marry or convert, according to 'Aisyiyah teaching, bear the blame for their action.

The Qur'an Lesson of Inside Boundaries

The issue of interreligious marriage opens the door to an issue that touches simultaneously on women's rights in Islam and that of children who disobey the religious rules. If 'Aisyiyah was battling ignorance about the rules in the old days, now the corruption of Islam comes from within. In the new Islamic climate, young adults themselves try to decide on the boundaries of intimacy.

Nancy Smith-Hefner's research shows that some young adults try to return to what they imagine to be the "original" Muslim customs of letting their family or peer group choose their partner. Some even go as far as refusing to meet their future spouse until the wedding day so that she or he will be a "surprise."[37] Others "legalize" their sexual relationship in unofficial ways. In the journal *Syir'ah,* young NU members acknowledge that "[f]ree sex among university students is not that strange. But it is shocking if it turns out that many practicing it come from the *pesantren.*"[38] "Free sex" here does not typically mean multiple partners; but it does mean students sleeping together without being married officially. For example, students far from home who do not want their parents to know that they are dating or sharing a house with their partner now opt for the secret marriage (*kawin sirri*) or the temporary marriage (*mut'a*). An Indonesian student in Australia wrote: "After I graduate from college we are planning to marry in secret so that my father will not be disappointed while we can realize our dream and most of all not commit fornication [*zina*]."[39] Others simply pledge to each other that they are married "with only God as witness."[40]

This new reality upsets Ibu Uswatun terribly, since the secret or *mut'a* marriage contracts are neither officially registered at the local Office for Religious Affairs nor publicly announced. She finds it upsetting not only "because nothing is legal and in accordance with the official Islamic rules," but even more because these marriage contracts can harm a woman. "What if he leaves her without a trace? What if she gets pregnant?"[41]

For 'Aisyiyah women, these practices are actually a reversal of women's religious rights that they struggled for decades to achieve. But the leaders are at a loss as to what to do; practically speaking, they cannot enforce their ideas. In the old days, people were not aware of the Islamic teachings; in contemporary Indonesia, students who want to get married unofficially know exactly what they are doing and can cite traditions supporting their actions. Few young adults are prepared to listen to 'Aisyiyah women, who are mostly older than they are and lack the charisma to move the younger audience. Although they can get furious about certain conditions, they can neither come up with viable solutions for this new generation nor enforce the official rules.

While some progressive thinkers have proposed reconsidering the institution of marriage, 'Asyiyah would never do that. The four legal schools express a range of opinions concerning marriage. The Hanafi school allows marriage without a *wali*, and the Maliki school considers a marriage without a witness valid.[42] 'Aisyiyah likewise would not readily agree with the Shafi'ite position: "For the Shafi'ite school the institution of marriage is similar to the transaction of selling and buying."[43] The concept of marriage that 'Aisyiyah upholds was formed during its first thirty years and after that became incorporated into the harmonious family model. In line with reformist teachings about marriage, 'Aisyiyah focuses on the laws and regulations of marriage, not on social analysis or new modes of human relations. Thus, to younger ears, its leaders seem to repeat old slogans rather than seek innovative methods.

Does this mean that 'Aisyiyah fails to address what it considers to be wrongs in society? Its leaders have been successful in reaching mostly uneducated women, those whom others overlook. Still, many of these are mothers of those practicing *kawin sirri* or *mut'a*. Perhaps this contradiction implies the need for increased and even more direct teaching, as building awareness is the first step in creating change. Reaching the audience as early as possible—in their own lives and in the emergence of negative social activity—has always been one of 'Aisyiyah's main goals. Reaching mothers is a clear first step, but I can think of no better place than preschools for children of tender age to start to adopt the Muhammadiyah patterns of believing and thinking.

Formal Education

Educating the Future Generation: Preschools

All involved in 'Aisyiyah/Muhammadiyah programs are in a process of continuous learning and on their way to become preachers and missionaries of

Islam. To instill "a Muhammadiyah spirit" in children and students is the ideal. Children in 'Aisyiyah preschools sing:

> Spirit of Muhammadiyah, deeply rooted in my heart,
> I have known you since I was small.
> You hold high the Law of God.
> You never know weariness, nor ever falter.[44]

Formal education is an important mission for Muhammadiyah parents, for their organization, and for Islam. It creates the future cadre. It helps preserve unified teachings about gender roles, morality, modernity, and the vision and mission of Muhammadiyah. In the end, it preserves the family and helps reach the goal of Islamizing society. Schools are the organization's strongest point. Muhammadiyah allows 'Aisyiyah only to operate schools deemed appropriate to women's *kodrat* (innate nature). These are preschools, the Mu'allimat school, and the colleges for nurses and midwives. At the same time, 'Aisyiyah women manage the other Muhammadiyah schools, many of them serving as principals, teachers, and administrators.

Every district unit of 'Aisyiyah (*daerah*) must open a preschool (*taman kanak-kanak*). These schools visibly prove the growth and vigor of the organization. At official 'Aisyiyah celebrations the children are part of the program. They present songs and little sketches and march in drum bands led by toddler cheerleaders. Children are the future, and 'Aisyiyah's task is to raise them in the fold of Muhammadiyah.

Starting at elementary schools, children receive special instruction in "Kemuhammadiyaan," the facts and history of Muhammadiyah. Children memorize a wide range of information, such as the organization's goals, mission, important congresses, and the names and history of some of its leaders. They reflect on questions such as, What is the Muhammadiyah personality? This methodology assures a generation well informed about the roots and backgrounds of its organization.

"To instill the Muhammadiyah spirit [*menjiwa*]" is a phrase often used to describe 'Aisyiyah's educational goals. Teachers aim to instill not only the spirit of Islam and a dedication to service but also a spirit of politeness. Children learn the rules of Islamic worship, faith, and *akhlak* (morals). Ibu Lies Sulistyowati, an expert on early child development, explained this process as follows:

> In school, the children learn the ritual prayer [*shalat*] and practice fasting [*puasa*] so that they can continue this pattern at home with their families. They learn to help each other, to lend their toys. Children at that age are still

selfish, so we teach them that sharing their toys will yield great merit [*pahala*] later. God will reward them in heaven. Around us we hear children speak in impolite ways, saying rude things [*kasar*], and not behaving politely. God willing, this will not happen when they are trained in Muhammadiyah schools. Religion, good morals, and politeness are instilled in a child between the age of six months and six years.[45]

Proper morality in Java entails *sopan santun* (politeness)—to know one's place in society and how to address those who are older or superior. When children cease to be polite, 'Aisyiyah women believe that society will erode. Ibu Nibras Salim, the founder of a large preschool in Jakarta, reflected on this belief:

Parents and teachers are important models. Nowadays, the role of schools in preparing future generations of Muslims is becoming increasingly central. Modern society has become less "polite"; youngsters are spoiled, while parents (especially mothers) no longer live up to their role as primary caregivers. Mothers no longer stay at home; they have more money and hire a babysitter, so the children lack the example of their parents. There is not enough informal education at home.[46]

In preschool, children get acquainted with gender roles and learn concepts of modesty. According to an 'Aisyiyah handbook for preschools, boys and girls should get used to doing gender-appropriate activities from the beginning: "[B]oys will play with different toys than girls."[47] According to 'Aisyiyah, teaching children modesty helps them understand the rules about how men and women interact and works to prevent future sins such as adultery. Ibu Nibras Salim is adamant:

Girls have to learn that they should cover themselves. Boys learn that they are not allowed to peek when girls use the bathroom at preschool. By the age of ten, they should no longer be allowed to sleep in the same room. Girls have to know that it is not proper to go around without one's *mahram* [male family member who accompanies them]. Parents and schools have to apply these rules, since on TV all they see is girls going about by themselves and socializing with boys who are from outside their family. This leads to *zina* [fornication] and is against Islamic teaching.[48]

In spite of the stress on specific roles for men and women, 'Aisyiyah does not consider segregation to be a useful way to learn about proper roles. The schools follow the pattern of the Indonesian educational system, which is based on co-education. This is a given and natural; gender segregation, they say, belongs to the Middle East. It is frowned upon and considered an undesirable import from other Islamic countries. Years later, Professor Baroroh Baried remained upset that

> once in Brunei during a conference, I had to leave the room during the coffee break because the women were on the other side. We in 'Aisyiyah try to teach our women that all that is obligatory is proper Muslim behavior and that there is no separation between boys and girls. We have co-education. We wear the veil not to disturb the men.[49]

Mixing the sexes means it is the teachers' responsibility to prevent errors before they occur by showing children the correct way. Like mothers, they must teach children the correct rules before they go off and enter a secret marriage or worse.

Instilling the spirit of Islam as represented by Muhammadiyah starts early and ideally continues throughout a child's school years. Early training guarantees exemplary young women who agree on the goals, mission, and methods of the organization, but 'Aisyiyah loses access to their formation when they enter the upper-level Muhammadiyah schools, where little on the curriculum mentions the activities of women. This loss complicates 'Aisyiyah's task of shaping of gender, as during the years in which girls are most gender-aware, their teachers hold priorities different from those of 'Aisyiyah. It also complicates the process of finding new leaders. The emancipation picture has shifted: young women are no longer interested in devoting their lives to such an all-consuming mission. Yet, playing second violin behind the men is not attractive either. So 'Aisyiyah had to design new strategies to attract future leaders. The educational network still seemed the closest and most viable option to find them.

The University Level

In the past, new members could be drawn from Nasyiatul 'Aisyiyah (NA), which was part of 'Aisyiyah between 1931 and 1965. After it became independent, however, NA slowly drifted away from the mother organization. On a day-to-day basis, NA must cope with its own problems, and its members will no longer automatically join 'Aisyiyah when they reach a certain age. This has encouraged 'Aisyiyah to initiate several projects to nurture future leaders. The Mu'allimat is one of these—while finishing the high school curriculum designed by the state, girls at the Mu'allimat spend 60 percent of their time on religious topics. The director, Ibu Kholifah, considers their study a *jihad,* since the girls struggle for God, "applying the norms of Islam in their private lives, while also serving society."[50] "Serving society" means preaching at youth gatherings and teaching children Arabic and the Qur'an. At home on their infrequent vacations, the girls continue to preach sermons, teach lessons, and visit hometown Muhammadiyah leaders to benefit from their wisdom.

Despite these high ideals, the surrounding world, with its manifold temptations, is interfering. The Mu'allimat school is losing its attractiveness, since after graduation few of its alumni manage to secure a place at the top universities. Girls are no longer interested only in careers in elementary education. Ibu Uswatun's career pattern no longer attracts the younger generation.

To intensify the search for new membership, 'Aisyiyah has also tried to revive an old Muhammadiyah tradition of opening dorms for female university students. During the 1920s, Ahmad Dahlan's wife started a dorm to set girls apart from society with its distracting influences of family and surrounding culture. 'Aisyiyah hopes that these initiatives will foster a new generation that has solid knowledge of the reformist legacy yet is innovative in its thinking and can help reinvent its mission. Moreover, these students can also advocate the proper forms of marriage.

The pamphlet advertising the dorms states that their goal is "to prepare a cadre of young women of high quality and high morals." The graduates, according to 'Aisyiyah, will be intellectuals who are also female *ulama* (*ulama putri yang intelek*). Students come from all over Indonesia to study full-time at universities and follow the religious program at the dorm. They also actively promote 'Aisyiyah in their hometowns. The experiment seems to be yielding good fruit, excellent students with a deep commitment to Muhammadiyah.

I asked the students in the Yogyakarta dorm Pesantren Niyai Ahmad Dahlan to formulate their hopes for the organization. Several of them wrote a short essay summarizing their vision for the organization. The result was an interesting blend of the old and the new in language and ideas and provided a glimpse of what the future will hold. Many wrote that they hoped "'Aisyiyah will be present in every hamlet throughout the nation," and that when the reformist teachings are implemented correctly, "the position of women will be improved according to the teachings of Islam." Such language can be found in 'Aisyiyah publications dating back to the 1930s. These slogans alternated with contemporary language such as "gender ideology," "emancipation for both men and women," and "a woman's task is not limited to the domestic sphere; she can strive to become the president."[51]

'Aisyiyah has chosen to change its cadre at the same time that the paradigm of Indonesian Islam is changing. The task is daunting. Even as 'Aisyiyah tries to shed its image of conservatism and "uncoolness," its women cannot see into the future. Their approach is necessarily two-pronged: to instill the enduring values in the youngest of the Muhammadiyah family while reinventing the organization through the university level. The students in the dorm already have ideas entirely different from those of 'Aisyiyah leaders. In one departure from tradition, their essays hardly mentioned the Javanese/Islamic virtue of *ikhlas* (pure dedication to work done for God's sake alone). 'Aisyiyah women talk about this virtue nonstop and see it as driving their dedication. They learned from their mentors that it embodies the original ideals of the organization, when members offered all their material and spiritual riches. While the challenges of modern society continue to erode original 'Aisyiyah values, *ikhlas* may have become hidden, but it can never disappear. It is the essence of Muhammadiyah activities. Understanding its interpretation is crucial, since it shapes not only the Muhammadiyah work ethic but also its gender dimensions. Although men and women reflect on it differently, it has shaped the nature of women's self-control. So before moving on to 'Aisyiyah's life work of the harmonious family, I elaborate on *ikhlas* as presented by the women of 'Aisyiyah.

Work for God's Sake Alone

Controlling Body and Spirit: The Construction of Ikhlas

The core of 'Aisyiyah's struggle is to find the right discourse for the right time. Of the several obstacles I have mentioned so far, the greatest comes from the women themselves: their self-image and their idea about what threatens their mission. Self-discipline has led to an internalization of control, the creation of what Foucault called "docile bodies."[52] Controlling the body for 'Aisyiyah is not negative, however; it is the means to a set of positive goals. These include working and acting within societal limits to liberate women by liberating their souls, and to become noble models of morality and perfect servants of God. How to achieve these goals forms the challenge for all generations of Muslim women in Indonesia. Making the right choices within the limits of Islam is a challenge that has created a process of continuous interpretation. For example, when Mbak Ama, one of the NA leaders, joined me for a swim at a western-style hotel, she wore a full body suit with long sleeves and legs and a rubber cap to hide her hair. Of course, 'Aisyiyah women would never swim, but it is Mbak Ama's favorite sport. So she found a way to negotiate her modesty.

In the end, not only male authority but also their own total commitment to the practice of *ikhlas* holds the women back. Crucial to the well-being of both a Javanese and a Muslim, *ikhlas* shapes their self-image, the image they wish to convey to the world outside, and the status of 'Aisyiyah women within Muhammadiyah.

Ibu Uswatun's life is composed of several paradoxes. She is so accustomed to them that they hardly bother her, but younger women find them quite frustrating. Her organization preaches equality of women yet ultimately has to submit to Muhammadiyah. It sets up health clinics and trains nurses and midwives to staff them, but when the clinics are extraordinarily successful and become hospitals, Muhammadiyah takes over their management because according to its rules, 'Aisyiyah must confine its activities to clinics. Yet most of the directors and administrators at Muhammadiyah schools and hospitals are 'Aisyiyah women.

'Aisyiyah preachers work day and night, yet they are not visible. Many Indonesian Muslims have the impression that the organization is wholly ineffective, unaware that through its extensive educational networks many women achieved degrees of higher education. It contributed to the success stories of the women who became politicians, judges, and deans; but their professional activities remained divorced from 'Aisyiyah activities.

The bottom line for Ibu Uswatun is that her vocation is from God. She can put up with what appear to be contradictory conditions in her individual life by relying on what she believes to be a Muslim woman's spirituality, personality, and role. Apart from that, she is driven by the historic sense of belonging to a group that counts and forms its members in a vast network. "When I was in Surabaya, I felt at ease, there were so many friends; we were all united in 'Aisyiyah," she explained. Most of all, the internal sense of *ikhlas* convinces Ibu Uswatun that her reward awaits her later and elsewhere, not here and now.[53] According to Islamic teachings, *ikhlas* is explained as "the human embodiment of *tawhid* [making God one]." Sachiko Murata and William Chittick explain that those who practice *ikhlas* "purify their religion for God alone, and God in turn aids them by purifying them of attention to everything other than himself."[54] I started to understand how the concept of *ikhlas,* in the Islamic sense of working purely for God, works in daily life in combination with the Javanese sense of inward resignation when I asked Ibu Uswatun whom she considered a model 'Aisyiyah member. She answered:

> When I lived in Surabaya, the local chapter of 'Aisyiyah had a voluntary secretary who came in every day and worked incredibly hard for the organization. [At this point Ibu Uswatun demonstrated how the woman would stick stamps

on hundreds of envelopes.] The woman had nine children, and her husband was a civil servant at the Ministry for Religious Affairs [notorious for its low salaries]. They were very poor, yet when I asked her why she did not prefer an outside, salaried job, she said that she "wanted to serve 'Aisyiyah because God would reward that with well-being." Her motivation was worship [*ibadah*]. In the end, all of her nine children went to college and found good jobs. She herself even made the costly Hajj to Mecca.[55]

For this woman, serving 'Aisyiyah was an investment in good works. In the end, she expected it to yield more than a regular job. At the same time, the work provided an active way of accepting her poverty. Alternative jobs outside 'Aisyiyah would probably not bring her much income, as she was not well educated. But hard work done in sincerity yields blessings.

According to the Qur'an, those practicing *ikhlas* are the opposite of hypocrites, people with external piety who do not truly accept God's message inside.[56] You do not become secular or bend with the winds of global influences. Most of all, you do not allow yourself to mingle with corruption. You remain modest, living in simplicity.

Muhammadiyah men especially like to mention that "'Aisyiyah women do not seek glamour; they are not in the tabloids." For the women this kind of behavior yields *pahala,* a blessing that builds up in a kind of reservoir. This starts in the early morning, when Ibu Uswatun attends the early morning prayers (in Indonesia around 4:00 to 4:30 A.M.) in the prayer house for women. She says that it gains her extra *pahala.* Women who live according to this principle, busy gathering up *pahala,* worry about the continuation of their organization, not about creating a public relations system that would give 'Aisyiyah activities a higher profile outside its own circles. In fact, this type of spiritual work should remain hidden from the public eye, lest too much outside attention jeopardize the power of blessing. In a roundabout way, storing up blessing harms the public image, since the work remains hidden. Publicity is bad for blessings.

For 'Aisyiyah women, this means that a good Muslim does not make a show of good works but keeps a low profile. This behavior is fully in accord with the Javanese context, where inward stability is much admired, while it also suits the Javanese ideal woman, who is silent and serving. At the same time, the women reverse the spiritual power structure. In the Javanese context, mostly men are deemed capable of intense spiritual exercises. 'Aisyiyah women have developed an alternative, Islamic mode of spiritual excellence that is splendidly compatible with their gender or "nature" (*kodrat*).

Ikhlas also demands that 'Aisyiyah work cannot be halfhearted but must be hard work. Ibu Uswatun never gets weary of the multiple tasks assigned to her, and she does not question the logic behind some of these, even if they are boring or repetitive. She considers the work to be a calling, one she performs for the general good of Muhammadiyah. The embodiment of the best 'Aisyiyah leader she had ever met was the head of the Surabaya chapter.

> I worked with her for eleven years. She trained me, and I learned from her. She loved me. Her method was wonderful; she had high discipline and precision.

What matters is not the outward image but the inward conviction that one works for and within 'Aisyiyah. I heard the most praise for 'Aisyiyah leaders who have a zeal for work and attention for all the projects, who start meetings on time and hand in their reports before the deadline. All the work must be done with a loving, selfless attitude. Only a few individuals are mentioned for their creativity or high level of spirituality. In speeches and sermons, I often heard references to this specific work ethic: "Lots of good works keep you young," or, "All that is worldly will pass, but what remains are the good works."[57]

The lynchpins of 'Aisyiyah work are *ikhlas, rutin,* a high level of discipline, hard work, and efficient use of time. All these accord perfectly with the teachings of Ahmad Dahlan. Ibu Uswatun's week is organized according to a meticulous routine that she carries out with rigorous discipline. She performs extra religious practices, does religious readings, and says extra prayers on behalf of her children, family, others, and the work of her organization. Sleeping late or simply hanging out for an afternoon are not her idea of a good time. In 1929, an admirer of 'Aisyiyah wrote in verse:

> They worked with a dedicated heart,
> Never thinking of anything else
> But freedom and high morals
> That respects the status of our women.[58]

This approach to work has carried 'Aisyiyah through the decades. It can, however, convey an image of being "boring" and an inclination to smother creativity and new initiatives when they do not fit into the routine.[59]

Another aspect of the emphasis on *ikhlas* is that you do not join 'Aisyiyah for your own benefit or to gain fame or power. Inside the organization you do not expect that positions of power in its upper echelons will be thrown into your lap. This works for men and women and gives *ikhlas* a gender dimension. When I asked men what it means "to practice *ikhlas,*" they often answered that they should not strive for high positions within or through Muhammadiyah. The same advice is stressed in Muhammadiyah publications.[60] For men, the organization can be an excellent venue to success. Amien Rais, for example, who in the post-Suharto government became the speaker of the People's Assembly and a presidential candidate, built his political career on his position as national chair of Muhammadiyah; he rarely referred to his job as professor of political science. Since the end of the Suharto regime, the Pemuda Muhammadiyah (Muhammadiyah Young Men) have intensified their focus to create future political leaders. The women, in contrast, continue to "focus on the grassroots level."[61] 'Aisyiyah women with successful careers rarely refer to their leadership positions in the organization. Apart from its educational services, Muhammadiyah has offered them few venues to use the organization as a platform for high-profile careers.

Ikhlas in an "organizational sense" implies that within the overall structure of Muhammadiyah, women should take second place, tending to issues that suit them naturally and helping the men where necessary. Never mind that they were often among those who made the new Muhammadiyah schools a reality by donating their jewelry, energy, and time. An NA member put her finger on the inherent inequality when she wondered, "Why should there be a separate branch for women and not for men?"[62]

Even within their own organization, the women do not gain the respect they deserve. At official 'Aisyiyah functions, Muhammadiyah at times sends representatives who do not bother to hide their boredom. Indeed, they often talk loudly during the women's speeches. I met many of the younger generation, especially men, who never took a closer look at 'Aisyiyah, considering its members models of conservatism with little impact on the improvement of women's condition and position. But rebellion is stirring from within. During their national convention in 2000, the women decided that their focus for the coming five years was going to be to "change the face of 'Aisyiyah" by realizing the highest possible promotions for those women already working in Muhammadiyah institutions.[63] In 1995 women were admitted as members of the Majlis Tarjih, the body that formulates the *fatwas* and other religious advice for Muhammadiyah believers, and in the spring of 2002 Muhammadiyah decided that women could run for positions in its executive bodies. These are revolutionary steps for such a venerable institution. As men and women compete for positions and respect, *ikhlas* becomes contradictory to some of the aspirations and might have to take a back seat.

Because 'Aisyiyah struggles so hard to provide the future generation with the tools necessary to become Muhammadiyah leaders in the twenty-first century, it is easy to forget that it has other goals as well. Its ultimate dream is that all Indonesian Muslims follow the models espoused by 'Aisyiyah. To realize this goal, 'Aisyiyah has focused on the nuclear family—father,

mother, and (ideally) two children. Women, men, and children in this family embody the structure of Muhammadiyah and practice its ideals, serving
as tools to propagate reformist Islam in Indonesia. The model, like the organization, functions in a top-down manner, with the father at the head.

The Harmonious Family

During Muhammadiyah's formative years, intense discussions about the
role of women in the context of a true Muslim marriage were prominent.
Similar to the Muslim Brotherhood, Muhammadiyah considered the nuclear family to be the core of a vibrant Muslim society. For 'Aisyiyah, the structure of the devout Muslim family also became a powerful tool to liberate
women. Creating this structure, however, did not solve the abiding question of how to convince men to cooperate. 'Aisyiyah found its answer in
the creation of the harmonious family model (*keluarga sakinah*), launched
in 1985.

Because this family necessarily involves women *and* men, the model fails
when men are unwilling to participate. Within the power relationship between Muhammadiyah men and women, men have the upper hand. But
from theories such as those of Antonio Gramsci and Michel Foucault about
hegemony, we learn that power is never a one-way force; it is exercised in interaction between the dominating and the dominated party, where the latter tries to negotiate concessions and to shift the boundaries for protection.
Following this line of thinking, we can say that 'Aisyiyah tried to design a
family program that empowered women to be significant partners in this
process of negotiation.

'Aisyiyah realized that the program had to be compatible with several
views concerning women: those of Islam, Muhammadiyah, Java, and the
state. Trying to please all these competing forces earned 'Aisyiyah a tornado
of criticism, especially from the younger generation, much of it justified.
I will come back to this in the following chapter. Here, I will look at what
'Aisyiyah achieved with its harmonious family program. As far as I know, it
is the earliest model in the Muslim world by and for women, based on the
teachings of Islam, that aims at fundamentally improving the quality of life
for Muslim women. The model also grants them a measure of protection
within the family. The program took shape at a time when ideas about human rights and women's reproductive rights had barely touched Indonesian society. 'Aisyiyah slowly developed it and instructed its preachers how
to convey its ideas. Checklists were made so the preachers could see if a
family had halfway reached the goals of the harmonious family. Such fami-

lies, for example, performed the ritual prayers together, kept a household budget, and did not allow children to watch TV unbridled.[64] An interesting detail is that within the unifying vision of Muhammadiyah, this family model was never officially debated. The women went ahead, avoiding the risk of being obstructed by men who might want to change elements that the women held dear. The women preferred to remain "vehicles of power" themselves.[65] By the time the family model was in place, the Majlis Tarjih accepted it. According to Ibu Uswatun, it has also become the model for government family programs.

The point of departure for the harmonious family model is Surah 30:21: "By another sign He gave you wives from among yourselves, that you might live in peace with them, and planted love and kindness in your hearts. Surely there are signs in this for thinking men." In Muhammadiyah ideology, women are the key to a stable family life in which children can be raised harmoniously. The word sakinah is found in the Qur'an; depending on the context, it is translated as "security," "calm," or "tranquility."[66]

The focus on the family provides 'Aisyiyah with an opportunity to teach men about their responsibilities. The women identified the family as the center where male and female domains meet, cultural values are fostered, and future believers are raised. These topics have been discussed over the past fifty years, but usually only in general terms. Particular discussion about family matters seems to have been accelerated by the government's birth control drive that, beginning in the 1960s, suggested a limit of two children per household. At that time, Islamic leaders taught that interfering in God's design was forbidden, and Muhammadiyah was pushed into making a decision concerning this matter. With their approval of birth control in 1971, the concept of a comfortable family (keluarga sejahtera) emerged within Muhammadiyah circles. The idea was that the members of the keluarga sejahtera, the family with two or three children, could become the nucleus of a prosperous Islamic society by promoting its religious, social, and economic conditions. 'Aisyiyah preachers taught the importance of limiting the number of children. This was allowed when parents wished to give their children a better quality of life, education, and attention but forbidden when they feared only for their economic condition (meaning a lack of trust in God). 'Aisyiyah actively promoted the birth control program and saw it as tangible proof of 'Aisyiyah's true care for women. Ibu Baroroh Baried remembers that the women "were more advanced than Muhammadiyah, we were at the forefront."[67] Concurrently, 'Aisyiyah preachers started to talk about matters such as the proper Islamic way of choosing a partner, as well as the duties of man and wife towards their children, their parents, and each other. The ideal emerged that by worshipping together and following Islamic rules concerning a spouse's rights and duties, husband and wife could strengthen and improve their relationship.

The "harmonious family" designed and launched by 'Aisyiyah is one step ahead of the "comfortable family" in that its members no longer perform Javanese ceremonies. They read the Qur'an together and attend Qur'an studies (*pengajian*) frequently. Their house, like the house of Ibu Uswatun, has a special platform on which to perform the five daily prayers, and they greet each other with the Arabic *assalamu 'alaykum* (peace be upon you). They have good relationships with their environment and are economically comfortable and healthy, among other reasons, because they participate in immunization programs.[68]

In terms of gender relations, the harmonious family spells out expectations for both spouses, trying to improve the woman's position.[69] Men as well as women need to know a wife's rights and duties. The harmonious family model assigns duties and responsibilities to all members of the family, thus creating an organic body with interdependent members. However much they stress "interdependence," though, 'Aisyiyah does not eliminate Qur'anic teachings that give men authority over women: "Men are protectors and maintainers of women, because God has given the one more [strength] than the other. . . . [T]herefore the righteous women are devoutly obedient" (Q. 4:34). The words "protectors" and "maintainers" are conventionally interpreted to indicate that men are in charge of women, or have advantages over women. 'Aisyiyah acknowledges the contents of this verse by mentioning that a wife should exercise "obedience, and respect with honesty and self sacrifice [*patuh, taat, dan hormat dengan tulus dan ikhlas*] towards the husband."[70] But while using this language, 'Aisyiyah has introduced the notions of "mutual love," mutual respect," "mutual trust," "helping each other," and "giving each other rights" when referring to the marital relationship.[71] Teaching men to respect their wives invites them to redefine their authority over women by indirectly referring to Qur'anic teachings such as, "men and women are protectors one of another" (9:71). It also moves away from the Javanese opinions that consider women as inferior.

Mutual respect in this model of family requires that the husband not beat his wife. Although it is hotly debated, many understand that a husband is allowed to beat his wife in case of "disloyalty and ill-conduct" (Q. 4:34). Even more radically, the harmonious family model does not allow the husband to marry more than one spouse, although Qur'an 4:2–3 allows for a man to marry up to four wives. Polygyny has mostly been discouraged in Muhammadiyah circles, yet a man who wants a second spouse cannot be forbidden to take one. But accepting the principles of the harmonious family relieves Muslim women of the common worry that a grudging husband one day will come home with a second bride. "Obviously, when a family is harmonious, it does not need two wives," said Ibu Wardanah Muhadi.[72] As a judge in the Islamic court, she tries to convince husbands who want a second wife that the harmonious family model is far preferable and spares him much headache. Since the responsibility for the relationship and the family's harmony falls on both partners, in this model, the man has to face his responsibility as well.

This teaching also guides young adults in selecting a partner. This proactive strategy aims to prevent marital problems such as domestic strife and adultery by husbands. The harmonious family may also help curb problems such as drug abuse and juvenile delinquency. According to Ibu Uswatun's translation of this family model into real life, there are multiple layers of benefit: for women, for husbands and children, for their environment, and eventually for 'Aisyiyah as well.

> We have to increase women's knowledge, improve their economic conditions and their worship, or religious understanding [agama]. Religious knowledge is important because women often do not understand their rights with regard to their husbands and their duties towards their children, husband, and household. They also do not yet comprehend that Islam dictates that we always have to keep learning [mencari ilmu], and that we have to live as members of a community [bermasyarakat]. . . . After the women become involved in 'Aisyiyah's programs, they will be happy to open a kindergarten [taman kanak-kanak] in their village. Then 'Aisyiyah can set up official subdivisions [cabang and ranting] to attract more women. They will stand out because they are able to open a school.[73]

In its effort to expand the harmonious family model beyond Muhammadiyah circles, its leaders started to promote it through marriage counseling. To address the high divorce rate in Indonesia, the government made counseling sessions for future couples mandatory. In case the marriage fails and one of the parties applies for a divorce, the same procedure is required. Governmental offices for counseling (BP4)[74] have been set up since the 1960s. Since there were no trained professionals to work in these offices, the help of organizations like 'Aisyiyah was invoked. 'Aisyiyah women were ideal officers because of their knowledge of the Islamic religious texts and their teaching experience. Ibu Uswatun works at the BP4 office in the Kraton area. She shares the work with ten other women, most of them members of 'Aisyiyah. Their goal is to create Indonesian families that are wholesome (*sejahtera*) and harmonious (*sakina*) and that know their proper place in society.[75]

I observed one of Ibu Uswatun's counseling sessions. The young couple looked like youngsters anywhere in the West. The woman was dressed in black tights and a short-sleeved top with a tight shirt over it. The man was wearing jeans and a t-shirt. Although the woman held a bachelor's degree, she owned a small fabric shop because she found running a business far more lucrative than working as a teacher or civil servant. Seated on the lavishly decorated chairs for future couples, they looked bored, forced to listen to Ibu Uswatun's obligatory advice. In her talk she especially addressed the man about some of the prevalent misunderstandings in Javanese culture and Islam concerning the position of women. She also laid out the main ideologies concerning gender and the family in the *keluarga sakinah* concept.

> A man should respect his spouse and realize that she is a creature capable of independent thinking. The Qur'an says: "The [women] are your garments, and ye [men] are their garments" (2:187). This means that couples should love and protect each other. It also says in Surah 4:34, "Men are the protectors and maintainers of women, because Allah has given the one more than the other [strength], and because they support them from their means." The essence of this text is that providing for the family is the husband's responsibility, not that he has unlimited power over his wife, or that she has to obey him in irrational fashion [*berkuasa mutlak*].

Ibu Uswatun advised the woman always to please her husband, "because a pretty face that never smiles is no fun." If she wished to do so, she could work for additional income for the "benefit of the family, even to buy lipstick or fancy shoes as long as these are used to please her husband." She exhorted both to remain patient in the advent of adversity, also to accept the unpleasant things life brings and always to exercise *taqwa*, mindfulness of God.[76] After she finished her speech, the couple filled out the required forms and paid the fees. On their way out, Ibu Uswatun called them back to give a final message to the man. The couple returned to the fancy chairs, and Ibu Uswatun stated that the man should not leave all the housework for his wife, reminding him, "Although the Prophet Muhammad was a hero in war, at times he mended his own clothes."

For Ibu Uswatun, the harmonious family model represents the furthest liberation possible for women. NA members and younger feminists at times cringe at this vision. If we take the speech apart, many ideas emerge that are not that liberating. Several are promoted by the state. Although the woman ran a business, Ibu Uswatun had no qualms about portraying her as dependent on the husband. Some women take words such as "patience in times of adversity" literally and feel obliged to endure their husband's abuse. But when quoting the Qu'ran, Ibu Uswatun referred specifically to texts that stress the man's duties towards his wife. Overall, the speech was heavily influenced by Muhammadiyah gender ideology, which we now will consider in the context of the harmonious family.

Women in the Harmonious Family

Ibu Uswatun seldom discusses the subject of women's emancipation. To her, Islam is the solution. When its laws and rules are applied correctly, women will be given their rightful place. Since its beginning, 'Aisyiyah has stressed this idea. However, not even in 'Aisyiyah is woman's status unchanging; it has been reshaped and redefined from the beginning as the organization adapted to developments in society. From the start it taught that women have their rights and can earn the same merit as men when performing good deeds (Qur'an 3:193).

There was, however, a perpetual tension between women's private and public roles and duties. In 1925, 'Aisyiyah women stated that "running the household is 100 percent a woman's duty."[77] This line of thought has until recently remained the same, while women's areas of work and activities have gradually expanded. Paradoxically, 'Aisyiyah's expansion and success depended on women leaving behind their household duties to travel around and preach. Suara 'Aisyiyah has regularly declared: "Those who have the competence to preach are obliged to go out and do so."[78] In fact, running the household was replaced by the idea that women are first responsible for their religious duties and can delegate household chores to others. Ibu Uswatun's mother was active in several study groups in Yogyakarta and attended all 'Aisyiyah congresses wherever they were held, taking her children and a babysitter along. Nowadays, 'Aisyiyah women also teach that women should understand their duties and responsibilities as a spouse, but they need not be a slave to their husband.[79] One of the thorny issues was that before a woman could become an active preacher, based on Qur'anic instruction, the husband had to give his permission. Without this, women had to stay at home. Even Ibu Baroroh Baried, while serving as 'Aisyiyah's national chair, had to cancel trips because her husband refused to grant his permission.[80]

Part of this dichotomy comes from the reformist method of interpreting Islamic sources. Women in NU can demand a *fatwa* that clearly spells out a certain right or duty, but when thorny issues appear in reformist circles, women must rely on deliberations that at times are ambiguous. The women themselves then reproduce these ideas. Contemporary 'Aisyiyah documents portray "women as more emotional than men" and then explain this in a positive sense: women like to keep moving and "expanding their potential" so that their emotion is translated not into a lack of spiritual power but into giving "love, care, and self-sacrifice."[81] Such statements border on psychobabble and do not really benefit women. Ziba Mir-Hosseini found the same vagueness when interviewing the Iranian reformist thinker Soroush: "Like Shari'ati, his refusal to address the issue of women through *feqh* [Fiqh] leaves him little choice but to talk in abstractions."[82]

As for the harmonious family, ultimately its gender model is interpreted according to the individual ideas of its members. For a middle-aged Muhammadiyah member I interviewed, it meant: "My wife worked as a teacher, but after our children were born, I became a civil servant and she stayed at home to guard the education of our children." The family model also teaches the dichotomy that "women can be anything in public life, but in private life they obey their husbands."[83] In the *keluarga sakinah,* women bear all the household responsibilities, even though its advocates stress that the Prophet mended his own clothes. This imbalance in power is present in the governmental and Muhammadiyah gender philosophies. Supposedly a woman is always to perform the duties most in accordance with her "nature."

'Aisyiyah has often been accused of collaborating with the Suharto government in laying out a woman's duties, since those described in the harmonious family model seem akin to the *panca dharma wanita* (five duties of a woman). Upon scrutiny, however, 'Aisyiyah's model is far less one-sided than that of the Suharto regime. 'Aisyiyah's model also spells out the responsibilities and duties of the husband. Although it stresses that the man is the main provider, it does not exclude the possibility that women might take that role. This is more in tune with Javanese and Indonesian reality, where many women are the main providers for their family. Women cannot be constant companions of their husbands and accompany them on their work duties. Women must preach and teach, and 'Aisyiyah teaches that ideally spouses should be interdependent friends.[84]

All possible criticism aside, it remains remarkable that by highlighting certain teachings of Islam without changing one word from the holy writings, 'Aisyiyah managed to redefine the marital bond. It helped to improve the condition of women and reached for a degree of equality between men and women (*kejajaran*) through the application of the rules of Islam.[85] It released a woman's potential and allowed her basic human and religious rights to be respected. This unofficial exercise essentially reinterpreted the holy texts of Islam. Careful education of all those involved led to a slow change in attitudes towards women and created respect for the bond of marriage. It gave women a stronger voice within their nuclear families and allowed their voices to become more authoritative in Muhammadiyah circles.

This change became visible in Muhammadiyah when in the early 1990s it initiated a new committee to study gender relations from the Islamic perspective. The committee stresses equality between men and women by moving the focus from the famous Qur'anic text of 4:34 (that presents men as the protectors of women and more or less indicates that under certain circumstances beating one's wife is allowed) to 2:187, where men and women are spoken of as each other's garments. Considering these changes, the harmonious family project can be pronounced a great success.

Following the Muhammadiyah ideology that Islamic propagation should move from the individual to the family and on to larger units in society, 'Aisyiyah designed the next step and introduced the harmonious family program to larger communities. The results were the village projects—"the good village," or *qoryah thoyyibah.*

The Harmonious Family in the Good Village

Muhammadiyah was founded in the city and over time developed a network of mainly urban-based supporters. 'Aisyiyah women especially remained active in the cities because they depended on public transportation. Around the 1980s, 'Aisyiyah realized that it had ignored the rural areas of Indonesia and started a drive to develop programs for women in villages. Ibu Uswatun explained:

> In the early 1980s, 'Aisyiyah women from the city realized that we should guide women in the villages because many more women live in rural areas than in the cities. When these women do not receive any formation, their husbands and children are not in good shape either. This is an automatic consequence.[86]

The process of guiding families in villages to live in harmony is called *pembinaan desa* (village guidance or formation). The ideas for village formation arose around the same time as the harmonious family project, so trying to implement the harmonious family in the rural areas as well seemed a logical step. The good village project consists of two components: the *pembinaan desa* combined with the *keluarga sakinah.*

In a *pembinaan desa* project, inhabitants are guided towards a model of comfortable living based on four points: religion, education (religious and secular), economic self-sufficiency, and access to the basic health care, such as vaccination for children. These points are taken from international guidelines provided by the World Bank. Women in villages learn the basics of Islam, hygiene, and business. One of the project's founders explained: "We show them that opening the windows of their house is a healthy thing to do and that using the river as a toilet causes diseases."[87] Each village is provided with electricity and at least one toilet. Women receive help with modest income-generating projects based on their village's natural resources and can borrow interest-free loans to start a small business. For example, in areas with potential for raising soybeans, they make soybean sauce (*kecap*). The loans are of great help to women who normally pay over 30 percent interest when buying goods on credit or borrowing money from loan sharks. To 'Aisyiyah, charging interest is usury and forbidden by Islam.[88] An important goal of the village project is to empower the poor. The prime designer of the rural projects, Ibu Alfiyah Muhadi, used to repeat to me that, in the end,

> The most noble of all are those who fulfill their tasks as servants of God. There is a huge divide between rich and poor. Yet the rich have no reason to be arrogant but carry a responsibility towards the poor.[89]

Each province (*wilayah*) of 'Aisyiyah is expected to develop at least one *pembinaan desa* project; in 1995, there were forty-one such projects. The next stage of development is to add the harmonious family project, introduced in 1985. All the inhabitants will live harmoniously and daily apply the Qur'anic verse 3:104, the Muhammadiyah maxim that urges the village to become "a band of people inviting to all that is good, enjoining what is right, and forbidding what is wrong." All families in the good village live according to the *keluarga sakinah* model, striving for harmony within their nuclear family and among their co-villagers. Ibu Broto Mulyono, the national coordinator of the project, explained, "The ultimate model for this project is the life of the Prophet Muhammad."[90] Through the project, 'Aisyiyah prepares "a fundament for the people of Indonesia, . . . towards a harmonious, just, and prosperous society."[91]

Currently, the main pilot of a *qoryah thoyyibah* project is in Potorono, south of Yogyakarta, a carefully chosen site in the midst of several NU *pesantren*. Its 230 families are all members or sympathizers of Muhammadiyah, most of them farmers whose children have left for the city. The village's affiliation with Muhammadiyah goes back to the 1950s. Ibu Istiqoma, the project leader for the women, has impeccable Muhammadiyah credentials: her father initiated the first branch in 1957, her mother set up NA and

'Aisyiyah, and her uncle was for many years the chair of the national Majlis Tarjih. With great zest, she organizes seven *pengajian* per month, calls the meetings, sets up income-generating projects, and checks on the progress of the village's inhabitants.

One Sunday I visited the village to attend the five o'clock morning prayers. Coming into the village, we were greeted by the sound of Indonesian Islamic songs, sung to the tunes of Arabic music. The music was meant to motivate the villagers to attend the meeting, which is a mandatory step in reaching the status of a successful good village. After a talk by an outside speaker, Ibu Istiqoma came forward to read the announcements. She chastised the audience for being half asleep and wondered why the majority of those present were women. "Where are your men?" she called out.

According to Ibu Istiqoma the village project has already produced visible fruits:

Unfortunately, we do not really have a measuring rod. But we observe that now families do not fight with their neighbors as much as they used to, we have a Qur'an school for the children [TPA], and NA and 'Aisyiyah are growing. At first, we had to round up girls to come and listen to our *pengajian*. That was tough; they did not want to come. But the 'Aisyiyah women persisted in guiding them, talking to them, giving sermons, and organizing activities. Now we have an active NA section, so we have cadre for the future to continue the work after we will be gone. The chair of NA is studying at the university in Yogyakarta, but she also participates in a local NGO and gives talks in the Qur'an school. She is right in the midst of society and not only in university circles. That is the ideal; she gathers all types of knowledge, not just scientific, but also social and religious.[92]

According to Ibu Istiqoma's report, between 1990 and 1997 "healthy homes" and "vaccinated children" increased, villagers gave more to charity, care for those in need nearly doubled, and religious awareness and understanding increased in fifteen persons. Fewer people worked as farmers (the number diminished by 40 percent), while more opened small businesses (that number rose by 50 percent).[93]

Observers from other 'Aisyiyah branches come to learn about how to set up a good village in their area. A delegation from Jepara in North Java was impressed by the cleanliness of the environment and the discipline of those involved. After long discussions, however, they concluded that the main obstacle to having a similar village near Jepara was the intense presence of NU chapters with members who still practice rituals that are not appropriate for the good village.

'Aisyiyah's far-reaching dream can lead to the next level, the good country (*baldatun thoyyibatun*), where all live in harmony and follow Muhammadiyah principles. The dream harkens to the euphoric postwar expectations of the 1950s, when reformist Muslim politicians predicted that Indonesia would become a nation under Islamic law.

The village project has harvested severe criticism, especially from NA members. Some are appalled by the fact that 'Aisyiyah has completely ignored Indonesia's religious pluralism and the diversity within Islam. While publicly acknowledging the Pancasila state model, critics charged, 'Aisyiyah worked towards entirely reformist villages.[94] Mbak Terias Setiyawati, NA's national chair since 2000, wrote her M.A. thesis on the village and found it lacking. According to her analysis, economic projects were haphazard rather than catering to the village's needs, and she concluded that the current approach of "guiding" was not helping the villagers toward independence.[95]

I will leave criticism about this village project and the rest of 'Aisyiyah works to the next chapter. Here I wish to stress the positive: a group of women tried to come up with a model that could lift women in rural Indonesia out of a cycle of poverty and abuse. That the project did not become as successful as they hoped can be ascribed to several factors. One is the suffocating 'Aiysiyah bureaucracy that operates from a top-down model. Somehow, the "how to" link was missing in the endless documents produced by the leaders of the good village. Other problems stem from women's lack of power to implement such an ambitious program and the reality that not all of Indonesia wishes to be Muhammadiyah-minded. These setbacks do not deter Ibu Uswatun and her colleagues. At a time when most of them could enjoy rest and retirement, they devote more of their energies than ever to 'Aisyiyah and to the dream of recreating the Kauman in the rest of Indonesia.

The Kauman and the World

'Aisyiyah women started in the Kauman. The values, ethics, and morals practiced in this safe, protected, and mostly Muhammadiyah neighborhood subconsciously became the model for bringing Islam to the Muslims of Indonesia. Vices criticized by 'Aisyiyah, it assumes, could not happen in the Kauman. After nearly a century of reformist preaching and teaching, the physical Kauman has been transformed into myriad imaginary Kaumans inhabited by twenty million Muhammadiyah-minded Muslims. The model of Islam is strict, yet moderate. It guards against but also must guard itself against several detrimental forces in society. The themes recurring in sermons and writings by 'Aisyiyah leaders comprise a picture of those forces: *zina* (for example, free sex), Muslims who disrespect the proper Islamic rules, secularism, and globalization. Other forms of Islam, such as traditionalism and fanaticism, are equally considered insidious. Whenever I visit Ibu Uswatun, she has a new list of vices. Within five minutes of meeting me on June 23, 2004, she volunteered the following challenges in society:

> How to educate the children. They now want naked bellies and miniskirts. It is vulgar. They can't find work, their compass is disconnected. And show business is destroying their character and exploiting them.

To ward off trends of extremist Islam, 'Aisyiyah can continue to preach alternative models and to counsel individual women. Most women are deeply offended by extremist views. In her capacity as national chair of 'Aisyiyah from 1965 to 1985, Ibu Baroroh Baried regularly had to advise in marital problems that arose when a husband became what she called a "fanatic."

> A friend of ours went on the Hajj to Mecca and returned with a long beard after connecting with a fundamentalist group. Now he fasts on Monday and Thursday, he does not have a car but transports himself by bike, and only wants to eat with his hands. I think he is stupid [*bodoh*]. His wife came to see me in tears. He now wants her to dress like a Saudi. I proposed a compromise: don't make a big quarrel, and wear *busana muslim* [Muslim dress]. A nephew of mine went to the university and became a fundamentalist. His wife wears the *chador*. At their wedding, men and women had to be totally separated. We decided to boycott the marriage. There is no doubt about it, they have to comply with our culture. His wife, a teacher, stays at home. Why did she bother to go to college? We find these attitudes more and more these days. They are the negative influences from the Middle East.[96]

Although very conservative itself, 'Aisyiyah wants to be moderate. It coaches its followers to become committed Muslims and wants to gather them in the mosque, seeing great dangers when they fall prey to extreme ideas. Paradoxically, in Islamic behavior, young Muhammadiyah women as well as young men have become more conservative. Some NA believe that the loose veil (*kerudung*) is insufficient, but 'Aisyiyah forbids wearing the *chador* (the long veil that fully covers the body and often the eyes as well).

Among the major sins the Qur'an identifies as the cause for disaster is *zina* (Q. 17:32 and 60:12). According to 'Aisyiyah reasoning, staying away from *zina* and practicing proper moral behavior will root out sexual evils in society, such as prostitution, rape, and premarital sex. They believe that these vices will vanish when Indonesian society is thoroughly Islamized (according to the reformist model, of course, not the traditionalist one).

These ideas, akin to those of the Muslim Brotherhood, seem simple and straightforward. But complex social problems cannot be answered by such simplistic attitudes; to apply this statement to 'Aisyiyah's case, their emphasis on the inward and personal life must sometimes be translated into practical and outward action appropriate to what happens in contemporary society. For example, in May 1998 Jakarta experienced severe riots during which dozens of Chinese-Indonesian girls were raped and killed. 'Aisyiyah never publicly protested this horrendous crime against women or offered to help the victims. "We are already working on this problem by combating *zina*, our work is preventative," commented Ibu Djazman, the national chair at that time.[97] Younger activists for women's rights could not believe their ears, and the Muslimat NU spoke out condemning the incident and organized a public forum on the issue of rape. 'Aisyiyah's ultimate goal is to combat "the moral crisis" in society, a recurring theme in discussions with Ibu Uswatun.

'Aisyiyah women are trying to address a multilayered social and religious Indonesian reality. In some parts of the countryside time seems to stand still, and people live according to age-old patterns. In the cities, new ideas and technological options emerge daily. In their active responses, 'Aisyiyah can no longer simply rely on its well-tested repertoire of preaching, teaching, and fiery articles in *Suara 'Aisyiyah*. Society and its problems have become more complex, and so have the expectations of its audience. For example, to combat the rising drug use among Indonesia's youth, several NGOs have started programs to prevent addiction, research its consequences, and address the problem of HIV/AIDS. But 'Aisyiyah still tries to convince the audience mainly with the word. In 2000, a large banner hung over the street leading up to Yogyakarta's busy shopping district read, "'Aisyiyah anti madat yang bikin melarat. Sekarat di akherat dilaknat malaikat" ('Aisyiyah is against drug use. It keeps you poor and half-dead, and the angels will curse you in the hereafter). These are well-intentioned words, but they are ineffectual if not followed up by a program to address the problem of narcotics in depth.

Besides demands from society, the women must balance conflicting views on the role of women in Islam; they must be perfect housewives and carry on their work as leaders of religion and society at the same time. The view of Indonesian society adds another level of difficulty: not only must women balance multiple, vital tasks, they must remain in the background while doing so. And of course, 'Aisyiyah women know that much of the official language is unrealistic. Ibu Chamamah Suratno would never have made it to the position of dean had she followed Muhammadiyah rules. She did her

Ph.D. studies in the Netherlands, leaving her small children in Yogyakarta and ignoring her "primary duty" to them. The younger generation battles with these conflicts. Its different ideas about models of mission, development, education, and the role of women lead to regular criticism:

> 'Aisyiyah does not think in concepts yet but takes its ideas from the Majlis Tarjih. If, for example, there are concerns about reproductive rights, 'Aisyiyah will open a clinic [*balai kesehatan*] for women; they just regenerate their old models without analyzing and researching the problem.
>
> They seldom respond to strategic problems; for example, they did not issue a press release when during the May riots in 1998 there was systematic rape of Chinese women in Jakarta. This is the contradiction within Muhammadiyah: on the one hand, they say that women can get a high education; on the other hand, they hold very conservative ideas about the household.[98]

The NA members airing this criticism are considering the future agenda of their own organization. When they have to confront these issues, will they create an even more internalized, imaginary Kauman? Or will they choose another course?

Conclusion

'Aisyiyah is a large and diverse organization. Any attempt to describe its ideologies will inevitably omit important aspects. One thing is certain: its leaders operate within the confines of the Muhammadiyah organization. This stability has many advantages: they can draw from a huge network and benefit from high-profile leaders such as Amien Rais. It also has drawbacks, primarly that they have to work within the confines of Muhammadiyah's bureaucracy and religious ideologies. Similar to Muslim women leaders elsewhere, 'Aisyiyah women must apply a range of strategies of resistance and compliance to reach their goals.[99]

Studying the women's efforts, one readily concludes that they have had an enormous impact on Indonesian society. During the past two decades, Indonesian allegiances have shifted to a middle ground: Muslim believers are less interested in traditionalist Fiqh-based reasoning and have little patience for extended Javanese rituals, but the somewhat rigid Muhammadiyah patterns are not entirely acceptable either.[100] In this middle ground, some students have become interested in the Islam Baru groups, and others study Sufism, but the majority is simply trying to be more conscientious in practicing their religion, fasting regularly, reading the Qur'an, and learning about Islam. During this process of renewed Islamization, 'Aisyiyah preachers were ready, preaching, teaching, and providing Islamic alternatives for the indigenous rites of passage in the life cycles of women and children. At birth, 'Aisyiyah midwives knew the correct religious formulas to whisper in the baby's ears; at death its leaders prepared a woman's body properly for burial. They performed the rituals in simple, economical ways that saved time and money, precious commodities in Indonesia, now and in the past. The upshot was that women gained understanding of the Islamic rituals and principles without having to delve into the time-consuming practices traditionalists followed.

'Aisyiyah's educational network provided a viable alternative to the *pesantren,* especially at a time when those were closed for women students. Through these, 'Aisyiyah could cast its net wide. People may originally have thought that their message was strange (*aneh*) in comparison with traditionalist teachings, or that the women were rigid and conservative when compared with secular women's groups that did not try to make Islam a force of progress for women. But during the first fifty years, the sheer availability of 'Aisyiyah educational facilities drew in millions of women who were eager to learn and saw new vistas opening up for their daughters' education.

As part of a reformist organization, 'Aisyiyah had to comply with its religious tenets, ideals, and goals. That this connection was simultaneously a benefit and a drawback became clear when the familiar structures of Indonesian society began to shift. During the Suharto years urban areas grew, a middle class developed, the gap between rich and poor grew, the educational level rose, and Islam became a spiritual and ritual force in people's lives. Concurrently with these developments, the Suharto regime tried to curtail the religious organizations. 'Aisyiyah women produced a twofold, seemingly contradictory reaction: they strengthened the reformist tenor of their message while trying to respond to the new trends.

The strengthening took the shape of blasting everything the women considered to be "un-Islamic." In the numerous sermons I heard, un-Islamic behavior ranged from traditionalist practices, Sufism, extremism or fundamentalism, and unofficial marriages to materialism, tattoos, and miniskirts. 'Aisyiyah preachers hammered on the right conduct of behavior and mode of believing, infusing their message with the reformist ideals of the perfect Muslim woman. This message was clear and understandable to women from the lower social strata, especially those of the older generations. But it became unacceptable to those (mostly younger women) who no longer believed in essential differences between the sexes.

Although they stressed their reformist character in an attempt to set themselves apart from many "others," including those unquestioningly following the new trends, 'Aisyiyah women also adapted to some of them. However, in many instances they could not do that within the organization. As a result, we see that, for example, in the advocacy against polygyny, 'Aisyiyah leaders did not join on behalf of their organization but were involved "on a personal basis." For all we know, the majority of 'Aisyiyah leaders might be engaged in novel, progressive, or mystical activities not acknowledged by the organization. Since they are outside the official program, these activities will not reflect back on 'Aisyiyah; thus the organization maintains its solidity but loses the chance to reinvent its image.

When moving inside the organization, the women have to fall back on their personal sense of *ikhlas;* their work is done for God alone. As with nuns joining a convent, individual desires and aspirations must be put aside for the good of the organization and the soul. By calling on this sense of *ikhlas* that is ingrained in the Javanese consciousness, 'Aisyiyah could encourage other women to become active agents of change. Women transformed its Javanese meaning of inward resignation to what life had handed to them into an active call to change their lot.

'Aisyiyah women live their lives at the fault lines of interpretation about what it means to be a "good Muslim woman." While trying to strengthen a woman's position, they espouse the view that women complement men. With this primary tenet in mind, its programs make sense. Women working side-by-side with men can bring about the true Islamic nation. But the togetherness has its limits. Women can and do help build hospitals, elementary schools, and universities; but when directors of such programs are chosen, they have to stay in their own quarters with the clinics, preschools, and nursing colleges. They addressed the plight of women via the harmonious family model but had to perform hermeneutic acrobatics to create a spouse who complements her husband, yet is equal in some sense.

This lack of consistency does not go down well with younger feminists, male and female, so we see a storm of criticism over the family program. In their indignation, many of its critics forget the benefits the harmonious family has brought to thousands of women. Paradoxically, the criticism is a sign of 'Aisyiyah's success: it impresses on women the importance of knowing the Islamic sources that define their role and position. Students of the sources took them to a higher level; now they not only read these texts but reread them as well. And while rereading, they demand clear answers to their questions about gender, not unclear reformist talk that dodges the difficult points.

At the start of the twenty-first century, even Muhammadiyah's Majlis Tarjih and its national board have come to realize the importance of women's interpretations. Recently both bodies have been opened up to women—albeit a limited number. To ensure success on these new levels of influence, 'Aisyiyah invited Siti Ruhaini Dzuhayatin to the Majlis Tarjih. She holds a graduate degree in gender studies from Monash University in Australia and embodies the future generation that will reinvent 'Aisiyah to survive into and help shape the new century.

4 Nurturing the Future: Nasyiatul 'Aisyiyah

Nasyiah, its symbol the freshly planted rice,
Always learning,
Working for the glory of Islam,
Always working.
Nasyiah, its symbol the rice paddy,
Nourishing rice
For the whole world.
—Abbreviated version of Nasyiatul 'Aisyiyah's anthem

The Future Generation

It was easy to choose Ibu Uswatun as a model to portray her organization, since it was her task in 'Aisyiyah to "guide researchers." In the beginning, she was present during all the hours I read the organization's historical material and visited its projects. My map with notes holds more from and about her than any other 'Aisyiyah member. Even though I talked with many other members, this method of transmitting information illustrates 'Aisyiyah's bureaucratic and hierarchical model as top-heavy, trying to maintain control of all that goes on. It also shows that some of its members have time to maintain this model. NA women cannot even think about doing this since they are busy with study, careers, and/or small children. To save time, interviews with NA members often took place in small groups. My two main sources of information were Mbak Terias Setiyawati and Mbak Ama, but often interviews were more of a discussion among three or four women than information from a single perspective.

This reflects the changes Muhammadiyah women are going through. Although well-educated themselves, 'Aisyiyah women still largely cater to the poor and the less educated. According to the 2001 United Nations report, Indonesia belongs among countries with medium human development, ranking 102 out of 162 countries. In the long run, NA will have to cater to the same women as well, but that mission is only one of the several they might choose. NA's leaders direct an increasingly sophisticated demographic group that faces a variety of choices about how to spend free time and where to get Islamic education. In other words, joining NA is no longer a natural move, not even for those from Muhammadiyah background. NA juggles complex social and religious issues such as the Islam Baru (the extremist-minded groups at the university campuses), global forces, and influences of modernization. Mila Stivens recognizes these forces in her summary of Asian modernity: "[A]stonishing economic and urban growth, ... falling mortalities and rising income and levels of education; of massive consumption in huge postmodern shopping malls; ... widening gaps between rich and poor, ... a whole set of strongly voiced social anxieties across the region focusing on issues of 'family' and 'culture.'"[1] As one of its policy documents shows, NA women have reflected on the situation from the point of view of the group's specific concerns:

> The onset of development and technology, especially communication technology, eliminates borders between areas, countries, and cultures and has sped up processes of interaction and acculturation. The result is a shift in values, including religious values. Religious communities, especially the Muslim community, immediately have to formulate a response to this crisis in values. ... Without a young generation that holds high values [*yang berkepribadian*], the future of Indonesia will be vacillating, influenced by a foreign, destructive culture that is ever ready to destroy the Indonesian people.[2]

After identifying globalization and its ensuing crisis of values as one of the largest threats to their existence, the NA document goes on to state: "NA women are able to face any temptation or challenge."[3] This is true, yet they can only do so within the confines of their own reality, which is widely different from 'Aisyiyah's. 'Aisyiyah women can afford to undertake multiple tasks within the organization, but NA leaders have to choose. No longer can they work according to the top-down hierarchical model followed by most 'Aisyiyah leaders. Limited time forces them to delegate and democratize. Young people have no patience for *pengajian,* so NA must find other models to transmit its message. To be effective, it has to make crucial choices concerning its mandate. It does not run schools or clinics as 'Aisyiyah does, and with Islamic education provided in public schools, its former tasks of teaching children and adolescent girls the proper rules of Islam could become redundant. It is now reinventing itself, focusing on gender discourse and improving women's economic condition. It plays a crucial part in defining the role of women in moderate, reformist Islam. While creating a new generation of Muhammadiyah women, NA members find themselves in the peculiar position of being 'Aisyiyah's most severe critics and its future replacement. This is not a totally unique position; many of Indonesia's youth face the same situation, as the country's social makeup is changing with higher education and the emergence of new vistas unimaginable for the older generation. Mbak Terias Setiyawati, NA's national chair since 2000, embodies this duality in her lifestyle, choices, and activities.

Mbak Terias

Mbak Terias works full-time as a professor of management at one of Yogyakarta's Islamic universities. She has five children, each two years apart; the first was born in 1991. In Muhammadiyah ruling circles, she is a bit of an outsider. Her family lived in the countryside with no ties to the Yogyakarta core. Since her father and mother were elementary school teachers, the family of nine children lived on a modest income. Both parents devoted all their free time to the Muhammadiyah organization and expected the children to help. Mbak Terias's day starts at five in the morning, when she and her children get up to perform the ritual prayers. Until nine, she helps the children with their homework, gets them off to school, and discusses NA matters. From nine to four she works in her office at the university, teaching fifteen hours a week and working on her Ph.D. studies, begun in 2004. In the late afternoon she spends more time on NA business and practices Qur'anic verses and prayers in Arabic with her children. Then she cooks dinner, and when they all are in bed, she studies until midnight. Her husband has spent several years in Jakarta pursuing graduate studies. Twice a week she attends the meetings of NA's Central Board. In her capacity as national chair, Mbak Terias often travels outside Yogyakarta, for example to attend the installation of new leaders. She regularly preaches at religious gatherings and serves as a speaker at NA academic events. She is one of the prime forces behind NA's new model that seeks to empower women through economic independence.

Her house is next to a small mosque in the midst of a *kampung* (neighborhood). The local NA chapter holds it meetings there, and Mbak Terias and her husband serve as its janitors. Mbak Terias's sisters and their friends, all high schoolers, are active NA members. They often gather at her house or use it for special NA activities such as cooking snacks. Her living room serves as a library, play den, and prayer room. Shelves filled with books line the walls; half of the floor is covered with toys and children's homework, while one corner is reserved for prayer. Mbak Terias wears the *jilbab*, the veil that fully covers the head, and dresses in baggy, colorful outfits similar

to what many women in the Middle East wear. She transports herself by
motorbike and speeds through Yogyakarta with a bag of books on her back
and her veil blowing in the wind. In the photo albums of highlights of her
children's lives, dates are given according to the Islamic Hijrah calendar.

Although half of her week is spent in the service of NA, Mbak Terias's life
is not unconditionally bound up in NA. She continues to develop her academic career conscientiously, publishing as much as possible and studying
for her Ph.D. Mbak Terias grew up in a solid Muhammadiyah environment
and accompanied her mother in NA activities. When attending the university, however, she did not join NA but chose to become a member of an
organization for Indonesian Islamic students, Persatuan Mahasiswa Islam
Indonesia. In 1988 NA invited her to become a board member because it
needed her organizational skills and knowledge. She will not force her children to join NA but gives them the freedom to choose their own activities.
She embodies the typical and the nontypical Muhammadiyah member: she
wants to build NA, yet she is not averse to criticizing her organization and
understands and accepts those who follow other groups.

Nasyiatual 'Aisyiyah's History

Especially during the first fifty years, the story of NA and its activities is
closely related to 'Aisyiyah, since it grew out of Aisyiayah's teaching activities for its members and their daughters.[4] Apart from the academic subjects,
women also learned how to make *kerudung* (scarves to be used as veils).
Learning, religion, and business merged when 'Aisyiyah set up cooperatives
to sell the veils to raise money for new buildings. In 1919 Muhammadiyah
students started a group called Siswa Praja (good education for students)
to provide informal religious education for children at Muhammadiyah elementary schools. Its goal was to "foster a sense of unity, improve moral
behavior, and strengthen religious knowledge." The motto of its initiators
consisted of Ahmad Dahlan's words: "Speak little, work hard" (*Sedikit bi-
cara, banyak kerja*). Muhammadiyah urged its branches all over Indonesia
to start similar projects. In 1931, when Muhammadiyah counted over four
hundred branches (*cabang*), the local languages and Dutch were abolished
and replaced by nationalistic Indonesian and Muslim Arabic. The Javanese
Siswa Praja became the Arabic Nasyiatul 'Aisyiyah (Nurturing 'Aisyiyah).
NA girls were charged with the same task as the young men in Muhammadiyah. Called *pelopor* (pioneer), *pelangsung* (the one who continues), or
penyempurna (the one who improves or makes things perfect), they were
considered innovators who continued and perfected the work of Muham-

madiyah. For over three decades, until 1965, NA dedicated itself to this task through 'Aisyiyah.

The informal curriculum for the girls, in addition to religious formation, comprised courses about health, general knowledge, and social skills. Women and girls received advice, often taken from Dutch magazines for housewives, about how to keep their bodies healthy, because a weak body cannot perform well in learning and childbearing. Social skills included politeness (*sopan santun*) and a sense of responsibility towards one's work and others—the beginning of *ikhlas*.[5] Every Muhammadiyah school was urged to hold meetings for female students to "instill in them enthusiasm for NA."[6] NA's activities grew to include courses in vocational skills such as embroidery, cooking, domestic skills, and administration. The girls were also taught a number of songs. Religious formation remained the core of NA activities. Activities were tailored to three age groups: birth to six, six to twelve, and twelve to fifteen years old. At the age of sixteen, a girl would be married and join 'Aisyiyah.

As the culture has changed, the marrying age has gone up, and young children have ample opportunities to attend Islamic teaching at school, in the mosques, and at special religious schools (*pesantren, madrasah*). With these changes, NA has had to reconsider the age limits for its members. Until 2000 it was twelve through thirty-five, and now it has become seventeen through forty. NA no longer sees itself as responsible for children but is shifting its focus to adolescents and young adults. After achieving independence from 'Aisyiyah in 1965, NA began to chart its own course; as the educational level of its leaders rose, they became more interested in the intellectual and ideological discussions generated by Muhammadiyah than in the pragmatic activities undertaken by 'Aisyiyah. Concurrent with these changes, NA leaders shifted their focus to researching Islamic teachings about women through gender studies and rereading of Islamic texts.

The NA Works

Formation of Children

NA was set up to extend and maintain the Muhammadiyah female center by developing young women who would carry on its core beliefs, social network, customs, and conventions. Traditionally, several different venues were to build this core: early family influence, followed by NA's mentoring and teaching through the Muhammadiyah schools or regular religious gatherings. Leaders used to train their own children or those of friends by involving them in NA activities as early as possible to encourage future leadership. Mbak Terias remembers from her childhood:

> From the time we were still small, our parents guided us to participate in Muhammadiyah activities, for example we had to go around and collect the membership dues. We were expected to be present whenever there was a meeting or festivity. We knew that our parents earned little and worked voluntarily for Muhammadiyah. Yet when there was an activity, they provided snacks for the guest that we children helped prepare. We learned always to think about others first instead of ourselves, and we still feel uncomfortable when we perceive ourselves as being selfish. What people gave was voluntary. We would count the contributions and divide the money among the poor widows in our village. We felt compassion for them. Our main drive was our feeling of responsibility to improve society through Muhammadiyah activities.[7]

Mbak Terias's story testifies to how the Muhammadiyah sense of commitment became instilled in her personality through a combination of everyday work and learning from presentations. This has long been a successful method. Talking with older women about their 'Aisyiyah childhoods, I noted several similarities to Mbak Terias's experience. They too helped cook meals for those in need, made snacks for the gatherings (imperative to any meeting in Indonesia), and prepared foods to be sold in the market and in little co-ops. The proceeds always returned to the organization, never to the individual.

NA girls were taught always to be ready to help. In a story from 1940, a twelve-year-old member describes how she had written the slogan "be ready to help" on the wall in her room. In a diary she registered all her good deeds and things she had neglected to do. "If I had not offered my help to anyone that day, I felt very ashamed in front of God," she wrote. During her holidays she felt "unfit to be an NA child," since at home there was not much to do. A sick neighbor provided release from this predicament because the girl now had someone she could target daily with good deeds.[8] Following the same goal as 'Aisyiyah, NA's ultimate hope is that by doing good deeds it can help build the perfect Muslim society.[9]

Participating in countless meetings imbued the girls with a sense of Muhammadiyah discourse and responsibility. In a sort of job shadowing, future leaders followed NA women wherever they went. The girls were called upon to recite verses from the Qur'an, read announcements, and give short sermons. They too followed the directives from the central office in Yogyakarta. As a result of this training in text and speech, many NA women became skilful orators who are able to deliver a public speech without much preparation. The material that shapes their talks is a blend of transmitted Muhammadiyah knowledge and what they learn at the university.

NA children were expected to be active, never lazy, and for the most part their day was structured around school and religious activities. Holidays especially were considered prime time for extracurricular religious activities, providing an occasion for learning in a festive environment. The free days during the month of Ramadan used to be the most intensive period of NA teaching and preaching activities. To reinforce the learning experience, NA leaders would teach children about their Islamic identity by performing all rituals and instruct them about how to wear the veil. This was still the case when Mbak Terias was a child:

> During the fasting month there were all kinds of special programs for us. We had competitions such as who was best at performing the ritual prayers, or who could give the best speech. I regularly beat my older brothers at that one. We could also join choirs and dancing groups. My mother took me to as many events as possible. We would always wear the veil during these gatherings.

The curriculum for the Ramadan activities was rigorous and aimed at those who did not attend Muhammadiyah schools. Mbak Terias further remembered:

> We performed the prayers and broke the fast together. After that, we had lessons about God's unity [*tauhid*], morals [*akhlak*], and worship [*ibadah*]. We learned verses from the Qur'an, religious poems, and practiced giving speeches, discussion techniques, and what makes a good leader. There were also elective skills, such as how to become a secretary. Apart from that, we memorized facts about Muhammadiyah, such as when and where it was set up. At times we listened to stories. After that we went home for dinner. We came back for the *tarawih* prayers and practiced for the *takbiran* procession that was held with the Muhammadiyah Youth [Pemuda Muhammadiyah]. At the time of the processions there were contests between the groups, and the most orderly won [*baris rapi*].

During the *takbiran* procession, children still go around town on the eve of the feast chanting "Allahu akbar" (God is great). Ramadan was also the time to show commitment to Islam and Muhammadiyah. Children as young as three would bring daily contributions for the *zakat-fitrah* (the obligatory alms tax) that were given to the poor on the occasion of the feast. They also brought a small token contribution for Muhammadiyah activities. The fasting month became a time during which Muhammadiyah values, beliefs, and bonds were confirmed and strengthened. This bond was most symbolized by the annual *halal bi-halal* tours that NA members still make at the time of the feast. This is a custom that I have not found in the Middle East. It consists of roaming from house to house to pay respect on the occasion of the feast, or to hold a gathering for the same purpose. Family and friends are visited in a hierarchical order, ending with NA friends, to renew and strengthen the bonds among Muhammadiyah members across generations. *Halal bi-halal* is an important activity to show commitment to the organization, and NA members who attend Muhammadiyah schools are required to prepare a report of their Ramadan activities when school begins again.[10]

Not being lazy was the mantra to motivate the children to gain knowledge relevant to Islam and the organization. Even playing (*main*) became an activity with a special meaning directed at imbuing children with the Muhammadiyah spirit of thinking. This starts at home in the *keluarga sakinah,* at full-time Muhammadiyah schools, during special courses, reformist holiday *pesantren,* and finally in the organization. In Mbak Ama's family, for example,

> We were allowed to attend any meeting [of Islamic organizations] and come home at whatever time as long as it was clear what we were doing. Only just hanging around [*main*] was forbidden. For fun I climbed mountains and went camping. I also played hockey, basketball, and was a member of the provincial hockey team.[11]

Up to the 1970s, this model was effective in keeping children within the fold of the organization, where they would eventually move into positions of leadership. But times have changed, and as the speech of Minister Malik Fadjar (chapter 1) shows, his own children prefer to go into business and would rather make money than devote time and energy to Muhammadiyah. Similarly, finding ways to motivate new members has become one of NA's most urgent challenges.

Creating New Leaders

NA members work hard to create a new cadre that is willing to stay and devote its free time to the voluntary activities. Without these volunteers the organization would collapse; its whole structure depends on them. In several districts where NA does not have strong leadership, it simply ceases to exist or is absorbed by 'Aisyiyah. In the long run this situation also would mean the end of that particular 'Aisiyah branch. Since the larger Muhammadiyah family no longer automatically provides new leaders, NA has to look elsewhere. Ibu Baroroh Baried identified the problem as follows: "Nowadays we have more girls who just attend. They don't help build

NA."[12] The Indonesian landscape offers numerous choices for young people who want to engage in religious activities. A growing number of them consider these options with the attitude of consumers measuring the personal benefits without having to invest personal energy.

Schools remain the best places to recruit new members for NA. Its most natural venue, the Mu'allimat school, however, is off-limits because its students from the age of twelve are registered with 'Aisyiyah. Muhammadiyah schools in general are the best pool of resources, since they convey what it means to be a reformist Muslim. On the curriculum are topics such as Qur'an, *tauhid* (teachings about the Oneness of God), Islamic history, Arabic, moral instruction (*akhlak*), and Jurisprudence (Fiqh). Mbak Ama attributes her religious awareness and engagement with NA to the years she attended a Muhammadiyah high school. The teaching made her aware of the inner meaning of the Islamic rituals. She remembers that the stress on independent thinking especially appealed to her: "Use your brain, and as it says in the Qur'an, in Surat Luqman [31:15], don't just blindly follow rituals without understanding them. That is stupid."[13]

To pique the interest of students graduating from Muhammadiyah schools, NA stresses the long-term benefits of joining the organizational network: It not only prepares for future positions of leadership, it yields opportunities that most Indonesians do not have access to, such as traveling abroad. Mbak Ama recognizes that she owes part of her own professional success to what she learned in NA and to the Muhammadiyah network:

The organization gives you courage. When I am trained to speak and lead different groups, I gain in experience. I will neither panic easily, nor feel arrogant. In an organization this big you have to deal with all kinds of people. When a conflict arises, I am forced to look at the matter from different angles, through the eyes of older persons, through those who have a family, or through those with a different educational background. This helps me grow and gain in self-confidence.[14]

When speaking to high school classes, she tries to convey these potential benefits to the students. During a speech to a graduating class she urged the students to seek deeper religious knowledge and to adopt a lifelong habit of learning. She positioned these activities within the benefits one reaps when intensified religious and academic dedication fuses with commitment to Muhammadiyah:

After you graduate from here you have to continue learning. Perhaps you are not yet used to reading your Qur'an daily, but read the newspaper [*koran*] instead. You have to start reading the Qur'an every day. Don't only read the paper. In Muhammadiyah we are called to memorize and to recite the Qur'an. That is what impresses me in Muhammadiyah; the religious learning. I also like the involvement in an organization. It teaches me how to network, because creating networks is important. For example, if I want to phone someone, and she is a member of Muhammadiyah, I will not hesitate to contact her. I learned how to write proposals and to understand what is going on in society around me. I even sometimes phone a minister. Through my work in NA I travel all over Indonesia and meet many people of different backgrounds with whom I can exchange news and experiences. Through NA I traveled to places like Costa Rica and Japan.

It is important that you are motivated to get ahead, that you have a dream. Through struggle you can improve your condition. The Qur'an says this: "God will not change the lot of people if they are not willing to change themselves" [Q 13:11]. Learn English, learn Arabic, don't waste time watching TV, but read as many books as you can. TV is mindless. Don't live a mechanical life of going to school, sleeping, watching TV, but take the responsibility for your future in your own hands. Take responsibility for your environment: "Enjoining what is right and forbidding what is wrong" [Q 3:104].[15]

Mbak Ama underlines the benefits of becoming a member of Muhammadiyah in addition to the sacrifice it requires. As in the corporate environment, certain working habits help advance one's career. In NA these habits rest on some of the core Muhammadiyah principles: working hard, reading, not squandering time, being vigilant in religious duties, and knowing your responsibilities toward society. At the same time, people are responsible for their own condition and their environment, and they always have to follow the right, forbidding the wrong. Within the Muhammadiyah network, these habits and attitudes will help advance one's life: professionally, within the organization's leadership positions, and, of course, spiritual benefits abound.

Indonesian society is still based on models of patronage; having the right contacts is crucial for one's career. Institutions groom their own human resources, and it is nearly impossible to come in from the outside without having a solid contact. For example, the university where I taught handpicked its brightest undergraduates upon graduation and educated them to become its future professors. Mbak Ama appeals to this social reality when mentioning some of the perks that come from being active within the organization, further educational opportunities, and options for travel, even abroad. This is a powerful incentive, since Muhammadiyah members hold a broad spectrum of middle- and upper-middle-class jobs throughout Indonesia. When the president at a university is a Muhammadiyah member, this can greatly help NA members to find teaching jobs within that institution. With her indirect references to these options for upward mobility, Mbak Ama addresses one of the most common anxieties facing university graduates in contemporary Indonesia: Where to find a job?

Muhammadiyah schools are easy, as far as the challenge to create a new cadre goes. The next level for NA in the quest for members is in competition with other Muslim organizations for students or youth. Will it ever be possible to draw from their membership? NA competes with other Islamic organizations for students of a similar age level who concentrate on improving the quality of their membership by practicing skills such as management. They hope that the members will apply these skills in society and in the organization.

NA must highlight its differences and stress that, unlike the student organizations, it has direct roots in society. It tries to improve the quality of young women's lives from a holistic point of view that includes religion, management, and health. It provides its members with information relevant to their lives, not only as students, but also as women, future wives, and professionals. According to NA, its members will not act as academics or professionals only but will also participate in the development of society. In the words of NA leaders, "They are the future force for society, the nation, and the Muslim community [*Kader masyarakat, kader bangsa, dan kader ummat*]."[16]

It is implied here that NA members will not seek materialistic benefits only. To NA, one of the dreaded specters of globalization in Indonesia is the erosion of community values; they fear that individuals will stop caring for the good of the community. Instead of focusing on gaining wealth through their professions, NA members prioritize volunteer efforts. Analyzing society, they consider the mixed blessings of new technologies, forms of communication, and prosperity. While improving the quality of life, these influences have also changed the expectations of Indonesia's youth today:

> By taking on paid jobs and neglecting their social life, they hope to be [financially] comfortable as quickly as possible. They hate strenuous work, for example, raising funds or analyzing programs. Young people now like to have fun and relax. Another challenge is that the prototype of the ideal youngster has changed. Now the ideal is to be handsome, rich, and surrounded by the latest gadgets. Before, the ideal was to be intelligent and involved in activities. Nowadays, being intelligent no longer tops the list. Outward appearances come first; young people want to distinguish themselves from others [not to be average]. This change has to do with TV advertisements and what they read in magazines. The model of the ideal young person has changed. TV

also influences the times we can organize activities; sometimes people will not arrive until their favorite TV show is over. Many are no longer interested in Qur'an lessons, so we organize outings to play soccer and games first and then have a short lesson. Now people are used to good food, so if we serve cookies they are not impressed. We have to come up with chocolates, ice cream, and Dunkin' Donuts. Regular donuts are considered boring. They have to be Dunkin' Donuts.[17]

NA is not rich; its membership fees are only symbolic, so the goodies described as necessary are actually an assault on the budget. The homemade snacks of rice cakes and soybean crackers that NA women used to offer are now regarded with disdain. More seriously, the new attitudes fly in the face of the cherished Muhammadiyah values of modesty, moderation, and frugality, the organization's most basic philosophies that formed the cornerstone of its success and long-term survival. Now NA can do little but comply with the "modern" wishes lest it price itself out of the market. Of course, the new trends also influence two other important areas: young women's developing self-images, and notions of *ikhlas*.

Islamism and Jilbabisasi

The challenge to satisfy young peoples' palates with western donuts pales in comparison to the challenges of extremist groups, which greatly increased after the fall of Suharto. Influenced by teachings from the Middle East and other Muslim countries such as Malaysia, they pose a serious threat to NA. Their mode of interpreting the sources of Islam closely resembles NA's own reformist model: many extremist interpretations refuse priority to the Fiqh and primarily study the original texts of Qur'an and Hadith. Moreover, some Muhammadiyah members mimic the mindsets of extremists who, for example, studied in Saudi Arabia and do not allow their wives to leave the house. This restriction insults NA women, since it hinders their mission of empowering women, if not rendering it impossible. Enclosed wives cannot become active members, so it also cuts the number of NA leaders. Other extremist groups bring in ideas about polygyny. In the reformist *pesantren* Pondok Taruna Al-Qur'an in Yogyakarta, set up by Saudi-trained Pak Umar Budihargo, female students say, "If it is God's will that my husband take a second wife, I will happily accept that." Such an attitude devalues the entire 'Aisyiyah/NA struggle to increase a woman's protection within the marriage through the *keluarga sakinah* philosophy.

Yogyakarta is a university city, and several extremist-minded groups have formed around the campuses of its many universities, drawing on the same age group as NA.[18] Young women especially are targeted as potential spouses; special meetings are held to link up couples. Mbak Ama attended several of these meetings and observed that their target was "to increase the number of members by creating large families." One of her friends, Mbak Rini, accepted her husband during such a meeting. Now she wears the *cadar,* the long black robe and veil that cover body and face. She is not allowed to be in mixed gatherings, and her husband does not give her permission to leave the house without him, not even to attend a *pengajian.* According to Mbak Ama, Mbak Rini was especially vulnerable, since she never had extensive formal religious education and did not realize that the group has a narrow knowledge of Islam. They only use one book, the Arabic-Indonesian translation of the Qur'an published by the Ministry of Religion. The leader of the group presents his private interpretations as the final truth that all members must follow. Ironically, Mbak Rini is the one who earns the income while her husband "sits and studies the Qur'an." She works from her home using the computer.

Mbak Ama and NA have a dual response to this reality. First, they stress the specific character of Muhammadiyah that would prevent such narrow interpretations of Islam. Following the rest of Indonesia, in Muhammadiyah men and women mix freely during meetings. Also, extremist expressions affront the Muhammadiyah principles of moderation, of finding the middle way, and the call to think for oneself. The organization's success rests on the fact that it has always found ways to adapt to the surrounding culture and likewise has adjusted its methods of preaching Islam. Although heavily relying on words, it also uses choirs and even gamelan music. Second, NA uses the extensive religious knowledge of its leaders to counter religious ideas that it considers shallow. It maintains open communication with members of these groups, organizes meetings to listen to their ideas, and uses this knowledge to train special *da'i* (missionary preachers) who work among university students.

To resist what it considers extreme trends in Islam, NA enjoins a process of religious renewal, while firmly remaining within its conventional framework. How this framework is interpreted depends on the issues at stake. In matters of Islamic ethics, dress code, rules, and other outward Islamic symbols, NA women can be more conservative than the older members of 'Aisyiyah, as it represents an interesting blend of conservatism and progressivism. Its leaders abhor religious extremism, yet they dress in a more Islamic fashion than their 'Aisyiyah mothers, wearing the *jilbab* instead of the *kerudung,* even chastising Ibu Elyda Djazman when she was 'Aisyiyah's national chair for not covering her neck. The NA chapter in Lampung is experimenting with wearing all-black outfits that closely resemble those of some extremist groups.

In the general Indonesian trend of building a stronger Islamic identity, NA has been at the forefront of those advocating the *jilbab*. Until 1990, wearing the *jilbab* was forbidden in public schools. Observers of Indonesian Islam testify that since the 1980s the number of young women and girls wearing the *jilbab* has increased considerably. This is referred to as the "jilbabisasi" of society. Unlike the outside world, Muhammadiyah schools have always encouraged girls to "practice" covering their heads several days a week. As teenagers, many current NA leaders asserted their Islamic identity by wearing the *jilbab* consistently; several of them think that it should be obligatory. Women wear the veil for different reasons, but to the majority it represents the preeminent symbol of Islamic identity.[19] Mbak Ama comments:

> I always would wear the *jilbab,* although it was not obligatory at that time. In the Muhammadiyah schools girls were encouraged to wear it three days a week, while until 1990 it was forbidden in government schools and offices. I started wearing it in the first class of middle school and never took it off. Wearing the *jilbab* can be a challenge, for example, while climbing mountains. This challenge is similar to performing the ritual prayers while participating in sports or other activities. Wearing it also allows me to be in mixed company.[20]

Covering the head in accordance with Islamic teachings is part of NA's character or personality (*kepribadian*) as described in the organization's guidelines.[21] To NA women, this means practicing Islam in its right mode, stressing their identity and purity while conforming simultaneously to the rules of behavior for NA women. Covering the head to them is also consistent with the teachings of Muhammadiyah and belongs to the category of implementing the correct rules of Islam. It is on the same level as the Islamic injunctions concerning the division of inheritance between men and women. Although these rules are circumvented by many in Java, NA women consider following the rules of Islam a greater blessing than receiving a larger share of inheritance.

In the Islamic arena where many are competing for members from the same age group and for the same symbols of Islam, NA functions as a moderate voice that connects the school with society and mainstream Islam with the school. This is an important role for the many students who seek the "right type of Islam"; it is even more so when those lacking guidance might hear and follow the extremist voices instead.

Reinventing Leadership

NA leaders are deeply involved in the process of redefining Islamic identities and have spent years brainstorming about the right type of Islam for Indonesia. The process of redefining its place within the Indonesian Islamic landscape is closely connected with developments within the organization. Internally, it aims at strengthening its own organization and Muhammadiyah. This involves a total reinvention of its models of leadership and focus of work.

In the original model, which 'Aisyiyah still practices, positions of national leadership went to those emerging from the inner core of Muhammadiyah families only. For NA, the pool of possible candidates has traditionally been limited to long-term NA members, preferably those who grew up in a Muhammadiyah environment and went to its schools. In a time when Islamic education was not as readily available as today, this method guaranteed that leaders had sufficient Islamic knowledge and were deeply familiar with Muhammadiyah's history and teachings.[22] Starting in the 1970s, this model disintegrated for several reasons. More of the NA members took up salaried positions in Muhammadiyah schools. Although they were active in the organization, they no longer could devote much time to voluntary work. Demographic changes also influenced NA's membership. In 1974, for example, when Ibu Sulistyawati was NA's national chair, she lost her entire board because all its members moved to other islands outside Java, went off for study, or had to relocate because of their husbands' work.[23]

The most important change, however, became visible during the 1980s and brought in new leaders from the newly developing world of NGOs. Streams of money coming in from organizations such as the Ford Foundation and the Asia Foundation allowed NGOs to grow rapidly. The sum total of increased NGO activities was a changing focus in advocacy work. The general agenda of "empowerment of women" pursued by 'Aisyiyah and NA became subdivided into issues such as women factory workers, women's rights in divorce, and marital abuse. Since the organizations did not have enough knowledge or womanpower to address these issues themselves, several of their members became involved in NGOs that focused on specific problems. As a result, many Indonesian NGOs involved in women's issues were set up by activists emerging from the networks of Muhammadiyah or NU. For example, Mbak Nurdjannah, NA's chair from 1990 to 1995, was also one of the initiators of Yasanti, which advocated for women factory workers. She explained her dual membership: "My individual concerns I could express through Yasanti. More general issues, such as those concerning religion, society, and youth, I addressed via NA and 'Aisyiyah."[24]

Using their NGO experience, the new leaders reconfigured NA's model for leadership training in workshops called Darul Arqam. Formerly two weeks long, these workshops now last only three days and are divided into levels and taught to local leaders of districts (*daerah*) and provinces (*wilaya*). Finding good instructors for these workshops is difficult, and as a result, Mbak Terias and her colleagues must make frequent visits to the different provinces to lead them.

The lack of qualified leaders has forced NA to diverge from the traditional model of preaching and teaching and instead to educate its leaders to serve as consultants for economic development. While other activities did not completely come to a standstill, the emphasis shifted to economic community development for young women, while activities such as religious teaching and social activities for girls became optional. Mbak Ama explained:

> Since 1992, we have started training women to become instructors for motivating preachers [*instruktur muballighat motivator*]. Those in turn will teach the "motivator preachers" [*muballighat motivator*]. They are different from the traditional preachers. They are not just "preaching machines" but design small economic projects as well. For example, in Bengkulu, there is an embroidery project; in Balikpapan, a cooperative and several projects for small vendors; in Yogyakarta, there is a business for custom-made clothes. All the motivators receive basic business knowledge. The goal is community development. In Indonesia, for our type of organization, this approach is still new.[25]

Preachers have become organizers and strategic planners; *dakwah* (mission) has become *terpadu* (integrated or holistic). Women's empowerment no longer takes place through the word alone but by improving their material lives as well. Ibu Nur'aini, who was national chair of NA from 1995 to 2000, explained how this model, following traditional methods, equally addresses new concerns:

> We have five types of *dakwah terpadu*; all are aimed at increasing religious knowledge and improving the quality of life within communities. We try to increase Islamic knowledge and awareness in society and use the media to transmit our ideas. We want to empower the poor by helping them through small-scale projects to set up their own business. Through the harmonious family program we counsel girls, and we reach married women in the religious meetings [*tabligh*], where we also address health issues such as HIV/AIDS and reproductive rights.[26]

On a national level, the development of small projects and co-ops dovetails with the desire of Muslim organizations to increase their participation in Indonesia's economy. In the 1990s, the Muslim think tank ICMI started to address the issue of Muslim economic marginalization. It established an Islamic bank, the Bank Mu'amalat, and created a center for "small-business incubation" that opened a bank similar to the Grameen bank in Bangladesh. Started in 1976, the Grameen bank specializes in awarding small, collateral-free loans to women. Following this example, NA also set up banks for small loans.[27]

Together, these developments mean not only that NA leaders are modernizing their organization but that they are transforming some long-standing Muhammadiyah structures. Their work methods are shifting from individual hands-on projects to delegating authority. This approach erodes the model of "one vision, one mission," since diversification is now encouraged. It also implies new managerial methods but also entails a reversal of the hierarchical model, one of Muhammadiyah's most prominent characteristics. This reorganization requires a complete change in attitude for NA leaders and the rest of Muhammadiyah. For NA, success of the projects depends greatly on the educational level of the leaders; at present, their minimum level of education must be equivalent to an elementary-teaching certificate. This requirement is difficult in rural areas that still lag behind the intellectual life of the cities. Many of the leaders in places far from the center have little opportunity to gain experience in new organizational models. According to Mbak Terias, "All they want to do is practical work."[28]

Pervasive hierarchical models are tenacious within NA and Muhammadiyah. In the old days, those in the provinces would wait for instructions from the Central Office in Yogyakarta; taking initiative does not come naturally to all NA leaders, especially those trained in the old ways and those in rural Indonesia. NA tries to strengthen these branches through provincial research groups that help develop local human resources, and research programs at Muhammadiyah universities assist NA in surveying and analyzing its activities to close the gap between the urban center and the rural branches. Muhammadiyah universities that are opening in each province will also help to bridge the gap.

In the long run, these developments not only strengthen the Islamic presence of NA in Indonesia, they also equip NA to be on par with NGOs operating in similar fields that are much better funded, often from western sources. Their wealth enables NGOs to train their workers extensively, pay for people to attend the workshops they organize, and purchase equipment. NA will never be rich, as it does not allow itself to accept funds from outside. Funds would diminish the intrinsic religious value of the work and reduce opportunities to practice *ikhlas*.

Within the Muhammadiyah structure, these new developments turn the traditional work approach and hierarchy on their heads. NA girls used to "embroider handkerchiefs and fold paper flowers," while 'Aisyiyah women were their educators.[29] The NA women are now in a position to educate the older leaders. Still, many 'Aisyiyah women regard NA members as young beginners. According to one NA member, when NA leaders move up to 'Aisyiyah, they are considered small and expected "to become messenger girls" (*menjadi orang suruhan*). In the old days, it was the natural pattern, but the modern highly educated woman no longer finds it acceptable. This is probably why I often heard NA women remark, "I should be joining 'Aisyiyah now, but I will wait another five years." It is not surprising that the maximum age to be an NA member has stretched to forty.

These developments also have changed NA's position in relation to Muhammadiyah. Its leaders refuse to become invisible, as 'Aisyiyah did. Through their projects and activities they gain a reputation in their own right. They advertised their activities in the press and issued press releases daily during the 2000 national conference, where they competed successfully with Muhammadiyah for attention. Nearly a dozen newspapers covered their part of the national meeting. They used television as well, gaining a high profile with their public discussion of pornography. In 2000 these activities led one of the Pemuda Muhammadiyah to remark, "Why don't we just abolish NA?"[30] NA chose to accept this comment as a compliment, implying that Muhammadiyah no longer needs a special branch for young women because they have reached the level of the men. But the goal of NA women is not to imitate the men. In 1980 Pemuda Muhammadiyah moved its headquarters from Yogyakarta to Jakarta to be closer to the center of politics and facilitate its efforts to form future political leaders. NA women want none of that; they want to compete in goodness and stay at the grassroots level where women still need help in improving their quality of life. NA leaders have an important task in helping redefine the many gender issues that face Muhammadiyah women. The task used to be simply instructing women about their ritual duties; now it includes helping 'Aisyiyah refine its harmonious family project, albeit through severe criticism. The simple as well as the complex responsibilities are performed at multiple levels that shift between preaching in the local mosque and doing research at a women studies center at one of Indonesia's Islamic universities.

Pengajian and Kajian: Preaching and Study

Efficiency is one of the reasons NA leaders have moved away from a focus on preaching. They observed 'Aisyiyah *pengajian* and at times came to devastating conclusions:

> Regular *pengajian* don't really work any longer. They are tedious. Many of us in NA prefer to watch them on TV because those are more interesting. We studied the 'Aisyiyah meetings in cities and villages and found that the ones in the city are mostly boring. Women just see them as another formal meeting to attend. In villages the women are more engaged in their meetings, perhaps because of the social pressure. The 'Aisyiyah programs are within such a rigid top-down system: from the Central Office to the local neighborhood, everything is defined. That is why they are the same everywhere. 'Aisyiyah does not have enough human resources to supervise all its initiatives professionally. This is related to the educational level of its leaders. For example, its [former] national chair, Ibu Elyda Djazman, is an elementary school teacher and a preacher. She does not approach matters in an intellectual manner but is practical.[31]

Based on these kinds of observations, NA leaders decided to combine *pengajian* (Qur'an studies) with *kajian* (study and research). They organized special sessions in local mosques to discuss problems relating to women. An example of such activity comes from the mosque adjacent to Mbak Terias's house, where the NA neighborhood branch (*ranting*) holds its weekly meetings. The leaders are local, most of them still in high school. They already are the movers behind the first level of NA activities in the mosque. Several evenings a week, adolescent girls gather for Qur'an study, discussions, communal prayer, training, and activities that benefit their future roles as mothers and wives. They have their own administration, and parts of their meetings are devoted to discussing reports and finances.

The following is an observation of one of those meetings. The room has no air conditioning or fan, and only the open door provides a modest breeze. The girls sit on tiny chairs behind tiny benches, a sign that the room is normally used for teaching religion to small children. In front of them stands a plate with homemade snacks. They try to be serious, jotting down notes while peering at the blackboard, which has an edifying Qur'anic phrase written on it. The meeting lasts several hours, only interrupted by the call for prayers.

At this level of the *ranting*, lifelong bonds of friendship are strengthened, and the fire for NA is lit. (Here is also the first level of leader dropouts. One neighborhood reported that of the thirty-one leaders it trained, eighteen disappeared due to study, work, or "disinterest."[32]) It is also at this level that *ikhlas* is formed. The NA interpretation of *ikhlas* shares many of the definitions found within 'Aisyiyah: work purely done for God without expecting a reward in this life. Yet it has shifted according to NA needs and aspirations. "If you work hard, rewards will follow," said Mbak Ama, "for example in the growth of universities, but there will also be a reward in the hereafter."[33] Mbak Terias defined *ikhlas* by enumerating what it is not: "Not wanting to work but only enjoying sitting in events [*acara*]. Stressing one's rights but ignoring one's responsibilities. Accepting responsibilities but then ignoring them. Not keeping one's promise, staying away from events without notification, and being late."[34] *Ikhlas* for NA is related to its survival. Those who practice it by working as volunteers cannot relax their sense of duty because this would be detrimental to the organization. Hence, *ikhlas* has acquired a practical dimension in NA: one's devotion to NA has to be complete and demonstrated in being punctual and doing one's duties. Successfully fostering *ikhlas* in future leaders depends on following a strict routine; for example, by scheduling meetings regularly.

The meetings at the mosque offer informal religious education. According to one of the local reports, members engaged in study sessions on the following issues: dogma (*aqidah*), morals (*akhlak*), "fifty advices to my sister" (three sessions), "information about 'Aisyiyah, "information about NA," "the importance of religion in the development of the child's brain," psychology of adolescents," and "how to use your time." At times, the girls organize cooking contests or do crafts. As the report shows, several sessions discuss the religious rules concerning women. Mostly these have to do with matters of ritual purity and a woman's place in the family and society. It is a classic theme that is always relevant. This is how the leaders explained the study to me:

> For *pengajian*, preaching, and *kajian* [study], we still focus on verses concerning women. We read the Qura'nic verses about ritual cleanliness, because women give birth and menstruate. For example, the Qur'an teaches that a menstruating woman is not allowed to perform the ritual prayers. Menstruation nowadays does not mean that it is forbidden for her to enter a mosque, especially now that there are special hygienic pads for women. Those are clean and prevent pollution. Concerning problems in society, we discuss anything. We discuss them among us, but at a certain stage we also try to involve men in our discussions, because the problems facing us human beings can no longer be solved by only men or only women.[35]

At the grassroots level, the program is a mix of the old and the new. Faithful to its mission, NA members learn the basic tenets of reformist Islam, study the holy texts and rules of Islam, and combine serious with fun activities. The difference from the old days is that as NA members are better educated, they expect active participation in reinterpreting texts and rules. Female preachers always faced the issue of impurity during their monthly period. The younger generation is addressing this issue in the light of new products that efficiently prevent pollution. This is the seedling for future discussion at the Majlis Tarjih level and might eventually lead to new interpretations concerning woman's cleanliness. The women realize, however, that these kinds of discussions can only be held in cooperation with men. NA women can provide new interpretations; however, nothing they produce is binding unless ratified by the qualified Muhammadiyah bodies.

In combining the old with the new, NA women are also changing the way that they reflect on the essence of the teachings of Muhammadiyah's founder, Ahmad Dahlan. They generously quote his thoughts but try not to do so mechanically; instead, they continuously reflect on the essence of his message. This meditation leads to a renewed commitment to the essential ideas of Muhammadiyah and to new models of teaching. For example, instead of following the conventional model, where groups study a text from the Qur'an or Hadith in one session, NA leaders now take a longer time, developing a process of careful hermeneutics:

> We take three months to discuss one chapter from the Qur'an. Muhammadiyah stresses awareness [*kesadaran*]. Ahmad Dahlan did that when he introduced the Surat al-Ma'un [chapter 107] about helping the poor orphans. He taught it for three months until his audience fully understood what the message of the Qur'an really was.[36]

Although NA tries to create new models, many of its leaders still consider preaching and teaching to be important vehicles to convey the essential message of Islam. According to NA's philosophy, when people follow this message, the ills of society can be truly remedied. Mbak Ama explains:

> When I preach, I like people to understand the essence of religion, that religion is not about rituals or clothes only. If it were like that, it would be superficial, like our current government [the Suharto regime]. What is the use of people wearing nice clothes when their moral life is rotten? Also, we should not perform religious duties without knowing what they are about. For example, if children really understand the five daily prayers, they will do them wherever they are, when in a train, or when climbing mountains.[37]

To NA, awareness of the meaning of the text, combined with truthful intentions, is more important than performing the required rituals mechanically.

This has been the hallmark of Muhammadiyah teaching since its inception, yet many reformists converted the original ideas into lifeless slogans without paying attention to the authentic thought. Following innovative Muhammadiyah thinkers such as Amin Abdullah, NA stresses that Ahmad Dahlan advocated a continuous process of interpreting the Qur'an and tradition. Many NA leaders prepared themselves for reflection within a broad religious framework by combining many years of Qur'anic studies with secular training at universities. This framework helps them take the discussion about women's rituals further to the level of gender awareness. Especially at this level, their ideas contradict the models advocated by 'Aisyiyah. As a result, the NA vision on gender issues heavily relies on a critique of the old 'Aisyiyah models.

The Debate on Women

The new NA discussion on gender has come to rely on the general standards for human rights. It differs markedly from the old model, where they follow 'Aisyiyah yet critique it for its teachings about women, especially in the harmonious family. NA women firmly believe in the value of the nuclear and extended family and reject the individualism they believe that western feminism represents. For Mbak Terias, the core of a woman's self-expression is bound up with her position in society, the Muslim community, and the family:

> For us the word "feminism" means that the woman struggles alone to improve her condition [*memperjuangkan*]. We in NA want to build a harmonious society where not only the woman counts, but the whole family [*keluarga sakinah*]. Very few of our members think along lines of liberal or radical feminism. Our members don't consider it to be interesting because they feel more attracted to pragmatic issues that make a difference in their environment. So they prefer the realistic, pragmatic actions that count and are visible.[38]

In accordance with Muhammadiyah and Islamic views, NA locates a woman's position within her family. The usual issues are at stake here: women's position in society, women's private and public rights according to Islam, and the relationship between spouses. NA women have to deal with the reality that "Indonesian men still consider active and educated women as a threat; men feel that women should stay under them."[39] Yet reality forces traditional models to change. For example, Mbak Terias observed, "When we NA leaders have to travel for our organization, our husbands automatically watch the kids. So we get used to an egalitarian division of tasks."[40]

NA is trying to address women's issues at several levels. First, it tries to re-read and reinterpret the religious texts. Second, it borrows generously ideas and methods from NGOs, where women of Muhammadiyah background have developed problem-solving models based on Islamic teachings. An example of this change initiated by NA members is Rifka Annisa, Indonesia's first center for battered women. Third, armed with new insights, NA reevaluates, for example, the harmonious family and reformulates its teachings on gender. This at times results in sharp criticism of the existing Muhammadiyah models.

When rereading authoritative texts, NA women follow the Muhammadiyah principle of closely studying the religious texts and exercising *ijtihad* when necessary. They also look at the texts using insights generated by gender studies, resulting in the following action plan:

> We are now preparing material to teach our women about gender injustice in society. The women have to learn about their rights, such as in reproduction. After that we continue with the Jurisprudence concerning women and politics [*Fiqh siyasah*]. We are behind in this area and have to link up with other initiatives to catch up.[41]

This approach is partly inspired by NA's close contacts with Rifka Annisa. Using the vast experience of Rifka Annisa workers, NA leaders have refined their arguments on issues such as marital abuse and polygyny. Siti Ruhaini, who is active in NA and in Rifka Annisa, explained how NA's view on polygyny took shape:

> We do not fight polygyny but disapprove of it because our philosophy is to empower women. Polygyny is incongruent with that vision. Only extraordinary men can practice it, such as the Prophet Muhammad and some of his companions. These days there is not one man qualified for such a marriage. Why should men copy the Prophet in polygyny while they neglect to pray all night and do not fast frequently as he did? We also try to raise women's conscience not to hurt each other [by accepting a polygynic arrangement]. Half of the women who end up in such a marriage had no idea that their husband was already married, or that he was taking a new bride. Our problem is that social pressure in Java prevents women from talking about domestic problems. They bring shame upon you, and you ruin the family's name. 'Aisyiyah *dakwah* [mission] often is not aimed at really defending women but preaches how to raise children and how to be with one's husband.[42]

Siti Ruhaini refers to the fact that 'Aisyiyah never has openly disapproved of polygyny, although it has obstructed the practice indirectly through the harmonious family project. This will no longer suffice; NA leaders wish to spell out the pro and cons of polygyny to supply women with firm tools to prevent their husbands from taking a second spouse. Doing so actually stresses Ahmad Dahlan's original teachings that justice should prevail in society (Q. 16:90). Based on this verse, he taught that religion is not only a matter of conviction and belief; it must be "done," or actively practiced.[43] It is hard to keep such teachings alive, for they can easily sink to the level of mere slogans. NA followed the ideas of Amien Rais in trying to revive this essential teaching of Ahmad Dahlan by advocating what Rais calls *tauhid sosial*—to act on the Unity of God in society and translate it into social action. When one applies the doctrine of "God being One" correctly in society, wrong beliefs are abolished and social justice is created. "Through the glasses of *tauhid*," writes Amien Rais, "whenever one person exploits the other, this is denying that person equality in front of God."[44]

This interpretation allows NA leaders to use a powerful combination of the old, Dahlan's interpretation, and the new, Amien Rais's ideas, to shape a decisive argument against polygyny within Muhammadiyah. They can argue that its followers who take a second wife deny their first wife equality in the eyes of God, a direct affront to the social application of God's *tauhid* (God's unity). Seen in this way, taking a second wife ranks as a sin.

This reevaluation of the meaning of the holy text brings NA leaders to their stand on 'Aisyiyah's *keluarga sakinah* project. Before I dive into some of their forceful criticism, I must remark that here they find themselves in a dualistic situation. In spite of all their criticism, NA does teach the harmonious family project as far as it concerns the role of a woman as a daughter. It also follows the 'Aisyiyah summary of a wife's duties that are based on the Muhammadiyah interpretation of the holy texts:

> Serve God and husband. Be faithful and obedient to the husband. Guard a sense of honor and politeness. Provide enough and satisfying care for the husband [*pelayanan*]. Do this while being soft, [using] polite language, and holding a sweet face toward him. Manage and guard the household well. Guard your own and the husband's honor, defending all his interests. Do not receive guests the husband does not approve of. Honor your parents, both your own and your husband's. Motivate the husband to behave himself in accordance with the teachings of Islam.[45]

NA cannot deny the issue of *qawwama*, the husband's leadership over his spouse, and in theory fully acknowledges it. Yet NA does not try to justify it with talk about a woman's "nature" (*kodrat*) or with pseudo-psychological reasoning about woman's specific qualities. It tries to address the issues directly by holding them up to broader standards of human rights.

After several of its leaders graduated from gender studies programs at Indonesian or international universities, NA's reflections on the weaknesses of the *keluarga sakinah* project developed. The arguments progressed from critique on the basis of similarities with the policies of the Suharto government concerning the role of women to questions about women's dual role in the household and salaried work. While not questioning the Islamic teachings concerning a woman's duty, NA points out the inconsistencies this model produces when it is applied. NA demands that Muhammadiyah men join the considerations of gender issues, not only theorizing but applying their ideas in practice. As a last step, NA rejects those aspects of the harmonious family that deny a woman her basic human rights.

To demonstrate this process of building awareness within NA, I will cite several of its leaders' lengthy quotations about the 'Aisyiyah family model. Siti Ruhaini applied the criticism by Indonesian women activists of the "housewifezation" program of the Suharto regime to the *keluarga sakinah*:

> In the *keluarga sakinah* the mother stays at home, cooks while wearing a fancy veil, and the husband comes home smiling. This is not the realistic model, but the model taken from the colonial *priyayi* class [the elite group of upper-class Javanese who served the Dutch government]. The colonial government sent girls to school to prepare good spouses for its civil servants.[46] The *keluarga sakinah* program as adopted in 1985 takes as its basis the five pillars proposed by Dharma Wanita [the organization started by the Suharto government in 1974] and diminishes a woman's role. In Java, the non-*priyayi* women worked as farmers, batik sellers, and merchants. They were independent, like the first members of 'Aisyiyah. They worked in the batik business and were central in the household, powerful in the market; they controlled the money. After the batik industry collapsed, many 'Aisyiyah women became civil servants and started to follow the models of the *priyayi* circles. That is how they lost their independence. Since the designers of this ideology were Javanese *priyayi*, this model was carried over to the Suharto government and became the national model.[47]

Mbak Terias questioned women's dual role and the inconsistencies in the model of male leadership:

> We also pay attention to what is not covered in the writings about the *keluarga sakinah:* that women intellectually and economically can become independent instead of having the double role. The double role especially becomes visible in the *qoryah thoyyibah* [good village]. We advocate a holistic mission [*dakwah terpadu*]. Women's role in the *qoryah thoyyibah* is physical, educational, and economical. That is too heavy and still saddles women with a double role. In the harmonious family there is the issue of leadership [*kepemimpinan*].

What that means has to be fleshed out, because right now it is confusing who can be a leader. [Here Terias referred to the Qur'anic teachings that the man is the head of the family.] Changing a discourse is not easy. For example, now Muhammadiyah teaches that a woman can become a leader on any level, but inside the house the man is the leader. This is problematic. Also there is inconsistency; the book *Adabul Mar'a,* published in 1972, already gives women the right to become active in politics, but after that, in 1985, comes the *keluarga sakinah* based on domestic thinking. The first source says that a woman can become a cabinet minister; the second source says that she is dependent. The harmonious family model does not match the reality of 'Aisyiyah women either; they all have careers outside and work as teachers, civil servants, and in business. In the pictures of the harmonious family, a domestic servant does the work while the wife watches TV, sits nicely [*duduk manis*], and smiles.[48]

Another point of criticism is that leadership is assigned to the man, the woman carries the responsibility for the family's well-being and its success in applying the harmonious family program. For example, in the Muhammadiyah *pesantren* Sobron in Solo, lectures about Muhammadiyah require female students to read the materials about the harmonious family. For male students it is only "hoped for" (*diharapkan*) that they will acquaint themselves with these teachings.[49] This by itself is inconsistent with the basic models of equality in leadership.

In summary, NA critics deem the harmonious family model to be unrealistic, inconsistent with Muhammadiyah teachings concerning women's role, and ultimately harmful to women by expecting them to accomplish multiple tasks. As the underlying model derived from the Dutch colonial ideal from the early 1900s was unrealistic, the family model is incompatible with Indonesian reality. It also is incompatible with reformist teachings and with women's capacities in the twenty-first century. Apart from that, NA argues, close reading of the Qur'an reveals that its verses provide better protection for the woman within the household. Thus, Siti Ruhaini concludes:

> Cooking, cleaning, and washing clothes are the man's responsibility. Islam acknowledges that women's tasks of giving birth and breastfeeding are heavy. They might die for it. Giving birth and taking care of the baby are in principle tiring enough.[50]

In this view, to refer to the woman as the one in charge of the household is redundant, since the Qur'an considers it sufficient for her to focus on the tasks pertaining to childbearing.

Of course, NA leaders have found that few Indonesian men rely directly on the Qur'anic model, instead adhering to age-old habits, expecting their wife to arrange the household. These references to the Qur'an, however, highlight that it is crucial to involve men in women's discussions concerning the family. Within the Muhammadiyah model, and for that matter in any other Islamic model, true change can only transpire when the men participate. This point became clear when in 1995, pushed by its sections for women and by some of the young male scholars led by Dr. Amin Abdullah, Muhammadiyah's national congress decided that rethinking gender issues would become a priority of the Majlis Tarjih. At the same time, three women (two 'Aisyiyah, one NA) were added to its male-only constituency. Siti Ruhaini is one of the women who qualified as a member. She explained this move:

> The Majlis Tarjih now believes that it is impossible to ignore the issue of gender in this day and age. We have to reevaluate books and decisions published by Muhammadiyah about the family and the position of women. These were in 1936 [*Isteri Islam yang Berarti* (The Muslim spouse who matters)], 1972 [*Adabul Mar'a fil Islam* (Morals for Muslim women)], 1988 [*Keluarga Sakinah* (The Harmonious family)] and in 1996 a collection of presentations given at a seminar about gender. So we started this discourse in order to give a voice to all. That is why the name of the Majlis Tarjih was changed into Majlis Tarjih dan Pengembangan Pemikiran Dalam Islam [Council for Religious Consideration and Intellectual Development within Islam].[51]

Muhammadiyah members refer to the Majlis Tarjih for guidance in adapting to the requirements of their time. Members say that "the color of Muhammadiyah is determined by the Majlis Tarjih."[52] As Siti Ruhaini indicated, since its inception the council has been instrumental in giving women space to fulfill their religious calling for the organization. How this was done can be read in the *Himpunan Tarjih*, the collection of its *fatwas*.[53] In fact, I have regularly but indirectly referred to this collection, since 'Aisyiyah and NA base their publications about women on its decisions. The women themselves reflected on the council's guidelines and challenged them if necessary. For example, when the council mandated that a woman is not allowed to go out except accompanied by her *mahram* (designated protector), 'Aisyiyah forced the council to modify this rule, since its women had to go out for preaching activities.[54]

Within this new frame of study and deliberation, the Majlis Tarjih has for the first time in its history started to discuss the *keluarga sakinah* program seriously. This time, the men are participating as well. Priority is given to equality within the family. The discussions assume that the father is no longer the head of the household who decides unilaterally but that decisions are based on the input of all family members: husband, wife, and children. This is based on the Islamic principle of *mushawarah* (communal consultation). According to NA women, following the logical consequence of this principle, the family must be based on democratic principles; each member must be allowed to grow spiritually, educationally, and economically. Women in this family are protected by their rights to be free of physical, psychological, and sexual violence, and their reproductive rights are guaranteed. When elaborated within this frame of thinking, the ʿAisyiyah model seems ambiguous, since it does not clearly spell out and cannot safeguard women's rights.

The ʿAisyiyah harmonious family model is mostly based on practical guidelines that, when possible, are derived from Qurʾanic teachings. For example, the verse, "Do you enjoin right conduct on the people, and forget [to practice it] yourselves, and yet ye study the Scripture? Will ye not understand?" (Q. 2:44) is quoted in the section about "education within the family."[55] After answering the question of why such education is important, the ʿAisyiyah guidelines flesh out the methods of achieving it: "modeling good behavior," "preventing problems," "corrective measures," and "methods of guidance." Under the heading of "guidance," ʿAisyiyah enjoins parents to maintain open communication with their children, especially during the teenage years. Among the many tips for parents are: "Provide an alarm clock in the child's room," and, "Instruct your child to knock before entering a room." These are sound instructions, especially when one hopes to include Muslims in rural areas. However, the cursory examples show to what degree the ʿAisyiyah model is debatable. It is too simplistic and fails to address underlying issues of gender inequality. A better educated generation needs more sophisticated ideas, and most already have their own alarm clock or use the alarm function on their cell phone to wake up.

In the new model envisioned by NA leaders, the guidelines for the harmonious family derive from universal basic human rights, democratic rights, and women's rights. "Universal" is the key word here. Amien Abdullah stresses, "When you discuss what is limited to your own group only, and not look at those outside you, it becomes problematic."[56] According to him, this universality is not only an ideal for Muhammadiyah but for all Muslims. Learning about others has positive, global effects.

One of the obstacles for the future is the gap between the attitudes of younger women and older men. Many Muhammadiyah men are still prejudiced concerning woman's capacities. Their long-lived cultural influences, combined with traditional interpretations of the Islamic sources concerning men's authority over women, have shaped the conservative ideas of many

Muhammadiyah men. According to Mbak Terias, "In matters of science they are open-minded, but not in domestic matters. Most members of Muhammadiyah are not trained in religious institutes and lack comprehensive understanding of the texts; they only consider them as a tool of faith [*alat iman*]. We have to broaden their horizon."[57] This is a challenge that will take a long time to meet. Knowledge among men about the role of women in Muhammadiyah is still lacking, largely because its schools teach much about Muhammadiyah, while the curriculum contains little about women.

According to Mbak Terias, within the Muhammadiyah hierarchy, a man's role still is considered higher than a woman's:

> Men are the ones who do the talking when there is a ceremony or a presentation, during the Friday service in the mosque, and when there is a funeral. Leading those kinds of functions is considered a man's task. What is left for women is to pray. Men feel more important than the women.[58]

The strong impression still prevails that 'Aisyiyah is the faithful and obedient spouse of Muhammadiyah, with NA following the same pattern.

NA is trying to modify this pattern by suggesting, for example, that the traditional segregation of genders through men's and women's branches within the organization be abolished. This unity can better be accomplished now that women are allowed to become members of Muhammadiyah's boards. Conversely, they say, men should be on the boards of 'Aisyiyah and NA as well. That will give the organizations the option to include men in its decisions from the beginning. When the men are on board, the women's decisions will carry more weight, and women will become more visible.[59]

Conclusion

The activities of NA's women provide a small window into the competing forces young adults have to choose among when deciding on the mode of Islam they want to practice. They also reveal Muhammadiyah's struggle in the twenty-first century to educate a future generation of actively engaged women dedicated to its cause. NA women are its hope. They can help the organization shed its archaic image, questioning some of its interpretations of Islam that do not agree with contemporary standards for human rights. No longer can it be taken for granted that NA women will automatically meet the terms of the organization's "character," the essential identity it has tried to protect through education, rules, and constitution. The commitments of the younger generation are no longer confined to the narrow model Muhammadiyah prescribes. NA women have ample choices.

NA women stand at the fault lines of the various developments within Indonesian Islam. Sharing some of 'Aisyiyah's conservatism, at times the women have become even more conservative in their Islamic expressions. At the same time, NA stresses its moderate character to differentiate itself from extreme trends in Islam. Its documents and its goals of reinterpreting the holy texts of Islam place NA leaders among the progressive thinkers in the country.

While 'Aisyiyah works in a crisis-oriented mode and tries to make do with what the predominant situation offers, NA is changing its orientation from crisis to conflict; it aims at a total overhaul of regressive ideas about women and at reshaping the methods of understanding the message of Islam. Re-creating its vision is what Muhammadiyah needs to escape its colorless image. The question is, Can it keep up with NA women who want to join in the re-creating process?

Taking 'Aisyiyah's original message of women's empowerment, NA leaders seek to reorganize these teachings in the light of universal human rights. This shift can only be accomplished by a radical rereading of the holy texts of Islam in a religious, spiritual, and practical manner. To NA leaders, women must be shielded from polygyny and domestic violence, and their well-being must include health and economic considerations. Its leaders want to provide women with tools to strengthen their religious, social, economic, and even political life. On the religious level, NA encourages women to take ownership of the Qur'anic texts; on the social level, it gives them leadership training and venues for upward mobility. Politically, it makes women aware of their choices by joining many other Indonesian women's organizations in voter education. Around the time the Suharto government fell, glimpses were visible of NA's success in fostering women's political awareness: hundreds of its members traveled to Yogyakarta in 1998 when it organized an anti-Suharto rally. To their disappointment, they were too late: the regime had fallen just before the rally started. Going beyond the initial work of 'Aisyiyah leaders, NA women disagree with the old models and thus heavily criticize the harmonious family projects.

To legitimate their ideas, NA women also rediscover and reinvent the traditions of their organization. In their quest to promote universal human rights, they find backing in the teachings of Ahmad Dahlan, who preached compassion for the poor and practiced tolerance for others. This development has led NA in unexpected directions; in 2000, for example, the organization hosted its first interfaith event.[60]

NA women play an important role in guiding reformist-minded women through the landscape of contemporary Islam in Indonesia. By stressing moderation in Islamic belief and culture, they prevent young women from falling prey to extremist groups—or from becoming so disenchanted with religion that they stop being involved altogether.[61] NA teaches "mosque Islam" and combines solid Islamic knowledge with social awareness and critical capacities. It keeps the connection between school and society alive. The social consciousness of NA leaders moves many of them to become full- or part-time social activists. All these contributions serve NA's goal of saving Indonesia from destruction by foreign, global forces and local forces of grinding poverty, corruption, and extremism.

NA contributes to reformist Islam in Indonesia with a discourse that is slowly changing the paradigm concerning women's position and place. It teaches that women and men are equal and even entertains the revolutionary thought that they both are responsible for household work. Practical as ever, NA women realize that an in-between stage is needed, for example, about who does the dishes. So before they try to convince the men to do their part, NA women first think about how to minimize the amount of dirty dishes. Thus, one of their latest documents about the characteristics of an NA leader states that instead of doing the cooking herself, a mother "can get takeaway food to feed the family."[62]

NA leaders face many obstacles in reconfiguring the old into the new. They are part of a Javanese culture that considers them as children and inferior to the older generation. More progressive groups consider them as somewhat outmoded, while their stress on moderation alienates extremist circles. However, these realities do not deter women who excel in realism and idealism and insist on having "high ideals." To them that is precisely what the Qur'an represents, and they see it as their mission to transform its divine ideals into reality for women.[63]

PART 3

Women of Nahdlatul Ulama

5   Tradition Revisited: The *Pesantren*

If women pay attention to [religious] issues concerning women,
I think a new configuration will emerge."
—K. H. Abdurrahman Wahid, former president of Indonesia
and former chair of NU

Women Graduating

"Did you notice that not one man was present during the whole graduation ceremony? No man spoke, and all the female teachers used their own
names. Not once was a man's name mentioned!" A female teacher at an
Islamic boarding school (*pesantren*) whispered this observation in my ear
around midnight after a graduation ceremony for the women students who
had memorized the entire Qur'an and studied the complex science of its
interpretation. The ceremony had been a glamorous event; the graduates sat
on chairs decorated with golden bows. Their dresses were shiny green satin,
their slippers golden. They wore the makeup of brides: fiery red lips with
golden eye shadow. Their women teachers were dressed in shiny pastel outfits. The ceremony had been symbolic of the privileged position the graduates now had: they were "holders" (*hafidz*) of the Qur'an.[1] Their mothers sat
in front and stood up when their daughters' names were called. The fathers,
many of them respectable *kiai,* remained in the section to the right, reserved
for the male guests. This was the third year that the women had been allowed
to hold a public outdoor graduation ceremony. Earlier they had been forced
to celebrate in a dark building that could barely hold all the guests. The students' main teacher, Ibu Fatma, had started the drive to transform the ceremony into an event that allowed public recognition of the great effort of
the graduates. This was not a small feat in the world of *pesantren,* which are
sometimes called "age-old and somewhat archaic" institutions.[2]

A great part of the transmission of the Islamic faith and knowledge for
traditionalist Islam takes place in the *pesantren.* They form the heart of tra-

ditionalist education and are seminal for developments within NU. They are specific to Indonesia and in the past were mostly situated in remote rural areas. *Pesantren* used to be considered bulwarks of conservatism, and for most of their history they had no women students. A women's graduation ceremony in the open symbolizes the profound transformations that are taking place within the *pesantren*. Opening up to the world means the introduction of new ideas, new curricula, and reconfigurations of existing hierarchies and authorities.

For women, studying at the *pesantren* provided opportunities for direct participation in scrutinizing the NU tradition, which is challenging existing hierarchies. Many of the activists in the Muslimat and Fatayat NU were trained and/or work in the *pesantren*. This chapter illustrates how this education helped women to participate developing their position and role within the NU in particular and Islam in general. The women teachers at the *pesantren* work within the enclosed environment of their own schools, but trends spread from there when graduates continue their careers in other *pesantren*, universities, and schools. At the same time, ideas are transmitted to a larger audience through *pengajian* (Qur'an lessons), publications, and the many NGOs set up by the brightest of the alumni.

The two women who are the main focus in this chapter are both female teachers at a *pesantren*. Ibu Fatma lives in a large city and started a *pesantren* for female students during the 1980s in the large complex her father built. Earlier, her mother had already accepted occasional female students and so paved the way for a school. Ibu Siti set up her *pesantren* in a small village, also during the 1980s. The women are not related to each other and have only met in passing.

In women's circles Ibu Siti and Ibu Fatma have great influence in producing and transmitting reinterpretations of the holy texts and new ideas about the role of women. They guide their students in reflections on the many issues facing Muslim women in contemporary society. They also face an ongoing struggle to be accepted in the male *pesantren* world that traditionally has been filled with archaic ideas about women's position and rights. In many *pesantren*, male students still recite the poem: "Woman is a devil created for man. Let us seek refuge in God from this evil devil."[3]

Nobody knows exactly how much influence these women have on new developments within traditionalist Islam. Many male NU leaders do not yet consider women as equal partners. Male teachers in the *pesantren* might consider Fatma and Siti's role in transmitting Islamic knowledge as marginal. Even Ibu Murshida Thahir, one of the two women in the highest NU board of the National Syuriah, admits, "there is still a gender gap."[4] Male leaders are not the only challenges; many a conservative leader has a wife who shares his opinions about the role of women. At the same time, an undeniable movement within NU aims at allowing women more authority in teaching the Islamic sources and in the process of creating Fiqh. Once women participate in these processes, their influence is irreversible.

Women like Ibu Fatma and Ibu Siti work at emancipating Muslim women, yet they remain unknown, never reaching the national fame of many male *pesantren* leaders. They remain behind the backs of the male leaders. I do not know of one woman who has independently opened a *pesantren.* They depend on the support of fathers, husbands, or other family members.

One of the most fascinating aspects of the *pesantren* world is that the conservative and the progressive go hand-in-hand. A former student of Ibu Fatma considered her a real feminist. The student confided to me in a perfect American accent, acquired during her stay in the United States from birth until she graduated from high school, "Ibu Fatma has taught us to look at Islam in a more liberated fashion. I was lucky to have her as my teacher. She explained Islamic marriage to me in a way I could accept and never taught that the husband should suppress his spouse. She made me aware of the fact that women can have their place and rights in Islam."[5] At the same time, Ibu Fatma had encouraged the final speaker at the graduation ceremony to stress that above all the graduates should be "virtuous wives." She knows that she walks a delicate line in a world where perspectives about women are changing but are still ruled by conservative ideas.

To illustrate how local changes reach the wider environment, I will end this chapter with a description of the reinterpretation of a Fiqh text that is widely read in *pesantren* and has greatly affected perceptions about women during the past century. The text, by Muhammad bin 'Umar Nawawi al-Jawi al-Bantani al-Shafi'i (1813–98), is called *Kitab Syarh 'Uqud Al-Lujjain fi Bayan Huquq Al-Zaujain* (Notes on the mutual responsibility concerning the clarification of the rights of spouses). Indonesians refer to the text as *Kitab Uqudullijain.* Throughout this chapter I will call it *Kitab 'Uqd.* Through a process of explaining and reinterpreting this text, its deeply rooted authority within NU circles was challenged. It started within the *pesantren* and is now being transferred to the entire NU community, especially distributed by the Muslimat NU.

Before elaborating on the women's situation, I must introduce the *pesantren* world and describe the role of its male leaders (the *kiai*) and its female leaders (the *nyai*).

Pesantren

The Beginning of Perpetual Longing

Education in the *pesantren* is rigorous and can take over twenty years. Its students, both male and female, are called *santri*, and they are led by a *kiai*, a male scholar of Islam. The *kiai's* spouse or other women from his family, the *nyai*, often are in charge of the division for girls. Other teachers are called *ustadh* (male) or *ustadha* (female).

Students come from all over Indonesia and live together, obeying strict rules concerning schedules and conduct. In a period that can range from one to twenty years, they acquire Islamic knowledge and leadership and oratory skills. This qualifies them to work as leaders of Islam, ranging from learned authorities who are actively involved in interpreting Islamic law (*ulama*) to preachers and teachers of the basics of Arabic and Qur'an at local mosques. The graduates at Ibu Fatma's *pesantren* specialize in learning the Qur'an by heart, memorizing verses in the early morning before going to school and in the late afternoon before starting their homework chores and sharing a small, austere room with up to fifteen women.

Often a *pesantren* will have started around a small prayer house where a teacher attracted students because of his specific knowledge. There are almost ten thousand *pesantren*, mainly in Java, that have student bodies ranging from a few dozen to nine thousand students.[6] At the *pesantren* students learn the essentials of traditionalist Islam in order to maintain and spread Islam. These are the values of the Aswaja people, the Ahl al-Sunnah wa al-Jama'ah (People of the tradition and community). Hence, an NU-related *pesantren* is considered "a fortress for the defense of the Islamic community" and a "center for the spread of Islamic faith."[7]

Three basic elements are unique to the *pesantren* tradition: the *kiai*, the course materials, and the value system.[8]

The Kiai

The *kiai*, the leader of the *pesantren*, is perceived to be the ruler of "a small kingdom."[9] He is fully in charge of everything that goes on in his *pesantren* and shapes its identity. Its success depends on his knowledge, fame, and charisma. When a famous teacher dies without leaving a successor of equal capacities, the *pesantren* declines or closes down. Guaranteeing proper succession is therefore of great concern to a *kiai*. To transmit the intellectual tradition from one generation to the next, the *kiai* trains his sons or recruits top students as future sons-in-law to create a pool of leaders that will continue the *pesantren* after his death. As a result, its leadership is built around tight-knit family relationships, while intricate patterns of marriage inter-relate *pesantren* to one another. "Just knowing the Qur'an by heart is not enough to qualify as a husband for the daughter of a *kiai*," I was told while discussing the marriages of Ibu Fatma's siblings. The stories about love de-nied and eluded were worthy of a novel. None of the women was free to choose her own husband but had to follow her father's wish, as the spouse would become part of the *pesantren*'s social and educational grid.

A *kiai* exemplifies Islamic ideals with his learning, behavior, and role in society. Not all *kiai* reach the highest level of Islamic knowledge, but those who do belong to the elite of the *ulama*, the religious scholars who are con-sidered inheritors of the Prophet's charisma.[10] Such a *kiai* enjoys the great-est respect from his students, who hope that obedience helps them derive some of his power of blessing (*baraka*). Often students are afraid to ques-tion their *kiai*'s teachings. This attitude of obedience is rooted in the ideal of the traditional relationship of the Sufi master and his pupil, who is advised to be "like a dead body in the hands of its washer." It is believed that not challenging the *kiai*'s wisdom will protect his vast reservoir of knowledge. Many in Java believe that attacking a *kiai*'s words causes "his knowledge to fade away as a bird disappears from sight as it flies farther and farther away."[11] In the past, a *kiai* seldom wrote his teachings down in books but conveyed his wisdom orally. He also did not pay attention to cumbersome administration and filing. *Pesantren* used to be notorious for their admin-istrative bedlam. This has changed, as many *pesantren* have introduced a general curriculum next to the religious one and appointed someone to be in charge of administration.

A *kiai*'s role is not limited to religious affairs. He can be active in econom-ic and social development and/or in politics. In the past, many *kiai* worked as traders. They are not paid for their religious work, since according to a Tradition of the Prophet, asking money to teach the Qur'an diminishes the degree of blessing inherent to the work. As political organizers, *kiai* could resist the Dutch colonizers. Their schools were far removed from the colo-nial centers that held non-Islamic, Christian values. Many *kiai* supported or joined the NU political party until 1984, when NU decided to leave party politics and focus on religious and social development. Many were back in politics again in 1999, when NU created a political party. *Kiai* not only teach in their own schools but serve the community around them by holding re-ligious meetings, presiding over rituals for death, birth, and marriage, and by providing counseling. In rural areas, many still assign magical powers to the *kiai* and ask for prayers and amulets to ward off evil or disaster. Charismatic *kiai* continue to guide their students after death, when the *santri* visit their graves every Thursday night. According to Abdurrahman Wahid, the role of the *kiai* must be understood within the context of the Indonesian concept of the holy men who do not withdraw from the world completely but retain worldly functions and are also highly valued by the secular rulers as advisors.[12] This remark naturally represents the NU ideal and helps build an image of *kiai* as founts of wisdom and erudition. In real life, it must be admitted, there are many not-so-holy *kiai*.

Kiai are members of a male-oriented world. In 1926, Nahdlatul Ulama was set up as a network of *kiai*. It never occurred to the *kiai* to invite women to join their circles until women started to demand a place; in 1946, this resulted in the Muslimat NU, but before the 1970s few women taught in the *pesantren*.

The Texts

The NU variation of the Islamic faith is taught through classical Islamic texts that are "nurtured and transmitted from generation to generation."[13] All but one of these texts were written by men; the one written by a woman called Fatimah is published under her uncle's name.[14]

In the *pesantren,* the study of the Fiqh and the practice of Tasawwuf, intensified forms of worship derived from Islamic mysticism, are emphasized. The topics can be classified into several groups, and a teacher can be famous for excellence in one or more of these groups: syntax, morphology, Jurisprudence (Fiqh), the sources of Jurisprudence, Tradition (Hadith), Qur'an interpretation (*tafsir*), the Unity of God (*tauhid*), Tasawwuf, ethics, history of Islam, or rhetoric.[15] The texts in Arabic are called Kitab Kuning, yellow books made up of loose leaflets that can be taken out for study.[16] Many of these are commentaries on commentaries of older texts interpreting the Qur'an and the Tradition.[17] There are also Kitab Putih, white books that are more modern. The yellow books hold the scholastic tradition, the Fiqh texts that are considered sacrosanct, while the white books are considered modern, although some were written at the beginning of the twentieth century.

The teaching methods are specific to a *pesantren*. Two are predominant: *gandrungan,* where the *kiai* reads a text aloud in Arabic while the *santri* sit in a circle around him, or *sorogan,* where the *santri* read the text by themselves while the *kiai* or his assistant gives guidance. Students learn to give speeches (*pidato*) and practice the art of debate (*diskusi*). The system is based on rote learning with little room for creative thinking or questioning the *kiai*'s teachings. There are no final exams; when a *santri* masters a certain text, he or she proceeds to the next, more complicated one. Martial arts and other sports are popular, especially among male *santri*. Apart from the academic curriculum, many *pesantren* organize vocational training and agricultural work.

The materials and methods used in the *pesantren* reflect both the strength and weakness of traditionalist Islam. Students are able to read the original texts in Arabic and become acquainted with alternative ideas from the Middle East, but up to the 1970s, students who graduated from a traditional *pesantren* had little knowledge of nonreligious subjects such as math, sciences, and modern languages. This disqualified them from moving into positions of economic, medical, or technological leadership, confining their role to the religious, social, cultural, and sometimes political arenas. This is gradually changing, and many *pesantren* have started *madrasah*, schools that also teach secular topics. *Santri* attend these schools parallel to following the traditional lessons in the *pesantren*. Nowadays there are two types of *pesantren*: those teaching mainly religious topics, called *salafiyya*, and those with a mixed curriculum of religious and secular subjects. The *salafiyya pesantren* tend to be more conservative than those offering a mixed curriculum. They are also considered more correctly Islamic. Male students, for example, stress their traditional Islamic identity by wearing the Javanese *sarong* instead of western pants. Students graduating from the *salafiyya pesantren* cannot study in the regular universities, but those who studied a mixed curriculum often go on to take degrees in a variety of departments at religious or public universities.

Material, method, and schedule for study in the *pesantren* differ from those in schools run by the state or Muhammadiyah. A *kiai* follows a unique schedule: he teaches his first lessons very early in the morning and often sleeps during the late morning.

When a *kiai* dies, visiting his grave becomes part of the weekly routine. Once a year the *pesantren* organizes elaborate festivities to commemorate the day their *kiai* passed away. This is called a *khaul*. Thousands of alumni come from all over Indonesia to reflect near the grave of their teacher, to listen to speeches about him, and to recite the Qur'an. Those who cannot attend in person will "send" Qur'an reciting with a friend or relative. All living around the *pesantren* are invited and treated to snacks and drinks. The *khaul* is a time to reconnect the *pesantren* with its students and its neighbors and to reconfirm the traditionalist identity. "Muhammadiyah has large buildings; we have *khaul*. That is why we are perpetually out of money," is Ibu Fatma's analysis.[18]

Apart from respect for the learned man, the texts, and the tradition, the *pesantren* ideal stresses disregard for worldly concerns and pleasures. Spending money in honor of the teacher has priority over hoarding it for material goods. *Santri* eat moderately and sacrifice physical comforts such as a mattress. Eating too much is considered a hazard; it makes the student fat and lazy in study and worship.[19]

Prayer in the World

Students come to the *pesantren* to gain a deeper knowledge of Islam and to grow in moral superiority. Values are practiced by living a basic and simple life while practicing the daily religious rituals and spiritual exercises. The *santri* sleep with a dozen or more other students in tiny rooms: male *santri* must sleep on the floor, while female *santri* can use a thin mattress. Males and females are strictly segregated; they have their own classes and seldom socialize. Within each group deep bonds of friendship develop. Students pray together—the men in the mosque, the women in their own prayer house. Their day starts at four in the morning and ends at eleven at night. They share the strenuous schedule of seventy-two hours of religious learning filled with curricular and extracurricular classes, helping each other with homework, cooking, and cleaning. My friends refer fondly to this time together: "After you leave the *pesantren*, your heart longs back to this time for the rest of your life."

Abdurrahman Wahid has described how the specific curriculum instills certain attitudes and values within the *santri:*

> This unique educational structure with its particular characteristics cannot but yield a specific attitude concerning one's life and aspirations. The most important vision in *pesantren* values is to gain acceptance from God in the day to come; in *pesantren* terminology this vision is known as pure dedication to God [*keikhlasan*]. . . . This orientation towards the hereafter forms the essence of *pesantren* life . . . it is particularly stressed in detailed and extensive practices of the religious rules, and can be seen in its obligatory literature.[20]

Life in the *pesantren* is structured around the daily rituals prescribed by Islam. No *santri* can skip the prayers without a valid excuse. In many *pesantren*, additional praises are added as well. This emphasis on obligatory and extrareligious exercises could easily yield to a tendency toward otherworldliness, but moving away from the world is avoided by the philosophy that spiritual feats are useless when devoid of social actions. Abdurrahman Wahid explains this as follows: "The value system plays an important role in shaping the societal frameworks *pesantren* people desire for the society at large. Piety, for example, is one value often employed by *kiai* to promote solidarity among different social strata."[21] Although romanticized and not always practiced in real life, as it does not agree with the social stratification within Indonesian society, this theme is recurrent in NU teachings. It goes back to the earliest Sufi traditions that stress charity and equality. For example, in a sermon from 1978, a *kiai* taught:

> "Fastidious performance of religious rituals only can never replace one's social duties. Those who intensify their performances of religious rituals—such as recommended prayers, *dhikir,* and recommended fasting—but do not fulfill their social duties—such as *zakat* [alms] and *amal jariah* [feeding the poor and orphans]—are like trees that do not produce fruit. Those who perform obligatory rituals and fulfill their social duties but do not perform recommended prayers and rituals are still better Muslims than those who neglect their social duties but perform obligatory and recommended prayers."[22]

Although these ideals are sometimes difficult to apply, it this basic attitude allows the *pesantren* to carry the tradition while becoming initiators of change within their own walls, within NU, and in the society surrounding them.

Women in the Pesantren

Until the 1950s, *pesantren* rarely had female students. The role of women was confined to being the spouses of the *kiai* and producing future leaders for the *pesantren.* Women had occasionally become scholars of Islam, but they were exceptional. Sumatra offered the first options for girls to receive full-time religious education. The first Islamic academy for girls in Indonesia was the reformist Diniyyah Puteri, set up in 1923 by Rahmah el Yunusiyah. Her goal was to provide women with opportunities to learn to read and write in order not to be confined to the house. She also considered education to be a tool that would help strengthen the spread of Islam among women.

The first Javanese *pesantren* to accept female students was the Denanyar *pesantren* in Jombang. It had started in 1917, and in 1919 Kiai Bisri Syamsuri opened it up to female *santri,* "facing great obstacles."[23] Kiai Bisri later became an influential NU leader. His teacher was Hasyim Asy'ari, fondly called Hadratus-Shaikh, the initiator of the NU and considered one of the greatest *kiai* ever in Java. Kiai Bisri's motives were not necessarily to emancipate women. Most of all, he wished to ensure that girls would become "truly good women who were not just hanging around." He was opposed to women gaining influence in political and other public activities but reasoned that staying in the *pesantren* would prevent them from being too free. Also, he felt that it would teach them discipline. This concept attracted parents, since it was an opportunity to have their daughters educated in a safe environment. The number of eight girls in the first year jumped to nearly thirty in the second.

The main concern at the time was to keep the male and female students separate. Initially the girls were not allowed to learn the Latin script but could only read Arabic, so that they "could not exchange love messages in Indonesian with the male students," or they learned to write the Javanese language in Arabic (*pegon*). A former student recalled that her mother "used to steal knowledge from her older brothers to learn how to read and write [in Latin script]."[24]

Another problem was that the girls should have female teachers. Since those were not yet available, Kiai Bisri issued a *fatwa* that allowed one of his married senior students to teach the girls. Kiai Bisri's honored teacher, Kiai Hasyim Asy'ari, did not agree yet with the new concept. Whenever he visited the *pesantren,* female *santri* had to "flee and hide in the back." During the 1950s, his own sister, Ibu Choiriyah, qualified as a female *kiai* herself. After a long stay in Mecca, her knowledge was considered equal to that of a *kiai,* allowing her to teach male students.

At the 1934 national congress in Banten, the NU leaders finally allowed official education for women. This meant that women could broaden their education beyond the study of Arabic and the Qur'an. Kiai Bisri's daughter Shalihah was one of the first to benefit from the expanded education. Studying in one of the first groups of women students, she learned Arabic and *pegon* but taught herself the Latin script in secret. She later married one of Hasyim Asy'ari's sons, Wahid Hasyim, and became a leading force in the NU organization for women. Abdurrahman Wahid is her son.

The original women's curriculum started with the last part of the Qur'an (the thirtieth *juz'*), since that was often recited at wedding ceremonies. This also served as good public relations for the *pesantren,* as the girls could now give public recitations at weddings. Thus the public could become used to women Qur'an reciters. As a result, Indonesian women were allowed to participate at national Qur'an reciting contests, which paved the way for Maria Ulfah in 1980 to become the first woman to win the international contest in Kuala Lumpur. She has gained international recognition and set up an institute in Jakarta where around five hundred young women between the ages of eighteen and twenty-five learn to recite the Qur'an. From the Indonesian side, the path was cleared by a *fatwa* composed at the 1979 NU congress in Semarang that allowed women to recite the Qur'an in public.

Apart from the art of Qur'an recital, the girls studied the rules concerning their obligations and duties in marriage. At the age of eight, many had already left the *pesantren* to be married. According to Ibu Iskandar, who currently is in charge of the Denanyar *pesantren* of girls, early marriage was regular until the 1980s. After that, "girls would finish their schools and, praise be to God, even go on to high school and university."

Pesantren have become popular havens where parents send their female children. In some *pesantren* there are more female than male students. This increase is a result of a new trend of sending male students to secular schools that aim for the prestigious national universities, while female students study at the *pesantren* to become teachers of religion or to go on to an Islamic State Institute for Higher Learning (IAIN).

As the age of marriage went up and women started to spend longer years at the *pesantren,* the number of qualified teachers grew. In most *pesantren* today, women teach the female *santri.* As far as the *nyai* are concerned, some still limit their activities to being the spouse of the *kiai,* but an increasing number have started to play an active role in reforming the *pesantren* by, for example, introducing innovative ideas concerning the position of women. Ibu Fatma teaches and interprets the Qur'an. Ibu Siti guides her students in the mystical way and at the same time is a social activist who participates in seminars about women's rights. Both *nyai* are models to their students. The challenge to them and to those concerned with modernizing the *pesantren* is to create an alternative for women that remains faithful to the institute's original intentions. They try to translate the texts written by and for men to the contemporary conditions and expectations of women. Women live with the reality that the Fiqh texts are a given: they are considered sacrosanct and cannot be discarded. If a woman is serious about her *pesantren* education, it is vital that she knows the texts as well as her male colleagues do. Only then can she join the process of reinterpreting them. This situation worries young women activists who once studied at the *pesantren* themselves. "Much of what is taught in the *pesantren* comes from the Arab world and has no relationship with Indonesian reality," said the member of a center that tries to monitor and guide young girls in their development into womanhood.[25] The ideals about women and women's Indonesian reality do not match. Ibu Fatma and Ibu Siti have taken up the challenge to try and make ideals into reality.

The Nyai

The Nyai in the City: Ibu Fatma

In the traditional institutes in which Ibu Fatma was educated, nothing on the curriculum questioned the position of women in Islam.[26] When she was a young woman, her family selected a husband for her, and she joined him at his school in East Java. This marriage became the occasion for her to begin her life as an activist. She discovered that marriage can be "like the lottery": you can win, but many lose. She lost when after one year of marriage, her husband wanted to take a second spouse. To her surprise, he also ordered her to stay inside: "He was very traditional, very *salafiyya,* influenced by the mores of Mecca where women always stay inside the house. I was not allowed to meet with guests and had to ask him permission to see my parents."

After her daughter was born and her husband decided to marry a second wife, Ibu Fatma's spirit awoke. According to Indonesian family law, she could have refused the second marriage, but the customary practice in the *pesantren* was different. Especially since her husband was a *kiai,* the family did not dare interfere. She simply had no choice but to accept. Unwilling to do so, she disappeared into Jakarta, where she prepared for life on her own by getting a degree in Qur'an studies. It took years and the clout of her well-respected father before she could move back to her parents' *pesantren,* but there in 1982 she opened a Qur'an department for the female *santri.*

Ibu Fatma inherited her defiant spirit from her mother, who was the daughter of a *kiai* as well and had been twelve when her parents chose her husband. He and the wedding guests never saw her. For three days, she remained hidden in a rolled-up mattress that stood in a corner. The message was clear: she did not want him. Three years later she saw Ibu Fatma's father in a dream, and when she met him, she indicated that he was to be her husband. With him she built up the *pesantren,* focusing on the education of women. She learned how to read and write Indonesian while pretending to read the Qur'an. She also earned income for the family by running a business that sold clothes and food. "This was the model of the first *wali.* Islam was introduced to Indonesia by merchants," Ibu Fatma likes to point out. While supervising building activities for the girls' school, Ibu Fatma's mother organized religious meetings for neighborhood women and started the local branch of the Muslimat NU. Her children now refer to her as "superwoman." Guided by common sense and a fire to bring the message of Islam, this mother became the first model of feminism her daughters witnessed.

Ibu Fatma's father equally modeled respect for women. He realized that he had made a mistake by forcing his daughter to marry someone incompatible with her and did not force her to return to her husband but quietly helped her regain her status. At home he never behaved as the men portrayed in the texts, who want, as Ibu Fatma puts it, to be "idolized" by their wives. She recalls,

> My father sometimes washed my mother's clothes. He never pressed my mother to do household duties. My mother used to tell how he sometimes got up in the middle of the night to clean the kitchen. My father understood what the Qur'an said and feared the Day of Judgment. He always spoke about woman's high position and liked to mention in his sermons that the Prophet never ordered his wives to do anything.[27]

These two models inspired Ibu Fatma never to take the interpretations of texts or rules for granted or at face value. She combines astute social understandings with deep knowledge of the Qur'an and has reached the level of a well-respected *nyai*. The graduation ceremony was a visible symbol that her male colleagues must respect her wishes, even if reluctantly. Ibu Fatma's own development and the opportunities she forged stand in stark contrast to how she started out as an eighteen-year-old bride. This came home to her when she attended a graduation ceremony for women in a *pesantren* in East Java that was similar to the one of her former husband:

> All the women and their guests were hidden in a small, dark building. The space outside was reserved for men only. But I wanted them to show that we matter, so with the women accompanying me I walked through the rows of men all the way to the front in order to greet the *kiai*. The men looked at us as if we had just landed from Mars.

Ibu Fatma has worked hard to reach her current position. She is now in charge of the women's department for Qur'an memorization at a large *pesantren* that enrolls eight hundred high school and university students. This makes it one of the top *pesantren* in Java. What follows is an impression of her daily schedule and living environment.

Studying the Qur'an

It is 5:30 A.M. Twenty girls of high school age all dressed in their finest clothes are sitting on the floor of the classroom. Five of them have gathered around Ibu Fatma; the rest lean against the wall. Ibu Fatma sits behind a wooden lectern on the floor. As if by an invisible sign, the five girls start to recite aloud, each their own part of the Qur'an they prepared the night before. The rest recite in silence. The teacher seems absorbed in studying the attendance list. Suddenly she corrects one of the girls and asks her to start over. After all are done they kiss Ibu Fatma's hand, asking permission to take their place among those against the wall. When all have had their turn, Ibu Fatma gives each specific instructions about intonation and pronunciation. The lesson is over by 6:30, and the students hurry to their regular schools while Ibu Fatma gets ready for the next group, the university students. When they leave for their lectures, it is the turn of the *santri*, who focus on memorizing the Qur'an only. The classes will gather again in the late afternoon to go over the newly memorized parts.

This schedule is followed every day of the year. On certain days the students study the Qur'an interpretation or practice rituals such as preparing the dead for burial according to Islamic rules, a necessary task of religious leaders in the villages. Officially, there is one week of vacation, and on large feast days there is some remission of classes. Between classes, Ibu Fatma devotes time to her main source of income, her businesses. She owns a shop that sells everything a *santri* might possibly need, from notebooks to juice boxes. She also caters religious gatherings and does bridal makeup and flower arrangements. Apart from that, Ibu Fatma leads the prayers in the mosque for women and holds Qur'an meetings in Javanese for the women from the neighborhood. Before the *santri* meet again at 6:30 P.M., she has a study session for administrative workers at the *pesantren* who memorize the Qur'an.

Ibu Fatma has her own quarters in the *pesantren* complex. There are living quarters for several students, a lecture room, a large catering kitchen, and the quarters of her daughter's family. "A daughter always stays in the *pesantren;* the husband has to join her," she explains. The house is tastefully decorated. Flower arrangements adorn the guestroom. Large cabinets display elegant china back-to-back with Qur'an commentaries. Ibu Fatma always dresses immaculately, with full makeup, gracing the room with her elegance. In the dining room there is always food because "guests drop in at any time. They still behave as if the telephone was not yet invented and come without forewarning."[28]

Ibu Fatma knows the Qur'an by heart, an accomplishment that places her among those considered guardians of the text, under the obligation never to forget the holy words once committed to their memory. This is a great responsibility that few wish to carry. Of the eight hundred students in Ibu Fatma's care, only a few dozen a year memorize the whole book. Ibu Fatma belongs to an elite group. According to Islamic tradition, on the Day of Judgment, God Himself will test the prophets, the martyrs, and those who know the Qur'an by heart. Ibu Fatma handles this great merit in a matter-of-fact fashion, considering herself a facilitator: "I am here for those who are like Moses. He needed Aaron to speak for him [Q. 28:34] because as a child he burned his tongue, after which he could never recite properly. I help the students to loosen their tongues."[29]

Ibu Fatma knows that she can never claim the merits gained by the male *kiai* and always holds second place. After all, whether she is a teacher of Qur'an or sells fabric at the market, a woman is still believed to be "spiritually impotent" by many.[30] Women teachers in the *pesantren* are only allowed to teach female students, so as "not to bring men into temptation." Ibu Fatma is one of the few women in Java who also has male students, the *pesantren*'s administrators who study under her guidance. This is considered a breakthrough for women in *pesantren* in general.

Kiai can also gain great merit and practice the virtue of *ikhlas* to the full by refusing money for their teaching. As the director of one of the *pesantren*'s units, Ibu Fatma gets a small honorarium. In principle, this already diminishes the merit of teaching the holy book. She needs the money, however, since many *kiai* not only have the security of a working spouse but also receive donations, gifts, and other payments in kind for their teaching. In Ibu Fatma's *pesantren,* most of these gifts go to its *kiai,* her brothers. This does not bother her, since she is convinced that her merit can be increased by helping the poor around her. After all, a *kiai* must combine teaching with works of charity to make each of the two really count.

In spite of the drawbacks of being a woman, Ibu Fatma has reached a level of authority where she is sought out for advice. Women come to her for counseling, blessing, or prayer, especially concerning family matters. She seldom uses techniques derived from folk culture customary in the countryside, such as magical amulets, but relies on psychological and spiritual methods: "When a son has poor grades, I advise them to pray and to recite the Qur'an but also to check that the kid does his homework."[31] Due to her status as a divorcee, many women seek her help in marital affairs. Often they long for a divorce or have received the news that their husband wants to take a second spouse. Invariably, Ibu Fatma advises them to reconsider, since society will not accept them. "You have to be courageous to become a divorced woman. Many divorcees end up accepting a polygynic marriage. Then they are worse off than before."[32]

Ibu Fatma's opinions seem to contradict her own condition. She ignored the constraints of society; not only did she gain a degree in Qur'anic studies, but she now runs several businesses and has increased her skills by taking up sewing and car repair. She has reached a position under and above the rules. But she knows that Indonesian society is unkind to widows and divorcees, and she regularly comments, "A woman alone is perceived as a threat. When the husband dies, it often happens that the widow no longer receives invitations to marriages and other events. The problem for many women is that they do not have sufficient skills to make it on their own." She maneuvers carefully, since her world will always depend on men. For example, when making the pilgrimage to Mecca, she realized that without the assistance of men she could not gain additional blessings by making extra circumambulations around the Ka'aba. To get there, she could not take a taxi, as no driver would transport her without a male guardian. Most of the Indonesian men in her party had no interest in these extra trips, preferring to sleep instead. She never made the extra visit to the Ka'aba.

Balancing her own challenges with society's expectations and demands for women, Ibu Fatma has to teach the students in her care the values that facilitate their entrance into society. Being too radical is counterproductive for women. *Pesantren* teach students a set of ethics that rest on pure devotion to God (*ikhlas*), patience in adversity (*sabar*), and readiness to help others (*ridla*). The precepts of the Qur'an are the basis and inspiration for the students' behavior. Ibu Fatma's motto is: "We have to know the Qur'an really well. Then we must translate the message into daily life. If we do not do this, we behave like a governor who receives an urgent request from a mayor and simply files it. Nothing happens, and he is ineffective."[33] She tries to translate the message so that it will be congenial to the specific needs of women without flying in the face of men.

Pesantren Ethics for Women

To prepare male and female *santris* for their respective roles in society, the realms of action are divided along lines of gender-specific responsibilities, duties, and tasks. Ibu Fatma is the guardian of these ethics and duties. She must demand obedience from her students. They cannot leave the complex without her permission. Strict segregation is still practiced in most *pesantren*.[34] This specific social structure at times puts Ibu Fatma in an awkward position. While teaching her students ideas about women's emancipation, she still must play the role of a traditional supervisor, one that the *pesantren* leadership and the parents of the *santri* expect her to fulfill. So Ibu Fatma will not allow phone calls from male admirers, nor will she tolerate interaction between male and female *santri*. Her methods resemble those of the traditional *kiai*, who demand total submission from their students. Yet students do not necessarily interpret this treatment as negative. Ibu Fatma is their second mother, and they will not marry or choose a school without asking her blessing on the new decision. In many cases, they will solicit her help in finding a husband. "The relationship is deep and emotional. Alumni *santri* will never be in town without paying me a visit, and whenever I come through their hometown I have to stop at their house."[35]

Part of the teachings concerns the Islamic rules for women only. For example, how should the rule that prohibits a menstruating woman from touching the Qur'an be applied in this program that focuses on study of the Qur'an? To solve this issue while remaining faithful to the Islamic sources, the *nyai* can choose from several strategies. Instead of seeing the rule as a handicap in the women's learning efforts, some explain it as "extra vacation." During that time, according to Ibu Fatma, students will not come to class but rehearse what they already know by heart. Others use versions of the Qur'an that have the text in Arabic and Indonesian. The translation renders the text less sacrosanct because it implies human involvement. This allows women to use it during the time they are considered impure. Another way out is to benefit from the teachings of one of the four *mazhabs*. For example, the Syafi'te school does not allow women to recite the Qur'an during their period, while the Hanafi school allows it.[36]

These strategies—the use of dual language and the shift in legal schools—illustrate how a *nyai* can bring about radical changes in the fixed *pesantren* pattern. She can create alternative methods and expressions to reframe and reinterpret the texts, methods, and structures conventionally used in the *pesantren*. She can also point out how misogynistic myths based on local tradition have become part of the Islamic heritage and highlight instead teachings that liberate women. Gender segregation proves beneficial to pursuing this agenda. Ibu Fatma holds full responsibility over her section of the *pesantren*, which enables her to make her own curriculum. Following the tradition of the *kiai* who mainly conveys his ideas orally, Ibu Fatma is nurturing a new generation of women *santri* who have become aware of the many layers of culture and prejudice that have influenced the interpretation of the Qur'an. It is also to her benefit that the *pesantren* world is famous for its unconventional and eccentric leaders. She can afford to be different. To the traditionalist mind, eccentricity is the stuff of future saints; their behavior is meant as a lesson for those who observe closely.

Because this also leads to an abundance of criticism, Ibu Fatma must consider the limits carefully, as her final products still have to be virtuous women. During their years in the *pesantren*, girls grow from childhood to adolescence. A prime aspect of their training is the preparation to become a good spouse and mother. Gender ideals for women are framed in a moral and sacred order of Islamic teachings and are positioned in Javanese culture. They form the point of departure for any career within the religious domain, as a teacher of Islam to children, a professor at an Islamic university, or as a spouse and mother. Female *santri* who go on to become specialists of Islam will become instrumental in conveying the ideals and teachings learned in the *pesantren* to groups of women all over Indonesia. They need to know the rules and practices that concern women, such as those about hygiene, cooking, cleaning the house, receiving guests, teaching their children, and their behavior towards their husband. Society still favors men's rights and privileges. The *santri* must come to terms with several paradoxes within society and within their own circles. This is quite a challenge, and many young women still hesitate to accept it. In the end, some feel more comfortable with the conventional interpretations of women's role. For example, during a discussion with male and female *santri,* all the women said they were studying "in order to teach their own children." When I asked the boys if girls could become aviation engineers, they said, "Sure, but what about the household?"[37]

Changing the prevailing mindset takes several generations. Many leaders in *pesantren,* male and female, still believe that "God has given different mental capacities to women and men. They are not the same; men are still higher."[38] A move towards change is noticeable in the reactions of those who have studied gender issues more extensively. Ibu Siti's husband once remarked, "Of course, women have less brain than men," which led his wife to treat him to a full lecture on the origins of this prejudice. Ibu Fatma only says "hogwash" when asked her opinion of the half-brain theory. Yet this mindset remains a challenge to her work and often holds female students back. Many *pesantren* require a less rigorous curriculum for female students than for male students. Women study the same texts but, for example, read smaller numbers of pages than male students; thus they end up with less knowledge of the Islamic sources and teachings. Yet depth of knowledge is a crucial tool in reinterpreting the sources.

In spite of the odds against them, women teachers influence the *pesantren* landscape in many subtle ways. Standing where the old and new generations intersect, they observe trends that can emerge earlier among the female *santri.* Modernity battles with tradition for the attention and action of the female *santri.* Even if Ibu Fatma agrees with certain new trends, she must juggle the wishes of the parents and the *pesantren* establishment. Trends of modernization and globalization are deeply affecting life within the *pesantren,* in spite of the abiding yellow books. Students read newspapers, learn English, and use computers. Total obedience toward the *kiai* is erod-

ing, a change women teachers tolerate more readily than their male counterparts. Ibu Fatma takes pleasure in students with minds of their own. She
chuckles, "They now discuss and answer back, an attitude unheard of only
a few years ago!"

The Nyai in the Village: Ibu Siti

For Ibu Siti, whose *pesantren* is located in rural Java, it is even more challenging to combine the traditional religious notions that often evolved from
the country side with the specific values for women and the knowledge she
has acquired in the many gender-related workshops she has attended. She
aired her frustration during a seminar about sexual relations between husband and wife for young *kiai* and *nyai.*

> What is the reality in society? In spite of guarantees in the marriage contract,
> women suffer. Many burdens fall on the woman. On top of that, preachers
> take duties from the books used in the *pesantren* and impose them on simple
> women in their sermons. Many women go through one pregnancy after the
> other. Their health is in perpetual danger. Men and women should be like a
> pair of shoes. In practice they seldom are.[39]

None of the men present paid attention to what she said. In fact, some of
the participants started to chat during Ibu Siti's comments, as they seemed
to find them uninteresting because of their social-psychological rather than
legal character. Of course, Ibu Siti knew this would be the case, yet she continued unabashed.

Ibu Siti has come a long way since graduating from a traditional *pesantren*
in East Java. During the 1990s NU selected her to participate in courses
organized to modernize the *pesantren.* She is now an alumna of courses
about women's reproductive rights, women's jurisprudence, and political
jurisprudence. Not only the knowledge but also the methods used in these
workshops influenced her profoundly. Discussions and role play encouraged participants to express their thoughts freely. This kind of free expression seldom happens in any type of school in Indonesia, let alone in the
pesantren. Her newfound confidence is still fragile but shines through when
she attends events in her own environment.

Ibu Siti is in charge of a *pesantren* for girls in a village under the shadow of the ancient Buddhist Borobodur temple. The accommodations are
the bare minimum: mud floors, unpainted walls, and an outhouse. The
pesantren started in 1988 and has eighty students of middle-school age. Ibu
Siti, her husband, and five children have two bedrooms, while the rest of

the house is used for teaching. The students sleep on the second floor. Her husband teaches in the local high school and helps out after hours. Ibu Siti invariably dresses simply in a traditional *kain,* the wraparound piece of fabric, a Javanese tight jacket, and a cap on her head. She represents the model of a traditional *pesantren* leader who follows the mystical-ascetic path. She finds her main role in being a pure model for her students and community through fasting, praying, studying the Qur'an, and participating in social work and social activism. Her reputation has started to spread beyond her own village since she made the Hajj in 2001. "She came back with fewer pieces of luggage from Mecca than she went with," was the first comment made by NU friends when I asked about her well-being. Most Indonesian pilgrims engage in shopping sprees for jewelry and gold, but Ibu Siti had no time to shop. During the forty days prior to her departure, she was visited by those who knew her with requests for special prayers near the Ka'aba. After the official pilgrimage was finished, Ibu Siti spent every waking moment praying in front of the shrine to get through the pile of requests.[40]

That Ibu Siti takes her spiritual work seriously can be observed by the decorations in her guest room. Apart from some family pictures and an embroidered rendition of the Shahadah, long lists with her tasks and schedules adorn the walls. According to these, her permanent tasks are the following:

> 1. The Qur'an (private study); 2. Mujahadah [literally, perform peaceful *jihad* (by this, Ibu Siti means prayer in the middle of the night)]; 3. Ritual prayer and praise (with the students and the children); 4. [Pray for] my parents; 5. Be in charge of the *pesantren,* the branch of the Fatayat NU, and the Qur'an school for the village children; 6. Monitor my family and their economic needs; 7. Counseling; 8. Teaching; and 9. Social activities for the neighborhood.[41]

The first three duties form the fundamental mission of every *kiai* and *nyai.* Ibu Siti tries to remain pure in body, heart, and mind at all times: "I perform the ritual washings frequently, read the Qur'an, and remember death." She considers being a mother as her highest responsibility and never wearies of praying and fasting for her children:

> I fast during my pregnancies or make up for it after the child is born if I feel too sick or too weak. At 120 days, God breathes the soul into the embryo [*ruh*] and writes three things in its heart: material riches, works, and spirituality; if these will yield paradise or hell; and the day of death. Especially the first four months we have to pray a lot so that the writing will be favorable. I continually recite the Qur'an, especially the chapters about fathers and mothers, the Surat Maryam, Surat Yusuf, and Surat YaSin. When the whole Qur'an is

finished, I start all over again. I fast extra, but when I break the fast I take nutritional foods like milk, honey, ginger, and organic eggs. At six months the child already hears the mother's voice. Then it is good to recite the Qur'an, so the child will become mentally well. At the seventh month I organize a *slamatan* to ward off evil and to pray for an easy delivery. Originally, before Islam, Hindu Indonesians offered food to the spirits. I follow the Islamic way that was shown by Sunan Kali Jaga, the first Muslim saint [*wali*], pronouncing the intention [*niyyah*] to increase my charitable giving. When the children are born I pray for them. We believe that a parent's prayer equals the prayer of a prophet for his community. God will never reject such a prayer.

Ibu Siti uses this same mystical approach when counseling those who address her with their problems. Following the *kiai* tradition of practicing pure devotion (*ikhlas*) through her work, she never expects material compensation for any of her efforts.

The reward comes straight from God. In 1983 I prayed for a woman who had a terrible problem. I recited the whole Qur'an for her several times. I also went to the grave of Wali Yulloh Simbah in Kajen Pati Jateng. He is a strong saint because it was his hobby to recite the Qur'an as often as possible. That is why he loves to receive the gift of Qur'an recital at his grave. So I recited the whole Qur'an at his grave, all thirty *juz'*. I have never asked anything for myself. Often my problems just vanish. I forget about them. Also, as the years went by I tried to realize my dream of setting up a *pesantren*. When we were first married, we lived with my husband's parents, and all I could do was preach and organize Qur'an studies. Then, in 1988, the person I had prayed for in 1983 suddenly appeared and said, "I want you to build a *pesantren*." She did not know that there were already two *santri* living with us but that we did not have a building yet. The woman gave us a sum of money that we used to build the house we are in today.

From the NU point of view, Ibu Siti represents the ideal alumna of the programs designed to create deeper awareness about gender issues. She is deeply rooted in the original, rural *pesantren* tradition, in particular through her practice of mystical exercises. This creates a special bond with the Javanese Muslim villagers surrounding her school. In the summer of 2000 her dreams for her students were "that all can join me in fasting for one whole year." At the same time, she has gained a deep awareness of women's issues. For example, she counsels women who suffer domestic violence, which is still a taboo topic. Based on the Qur'anic verse, "As to those women on whose part ye fear disloyalty and ill-conduct, admonish them [first], [next] refuse to share their beds, [and last] beat them [lightly] (Q. 4:34), many women assume that the husband is allowed to beat his wife, even severely. "I am now teaching that violence against women is not good," said Ibu Siti. When she counsels women, she combines the mystical with the modern.

> First I try to find out the story. Is she a good wife, is he a violent husband? Then I instruct them to pray so that their household can thrive. Forty times saying the Fatiha for forty days is the first step. They also have to perform extra prayers together and, of course, always the five ritual prayers. Then I pay a follow-up visit. If the problem still is the same, I suggest they make a trip to the grave of Wali Yulloh Simbah and recite the whole Qur'an there. If they feel they cannot do that, they have to ask for help through prayer. When our heart is good, God will help. When the problem persists, I make an appointment for them at the Rifka Annisa crisis center.

Rifka Annisa received immense criticism from traditionalist and reformist circles when it opened in the early 1990s. Some leaders called the women "advocates of divorce."[42] Most of their methods were said to be imported from the West. Since there was no precedent for the work in Indonesia, Rifka Annisa workers made trips to the Netherlands to observe successful projects such as the "Blijf van mijn lijf" (Don't touch my body) houses and to study western methods of psychological and material support. But Muslim women activists from NU and Muhammadiyah guided the center in developing an Islamic approach to solving problems. In many cases, women endured long-term abuse based on their interpretation of the Qur'anic verse that speaks about beating. Along the same lines, women think that they must accept a second spouse, even if their husband's choice causes them to suffer psychological violence. When Ibu Siti sends a woman to the center, she is breaking age-old conventions. She risks being accused of tarnishing Islam. Both the Islamic faith and Javanese culture teach that a woman's duty is to protect the honor and respect of her husband and family. Admitting that domestic violence occurs is considered a serious breach of this duty. Yet for Ibu Siti, the well-being and basic human rights of those who seek her advice prevails. She derives courage for her actions from the many workshops she has attended.

Although Ibu Siti never heard of the term "empowering women," her dream of many years has been precisely that: empowering them to become fully human in the eyes of God, as the Qur'an teaches that they are. As a way to increase this activity, she decided to set up a branch of the Fatayat, the young NU women. Since the 1980s, Fatayat were encouraged to move away from organizing ritual meetings and to take a stronger focus on gender issues. This was not easily done in the countryside, where ideas that are too advanced often go over the heads of great numbers of women and men. The Fatayat are young, many of them educated at the *pesantren*. Ibu Siti realized their potential force for change and started to convince young women around her to join in creating a branch that would transmit new ideas about gender as well. Three times a month she meets with Fatayat groups in her region, passing on her newfound knowledge. They pray, discuss, eat snacks, and chant mystical songs. The women are often insecure when talking to other women in their village. Ibu Siti encourages them through regular meetings, counseling, and when they cannot reach her (until 2002 she had no telephone), she occasionally speaks to them in their sleep through dreams.

Javanese-Islamic Values for Women

Similar to Ibu Fatma, it is one of Ibu Siti's primary responsibilities to teach her students values for women. Most of her students will remain in the countryside, and few of them will ever reach the university level, so she must tailor her teachings accordingly. Although it is not easy, Ibu Siti uses one of the advisory texts composed especially for Javanese women. They are written in Javanese using Arabic script (*pegon*). The text is called *Al-Mar'a al-Salihah* (The Virtuous Woman)[43] and spells out the religious and domestic duties of a good Muslim woman and how she should behave not only towards her husband, but also towards her children, parents, neighbors, and guests. The text consists of lists with admonitions concerning issues from gossip, foul language, and spending too much of the husband's money to wasting the family's money on foods that are too expensive.

Ibu Siti explains the detailed instructions spiritually: "The Prophet taught us that we first should improve our personal environment. That means we first have to be good to those nearest to us. These are parents, sisters, brothers, neighbors, and friends." She also interprets the injunctions as helpful to create a wholesome family (in NU terms: *keluarga maslaha*). "The rules invite us to talk with each other, visit our family, and see how we can improve our relationships."[44] Her own monthly calendar reflects the value of taking care of this spiritual environment, as she has planned visits to groups and individuals five days a week.

Being polite and knowing what to say and what not to say at the right time is important in Javanese hierarchy. The text combines rules for social behavior with religious instruction for women, speaking of the obedience she owes her husband and parents in daily life. She should, for example, speak politely in proper language, not the vernacular form of Javanese, as polite women are at peace with their husband and social environment. "Never lie, neither about small, nor about big things"; "Being envious is never allowed"; "Never be too impertinent to husband, parents, parents-in-law, teachers, and leaders." Issues of ritual and general cleanliness are connected to housework. "Remember that cleanliness is half the soul of religion, which means that it has to be observed seriously," the section starts. Women are advised always to wash their hands, especially when they are ritually unclean. "Wash hands before going to sleep"; "Don't bite your lips."

One of the first rules mentioned with regard to the husband, however, is profoundly Islamic and states that the wife always must receive his permission before going out. Obedience to the husband is based on Qur'an 4:34: "Men are the protectors and maintainers of women." This is an issue of intense discussion among NU women because the majority of the male *kiai* will not allow much diversion from the prevailing opinion that this verse allows men authority over women. Many conservative *kiai* still do not accept that this rule could be changed. This means that both men and women leaders in NU have to move carefully when pushing popular understandings of such injunctions. The influential Kiai Sahal Mahfudh (chair of Majlis Ulama Indonesia and of the Syuriah NU since 1999), interprets this verse as follows:

> A woman's first responsibility is obedience to her husband; no discussion is possible about this matter. According to a tradition, this obedience is comparable to the duties of human beings towards the Creator, such as obligatory prayer and fasting. Obeying here is similar to respecting the husband. The husband deserves this respect because he shoulders heavy loads and responsibilities. The husband is in charge not only of his own spiritual and worldly affairs but also of those of all the members in his family.[45]

When preparing women for their proper role in life according to Islamic guidelines and the expectations of local culture, Ibu Siti must take this opinion into account. She also believes that she must help her students understand how to be a good spouse: "Many women don't know how to take care of their husband. It happens a lot that the man just wants to marry someone else. That is why it is very important for the girls to learn about their duties and work."[46] This means that in spite of winds of change that are blowing through the *pesantren* world, one of Ibu Siti's goals remains to prepare students to be "good wives, mothers, and worthy members of society."[47] This does not, however, render all the new teachings about gender issues defunct. Ibu Siti emphasizes, "In the old days, we would deliver women who were excellent public speakers; now we educate women who are excellent speakers with skills of independent and innovative thinking."[48]

Such developments evolve in the private environments of *pesantren*, first challenging and then changing the interpretations of Islam concerning the role of women. Not everybody agrees with the ideas and visions of Ibu Fatma and Ibu Siti. Many Muslims, not only in Indonesia, continue to be influenced by classical Fiqh texts that place a woman in the position of her husband's handmaid, owing him total obedience without room for her own personality.

Because men have studied and been the main interpreters of these texts, male mindsets must change before women can successfully regain their God-given rights. Women cannot take on this task by themselves. That would alienate many Muslim men and women. In Indonesia's NU circles, they could ride on the winds of change initiated by religious leaders who saw a need for change. This started a process of reinterpretation and adaptation that has been going on for over three decades and is still evolving. At the cradle of this process were independent-minded leaders who created institutes that tried to strengthen progressive Islamic thinking within the NU community and in society. In the following section I will introduce one of these institutes that was formative for thinking about the roles and rights of women: P3M (pronounced "Pay-tiga-em"), the Center for the Development of *Pesantren* and Society.[49]

Authority Revisited

Social Fiqh and Social Activism

The rigorous spiritual, religious, and secular formation in the *pesantren* has long been the backbone of strong NU leadership. These leaders, however, were never merely preachers or religious teachers but also served as leaders of society. To strengthen and formalize this process of formation, during the 1970s discussions started within NU circles about ways to modernize the *pesantren* and help produce leaders who could negotiate the rapid changes of modern society and be instrumental in social change.[50] One of the instigators of these discussions was Abdurrahman Wahid. He saw as the main challenge a transformation of the *pesantren*'s potential of dedicated people who were well versed in Islamic knowledge into instruments that could propagate Islam as an innovative way of life. The answer was sought in teaching Islamic ethics and ideologies that could strengthen the Islamic intellectual potential and concurrently shape new community frameworks based on Islamic principles and values.[51] During the 1980s, progressive NU leaders launched two types of initiatives to reach this goal. For their ideas to gain a authority within *pesantren* circles, they had to support them with relevant Fiqh texts. This made them realize that they must explore a new approach towards these texts, which led to the development of the so-called Fiqh Sosial school. The leaders then set up several institutes that facilitated introducing the new ideas and methods into NU society.

Over the past three decades, Fiqh Sosial has become one of the hallmarks of NU jurisprudential thinking. Kiai Sahal Mahfudh became one of its most influential proponents. The editors of one of his books on the topic, *Nuansa Fiqih Sosial,* outline the agenda of this type of legal thinking.[52] According to them, thinking about Fiqh in NU has shifted from "being a paradigm of 'orthodox truth'" to "a paradigm of 'social relevance.'"[53] Fiqh thus has the potential to become a counterdiscourse within society. Reinterpreted within the contemporary context, Fiqh texts can provide a system of social ethics that uses philosophical methodologies to analyze cultural and social problems.[54] According to the editors, the interpreters do not follow a *madhhab* in its literal teachings but in its methods. They distinguish between the "roots" or essential (*pokok*) teachings of the *madhhab*'s legal methodology (*usul al-fiqh*) and its branches—that is, its theoretical aspects (*furu'*). Thus, they consider Fiqh to be a hermeneutical tool that has the potential to manage a plurality of truths.[55]

To process the results of the new jurisprudential approaches, the Center for NU Documentation, Information, Research and Human Development (Lakpesdam) was created in 1985 to support NU leaders academically, and it has developed widespread activities, such as monitoring national elections, that benefit the NU community at large.[56] P3M was set up in 1983 to help *pesantren* configure their curriculum and provide information that would equip *santri* to face the demands of contemporary society. Considering the central role of the *kiai,* P3M aimed at raising their awareness about social-religious issues. This resulted, for example, in courses in writing and reporting as well as seminars about topics ranging from human rights and democracy to how to reinterpret Islamic Jurisprudence.

During the 1990s, P3M also started to organize workshops for women leaders and students to discuss matters such as reproductive health and rights, the status of women in Islamic Jurisprudence, and its reinterpretation. Ibu Siti was one of the first to attend a series of these workshops. The focus on women and reproductive rights in Islam was unique, the first initiative of its kind in the world. The rereading and reinterpretation of Fiqh texts dealing with women's issues led to another exceptional project, the publication of a critical annotated edition of the *Kitab Syarh 'Uqud Al-Lujjain fi Bayan Huquq Al-Zaujain*.[57] Nawawi lived and taught for over four decades in Mecca, where he wrote several commentaries on the Qur'an that gained prominence throughout Southeast Asia.[58] In Mecca he taught Indonesian students who sought him out for his erudition and for his resistance against the Dutch colonial power.[59] The *Kitab 'Uqud* is not an original work; Nawawi compiled the teachings concerning women that he found in a total of nine classical books.[60] It is not clear what moved him to write the text; some speculate that it had to do with the fact that he married a much younger wife after his first wife of many years passed away. Others think that for a few years he was married to both wives. Regardless of Nawawi's reasons for composing the text around 1874, the result is so misogynist that, according to the respected NU *kiai,* Bisri Mustofa, it "went to a man's head" (*membuat lelaki besar kepala*).[61]

The methods and results of P3M's work deserve a separate study. Here I will provide a glimpse of the process set in motion by its workshops, publications, and seminars and its influence on gender teachings in the *pesantren.* I will end this section with a recent, highly visible success story, the publication of the revised *Kitab 'Uqud.*

Triggering Silent Revolutions

P3M has to be careful, as Ibu Fatma and Ibu Siti are not to trespass against age-old boundaries and to remain faithful to the *pesantren* goals and values. To legitimize its activities guided by its director, Masdar Mas'udi, P3M sought the support of respected *kiai* who helped develop a theoretical and philosophical framework based on Islamic teachings. Thus Mas'udi, known for his unconventional ideas, gained the approval of those who did not agree with all of his teachings. P3M's basic model of teaching is based on the assumption that the position of women in Islamic thought is not shaped solely by religion. It is constructed by culture, society, and erroneous religious interpretations. From this basic philosophy, P3M wants to rewrite the Islamic definition of wives and mothers. Moreover, it strives to make women knowledgeable about their rights. P3M also holds that women who have studied Islam for many years should be able to become equal partners in the religious NU debates, similar to female *'ulama.*

Regarding society at large, P3M believes that by empowering male *and* female Muslim leaders, a democratic civil society can develop that eventually will replace the hierarchical models conventional to Indonesia. Masdar Mas'udi explains this as follows: "In the old days, changes in society were brought about in a top-down model. The king issued a decree, and all obeyed. Nowadays we try to initiate change by working from the bottom up. By teaching *santri* new ideas we eventually will change the way society thinks. That is the model of P3M."[62]

During the past five years, with support from the Ford Foundation, P3M has focused on women's Jurisprudence (Fiqh an-Nisa') and political Jurisprudence (Fiqh Siyasah). Meetings use methods that are still unconventional for Indonesia and provide a mix of information, discussion, and role play. Participants analyze the rules of Fiqh for women by looking at the original Qur'an texts, the Traditions, and the different forms of interpretation. Words such as "feminism" are carefully avoided and replaced by terms such as "Fiqh al-Nisa'."

P3M has identified a main obstacle to women being considered fully human: Jurisprudence has failed to apply to women the basic rights that the Qur'an provides for all people. These ideas are inspired partly by the writings of the Sudanese intellectual Abdullahi Ahmed An-Na'im, who argues that the status of women became governed by verses from the Qur'an revealed in Medina that rendered the more egalitarian and universal verses from the Mecca period obsolete.[63] Following this line of thinking, P3M programs stress the five universal human rights that coincide with the rights the interpreters of the Qur'an have derived from its teachings: the right to live (physical well-being and safety) or the self (*al-nafs*); the right to think (*al-'aql*); the right to attain wealth or comfortable living (*al-māl*); the right to be religious (*al-dīn*); and the right to have offspring (*al-nasl*). In the marital relationship, three rights are guaranteed for women: the right to be provided with food, clothing, and a place to live. These rights derive from the medieval Maliki jurist Abu Ishaq al Shatibi (d. 1388) and were reformulated and reintroduced in P3M teachings by Abdurrahman Wahid.[64]

Since these rights are directly connected with a woman's role as mother, P3M has identified reproductive rights as an area in women's Jurisprudence that needs special attention. Because women bear children, P3M argues that the basic right to life for women means the right to safety and health. Islam teaches that in the marriage, the husband is obliged to provide food, clothing, and housing. In principle, a woman can keep her own income to herself even if it is more than that of her husband. If a woman cares for the children, according to P3M, she can demand compensation, since it is the husband's duty to provide. Finally, the most contested point made by P3M is that women have the right to make their own decisions.[65] This conclusion is based on the right to think and P3M's firm belief that Islam grants equality to men and women. Referring to the Qur'an text, "Men are the protectors and maintainers of women" (Q. 4:34), however, many conservative Muslim leaders hold that the husband should make all decisions in the family, including those concerning his wife.

P3M workshops serve as a laboratory to test these new ideas of women's equality and God-given rights. Discussions are detailed with abundant quotes from the Qur'an, Tradition, and Fiqh. Qur'anic verses are carefully analyzed and placed in the original context of seventh-century Arabia. Thus a theological basis is constructed from which to reconsider women's position in contemporary Indonesian Islam and society. The participants debunk myths, such as that women were created as temptresses of men and that their *nafsu* (desire) is more intense and less controllable than men's. The meetings open the opportunity for women to question opinions that prevail in society and to speculate on their inconsistencies:

> Okay, so the man has to guide the woman. Now who will guide the man? What if he needs guidance as well? And what about a woman's responsibility to guide her husband? So what really is a virtuous [*sholehah*] wife? Will she still be considered virtuous when she does not accept it when her husband takes a second spouse? And why should only the wife be virtuous and obedient to the husband? What about him? What if the husband does not work, and the wife provides for the family? [One in eight Indonesian households is headed by a woman.] Will he still be the protector?[66]

This process helps participants become aware that the ideals the *kiai* preach often differ from reality. This is challenging not only for the men but also for the women present. Most of the issues tackled during workshops are still sensitive, and the older generation especially finds it difficult to discard the values and ideas they were raised with. Some participants consider the views espoused as utterly extreme. During final reflections at a meeting held in 1997, one of the participants, Ibu A'isyah noted, "We women tend to throw the difficult matters to our husbands." She considered the newly found rights and obligations both a challenge and a promise. On behalf of the men, Pak Rosyadi stated: "We all have to be aware of our rights and duties. Let it not come to what we see in the soaps on TV where women constantly flaunt their rights while brushing over their duties."[67] Kiai Hussein Muhammad, who has become one of the most avid supporters of the P3M method, looks at the bottom line. In his analysis, the ritual worship is ultimately more important than social convention:

> The *Kitab 'Uqudullijain* says that on the Day of Judgment a man will be confronted with his family and children. They will accuse him: "Oh Lord, we

punish him since he withheld from us our right to guidance in religion." That means that the obligation rests upon a man to teach his wife and family about matters pertaining to worship.[68]

Discussions initiated by P3M and supported by the Fiqh Sosial models have inspired others, such as the Fatayat Welfare Foundation (Yayasan Kesejahteraan Fatayat; YKF), and are slowly but steadily influencing the younger generation. They realize that what the classic Fiqh books teach can be approached with multiple levels of interpretation and that they do not necessarily contain one-dimensional truths for all time. One crucial awareness is that human factors shaped the contents of the Fiqh books. P3M uses universal teachings about human rights and aligns them with the timeless teachings about rights in the Qur'an.

The old Fiqh books cannot be discarded; rather, they take on another role that allows *santri* to receive the part of their teachings that is still valid and consider the rest as tales from another time or culture. This is an irreversible trend. Once the *kiai* and *nyai* grasp the newly gained knowledge and awareness, they will use it in their classes and Qur'an studies for women. Ibu Djudju, a *nyai* from Tasikmalaya who took several series of P3M courses, painted this classroom scene at the high school in her *pesantren*. Her students are sixteen-year-old male and female *santri*.

I fish a bit around to see what they think about the differences between men and women. Then I simply add fuel to the fire. [I say,] "Boys can be emotional, too." That makes the girls feel good; they feel someone is defending their case. [I ask,] "Can girls drive cars?" They can, just as boys. "Can they have babies?" They can, but boys cannot. So we arrive at the conclusion that the only difference between men and women lies in their reproductive functions.

I recite with them Surah 49:11: "Let not some men among you laugh at others: It may be that the [latter] are better than the [former]. Nor let some women laugh at others: it may be that the [latter] are better than the [former]." Then we talk: Why does the Qur'an specifically mention women [as well]? The girls then answer, "Because women are outstanding [istemewanya]." The boys answer: "Because women like to talk too much." This makes them all think. Sometimes there is really mayhem in the class. But in the end they start to think. . . . Another example: society has a word for female sex workers: "prostitute." But there is no word for men who sell their own bodies. Society does not mention the male prostitutes. I explain to the students that from a sociological point of view, this is the hallmark of a patriarchal society, a society that chooses the side of men only.[69]

At the high school level, Ibu Djudju builds new awareness about gender issues. Ultimately, she challenges not only the thinking patterns but the religious authority underlying these patterns. The process is irreversible, part of a silent revolution. The next step is to prevent that student's return to the former, biased ways of thinking when they start serious study of the Fiqh texts and become convinced that those convey a sacrosanct truth. To accomplish this continued openness, the next level of activity identifies texts that hold teachings biased against women. *Kitab 'Uqud* was the text most used in the *pesantren;* filled with gender-biased teachings, it was a natural choice for first analysis. *Kitab 'Uqud* is only twenty-three yellow pages long, but it has imprinted ideas about women in the minds of thousands of *santri.*

Reconsidering the Texts

Within the *pesantren* world, female *santri* are subjected to biased textbooks written by men that cast women mainly in the role of spouse and mother. As mother, she is often put on a pedestal. Traditions are quoted, such as, "Heaven rests under a mother's feet." Masdar Mas'udi observed, "Apart from being part of the interpretations found in the yellow books, these types of opinions do not further equality [between men and women]."[70] After scrutinizing the books traditionally used in the *pesantren,* Mas'udi concluded that their basic teachings hold

> men as the standard for everything. Differences between men and women are interpreted in terms that women never reach that male standard. It is as if a woman exists only to serve the man and fulfill his sexual desires. Man's status, both in this world and the next, is above woman's status, and . . . it is as if one man equals two women.[71]

Many argue that the quintessential problem with the texts is that they not only reduce the status of women but also give the impression that all that matters are issues such as "menstruation, ritual purity, the veil, and inheritance [a woman's share being half of a man's]. The texts ignore important matters such as woman's right to work, the social status of widows, and woman's participation in education, the economic and political life."[72] Since the 1980s, this has given rise to pertinent discussions about the influence of the *pesantren* in creating gender-biased discourses. The reality is that most texts were written before the twentieth century and carry cultural baggage that has long been abandoned in other areas of life. Also, the majority of the texts stem from the Middle East and reflect its specific culture. It is clear that reinterpretation of these texts is called for. This is a complicated matter, however, since even if a text is declared unsuitable for this time, it cannot be discarded. Because it is sacrosanct, great care must be applied in researching and criticizing it.

The process of reinterpretation is necessarily careful and long. It consists of several steps: 1) identifying the harmful text; 2) discussing its contents (including holding workshops about detailed elements of the text); 3) researching its truth claim; 4) reinterpreting its quotes from the Qur'an and Tradition; 5) editing the original text with footnotes that correct faulty information; 6) trying to introduce the critical version into the *pesantren* and familiarizing NU leaders with its contents through discussions and workshops; 7) using the corrected version in sermons and discussing it with women's and men's Qur'an study groups all over Indonesia. The text of *Kitab 'Uqud* went through this process. A team of twelve men and women with specialties in Tradition, Fiqh, Qur'an exegesis, Islamic history, and anthropology, calling themselves Forum Kajian Kitab Kuning (Forum for the Research of Yellow Books; FK3), took several years to prepare the new critical edition that came out at the end of 2001.[73] Nuriyah Abdurrahman Wahid was one of the driving forces behind the project and became its powerful patron during her time as first lady (1999–2001). After the book appeared, she continued to explain its contents in the national media.

The critical edition was prepared following NU principles of research. For example, to separate truth from myth, the Traditions (Hadith) used in the texts and their chains of transmission were carefully scrutinized. Traditions complement the information given in the Qur'an and thus are vital in shaping legal opinions. Teams of Tradition specialists found that more than half of the Traditions quoted in the text were fabricated or weak. Since the intended audience had no knowledge of this, these Traditions were taken for granted and applied to daily life with detrimental consequences, especially for women.[74]

In explaining passages quoted from the Qur'an, the NU method distinguishes between texts that apply only to the time and place of the Prophet and texts that are of universal ethical value. The texts containing fundamental truths (*qath'i*) are those concerned with basic values of human equality and justice between men and women. Their meaning is clear and unambiguous. The texts that are contingent upon time and place (*dhanni*) are those that concern private, social, cultural, or political matters. These are less clear and must be interpreted via *ijtihad*.[75] An example of the latter is slavery, which is condoned by the Qur'an but has been abolished in contemporary Muslim society. Another example is that the Qur'an requires two female witnesses, in contrast to one man, in the case of business disagreements (Q. Al-Baqara 2:282). According to Masdar Mas'udi, this was necessary at a time when women were not actively involved in business transactions and one woman could have made faulty observations due to lack of experience. Today, however, this condition has changed.

According to Mas'udi, the challenge to contemporary interpreters of the texts from the Qur'an and Tradition is to make sure that texts that arose from a certain context can be brought into alignment with those that hold eternal truths. Texts that cannot pass this test are not suitable for universal use in the twenty-first century. To make decisions in this process of reevaluation, a person is allowed to exercise his or her own judgment (*ijtihad*). Of course, this is done with the assumption that the conclusions scholars arrive at will be discussed with the community of NU scholars at large.[76]

Guided by this combination of classical and new principles, the team annotated the original text of *Kitab 'Uqud*. The text is divided into segments that are first presented in the Indonesian translation of the original Arabic. Then follow the results of the team's research of Traditions and the classical Fiqh texts. The segments end with commentaries by FK3 and quotes from contemporary scholars of Islam. For example, *Kitab'Uqud* writes that a woman

> should know that she is like a slave marrying her master, or a weak prisoner who is helpless under someone's power. . . . A wife has to feel timid [*malu*] toward her husband, she may not contradict him, she has to lower her head and gaze when in front of her husband, she has to obey her husband no matter what he asks her to do, apart from what Islam forbids, she has to remain silent when her husband talks, stand up at his coming and going.[77]

The team concludes that "the above explanation forces us to scrutinize once again what the goal of marriage is." This is followed by a quote from one of the greatest scholars in Islam, al-Ghazali (d. 1111), according to whom the first goal of marriage, when considered from the point of view of the law (Shari'ah) and the general religious teachings, is to perform one's social duty. Furthermore, the team points out, al-Ghazali mentions five benefits of marriage: "procreation, to protect religion and limit one's desires [*nafsu*], to develop closeness to women, to have someone who can take care of the household, and to practice the development of good character."

In the third section, the team draws its own conclusions: "From the aforementioned explanation [it becomes clear] that there is not one word mentioned that places a woman in the position of a slave." Then it quotes two respected Muslim leaders, Quraish Shihab and Tolhah Hasan, who teach that within a marriage there should be harmony and mutual understanding.[78]

At the end of the book, Shaykh al-Nawawi defends the seclusion of women with a Tradition that indicates that the companions of the Prophet closed the window and holes in the wall so that the women could not spy on the men. The team refutes the Tradition, as serious flaws have been found in its chain of transmission. Fierce criticism follows the official part: "Closing the house like that turns the woman into a convict. It is clear that this is not human. Apart from that, from the point of view of health, a house without ventilation is not healthy, especially not for children because no fresh air comes in. A woman becomes like a frog in a coconut shell who cannot see how wide the world is and how deep the sea."[79]

Analyzing the project of reinterpreting *Kitab 'Uqud*, we see that the team relies on a combination of methodologies, some old and some revolutionary. When scrutinizing the Traditions, they revisit the chain of transmitters, which by itself is a classical method. While staying within the framework of the Shafi'ite tradition of learning, they propose a shift in understanding the meaning of *qath'i* and *dhanni* texts. Thus they create a new legal foundation for their findings, backing them up with teachings from the four schools of law and scholars such as al-Ghazali, who lived after the time the *madhhabs* were formed. While the traditional authority of the Fiqh is being deconstructed, the new interpretation remains firmly grounded within the framework of the NU Shafi'ite tradition. These hermeneutics challenge the old authority by replacing it with another, more modern one. Using the traditional techniques, however, facilitates the acceptance of the new ideas.

The results of these reinterpretations had to be presented with great tact. For example, the team found that over 50 percent of the Traditions quoted were weak or false. This meant that for over a century, *santri* had memorized incorrect teachings, which they passed on in their sermons once they became *kiai*. As a result, the text greatly influenced thinking patterns, especially about marital relationships. *Kiai* like to quote this text in sermons to married women. Simple transmission of this text leaves most people utterly confused, since it imposes unrealistic, sometimes inhuman requirements on women. Many progressive *kiai* agree that

> [t]his text hurts women. The problem is that it is the only text that covers the Fiqh concerning women. Other books for or about women are merely considered instructive or advisory. Very few *kiai* manage to translate what this text teaches into the contemporary, Javanese context. From the gender perspective it is no longer suitable as educational material in the *pesantren*.[80]

In many instances, however, tradition overrules common sense.[81] Until the new edition reaches them, most *kiai* do not have access to or are not aware of sources that are less biased. This dawned on me when I was one of three speakers at a seminar organized by Ibu Siti's *pesantren.* The audience consisted of female *santri,* alumni, and young NU women (Fatayat). Kiai Muhyiddin Sofyan was the first speaker, followed by a young professor of women's studies from the Islamic State Institute for Higher Learning and myself. The *kiai* peppered his speech with comments such as, "When a woman does not seek her husband's permission for everything she plans to do, all she does will amount to nothing and she will be cursed by God," "Women can only have a career while serving their husband wholeheartedly," "The man totally controls the wife," and, "The best spouse is she who always pleases her husband. Whether there is money or not, she will always smile."[82] The speech elicited an immediate question from the professor: "Where is a woman's value and equality as a human being?" In her own speech, she stressed that a Muslim woman's potential is unlimited and does not necessarily interfere with her religious duties.

Kiai Sofyan derived his knowledge from the *Kitab 'Uqud.* The text teaches ideas that are hard to stomach, such as that a wife should clean her husband's feet with her face. Even when aware of the incompatibility of these kinds of rules to contemporary conditions, *kiai* continue to use the text. At the bare minimum, they use it "for the sake of comparison to see what can still be learned from it for modern times."[83]

Many *kiai* simply do not know about alternative interpretations because they seldom attend study sessions about this topic. Debates about women's issues draw less interest from influential *kiai* because these issues, according to them, do not belong to the core religious concerns, such as worship (*ibadah*).[84] Kiai Husein Muhammad explained this as follows:

Compare it to Catholicism: women cannot become priests, but nobody protests against a female president in Ireland. The *kiai* are more interested in the rule that women cannot lead the ritual prayers when men are present than they are in questions of limits to women's careers.[85]

Some *nyai* return to the text and try to see how it can be meaningful in spite of all its drawbacks. For example, a *nyai* at a large *pesantren* suggested,

Sometimes the text exaggerates in order to reach its goal, which is to teach women not to be too free. It shows us how to be truly obedient to our husband. From that point of view there is nothing wrong with following its instructions without forgetting that the Prophet Muhammad was sent to improve women's lot.[86]

Ibu Fatma and Ibu Siti have wrestled with this text for many years. Ibu Fatma has discarded the *Kitab 'Uqud:* "I will never teach that in my school."

She flatly refuses to teach books that contain teachings negative to women: "Women are constantly reminded of their duties, such as praising their husbands. In those books a man is never reminded of his responsibilities. They make the man into a semi-god." Ibu Fatma will never miss an opportunity to explain this in her teachings. Her goal has always been to highlight variations of Qur'an interpretations that are favorable to women. In her view, verse 4:34 ("Men are the protectors/providers of women") can never be used to discriminate against women. She argues that the verse must be read without the potential consequence of men suppressing women: "Women should take hold of this verse and remind the husband! Suppression was an element added by male interpreters over many centuries. All those texts remind the woman of her duty without ever reminding the man." Including women in the process of forming new interpretations of the age-old texts is precisely what institutes such as P3M try to bring about. This is not easy, but when individual *nyai* can join hands, they create new openings.

Ibu Siti cannot ignore the text, since in the rural environment the gender views of many *kiai* are shaped by the teachings of *Kitab 'Uqud*. This means that she must familiarize her students with its contents. They read it during Ramadan, but, Ibu Siti stresses, "with justice." When I probed to see how much of the book the students actually discuss, it turned out that a superficial survey of the text suffices. She has new gender-friendly material from the P3M workshops that she uses for discussions about marriage. At the same time, she tries to instill in her students the profoundly Javanese values that emphasize the importance of maintaining social harmony and respecting the existing social hierarchy. She has interpreted these ideals according to the virtues taught at *pesantren* that imply that a woman (as well as a man) should be looking out for the general well-being, rather than her own personal good, desires, and will.[87]

In the meantime, the revised version of *Kitab 'Uqud* is being shipped all over Java. Institutes such as YKF organize workshops to familiarize young *kiai* and *nyai* with its contents. Hopes are high that, within a few generations, gender equality will be a matter of fact, even in the *pesantren*.

Conclusion

Although no longer a world of their own, the *pesantren* continue to embody the ideal fount of learning for NU Islam. Students not only continue to mull over ideas that have been studied for centuries, they study modern concepts of rights and choices for women. With women participating in these processes of learning, men *and* women students are moving toward a gender ideology that is compatible with the demands of modern life and firmly rooted in the traditionalist Islamic teachings. Although older and conservative *kiai* still reject many of these new teachings, they are gaining acceptance because of the soundness of their theological and philosophical basis.

Ibu Siti and Ibu Fatma are important actors in this process of reinterpretation and adaptation. They are two of a growing number of *niyai* who teach about a woman's potential in Islam to claim her God-given rights. When after their graduation the students at Ibu Fatma's *pesantren* leave the podium in their golden shoes, each kissing her hand as a sign of respect, many go on to an Islamic State Institute for Higher Learning and pursue graduate work in Islamic studies. Those who cannot afford further studies will return to their hometowns to become teachers in the local mosques. They will be considered authorities and leaders. Their reality and ideals remain at the point where the traditional and modern elements of their education intersect. They have to apply new ideas in contexts where the old still reigns. Having been trained by women who applied the paradigm shifts that leaders such as Masdar Mas'udi created, their views have changed profoundly. Their education has provided them with solid arguments from the tradition of Islamic learning to defend their new ideas. The reality of conservative ideas can be strong; even in their marriage, the young women might face a husband whose ideas about women are rooted in the literal world of the *Kitab 'Uqud*. However, in their struggle for justice and more freedom, the women can use the weapons of education, referring to the freshening opinions of their teachers.

The winds of change in the *pesantren* cannot be halted. The specific nature and structure of the *pesantren* and NU should be credited for allowing multiple levels of progressiveness to exist side-by-side with ultraconservatism. Kiai Bishri was educating girls for nearly twenty years, while other *kiai*, including Hasyim Asy'ari, were still against women's learning. NU education now produces women judges, professors, and award-winning Qur'an reciters. And these developments took place with the support of men, a fact that grants them stronger authority.

NU is a grassroots organization with the potential to reach millions of Muslims, helping them to begin listening to and discussing new ideas. This structure allows the creation of a true form of feminism based on Islam that will not break down because it is carried only by elite circles of western-educated Muslims. The NU organizational model allows for the new Fiqh interpretations to leave the rooms of the scholars of Islam and become translated into real life. In the remaining two chapters, I will further illustrate how people in villages and at other grassroots levels process the new teachings of the *Kitab 'Uqud* into their daily lives. This is an example of Fiqh in action. Due to the educational policies of the Suharto regime, most Indonesians have some level of literacy. This means that traditionalist men and women from all ranks of society can engage in activities previously reserved for *santri* and their teachers. Nonspecialists can learn to understand the essence and meaning of the sacred teachings of Islam. Part of this religious knowledge distributes new ideas about gender, subtly challenging religious authorities that seemed immutable less than half a century ago.

6 Tradition in Action: Muslimat NU

> It is my dream to start an M.A. program with a comprehensive curriculum in Islamic and other sciences for the brightest young women *santri* so that in a short while we will have women *kiai*.
> —Dra. Hj. Sinta Nuriyah Abdurrahman Wahid

Speak to one Muslimat NU woman and you might find the dutiful spouse of an ultraconservative *kiai*. Engage another in conversation and you might find yourself speaking to a socially active member of Parliament in Jakarta. The first may have initiated the construction of a birthing clinic; the second may teach the Qur'an in her free time. Many Muslimat NU women, barely a generation removed from the old ways, now work against practices their parents or grandparents considered natural—child, forced, and arranged marriages, polygyny, refusing women an education. Whatever their background or current position, a wellspring of personal experiences has firmed their common goal to improve the lot of women.

As a child in Kalimantan, Ibu Asmah Sjachruni, Muslimat NU's national chair from 1979 to 1995, one day overheard her parents decide that elementary school was enough education for her as a girl. She later taught herself, finding teachers when necessary, and had an astonishing career as a member of Parliament and chair of Muslimat NU. Fifty years ago, she spoke in segregated meetings and had to discuss matters concerning NU women from behind a curtain so as to shield the men from temptation. Ibu Aisyah Hamid Baidlowi, Abdurrahman's Wahid's sister, knows firsthand how her mother, Solichah Wahid Hasyim, was forbidden to study the Latin script but taught it to herself in secret. Ibu Umroh Mahfudzoh's grandfather and a cofounder of NU, Wahab Chasbullah, practiced serial polygyny on such a large scale that his family is still uncertain about the number of women he married—some estimate more than twenty.[1] Ibu Lily Munir Zakiyah, the founder of the Muslimat NU Women's Studies Center, is a grandniece of the legendary NU founder Hasyim Asy'ari. Her grandmother, Ibu Choiri-

yah Hasyim, had such extensive religious knowledge that she was appointed a member of the NU Central Religious Council (Syuriah). Moving to
Mecca with her second husband, she forced her daughter Abidah to marry
at the age of twelve. Honoring her great intelligence, her illustrious uncle
taught Abidah the principles of Qur'an and Fiqh so thoroughly that she became a member of the Provincial Parliament, joined the team that drafted
Indonesia's first independent constitution, and was one of the first women
Shari'ah judges.

The lives of these powerful women seem to have been nurtured on con-
tradictions. They have seen it all and then some, but they never stopped
fighting to improve the condition of women. Spurred on by the younger
generation of NU members, Muslimat NU are now trying to forge ahead:
they nearly rejected the practice of polygyny, several of their leaders are involved in a revision of the marriage law that wants to propose marriage as a
monogamous bond, and they are assertive in defining their role as women
within the traditionalist paradigm. This chapter describes how they negotiate the various layers of "NU culture." Neither impeded nor aided by a
"one vision, one mission" ideology, they have abundant freedom along with
abundant restrictions. They have truly inspired the younger generation by
their suffering, their courage, and their vision. Their very bodies seem poised
between future and past: young NU members who advocate new ideas about
gender stand on their shoulders, their feet surrounded by village women,
many of whom remain stuck in marriages with virtually no rights.

The women's experiences gave birth to courage and persistence but also
to a keen sense that women should be actively involved in shaping the politics around them, from the kitchen level to the Parliament. As I met NU
women inside and outside Java, it struck me how many were active in local,
provincial, and national politics. The current Muslimat NU national chair,
Khofifa Paraningsih (2000–), and Asmah Sjachruni held seats in the National Parliament. Khofifa served as minister of women's affairs during the
short presidency of Abdurrahman Wahid and is on the board of the NU-
related Partai Kebangkitan Bangsa (PKB; the National Awakening party).
It also struck me that several defining moments in Muslimat NU's history
hinged on highly charged political events such as the fight against Communism. And when speaking to its leaders about the contemporary situation, many seemed to consider local politics more important than what
was happening on the national level. In the post-Suharto era, when Indonesia was redefining itself as a democracy and national politics were still in
a state of transition, with corruption rampant and a struggling economy,
many Muslimat NU politicians deemed spending their energies on the lo-

cal level more judicious and more practical. They chose to address crucial long-range matters, such as voter education and drawing more women to careers in politics.

I chose to focus on Ibu Umroh Mahfudzoh's life story in this chapter because of her interesting blend of submission and politics. She is a member of the National Parliament and among the founding members of the PKB. She also embodies the elite of the NU network, as she belongs to one of its "blue-blood" families. Her biography reflects the sharp turns the lives of many NU women have taken, especially those who were born before the era of independence. As Ibu Umroh's life unfolded she took various, sometimes repeated roles—student, NU activist, mother and housewife, student, religious leader, politician, retired grandmother, and now a politician again. Her biography illustrates a woman of great curiosity, passion, and energy, but she is not alone in these gifts. She shares the stage with several other influential Muslimat NU leaders, together with whom she provides a glimpse of the character, work, and ideologies of women leaders who congregate under the enormous umbrella of NU.

Ibu Umroh Mahfudzoh

Shortly after Suharto stepped down, Ibu Umroh Mahfudzoh became unexpectedly busy. At the age of sixty-two, having just retired from a political career, she had been enjoying her grandchildren and staying involved as one of the national vice presidents of the Muslimat NU. In 1999 she decided to come out of retirement to help establish the PKB. NU chairman Abdurrahman Wahid himself convinced her that she was needed to give NU a voice and a place in the political arena. The party won 12.6 percent of the votes in the 1999 national elections, and in the summer of 2000 the party chose her as one of its top leaders. This made her one of the few women in an ocean of men playing a major, yet largely unnoticed, role in Indonesian politics.

Ibu Umroh used to live one block away from my house in Yogyakarta. I hardly ever saw her, since she spent her time shuttling between Jakarta, Yogyakarta, and East Java, where a large part of her family lived. Her house was roomy, its foyer filled with souvenirs from faraway countries testifying of frequent travels. In between the souvenirs hung the name of God carved in wood and the Islamic confession of faith. Ibu Umroh was petite, just over five feet tall, and kept herself slender by jogging several miles a day. She was unassuming, easy to miss in a crowd, but her inquisitive eyes seldom missed a thing and revealed a keen intelligence. Her answers were always short and to the point, those of an efficient, very busy person.

Ibu Umroh is a granddaughter of Wahab Chasbullah, one of NU's founders and, beginning in 1947, its national president (Rais Am) for over twenty
years. He was a flamboyant man who in the 1930s drove a Harley-Davidson
motorcycle and whose fascination with beautiful women is the stuff of juicy
NU myths.[2] His base was the Tambakberas Pesantren in Jombang, East Java,
where many of Ibu Umroh's family still live. She was born and raised in the
pesantren. Her generation was among the first to receive extended education. After her religious training at the *pesantren,* her parents allowed her to
attend a teacher-training college in Solo, where half of the curriculum was
devoted to religious subjects. This was in 1952; Muslimat NU had just started in 1946, and Ibu Umroh was a fifteen-year-old with an intense awareness of NU's need to recruit more women. To interest high school girls in
NU activities, she helped create an NU body suitable for young students:
the IPPNU (Ikatan Pelajar Putri NU), the association for female students.
This is how she met her husband. In 1951 he had been part of the collective
that started the IPNU (Ikatan Pelajar NU), the association for male NU
students. The idea was to provide students outside the *pesantren* a way of
remaining attached to NU. Ibu Umroh was the head of IPPNU in 1952 and
at the same time the local leader of the NU branch for young women, the
Fatayat. Her husband, who died in 1986, was the head of the NU in Yogyakarta and a professor at IAIN.

All of Ibu Umroh's seven children but one are active in the NU. Her son,
Fajrul Falak, is among its promising young leaders and a member of the
NU National Executive Council (Tanfidhiyah). He holds two M.A. degrees
from England and is a lecturer in political science at the prestigious Gaja
Madah University, thus representing a new generation in NU leadership.
Her daughter Rosa was national chair of the IPPNU, and her daughter Yun
is a member of the Provincial Parliament and active in the Fatayat NU. The
family is close to major NU figures, with direct or indirect family ties to
most of the leadership. This is typical of NU, where everyone seems to be
connected by marriage, blood relationships, or teacher-student bonds.

This chapter can only begin to portray some of activities Muslimat NU
engage in. Based on what came up most frequently during interviews with
Ibu Umroh and other leaders, I narrowed my choice to their day-to-day religious activities of preaching and chanting, some of their political involvement, and their work for women's position within NU. Muslimat NU are
married, most of them around middle age. They represent a world where
the women's obedience trails their independence; thus, like 'Aisyiyah, over
time they have tended to focus on remedying problems within the existing systems rather than aiming directly at fundamental change. Challenged

by the younger generation, however, Muslimat NU women are becoming bolder in creating programs that aim at transforming conditions detrimental to women.

Since the Fiqh from the *Kitab 'Uqud* aims at married women, I looked at how some Muslimat NU leaders handle its teachings when speaking to women. This includes the issue of polygyny, which comes up frequently in NU circles. Muslimat NU often counsel women whose husbands marry second wives, and many of them use this experience to ground the Fiqh discussions around polygyny. Not coincidentally, these discussions escalated when Islamist groups started to advocate the practice after the fall of Suharto, and Hamzah Haz, a longtime NU member with three wives, in 2001 became vice president in Megawati Sukarnoputri's cabinet.

Creating Space for Women

NU began in 1926 as a network among *kiai* who wanted their voices to be heard in the national and international Islamic scene. Unlike Muhammadiyah, it did not launch a conscious endeavor to spread Islam or set up a network of schools, hospitals, and social services. NU was based in the *pesantren,* where women did not yet play an important role. "Although outside the NU [in the 1920s and 1930s] there were already many organizations for women, NU women were not given permission to leave the house."[3] Women could be part of NU and played important roles in strengthening the organization with their donations and activities for women, but they had no official body, voice, or position. As women's Islamic education improved, independent female preachers started to emerge from traditionalist backgrounds. One of them, Ibu Djunaisih, in a sweeping speech during the thirteenth NU congress in 1938, impressed upon the male *kiai* that "there are not only men in Islam."[4] She spoke plainly: "Without women, the organization's struggle cannot succeed. If the NU will not make room for women, they will lose many members, since the women will leave in masses."[5] Two thousand women attended this meeting inside the building, while six thousand had to remain outside. They gathered from all over Indonesia, carrying pillows and blankets for the night and paying their own way. The NU men were not prepared for this multitude of women and tried to pacify them with solid male advice. As one of the NU members stated: "It is absolutely imperative to women to obey the directions of men, because a woman who ignores the man's advice or orders, fails to worship God who thus despises her and she surely will fall prey to the flames of hell."[6] In the end, some of the most influential *kiai*—Kiai Wahid Hasyim, Kiai Wahab

Chasbullah, and Kiai Mohamad Dachlan—convinced NU leaders to accept women.[7] The struggle ended in a stalemate; the women were denied places of authority within the NU but were allowed as "observers and participants."[8] Women were driven to defy the inhospitable atmosphere by a sense of calling to work for the plight of women in their circles. Ibu Aisjah Dachlan, the wife of Kiai Mohamad Dachlan, expressed this feeling of urgency in her writings:

> A woman's lot is hopeless. She suffers from lack of education and ignorance, carrying the burden of many duties while being denied her basic rights. In her own house she has neither rights nor a voice. It is the husband who decides, and she has to obey unconditionally. Within the marriage the man often abuses his right to divorce, leaving the wife powerless. . . . Many children and young women thus are left behind, becoming a burden to society that is not lifted easily. Women now realize that in order to change the fate of those suffering there has to be an organization that focuses on this plight.[9]

At the sixteenth NU congress in March 1946, more than two decades after the NU started, the Muslimat NU finally gained recognition as an official NU organization representing women in traditionalist milieu. However, until 1959 the women had to sit behind a curtain during joint meetings.[10] They suffered fifteen years longer than 'Aisyiyah women, who in 1944 received permission from Muhammadiyah men to be visible. This did not inhibit the women from raising their voices. Ibu Asmah Sjachruni stated: "I would stand up and say what I wanted to say. We were five women in a meeting with over a hundred men. I did not care about the curtain; they had to listen to us."[11]

Their goal as described in official publications was "[t]o make Indonesian Muslim women aware of their responsibility to become true mothers, so that they can join in strengthening and helping the work of NU in affirming the religion of Islam."[12] It sounds akin to what other Muslim women were called to do in Indonesia at that time: to help strengthen Islam and build the new nation. Over and above this, the unwritten goal was to raise awareness among Muslim women about their equal rights. Looking back in a 1971 speech, Ibu Mahmudah Mawardi, the national chair from 1952 to 1979, acknowledged that the revolution in 1945 was the watershed event that impressed upon NU men the need for extra female workers who could address social and medical needs.[13] During the Dutch colonial period, NU's activities had been mainly religious. The Japanese occupation (1942–45), while harsh, gave Indonesians unprecedented opportunities to participate in politics and the military. A large number of *kiai* received military training from the Japanese for the war against the Allies. After 1945, NU and Indonesia needed human resources in every segment of society: politics, economics, and social work. At first, the Muslimat women were directly involved in the *jihad* (struggle) for freedom against the Dutch (1945–49). But the women were expected not to move beyond their traditional roles. They led army kitchens and hospitals and "were expected to sit and type behind the fighting lines or act as couriers."[14]

In the stormy years following independence, women's help became increasingly vital for the continuation of the NU organization. During these years, NU women developed a high level of political awareness, and a relatively large number of them became involved in local or national politics. The Muslimat NU issued a pamphlet listing the main national events that influenced their development: 1) the Communist uprising in Madiun (1948), in which many NU women and men were killed; 2) the break between NU and reformist Masyumi in 1952, after which NU set up its own political party; 3) in 1964, Muslimat NU volunteered for military training in preparation for a possible conflict with Malaysia; 4) the following year they participated in what amounted to a war against the Communist party (PKI); 5) the birth control issue, which in 1967 became a topic of discussion in NU circles; 6) in 1984, NU severed its formal ties to political parties. This did not mean total withdrawal from politics; many individual NU leaders—for example, Ibu Umroh Mahfudzoh—kept their parliamentary positions and remained members of non-NU parties. The organization, however, shifted its focus to its religious and social role (*kembali ke khittah*, returning to the original charter). For the NU men this meant working in an entirely new direction; until 1984 the women had carried most of the NU social work and set up kindergartens outside the *pesantren* system.

The number of current Muslimat followers is estimated to be around five million women. At first sight, there seems to be little difference between the activities of the Muslimat NU and 'Aisyiyah. They both carry on religious, social, and medical activities and operate on the microeconomic level, providing small loans and running cooperatives that provide affordable commodities for the members. Both are faithful to the charter of the parent organization, and both seem to conduct their meetings and administration in similar—that is, Indonesian—ways. Once I attended a regional Muslimat meeting in Pekalongan after visiting the local 'Aisyiyah branch. A senior 'Aisyiyah member insisted on accompanying me. What I remember most of the seven-hour-long session was her exclaiming every fifteen minutes, "We do this exactly the same way!" This went from opening the meeting with the organization's anthem to the remark that a copy of every important decision must be sent to the parent organization. The largest difference was that Muslimat NU started their meeting over an hour late. This lack of punctuality greatly annoys Muhammadiyah women. Also, Muslimat mostly chant religious texts; as a result, only a few could produce the opening song without hesitation. Muhammadiyah members do not chant but sing specially written songs instead. These are superficial similarities and differences, however; the two organizations differ fundamentally in their institutional models, one traditionalist and the other reformist, which results in alternative models of teaching, preaching, and strengthening the position of women.

Muslimat NU Works

Hearing the Sound of Islam: Dakwah

THE WORDS *Dakwah* in NU does not bear the connotation of converting non-Muslims to Islam, nor does it strive to bring Muslims to NU thinking. It is directed at providing guidance for those who consider themselves Muslim, whether they are dedicated followers or only nominal believers. This guidance stretches from teaching people how to perform their daily ritual duties to deciding what indigenous rituals can be accepted by Islam and what rituals are counter to its basic teachings. Although there are no official counts, the majority of Muslims in Indonesia, especially on Java, are attracted to Islamic pluralism rather than extremist Islam. There are no hard numbers available to indicate how many of these are traditionalist-minded. Based on the outcome of the 1999 elections, the Australian political scientist Greg Fealy estimates that the division between traditionalist- and modernist-minded Muslims has become about fifty-fifty. This estimate reflects the fact that the Indonesian Islamic landscape is changing as differences between traditionalists and modernists erode and members of both groups move towards a middle ground.[15]

Yet "being NU" to many is considered the natural, indigenous mode of being. Ibu Asmah Sjachruni expressed this natural feeling of belonging when describing the village where she was born in Kalimantan. "We were already *ahl ussunnah wal jama'ah,* we were NU although we were not members yet."[16]

In its teaching methods, NU at first did not aim at creating new models or paradigms. Individual members developed these whenever needed. NU tries to follow the model of the *wali songgo,* the nine saints accredited with bringing Islam to Java. According to legend, they built the first *pesantren* and designed methods of mission suitable to the Javanese culture. For example, the most famous *wali*, Sunan Kalijaga, is credited with Islamizing the Javanese shadow play accompanied by gamelan music to bring the message of Islam to the people.

The theme of using music to spread Islam still flows through Java and moves the hearts of thousands who hear its sounds. For example, in Yogyakarta, once a year at the time of the birthday of the Prophet Muhammad (Moulid an-Nabi) a monthlong fair called *sekaten* is held on the plaza in front of the Kraton. On certain nights a gamelan that normally is stored inside the Kraton is brought out. According to the tradition, the *wali songgo* themselves changed the composition of this gamelan by adding a *bedug*, a drum used to call for prayer. This gamelan has been used since the Muslim kingdom of Mataram started with Sultan Agung (1613–46).[17] In the past the gamelan would play during the fair to attract the peasants from the surrounding villages. To them its sound represented Islam and was so powerful that many felt moved to convert to Islam on the spot by pronouncing the confession of faith, the *shahada*. The word *sekaten* is a Javanese rendition of the word *shahada,* and the *sekaten* fair still provides a mix of religious and worldly entertainment. While preachers give moving sermons, worldly attractions ranging from karaoke singing to merry-go-rounds vie for the visitors' attention. Most Javanese have long since converted to Islam, but many still stand spellbound in front of the podium on which the gamelan is played on certain nights.

Hearing the sound of Islam has remained a powerful tool in NU activities. To its followers, *dakwah* does not mean passively listening to sermons and theoretical explanations of the faith. They believe that this alone does not move the heart or motivate them to seek deeper meaning within their religion. Listening to recitations from the Qur'an, to poems about the life of the Prophet Muhammad, and to prayers of praise invites them to participate. NU members believe that repeating the words will awaken a desire to shift to actions such as charity due to an overwhelming longing to be part of the body of believers. This to NU is *dakwah.* According to the Muslimat NU, repetition of the sacred words and rituals is the starting point for their religious work. When the economic crisis started in 1998, Ibu Asmah Sjachruni reflected on the power of the rituals and traditions practiced by NU:

> There is great wisdom in our religious traditions. During these turbulent days, we hold mass prayers for forgiveness [*istighosah*] and mass gatherings of praise [*tahlil umum* and *tahlil kubra*]. The majority of Indonesia's Muslims come to join the chanting. Go to some of the villages, go to some of the

NU areas like Jatinegara [east of Jakarta]. When they recite the Prayers of the Prophet Muhammad [Shalawat Nabi], feelings of sadness disappear, and sometimes we are moved to tears because of the words. It is as if those prayers call us. They are a call [seruan] not to give up, to hold on to faith. They call us to live a life of high morals and ethics [berakhlakul karimah]. We also give sermons, but we can never ignore these traditions. They give meaning to our religion. Just listening to sermons does not move your heart; it gets boring.[18]

The belief that the sound of Islam is not for the living only but includes the dead as well is particular to NU philosophy. Once a year, the Muslimat NU organize commemorative prayers for the deceased (khaul) where families are invited to write down the names of those who have died recently or long ago. During a litany of prayers, each name is mentioned out loud. According to Ibu Asmah, "This creates an extraordinary bond between NU members; at that moment we feel united in unique fashion."[19] The relationship starts at the time a person passes away and the body is prepared for burial; it continues as long as those who remember are alive. Preparing the body is a prime activity for Muslimat NU women. They know the proper procedures for washing and wrapping it in pieces of white fabric. They also have memorized the accompanying prayers and chants. Often they will stay with the family the whole night until the time of burial.

> When we prepare the dead for burial, we recite prayers and the Fatihah. We must pray for those who died, but the prayers are not only for them. For us they represent dakwah, because one day we will die as well. That day, we will not be able to take a thing except for our good and bad deeds. Moreover, instead of just chatting about trivial things, it is better to present the deceased with a gift of readings from the Qur'an. This is truly dakwah. At the grave we chant tahlil [praise]. This again is a reminder that our turn will come. These prayers are for both the living and the dead. We say, "Wash before your own body will be washed, and pray before you will be prayed for." This is dakwah.[20]

This model of dakwah is rooted in the mystic origins of Indonesian Islam. For centuries, students in pesantren have been involved daily in chanting prayers and praises. The heart is emphasized, not the brain only. The Muslimat NU expressed this sentiment when on the occasion of their fiftieth anniversary they tried to distill the most important aspects of their religious life: "The Islamic doctrine for our daily lives is a combination of law and mysticism [Fiqh and Tasawwuf]; thus the cerebral head is connected with the feeling heart."[21]

THE RITUALS   Another central activity for Muslimat NU leaders is guiding rituals that follow people from birth to death. Even if the actual ritual
is dominated by men, as is the case at many *slametan*, women have important roles. They cook the food, plan the gathering, and decide when to
hold it. Many of the rituals for and by women are embedded in local culture, real-life situations, and Islamic religion.[22] For traditionalist Muslims,
rituals are soothing to body, mind, and soul; reformist preachers, however,
abhor them and frequently mention the many non-Islamic rituals followed
by "others" (NU members). Reformists seldom differentiate between indigenous Javanese rituals and those adapted to Islam.[23] They also ignore
the fact that the participants' interpretations of a certain ritual primarily
depends on their background and knowledge.[24] This makes it even more
important that the Muslimat NU offer religious guidance and education
concerning these rituals.

Hence, Muslimat NU women are keenly aware of their role in guiding
rituals, such as *slametan*, that stem from pre-Islamic Javanese culture. One
of the possible definitions for a *slametan* is "a ceremonial meal consist-
ing of offerings, symbolic foods, a formal speech, and a prayer."[25] Originally, during the *slametan* an offering of food was made not only to those
present but also to the spirits.[26] This is not allowed in Islam. So for Muslimat, the *slametan* has become a meal of many meanings, depending on its
function. For example, Ibu Fatma's daughter explained that her mother
organized three *slametan* in 1999–2000 for her second pregnancy. Because
the first pregnancy had ended in miscarriage, the family felt a deep need
to organize a ritual that would strengthen the mother-to-be. Birth *slametan* are customarily held at the third month of pregnancy, at the seventh
month (*tingkeban*), and to name the child on the seventh day after birth.
The daughter especially valued the one at the third month because she felt
sick regularly. "I needed extra spiritual and psychological help through the
prayers of those joining the *slametan*." These prayers are perceived as especially beneficial when several notable or charismatic *kiai* are present as well.
In different areas of Indonesia, I observed several *slametan* that were held
to invoke extra strength and blessing. For example, in Sumatra I was invited
to a large *slametan* to name a baby. The baby was already a few months old,
but the parents had waited because all its siblings had died after only a few
weeks. The baby's mother was anxious to invite as many guests as the house
could hold to increase the potential strength of blessing.

While they follow the principles of the original Javanese rituals, NU leaders modify their content and intentions. For example, according to Javanese

beliefs it is crucial to hold the *slametan* on a date specified in the Javanese calendar. The date does not matter in NU circles; the *slametan* is held when it fits the schedule of those involved, and no one time is superior to another. While in Java each dish served has a special meaning, following traditional patterns, Muslimat NU simply offer foods they like. The different dishes are presented in small carton bowls. Whereas in the original ritual, bowls with food are offered to the spirits (*sesaji*), Muslimat NU dedicate the dishes to Islamic saints, such as the first four caliphs: "This dish is for Abu Bakr, this is for Umar, this is for Uthman, and this is for Ali." Ibu Fatma explained:

> We in NU emphasize the teachings of Sunan Kalijaga. We follow his exam- ple to respect local culture. This does not mean we just follow local culture blindly, we shape it [*mengisi*]. This is in accordance with the original teachings of Islam. The word of God was revealed gradually in order to give people a chance to adapt and to get used to the new rules. It is evolution, not revolu- tion. Take, for example, the teachings about using alcohol. At first God sum- moned the Prophet's companions to be moderate with drinking [Al-Baqara 2:219]. Sometimes they had had so much that the call to prayer was chanted in slurs. Then God forbade them to drink before the five ritual prayers. That left only the night for them to get drunk [An-Nisa' 4:43]. Finally, the command was revealed that forbade drinking alcohol altogether [Al-Ma'ida 5:90]. Sunan Kalijaga took this wisdom of God as his guideline in negotiating Islam with local culture. Later this became part of the NU teaching.[27]

What might appear to be a random process of absorbing local rituals in fact follows a keen strategy for *dakwah* that aims at providing meaning- ful rituals acceptable to Islamic teachings. Women play an important role in this process of Islamization. They instruct the local communities about what rituals are wasteful or against the spirit of Islam and what rituals are religiously meaningful and allowed.

Muslimat NU preachers all over Indonesia have developed ways to con- vince the women that giving up certain indigenous rituals makes them "better Muslims." Economic and social considerations play an important role in this process. For example, Ibu Ismawati, a local Muslimat NU leader from North Java, reinvented the contents and economic aspects of the ritual surrounding Ruwah, the month preceding the fasting month of Ramadan. At that time, people customarily visit the graves of ancestors to clean them, offering prayers and food. After these visits, the Muslim fasting of Ramadan begins. At the end of the fast, it is strongly recommended that all Muslims, including women and children, gather for public prayers to celebrate the beginning of the feast (Lebaran or Idul Fitri). Villagers with only a superficial knowledge of Islam, however, ascribe more importance to visiting the grave and will skip the prayers, especially if a loved one has died during the year past. Knowing the strong beliefs surrounding visiting the graves, Ibu Ismawati started to address the economic aspects of these rituals and convinced her NU community "not to hold a *slametan* for the spirits because they no longer eat. In fact, sending food that is not meant for consumption is a great waste."[28] When the participants in her Qur'an circle could accept this, Ibu Ismawati suggested collecting the money thus saved for the educational project of the local Muslimat. Then she persuaded the villagers to skip the visit to the graves altogether and to hold a mass gathering of prayer and praise instead. Those who still wished to pray for members of their family could write the names on a list to be distributed among all the participants. In that way the dead received more prayers than when visited by a few of their beloved ones only.[29] Now, according to Ibu Ismawati, all are happier. The community feels that it has moved closer to Islam, and from the community's devotion the Muslimat NU can finance a building for their new educational projects.

Words and Action: Majlis Ta'lim

In NU circles, regular religious gatherings are called Majlis Ta'lim. Women's Qur'an groups begin with women chanting with hands raised and eyes closed. The prayers seem to move them from the secular into the religious realm, and for some moments all present are united in communication with God. Especially in the NU strongholds of East Java, Majlis Ta'lim attract hundreds of women. Gatherings held on the occasion of a feast or commemoration can draw thousands. When all participants are present, a sermon, speech, or short reflection follows.

Originally, preaching was a side activity of itinerant merchants. Ibu Mahmudah Mawardi (the first Muslimat NU chair), widowed, went around as a batik seller, giving sermons after market hours. She exemplified the Muslimat NU teaching: "The method of *dakwah* was simple, connected with daily life. For example, how to clean the water for the ritual washing, how to perform the ritual prayer. There were no microphones so meetings were small, up to one hundred women. The main philosophy was that all who called themselves Muslim indeed would perform the prescribed worship rituals."[30]

Over time, the Majlis Ta'lim became a tool of nonformal education, women's empowerment, and teaching religion. At first they addressed Islamic matters only, but they eventually came to include information about

topics such as health, birth control, and children's nutrition. It was especially important to address health issues in the countryside during the 1960s
and 1970s, since many were deeply suspicious of state-run facilities such as
hospitals. These sentiments stemmed from colonial times, when most official health providers were Dutch. According to Ibu Muhammad Baidawi
from Jombang, "Women simply refused to see a doctor. They believed that
if you went into a hospital you would die, and the doctors would take your
brain out."[31] Muslimat NU leaders used practical preaching to overcome
suspicion and prejudice.

The Majlis Ta'lim always served as a tool of *dakwah*. The many methods for this kind of mission ranged from holding public or private prayers
for forgiveness (*istighosah*) to frequent public recitations of the Qur'an. In
1998, when the economic crisis had become apparent in all sections of Indonesian life, Muslimat distributed booklets with the text of the prayer for
forgiveness and urged its leaders to say those daily in private. NU leaders
organized and led the public sessions of these prayers. Not only an act of
praising God, reciting the Qur'an is also believed to reinvigorate the commitment of NU members and to strengthen the bonds among them. For
example, the charismatic preacher Ibu Chunainah used it as a tool to revive an NU community in a Jakarta area where NU adherence had greatly
diminished during the 1970s. Over twenty years ago, she started a Majlis
Ta'lim that still rotates its meetings among the different mosques in her
neighborhood. Her aim is to get women interested in becoming Muslimat
NU leaders by teaching them not only the contents of the Qur'an but also
the art of reciting. To give the women a strong grasp on the text, Ibu Chunainah arranges daily gatherings in one of the homes to recite parts of the
Qur'an. Thus the whole book is completed once a week.[32] Ibu Chunainah
has so far succeeded in guiding and training seventy-five women, each of
whom set up a Muslimat NU section in her own neighborhood (*ranting*).
Counted together, they represent a new chapter of the Muslimat NU.

NU communities all over Indonesia initiate rallies of reciting holy texts
before and during the month of Ramadan. This underpins the holiness of
the fasting month while welcoming in the festive mood of the feast to come.
A young NU woman remembered how in her village near the sea in North-
east Java, "Twelve days before the feast started, morning and evening, we
would move from house to house and recite the history of the Prophet and
sing about his *burda* [mantle]. This invited us to ponder how as a Muslim
community we could live in harmony and enter the feast in a unified spirit.
After all, that is what NU is about: unity and brotherhood [*kesatuan* and
persaudaraan]."[33]

Like the *pengajian* of other groups, Majlis Ta'lim have become a vehicle for economic improvement. NU members in the villages are mostly poor. This challenges the preachers to find nonmonetary ways to collect income for certain projects. For example, in Sidoarjo, Muslimat NU designed the so-called *jimpitan* project: each member of the study group sets aside one spoonful of rice a day. As much as five hundred kilograms of rice a month can thus be collected. The rice is sold, and the proceeds are used to build new houses for members of the group. The project turned out to be so successful that it was copied by similar groups in Cambodja.[34]

Since most Muslimat members live in rural areas, they are familiar with the problems of poor villagers. Social work naturally emanated from what the preachers observed during Qur'an studies and became inseparable from religious activities. Ibu Asmah Sjachruni, who herself rose from poverty, often reflected that

> Islam itself acknowledges that a poor person can be in danger of becoming an unbeliever. When you live in poverty you are overwhelmed by financial problems. Think of how a father or mother has to work all day to feed their family. When do they have time for the ritual prayer, for praises, how can they find time for their religious duties?[35]

Up to 1984, when NU formally left national politics to renew its focus on religion and social work, the bulk of its social welfare programs was carried by the Muslimat. Most NU activities did not generate income for the organization, while the schools and projects of the Muslimat yielded extra funds for the members. "When we had the joint conference with NU in Yogyakarta [1988], we drove back to Jakarta with a minibus filled with money, while the NU had nothing to transport," remembered Ibu Asmah Sjachruni.[36] The projects in combination with the birth clinics and kindergartens make Muslimat NU more prosperous than NU. This is especially the case in rural areas. Ibu Maryam, a Muslimat NU leader in Yogyakarta, explained: "NU in the cities is becoming more intellectual, while at the provincial level [*wilayah*] the programs are aimed at economic improvement. For example, the revenue of our co-operative An-Nisa in Malang is several million rupiah. The Muslimat as a whole moved into social work through economic activities. These are the best tools to improve women's condition."[37]

Majlis Ta'lim groups also have become vehicles to implement worldwide programs sponsored by the United Nations, such as immunization of children and preventive health information for mothers. Following the general trend, Muslimat NU also became involved in the national drive to curb birth rates and with NU went through lengthy discussions surrounding birth control. NU officially permitted it in 1972, around a decade after Muslimat NU began to encourage it. NU is an aggregate of individual, independent *kiai* who may or may not follow decisions of its Central Boards. This model leaves room for individual *kiai* to allow certain practices before the national boards approve of them. This process is illustrated in the ways that individual Muslimat NU handled the matter of birth control before it was officially decided upon in 1972 by the Syuriah. The example comes from Jombang, a town in the heart of NU land where every other house seems to host a *pesantren*. The local chair of the Muslimat NU, Ibu Muhammad Baidawi, decided it was time to present her ideas in the Majlis Ta'lim and help the women control the size of their ever-expanding families. She asked the local NU chair, her husband, to issue a *fatwa* that permitted birth control and specified methods that were permissible. After studying the matter, the only method allowed was the oral method, the birth control pill. The women started to promote the pill but still met with fierce resistance because of suspicion towards formal medical services. So they built their own clinic for women. After studying other legal texts, a second method was added, coitus interruptus, with the requirement that it be *halal,* permissible and not in disagreement with the Islamic law. This meant that both partners had to agree to it. By the time NU issued its official statement concerning birth control, the program in Jombang was already approaching its tenth anniversary.[38]

The birth control issue illustrates how local and national NU politics mutually influence each other. According to NU philosophies, the local is considered politically as important as the national. There is politics in a broader and in a smaller sense; for the good of society, everybody has to join in, even at the microlevel. Muslimat NU had the advantage of starting in 1946, after the Dutch colonial period was over in Indonesia. A new society had to be constructed from the postwar chaos. These times offered new and exciting opportunities for women, not only in the private and unofficial sections of society but also in the public arena of politics.

Muslimat NU in Politics

Muslimat NU skillfully took advantage of the unprecedented climate in newly independent Indonesia. In a history of the Muslimat NU written in 1968, Ibu Aisjah Dachlan, one of its national chairs during the 1950s, called on each member to "[i]ncrease your knowledge and grow smarter. Join the political developments of the fatherland like all those who are members of a political party."[39] Participating in the political process was vital for the

Muslimat NU to have a voice in the future development of the Indonesian state. Moreover, political involvement gave access to power, networks of patronage, and resources that helped NU women to catch up with the ever-growing activism of Muhammadiyah women.

Many Muslimat NU women became active in politics while serving their organization, participating in the formation of the governmental system. Ibu Sinta Nuriyah, Abdurrahman Wahid's wife, described their goal as "help[ing] the government . . . in strengthening civil society, especially for the interest of women."[40] This was one of the reasons Ibu Umroh became involved in politics. As early as 1955 she was campaigning for the NU party, which at the time garnered 18 percent of the national vote. Together with the other young members of NU she received training in party doctrine and politics and in the NU political program.[41] NU leaders urged her to quit school for a while to join the campaign and convinced the young students that the struggle against atheist Communism was a matter of life and death. Ibu Umroh was told, "If you do not help NU win and find studying more important, the Communist party will win, and you will end up being hacked to death. Only by building a Muslim party can we develop Islam." She remembers, "At school I was on leave for almost a year to have time for campaigning. On horseback we visited the remote villages to lobby for votes; Anshor, the NU branch for young men, provided guides and protectors."[42] She had had experience in going to the rural areas when she initiated IPPNU, visiting the different areas of Indonesia by boat and train to speak to potential young members and their parents. She could travel so widely because of her grandfather's reputation, yet it remains remarkable that a young girl was allowed to do this with her sole protectors the young men of Anshor. These were the postwar days when reformist 'Aisyiyah writings reflect immense concern over "national morals" and "men and women freely socializing." It could be that people deemed Ibu Umroh "protected" by her famous grandfather. It is also an indication of the potential opportunities within NU for the persistent individual who has the right credentials. NU's structure allows the charismatic or forceful individual who has a vision or a dream to strive to attain her goal. This is a recurring motif in the story of the Muslimat NU. At the time, Ibu Umroh was a *pemudi*, a female adolescent. This term for young persons held special meaning during the time of the revolution: "The [male] *pemuda* were the young-at-heart who were willing to devote their entire being to the struggle, in contrast to what was seen as the more cautious, less committed older generation."[43] They shaped the new Indonesia and had the courage to go where others did not dare.

After the NU party won several seats in the 1955 elections, Ibu Umroh, at eighteen years old, was too young to be eligible for office. Five of the forty-five NU seats in Parliament were given to Muslimat NU. That was the same quota given to women in the Communist party, while reformist Masyumi assigned only three of its fifty-two seats to women.

Political anxiety resurfaced in 1964 and 1965, but this time Ibu Umroh was not involved in the public sphere; she was busy raising her small children. The Muslimat NU joined the military preparation to resist possible Malaysian aggression. Concurrently, they started a drive against increasing Communist influence in society and government. Ibu Asmah Sjachruni observed the "ideological discipline, fanaticism, and militant behavior of the Communist women, and the fact that they were involved in military exercises."[44] As the Muslimat NU held the ideal of an Islamized Indonesian society, they organized semi-military training for members to counter the activities of the large and influential Communist women's group of Gerwani. Fear and hatred of Gerwani drew two hundred thousand women from all over Indonesia. Special forces, dressed in traditional wraparound skirts (sarong) and wearing veils, assembled to learn how to handle guns and jump over roads on fire. "When they can carry arms, why can't we learn how to shoot?" said Ibu Asmah Sjachruni, who could not join the physical activities because she had just given birth but became a commander instead. The Communists used songs to arouse enthusiasm in their followers. The young NU women, the Fatayat, wanted to create a drum band that could accompany Muslimat NU marching through the streets in shows of force. Initially the top NU leaders were against this because it meant that the women had to wear long pants.

When the campaigns against Communism began in September 1965, Muslimat NU members joined the fight. Looking back, its current leaders believe that these activities changed the direction of their organization:

> We moved from an unruffled existence of preaching and giving courses in preparing a corpse for burial to rallying in the streets against the Communists. We climbed barricades and demanded that the Communist women's organization, Gerwani, would be removed from the National Association for Women's Organizations [Kowani]. We went ahead at high speed, and after that we could never go back to the traditional Muslimat NU activities. We were now fully involved in society and politics.[45]

While the mindset of Muslimat NU leaders was set on destroying Gerwani, they learned much from the organization's efficient and innovative methodologies and programs. For example, in the field of education, the

Muslimat NU observed how Gerwani women stressed the importance of kindergartens in the formation of children. Consequently, they opened kindergartens that featured a broad religious curriculum.

The next politically sensitive issue was the debate surrounding the contentious marriage law. From the 1950s until 1974, they battled over its contents, such as the age of marriage and polygyny. Polygyny remains an especially problematic issue that underscores the deep disagreements between Muslim and secular women's groups about how women can secure their rights and find justice in the Islamic teachings. According to devout Muslims, the Qur'an allows men to marry up to four wives (Surah 4:2, 3), so abolishing polygyny through the marriage law could never be an option to the Muslimat NU. Such inevitability urged women to participate in the discussion about how to frame the issue in terms tolerable to women. Since much more was at stake for women than for men, an observer wrote: "In the debate on polygamy it was mainly the female members of Parliament who took parts."[46]

Another big issue on their agenda was the working conditions of female and child workers. This resulted in a law that (ideally) granted women a leave of absence after birth and when menstruating. It also protected female factory workers from working night shifts. Muslimat NU created a special department to monitor the plight of female NU workers and negotiate directly with the ministry on their behalf, similar to a labor union. It is not surprising that when Ibu Umroh became involved in founding the PKB, one of her first concerns was to negotiate with the male party members over the party's stance towards women and specify how to improve women's level of sustenance, independence, and participation in the economy and politics.[47]

Interest in politics escalated in 1998 when the door opened for democratic and free elections. When the United Nations provided funds for voter education, the Muslimat NU joined dozens of Muslim organizations and organized fifteen thousand leaders in eleven provinces to motivate women to vote. Not only were the women encouraged to leave the house and cast their vote, they were also taught that they could choose according to their own preference. Muslimat NU impressed on them that it was not an act of disobedience and thus not a sin to deviate from the husband's choice, as was taught by conservative *kiai*. During the 1950s and 1960s, women had participated in developing the political process, even though their education was not very advanced yet. Voices were then muffled by the Suharto regime, but in 1998 women joined men in creating the NU-related PKB.

While they have been active and successful in political life, NU women face many dichotomies in their inner circles. Within the organization of

NU and within their family, men have the final word. When she was a member of the National Parliament, Ibu Asmah Sjachruni would not attend official functions without her husband's consent. At times he did not grant it. The following sections will focus on the obstacles NU women face within the organization and within the circle of their nuclear family.

Women in NU

The former chair of Muslimat NU, Ibu Aisyah Hamid Badlowi, is a seasoned politician and a keen observer of NU's ambivalence towards its women members. She knows what she is talking about: her grandfather, Hasyim Asy'ari, was one of the founders of NU, and her brother, Abdurrahman Wahid, was the chairman for several decades. In 2000 Ibu Hamid Baidlowi presented a paper at the Muslimat NU meeting about polygyny in which she analyzed the position on NU women within the organization. The title of her paper refers to the years when women were forced to sit behind a curtain during NU meetings.[48] She concludes that in spite of several documents NU produced concerning women's position and rights, its stand is still ambiguous. As the male head of the family monitors his spouse, the NU monitors the Muslimat NU. The election of Ibu Hamid Baidlowi's successor revealed this ambivalence: the Muslimat NU were not allowed their own choice. When the time of electing a new chair came around, news was brought from NU headquarters that its preference was to choose Khofifah Paraningsih, NU Minister for Women's Affairs at the time and an influential PKB member. This situation provided some ugly moments of internal power politics. The Muslimat NU did not approve of this choice: in her mid thirties and pregnant with her fourth child, Khofifah was considered too young and inexperienced and too busy because of her position as minister. Yet NU preferred the potential political influence the choice of a minister would yield, and the Muslimat were overruled. All, including Khofifah herself, were forced to accept the NU decision.

The Muslimat NU have been aware of this situation for a long time. At the beginning, the men made most of the decisions, since the Muslimat lacked strong leadership. Ironically, NU leaders themselves tried to strengthen the women's organization. In 1949 they called on Ibu Mahmudah Mawardi to become the national chair. She was thirty-seven years old, widowed with young children, and a teacher who had set up one of the first schools for NU girls in Solo, where she taught secular and religious subjects to women *pesantren* graduates. Ibu Umroh Mahfudzah was among her first students. In the 1940s and 1950s, teachers were among the highest educated members of Indonesian society and hence commanded immense respect. Ibu Mahmuda was also a well-known preacher. Despite her credentials, NU leaders did not appoint her until they had examined her preaching skills during a mass gathering in Madiun.[49]

The Muslimat NU's autonomy was not always accepted on the local level. The struggle for recognition continued for several years, as many local NU divisions forced women to register as NU members, an affront to their status as an independent organization within NU. After several futile attempts to change this situation, the leaders in Jakarta came up with a suggestion that scared the NU men into allowing the Muslimat membership cards: "We said, 'Okay, if women hold the NU card that means that they are eligible to be elected to local [male] NU councils.'"[50]

The women realized that their presence in NU bodies would be the most efficient way to receive attention for their issues. They struggled for membership in the NU Central Religious Council (Syuriah) and in the Central Executive Council (Tanfidziah). Membership in the Syuriah, whose members are commended for their outstanding Islamic knowledge, in principle is open to women, provided they hold the required level of learning. During the 1950s and 1960s three women were members, of whom Ibu Mahmudah Mawardi and Ibu Choiriyah Hasyim, the sister of Hasyim Asy'ari, were the most prominent. It was nearly four decades before two more Muslimat NU women were added to the Syuriah during the 1999 NU national conference in Lirboyo (albeit without voting power): Ibu Huzaemah Yanggo, a full professor of Shari'ah at IAIN Jakarta, and Ibu Mursyidah Thahir, a teacher at the Institute for Qur'an Studies (Institut Ilmu al-Qur'an; IIQ). NU itself wishes more women to participate in this council at different levels and runs a program to educate female *ulama* (religious leaders). The presence of women members in the Syuriah allows Muslimat to participate in decision making and to take religious issues directly to the council.

For the Muslimat, this was a modest victory but not enough. During the 1999 meeting, their most distinguished member, Ibu Asmah Sjachruni, decided that she should run for a place in the Tanfidziyah. She wanted Muslimat NU to take part in this council since it is the platform where crucial decisions about nonreligious policies are made. Ibu Asmah did not gain a place; it seems the men were not ready to receive a woman, even one as distinguished as she. To the Muslimat's chagrin, they were only invited to "join the plenary sessions" where outsiders are welcome. Some of them were also allowed to chair one of the conference's subcommittees. This small breakthrough allowed them to show "historical courage" by presenting the results of research about domestic violence in the *pesantren* world. This extremely sensitive, taboo topic revealed the embarrassing reality that in many families of *pesantren* leaders, violence against women is taken for granted.[51]

This was not the first time that NU provoked its women members into pressing the point of its inconsistency towards their role. Many referred to the question concerning women in positions of public leadership raised at a national NU consultation in Lombok in 1997. All present at that consultation were aware of the political implications: Suharto's daughter Tutut was emerging as a possible replacement for her father. The question at hand was, Can Indonesia have a female president? In spite of vehement objections among certain *kiai*, NU decided that according to the principles of Islam, "'women can hold public positions, provided they have the required capacities . . . at the same time not forgetting their female tasks and nature.'"[52] The consultation resulted in a flood of discussions nationwide. *Kiai* all over were compelled to insert their own precise definition into this statement, ranging from "women in leadership should be under a man, hence can only be vice president," to "the ruling for a man to be head of state only applies to the caliph."[53] Despite the dissenting voices, the original ruling gave room for some optimism concerning the women's chances to win a place in the Executive Council in 1999. Yet this appointment once again proved impossible.

Ultimately, the way the NU conference at Lirboyo decided on women's issues was disappointing for its progressive men and women. It was meant to showcase NU's progressive agenda concerning women, but conservative *kiai* barricaded the road to true representation with the election of the Executive Council for women.

The Muslimat's perplexity increased when in 2000 they were forced to approve a new chair who was not their first choice. Ibu Khofifah explained two years prior to becoming the Muslimat NU national chair that "in principle the Muslimat NU have to obey NU rulings. Everywhere in the NU there is still a high degree of obedience to those at the top. People fear that disagreeing with those in charge, with the *kiai*, can result in being punished by a higher power. In the *pesantren* they call this *kualat*."[54] In the end, the male *kiai* rules with all the powers from this world and the other world.

Kualat are hard to surpass as part and parcel of NU reality. Research, however, is becoming an equally powerful instrument to attract attention and power, as the presentations in the subcommittees showed. Now that the Muslimat NU members have more scholars in their ranks, they have started to study gender issues. Ibu Lily Munir Zakiyah, one of the national chairs, hopes to realize the dream of adding a Women's Study Center. In July 1998 she organized the first official event of this new initiative: a seminar to discuss the rape and murder of dozens of Chinese women during the May riots in Jakarta. In 2000 she guided the Muslimat NU into discussions about the implications for women of the introduction of Shari'ah law and the newly emerging lobby for polygyny. Knowledge has always been a sure way to gain access into closed male circles. The Muslimat NU used to focus on religious knowledge to get behind closed doors; now they combine religion with studies on gender and sexuality, published in the *Jurnal Pemikiran Islam tentang Pemberdayaan Perempuan* (Journal for Islamic Thought about Women's Empowerment). Begun in 2000, it is sent to the nationwide leadership. Knowledge about religious and Fiqh rules is one of the keys to strengthen a woman's position within her private familial surroundings.

Women, the NU Family, and Fiqh

Muslimat NU women are accustomed to ambiguity, and they have a long history of getting past NU rulings they perceive as ambiguous. Adversity in gaining full recognition never implied they were defeated or even inclined to give in to NU wishes. As with the birth control issue, they could always find a way, through a supportive *kiai,* a foundation, or independent studies. The foundation (*yayasan*) provides a sure escape from the control of the dominant organization. What cannot yet be done within the organization can be pursued by setting up a separate foundation, similar to an NGO. For example, when NU refused permission to open a school for nurses in the Muslimat clinics and hospitals, a foundation has taken up the construction of a nursing academy.[55]

NU's internal structure allows seemingly impossible situations to be overcome with the help or interpretation of a powerful *kiai.* What seems conservative can turn modern through reinterpretations of Islamic law and scripture. At times, silence can prove golden for women, as they can benefit from the fact that no NU leader has pronounced pro or contra about a certain topic. Silence, for instance, led to the current prominence of female Islamic judges in Indonesia. When in 1951 the state opened Islamic colleges to train future clergy (what later became IAIN), the minister of religious affairs, Wahid Hasyim, simply did not mention whether or not women were to be allowed into the program for Islamic law. As a result, women began to graduate with degrees in this field, which in most Muslim countries is reserved for men. In 1954 the Muslimat NU officially requested the government to allow female judges in the Muslim courts, arguing, "What does a male judge know about women's suffering in marriage, in the household, and in situations of inheritance?"[56] Their request was granted only in 1977.

When denied formal access to NU forums, women can approach the Forum for Religious Matters (Bahs ul-Masa'il; literally, the examination of questions), which prepares matters to be brought to the attention of the Syuriah. In principle, women can participate in and also set up their own forums. Benefiting from members with a background in Shari'ah studies, the women organize their own discussions about issues such as cloning, test-tube babies, reproductive rights, marriage under the age of sixteen, temporary marriage (*mut'a*), or the plight of women working in prosperous Muslim countries such as Malaysia and Saudi Arabia. The discussions are published among the members and used to prepare suggestions to the national Syuriah at official NU meetings. By making new information available, women can strengthen their case in local platforms. Furthermore, these forums support the activities and publications of the Women's Study Center, a platform for discussions concerning women and the family. The newly acquired information can be used by preachers to help women gain stronger positions in their home environment.

Women and the NU Family

NU's model of the private family is not as clear-cut as the harmonious family advocated by Muhammadiyah. NU has developed a model of the "good family" (*maslaha*), but this model has not been spelled out with rules and guidelines. The implications of this model will be discussed shortly; the relevant observation here is of the great variety of models, all acceptable and related to NU religious standards.

Within the family, women are both bound and free. They strive for emancipation, yet fully obey their husbands. Women take up positions of leadership, yet remain subordinate at home. Questions such as where to draw the line in obeying the husband recur within NU as topics of countless seminars, discussions, and articles. What to do when the husband forbids the wife to go shopping for groceries? How many meals should the children forgo before the wife can leave for the market without her husband's consent? To an outsider, many of the points seem beyond argument, since in Indonesia women dominate the marketplace as sellers and buyers. Women constantly negotiate between giving up some of their freedom for their husband's wishes and taking it back in other ways. Ibu Umroh Mahfudzah's biography provides an example.

> My husband encouraged me to study Islamic law when the children started to grow up. But he did not allow me to accept a position as judge in the Islamic court. In fact, he did not allow me to work in government service, because

in his opinion this would tie me down too much. So I gave up my dream of becoming a judge. Islam teaches that although a woman does have the capacity and chance to work a certain job, her husband can withhold his consent for the sake of the family's harmony. Before he passed away in 1986, however, he advised that if ever I had to choose between a seat in the local or National Parliament, I should go for the national one. When I was invited to join the National Parliament, I accepted after a long discussion with my children.[57]

Ibu Umroh's situation illustrates the NU principle that counsels women to find agreement about their role through discussion (*musyawarah*) that discerns solutions in the interest of the majority.

Discussion is easiest within the confines of the nuclear family, but those outside the domestic sphere must always contain references to Qur'an, Tradition, and Fiqh. This model in NU methodology can go two ways: It can become very rigid when scholars insist on choosing certain opinions or following one school of thought only, but it can also be flexible precisely because of the wealth of resources. An alternative opinion that opens up new forms of interpretation can always be found among the many available.[58]

NU women benefit from this model because in principle everybody is allowed to discuss these matters within their own circles, such as during Forums for Religious Matters. Even when they are not officially involved in decision making, women always have access to the *musyawarah* (discussion). Their education in *pesantren* and IAIN has given women in NU knowledge of the Islamic sources, and educational programs such as those designed by P3M have created growing awareness about gender issues among women leaders. They have gained the clear sense that women must negotiate within a matrix of tradition, theory, ideals, and reality. The teachings of many male *kiai* who generously quote the traditional, gender-biased sources represent the traditional ideal of a good Muslim wife. NU women themselves needed to develop the realistic model about their role and position in Islam.

NU has primarily affirmed that the position of a woman is equal to the man's except for certain matters. As Kiai Abd el-Aziz Mashkuri explained, "Because a woman's abilities are limited, there are certain matters where she cannot be considered equal to a man."[59] This opinion has contributed to the prevailing opinion: "According to the conventional Fiqh teachings, a woman is surely not equal to a man. The *kiai* in the *pesantren* teach girls to be obedient wives."[60] The thorny question remains how to negotiate and interpret phrasings like "tasks" and "certain matters." Many men and women still hold that "men and women are not the same, since the man is considered higher because people assume he is more intelligent."[61]

The Muslimat NU seek to overcome such gender bias. They must wage a battle of words concerning women's role, seeking to reach women who live in a state of confusion because of unrealistic preaching delivered by *kiai* who rely only on gender-biased texts. None of the women who hears those sermons wants to end up in hell as a "disobedient wife." To change these attitudes and remove misconceptions, the Muslimat NU went to the heart of the NU tradition, the Fiqh. Since the *Kitab 'Uqud* is one of the primary texts perpetuating these confusing ideas, they tackled it first.

Reinterpretations

Kitab 'Uqud

The Muslimat NU leader Ibu Ismawati works mostly in villages, where she counsels women who fear they are destined for hell after hearing the sermons of the *kiai*. While in graduate school, she decided to combine practice and scholarship by writing a paper about the *Kitab 'Uqud*. She studied its content and the role it has played in the lives of village women. In her paper, she translates the text into Indonesian and points out its negative influence on the psyche of women in the villages she serves. She especially highlights the traditions used by Shaykh al-Nawawi concerning a woman's behavior in the company of her husband. Ibu Ismawati translates this section, which I refer to in chapter 5, as follows:

> A wife should always feel timid when in the presence of her husband, obey his order, be silent when he speaks, stand up to greet him when he comes and goes, adorn herself at bedtime by using perfumes and washing her mouth, always wear makeup in the husband's presence, but leave it off when he is not around, not harm his honor or possessions when he is not at home, respect his family and friends, when he brings home a meager income still consider this as big, never reject his advances even while sitting on the back of a camel, not fast or go out without his permission. When she trespasses any of the rules mentioned, the angels will curse her until she becomes aware [of her bad behavior], [she must obey these rules] even when her husband is abusive.[62]

The text is a mix of true Islamic injunctions and Shaykh al-Nawawi's personal ideas about a woman's behavior. Although at the time she wrote her paper, Ibu Ismawati did not have access to the vast knowledge the research team FK3 brought together in the new edition, she was aware that several of the Traditions quoted were fabricated or weak.[63] For example, the claim that a wife will be cursed if she refuses to please her husband is based on what some Islamic scholars had already found to be a fabricated Tradition. She pointed out that the text quotes such Traditions to scare women into behaving well. For example, it states that a wife who steals from her husband commits a sin equal that of seventy thousand thieves, an equation outrageously out of proportion.[64] It led Ibu Sinta Nuriyah Abdurrahman Wahid to conclude that women might as well rob a bank, since the punishment for ordinary thieves is less.[65]

Some textual statements are simply puzzling, such as the counsels that a wife should clean the dust of the soles of her husband's feet with her face and lick up blood and pus from his nose. Especially in rural areas, women with little education learn Shaykh Nawawi's ideals about spouses during *pengajian* held by male *kiai*. The authority and charisma of these men seemed to motivate young, unmarried women to follow the teachings almost literally; however, married women recognized that these are impossible ideals. According to Ibu Ismawati, only women with a high school education questioned the text. They considered the large number of Indonesian women who earn the main income that provides for the children's education and helps build the family house.[66]

Ibu Ismawati and others like her are women of action. As their education has made them aware of the influence of tradition and culture on women's lives, they use that education to question and demystify the rules formulated by centuries of male scholars. The Muslimat NU are in fact not leaders in this process; the younger generation initiated these academic exercises of reconstructing religious teachings. Muslimat NU women were more involved at the grassroots level. That level, however, is hardest to reach, and it is where prejudices and misconceptions are kept alive by fathers and mothers who transmit them to their children. Because the academic level is far removed from the little villages, the contribution of the Muslimat NU is vital as the closest contact for women to discuss religious issues. In the home and in private lives, Islamic teachings are the most significant influence on the majority of women, who strive to be virtuous wives and mothers according to the teachings. Here, too, the teachings of *Kitab 'Uqud* can set the stage for a devastating drama: a husband's choice to take a second spouse.

Polygyny and Well-Being

Nobody knows exactly how many NU members have more than one wife. Polygyny is still practiced, especially in circles of *kiai* and preachers. Some women want to become the second or third wife of a charismatic *kiai* to benefit from his knowledge. During the past decade polygyny also has become fashionable in limited upper-class circles. Famous artists or high-placed officials who can afford to provide for two families set this trend. But in most cases, women are forced to accept such a union. In the past, a woman's own brothers, acting on behalf of their family, would threaten to kill her if she chose to shame the family with divorce rather than obeying her husband's wish for a second spouse. Before 1974, a woman did not have the protection of the law, and a husband could leave or take a second spouse at will.[67]

Since the introduction of the marriage law, the first wife must approve of a second spouse, and the marriage must be registered officially. Yet it often happens that men marry in secret without their wife knowing. I met several women who were forced to accept a second spouse or whose husband married in secret. Not registering the marriage also hurts the second wife. Her legal position will be extremely weak, and her children will be considered illegitimate.[68]

As it is ordained in the Qur'an, according to the Muslimat NU, polygyny cannot be forbidden. Each individual NU member is free to practice it. In principle, Muslimat NU cannot challenge it. When asked to comment, their first reaction invariably is, "It is a very private issue. It is between husband and wife." This reality has consequences for the concept of family within NU circles.

NU does not have the concept of the harmonious family that 'Aisyiyah has tried to promote among its members. NU members maintain that the word *sakina* is too static to describe family life. Instead they use the concept of *keluarga maslahah,* the family in well-being. *Maslahah* means "benefit" and is central to the NU philosophy of making decisions that pursue the community's benefit and avoid harm (*mafsadah*).[69] According to the Muslimat leaders, this family model must be interpreted in view of its benefit to the community. It not only means living well within the nuclear family but entails visiting NU members, helping each other, and taking care of the living and the dead.[70] It also includes advice about family planning, children's education, and preventive health care. As for the core members of a family, parents and children, Afif Rifa'i, the head of the Yogyakarta NU program for family welfare (LKKNU), explained:

> Based on the Tradition the family consists of four components. First, the God-fearing wife [*sholehah*]; secondly, children who behave well towards their environment and friends. The third component is the environment: a healthy family creates good relationships with its environment. Finally, the members have to work within the country where they live [they cannot work abroad]. It is a dynamic view of the family because it not only cares for the well-being of oneself but also for others.[71]

In view of the reality, this answer is ambiguous. Only the wife is mentioned as virtuous (*sholehah*). When I asked further about the role of women in this family, Rifa'i left out recent NU *fatwas* about the potential role of women and answered: "Apart from her role as housewife, according to the teachings of the Fiqh, the woman is not allowed to leave the house unless it is for her activities in an organization [such as the Muslimat NU]." Yet the phrasing of this model does not leave room for polygyny, since according to women activists this seldom results in harmonious relationships. In other words, the NU family model does not accomodate polygyny, while the Fiqh teachings used by many *kiai* leave ample room for it.

Polygyny remains a thorny issue, one of the few topics Abdurrahman Wahid has not discussed in his prolific writings about NU. So far he has refrained from commenting on it, as he fears hurting the feelings of many NU members who have more than one spouse.[72] Muslimat NU try to address the reality of multiple spouses with what appear to be preventive measures. Ibu Nuriyah Abdurrahman Wahid dryly remarked: "If you want the men not to commit polygyny, tell the women not to accept the position of second wife."[73] To equip women with the appropriate knowledge to reject such a match, the Muslimat NU organize seminars and Qur'an studies that discuss the historic, social, religious, legal, psychological, and cultural aspects of polygyny. They point to the historical context in which the verses that allow a man to marry up to four spouses were revealed: the battle of Uhud (625 C.E.), which left many women widowed in a budding Muslim community. They discuss the psychological stress for those involved, how it undermines the essence of marriage, and that the requirement to be just to each of the spouses is above mere humans. In their view, only the Prophet could treat his wives with true justice. And they wonder why men follow the Prophet's example in marrying more than one spouse but ignore other aspects of his way of life, such as his asceticism.[74]

Ibu Sinta Nuriyah Abdurrahman Wahid is one of the most ardent fighters against polygyny. She approaches the matter from the angle of basic human rights and psychology. According to her,

> The teaching of just treatment can be interpreted in a material and a spiritual sense. Traditionally, justice here is interpreted in a material sense. If you can provide a house and a car for all your wives, you are okay. But that interpretation ignores other verses in the Qur'an that call for harmonious living also for women. This includes giving love and affection. It is difficult to be fair in dividing one's love, so here a man would be unjust. This injustice creates great suffering for women and can be considered as a form of psychological violence against them. Men say polygamy is to help them not to commit the sin of adul-

tery. But they forget that in this case they commit the sin of making a woman suffer to the point that she sometimes is ready to commit suicide. Apart from that, men who take a second wife cause great harm to their children.[75]

Like Ibu Abdurrahman Wahid, a growing number of women activists try to address the issue head-on. Yet they face an uphill battle. NU itself has regular discussion about polygyny. Ibu Noer Cholida Badrus Sholeh, a female *kiai* who is the head of a *pesantren,* has participated in such discussions during NU national meetings. She managed to enter these forums because of her late husband's presence and observed the following:

> There were those [during the forum] who wanted to throw the door to polygyny wide open. When that came up, I raised my hand and said, "Why do you want to run to polygamy?" The Qur'an states that you can have four wives but that you should refrain from it if you fear you will treat them unjustly. When I study polygamy, I see that people always mention two or three [wives]. But they have to get past wife number one first. We have to take her condition into consideration. If the first wife fits the Islamic criteria—as it says in the Qur'an [2:187], "you are each other's garments"—that means that all wives are like their husband's garments and vice versa. Also, what if the first wife fulfils the criteria of a good spouse, as taught in the Tradition? These are that she always pleases her husband, always fulfils his requests, never trespasses the rules of religion, and guards herself and what belongs to her husband. If she already applies all of these, she should be treated well. Also she deserves love when she already has given birth to offspring. If all these criteria have been fulfilled, surely there is no place for polygamy [in this marriage]. But if a husband is not treated well by his wife, he will not feel compelled to treat her well either.[76]

Ibu Noer Cholida's account seems to put the responsibility to prevent the husband from taking a second wife on the woman. Indeed, women are encouraged to treat their husbands well so that they will not have reason to look for a second spouse. This practice also reflects the Muslimat NU ideals for themselves as women: to be good wives and mothers, most of all obedient. "Always be a good mother, be there for your family."[77] Obedience is even enshrined in the secular-based Indonesian marriage law. It states that the spouses must love and respect each other, but obedience is only required from the wife.[78] Polygyny, it seems, can be warded off by model wives. Of course, it is not so easy in real life. When I asked who could serve as such an ideal, some Muslimat NU mentioned Ibu Mawardi as an example: "She was a total leader, of the Muslimat, of her family and of her children"; "She gave herself to all with total *ikhlas,* devotion." The irony here is that Ibu Mawardi was widowed at a young age and never remarried.

Most Muslimat NU fully agree with all the arguments laid out by Ibu Noer Cholida and Ibu Nuriyah. Yet they are powerless to change the practice in the face of overwhelming male sympathy with those who marry more than one wife. Some reasons are considered urgent: when the first wife remains childless, or when a man falls in love and is in fear of committing adultery. In such cases, the feelings of the first wife and the potential harm done to the family are not considered serious enough to prevent the additional marriage. In the religious domain, the Muslimat NU can do little apart from raising awareness among their members that the first wife should at least claim her rights to justice. Even if Parliament would pass a revised marriage law that forbids polygyny, many men will still appeal to their right to have more than one wife as granted to them by the Islamic law. Some say that such suffering allows women to become models of Islam and practice the virtue of *ikhlas*. However, this virtue of pure devotion, according to the Muslimat NU, should be first practiced towards God, not the husband.

Reinvention and Ikhlas

Ibu Iskander, a *pesantren* leader in East Java, remembers,

> I had to marry so early that I could not become smart [*pinter*]. So I remained stupid. If my father would not have married me off so early, I could have finished a B.A. and been smart. But I stopped worrying about that and kept reading books, any book I could find to increase my knowledge.[79]

This pattern of education is common for NU women in their seventies. Only since the 1980s did a significant number of NU women start to enter general public education. Before that time, many relied on informal education. Yet they were encouraged by individual *kiai,* husbands, or fathers to continue their studies, even if those took place outside of official schools. This reality forms the basis of how older NU women operate within and outside their families. Negotiating obstacles, they find ways out of long-term conditions that to others seem hopeless and in many instances could lead to dire poverty. Molding adversity into an advantage is a talent shared by many Indonesian women, but in my observations it is particularly striking in NU circles. NU women have learned not to give up or give in, and this has become the hallmark and aim of their messages, trying to improve women's self-esteem by insisting on the value of education, even if it is informal. This is not an easy task in Indonesian society, which especially respects diplomas, even for a day-long course. Yet Muslimat NU have many models to refer to. The most famous is Abdurrahman Wahid's mother, Ibu Solichah, who as a highly intelligent child was forbidden to learn to read or write. Encouraged by her husband, Wahid Hasyim, she caught up and became a voracious reader; she is now well known for pushing her children into the pursuit of knowledge.

Encouragement is the key. When one of the leaders of the Muslimat NU in Yogyakarta, Ibu Zaini, wanted to organize a workshop for women in the villages, she could have invited educated speakers from outside. Instead, to show the women that they had the capacity to make a presentation, she wrote the papers herself and convinced the women to present them.[80] Ibu Zaini herself has had the bitter experience of being denied access to a graduate degree. She was accepted for a place in a respected medical school, but her parents decided that her place should go to her brother, who was less intelligent and had failed the entrance exam. Of course, the university did not allow this, and Ibu Zaini lost her opportunity to become a medical doctor. Her passion for mathematics landed her a job as a teacher. She quit when her parents chose her a conservative *kiai* as a husband, whom she married after a brief meeting with him. Accepting the marriage as the will of God and eager to please her parents by accepting their choice, she reinvented herself. She became a beautician, caterer of cakes and cookies, *pesantren* manager, co-chair of the local Muslimat NU, preacher, director of a food co-op, local politician, and graduate student preparing for a master's degree in psychology. She does all these jobs simultaneously while raising her children.

Like women in other Muslim organizations, Muslimat NU are carried by the sense of *ikhlas.* "We sacrifice our possessions and our energy for the work," said Ibu Umroh.[81] "Don't feel desperate if things do not work out."[82] When work is done with *ikhlas,* it implies that it is not a hobby or just for fun. "You do the work for God most High, not expecting worldly rewards but spiritual benefits that remain hidden from the public eye. We are not allowed to show off our work. It is the same principle with *kiai* who are famous for their spirituality or knowledge. They want to stay in the background. Women keep themselves even more away from public recognition."[83] *Ikhlas* in NU circles is not discussed; it is taken for granted as something a good Muslim does. "It is a way of life, you learn it at home."[84]

Ikhlas is a common concept for Islamic believers that in the Javanese context has become stressed and intensified by local philosophies. Taking a closer look at the concept of *ikhlas* in NU circles, several aspects stand out. The stress on hiding one's good deeds, special skills, or knowledge is shaped in the *pesantren,* where education stems from and is still influenced by Islamic mysticism. The mystic is averse to publicizing his or her efforts for God. This does not mean that Muslimat NU hide themselves. Their history shows them to be capable of speaking up and drawing attention when necessary. With the sound of Islam continuously present, one simply continues to work for God without dwelling on the why and how. To NU women, *ikhlas* means strengthening the NU community and solidarity. When you visit the remote areas, you bring food and a mattress to sleep on. You do not shy away from the poor and dirty dwellings but join members whatever their circumstances might be. "It takes a long time to help those at the bottom of society. In these days of globalization we should never forget those who are at the bottom."[85] Finally, part of *ikhlas* is to show initiative and reinvent oneself when necessary. When it serves the benefit of the NU community, women should not remain silent or passive but initiate what they deem necessary. This initiative ranges from taking a course or setting up a support group to visit patients in the hospital to participating in a nationwide preventive health care project sponsored by UNICEF.

Conclusion

Muslimlat NU embody the struggle of many Indonesian Muslim women of the generation that grew up just after independence and during the Suharto era. Their ongoing struggle to improve the condition of women remains firmly rooted within the traditional boundaries of local cultures and Islamic and local hierarchies. They are careful to only challenge the religious authorities openly at times when a critical mass of protesting NU women has been formed, such as in 1938, when they demanded their own organization within NU, or at times of crisis, as during the postwar years when their human resources were needed all over Indonesia.

Although within the framework of NU, individual men and women can rise to positions of great official or unofficial power, women always remain careful to push the boundaries gently so as not to be shut out altogether. Individual initiative is valued, and with the support of powerful *kiai*, women can initiate most of the programs they envision. The issue of birth control is a telling example of the simultaneous simplicity and complexity of this process.

The impact of Muslimat NU activities, whether political, religious, or medical, tends to be powerful yet indirect. Muslimat NU intuitively identified the problems of women within society but often lacked the tools to address those problems in a structural fashion. For example, while quietly working to strenghten women's legal position in Islam, the Muslimat NU seldom openly challenged religious or government ideologies that reduce a woman to a "domestic, dependent, and weak creature that needs protection."[86] Their approach was not simply a sign of inertia; it reflected the vast differences of opinion among Indonesian Muslims as to how liberation and justice for women should be defined.

On their own level of traditionalist Islam, Muslimat NU did try to bring about fundamental changes in teachings about women by challenging the sacrosanct Fiqh texts from the bottom up. This was a potentially effective tactic. Yet on all levels a final seal of approval by the male *kiai* is needed to transform the grassroots efforts into structural programs. The younger generation is keenly aware of that reality and, inspired by initiatives such as those of P3M, has started to apply methodologies that include the top of the hierarchies and the grassroots level. Young NU members, women and men, have run out of patience with the status quo, especially after the repressive Suharto years. They are more vocal in addressing opinions that reduce women's role and capacity and consider these symptomatic of structural roadblocks for women within society. To make their voices heard, they join the Fatayat NU, the IPPNU, or an NU-related NGO, where they apply the skills and beliefs of the older generation while searching for ways to translate their ideas for women's empowerment into efficient initiatives. Their challenge is to combine the old with the new. Fatayat have deep knowledge of the Qur'an and its recitation techniques; they chant praises in Arabic and have a keen sense of NU's role in society. They continue to value local rituals but are less interested in the preaching groups (Majlis Ta'lim). They are as active as the Muslimat NU in politics.

NU women are no longer limited to Muslimat NU but can join whatever subgroup is affiliated with NU. It is not a rigid body where they must accept structures they do not agree with. Many among the younger generation have become more intellectual and are not satisfied with the practical work of the Muslimat NU. They have moved into areas such as publishing and advocating women's reproductive rights. The final chapter will discuss one of those "activist" groups. This diversity is intrinsic to the character of NU and does not disconcert the Muslimat. What matters most to the Muslimat is never to forget those at the bottom of society. Remembering can be translated into political or social action or might simply move a woman to change her personal behavior when hearing the sound of Islam.

7 Post-Tradition: NU Activists

> One of the aspirations of NU members is to build the best of commu-
> nities. Development of critical thought can only take place through the
> creation of such a community and should involve the social, political,
> educational, health, law, and economic areas [of society]. Ideals alone
> are not enough to realize the creation of an outstanding community.
> It needs concern and solidarity paired with valid projects that work
> within society.
> —Yayasan Kesejahteraan Fatayat, *Agenda 1998–2002*

Traditionalisms

The young NU generation practices an amalgam of new trends of thought
and interpretation of Islamic texts that have entered the NU discourse since
the 1970s. These ideas, many of them proposed by Abdurrahman Wahid,
were converted into action when P3M and the think tank Lakpesdam arose
from the folds of established NU leadership. The young generation that
learned from the P3M workshops and studied publications by Lakpesdam
became dissatisfied with the traditional models of leadership and interpretation within NU and spearheaded their own initiatives. Remarkably, some
of the most intense and creative of these NU activities originated in Yogyakarta, where the leaders were interconnected through bonds of friendship, marriage, family, and professional cooperation. The Fatayat, the NU
branch for young women, set up the Yayasan Kesejahteraan Fatayat (Fatayat
Welfare Foundation; YKF) in Yogyakarta in 1991. Young NU men (Geraken
Pemuda Ansor) launched Lembaga Kajian Islam dan Sosial (the Institute
for Islamic and Social Research; LKiS), which has translated and published
numerous pathbreaking books, while women and men learned methods
of activism in the Lembaga Kajian dan Pemgembangan Sumberdaya Manusia (the Institute for Research and Development of Human Resources;
LKPSM), established in 1986.[1]

These activists strive to develop a model of Islam that they call "transformative, egalitarian, and tolerant," each term indicating a particular focus. Following the NU model of *tawasuth* (moderation), *tasamuh* (tolerance), and *tawazun* (balance), these groups develop models and projects that are consistent with basic human rights and promote social justice. Specifically, they aim at strengthening NU's position in Indonesian civil society through activities that range from the critical study of politics, social structures, religion, and local cultures to radio shows that promote awareness about gender issues among villagers.

In its search for alternative visions of Islam, LKiS translated and published works by Islamic thinkers who suggested new frames of reference for Islamic scholarship, including Abdullahi Ahmed an-Na'im, Nasr Hamid Abu Zayd, Farid Esack, Hasan Hanafi, Muhammad Arkoun, and Muhammad Abid al-Jabiri. The list includes multiple works about gender, for example by Asghar Ali Engineer and Fatima Mernissi. Their publications and translations were not limited to Islamic thinkers; influential western philosophers such as Michel Foucault and Jurgen Habermas received ample attention as well. New thoughts were always held against the light of traditionalist Islam and local cultures, thus moderating the influence of Arab culture and excluding extremist thought. This vibrant scene increasingly helps shape a platform where NU and Muhammadiyah minds can meet. For example, the Jakarta-based project called Liberal Islam (Islam Liberal, founded in 2002) has become a clearinghouse where NU and Muhammadiyah activists and intellectuals join together to counter the increasing influence of Islamic extremism. Publications, a Web site, and radio shows that air throughout the archipelago broadcast moderate and liberal voices.[2]

This liberal network of activists and intellectuals has provoked fierce reactions from extremist groups, who accuse it of destroying the faith and law of Islam and allege that it is backed by an amalgam of "Christian," "neo-imperialist," and "Zionist" sources.[3] Liberal Islam disturbs its opponents' belief in the literal meaning of the Qur'an; they also seem upset that the network is not clearly identifiable. "It does not have a definition," writes Adian Husaini.[4] What had seemed clear in the organizations of Muhammadiyah and NU is slowly becoming diffuse, as activists from both sides initiate evolving configurations of cooperation and networks. The reactions also show the strength of the liberal networks. To extremists, this is cause for alarm: now that liberal groups join hands, their strength and potential influence suddenly hits home.

In addition to extremist groups, many conservative NU scholars are not yet ready for radical ideas. Many are reluctant to accept ideas such as those published by Masdar Mas'udi, for example, based on his work in P3M about the reproductive rights of women.[5] A young *kiai* remarked: "It is very difficult to change the standards used in the *pesantren;* we will always have to return to the interpretations of the scholars who went before us."[6]

For the activists, the tradition as taught by NU remains central, but it is developing into an amalgam of discourses that not only rest on religious arguments but include theories on economics, politics, sociology, and culture. They deliberately choose this hybridism and heavily draw upon the ideas of Abdurrahman Wahid, who since the 1970s has advocated the Islamization of every aspect of society to counter the suppressive Suharto regime. Their aim is the formation of a liberal, tolerant type of Islam that "maintains what is beneficial in the historic discourse [*wacana terdahulu*] and takes what is beneficial from the contemporary discourse."[7]

YKF was created in this context to address issues concerning the status and role of women. During the past decade YKF developed into a platform for women's issues, especially those related to the *pesantren.* Following the model of P3M, YKF created programs that advocate women's reproductive rights. In tune with the discourses developing globally about these rights, they widened their scope to include issues such as HIV/AIDS, prostitution, violence against women, divorce, and child marriage. The inspiration for these activities came from the ongoing debate concerning human rights, in particular about the reproductive rights of women as developed by the United Nations. The Beijing conference on women provided strong inspiration as well. The essence of the activities is to align these insights with Islam as taught by NU so that they can be transmitted to the *pesantren* and other educational institutes. The visionary and driving force behind YKF was Mbak Masruchah, its director until 2002. She helped lift YKF to a national model of advocacy for women's rights. YKF's work epitomizes the methods and approaches of the many NU-related initiatives that are budding all over Indonesia. The remainder of this chapter will trace the development of YKF and some of its numerous activities.

Leading Women

Mbak Masruchah

Mbak Masruchah was born into a *pesantren* milieu in a small town on the east coast of Java. Her grandfather, Kiai Sholeh, served as a senior adviser to the national board of NU during its initial years. He set up a *pesantren* in the town of Kudus, married four wives, and was a social activist, especially resisting the Dutch colonizers. Mbak Masruchah's mother was the first-born of Kiai Sholeh's second wife. Former *santri* still visit his grave, and once a year more than 250 family members organize a *khaul* in commemoration of his death. Neither of her parents followed in the footsteps of her grandfather but taught the Qur'an in their spare time and held frequent retreats in the *pesantren* to strengthen the inner life. Mbak Masruchah greatly admires her grandfather, although she strongly opposes polygyny. She considers his marriages in their historical and cultural context: "He took pity on some of his poor *santri* and married them." She sees this as consistent with the initial spirit of marrying more than one spouse: "It was to help the widows and the orphans, not out of sexual desire or physical attraction."[8]

Mbak Masruchah has a solid religious education that she mostly received from her parents. But her probing mind led her into unconventional paths: "My whole childhood I protested, wondering why I was born a woman. I liked to play soccer, to participate in radio plays and contests. I just wanted to experience it all."[9] Naturally, Mbak Masruchah was destined to study in her grandfather's *pesantren*. But the rote learning and unquestioned obedience did not agree with her personality. Her parents insisted on the minimum—short stays in the *pesantren* during Ramadan—and sent her off to Kudus with some money and rice. Upon arrival, she would sell the rice and be back on the next bus. "Life in the *pesantren* simply did not become me," she remembers. The methods of teaching and administration used in the *pesantren* went against her penchant for organization and efficiency. Over time, intolerance for sluggish and unfocused activities within NU became one of the most powerful motivating forces behind her actions and one of the secrets of her accomplishments. Efficient management and focus on vision are becoming the hallmarks of a new NU generation.

Mbak Masruchah's career embodies the rapid changes Indonesia has been going through since the mid 1990s. She held four positions in five years, each a step higher than the previous. She accepted them because each called on her from an urgent need for action vis-à-vis extremist influences. When I first met Mbak Masruchah in 1996, she was the coordinator of the LKPSM projects. Her de facto position was executive director, but the Yogyakarta branch of NU had voted against placing a woman in charge. In 1999 she became director of YKF, and seeing her abilities, in 2002 NU asked her to be the first female director of its Family Welfare Foundation (Lembaga Kemaslahatan Keluarga; LKK). In the summer of 2002, she had great plans for this foundation, projecting to change the ratio of its staff from 25 percent to 60 percent women. She also planned to introduce many of the programs developed by P3M and YKF so that they could become known among a wider audience, such as high school students and village *kiai.* With calls for the application of Shari'ah law increasing, she soon was called upon to join the Koalisi Perempuan Indonesia (Indonesian Women's Coalition) in Jakarta.

With Mbak Masruchah in charge of the Family Welfare Foundation, the cycle of NGO-Ormas activism had come full circle. She started as a member of the Fatayat that founded YKF as an NGO to meet needs that the Fatayat could not address because of its position within the NU hierarchy. Then she moved to the top echelons of NU bureaucracy, equipped with NGO knowledge and methods, and now she applies on a national level the skills honed in the Fatayat and YKF.

The Fatayat remains the constant in the story of Mbak Masruchah's career. Most of the women working at YKF are Fatayat members, and the organizations are interlinked through a continuous flow of ideas and projects. A brief description of their history and ideas is fitting in this context.

The Fatayat NU

The Fatayat NU (Young Women of NU) was founded in February 1950 and became an independent NU-related organization in 1959. As with the Muslimat NU, acceptance did not come easily and was greatly influenced by external political circumstances. As early as 1940, women played an active role in the fifteenth NU congress in Surabaya. Young women questioned why Geraken Pemuda Ansor for young men had started in 1934, yet there was no place for young women, especially not for unmarried women. They complained in a song about their situation:

> Young women of NU prepare yourselves
> To defend your country and religion.
> Because you are the backbone of the older generation
> That has trouble remembering you exist.
> At the right time [you are] always ready [for action]
> Because the homeland needs healthy workers.[10]

After independence, three women—Murthosiyah, Chuzaimah Mansur, and Aminah—set up a branch for young women related to NU in East Java. They called themselves the Triumvirate (Tiga Serangkai). Later analysts admit that political motivations moved NU to encourage this group to join the organization as an official branch. During the 1950s, with the advent of Masyumi (the Islamic political party that initially had NU in its coalition), NU needed members of all age levels to participate in the political process.[11] Originally the Fatayat's activities were limited, and its members were young, between twelve and twenty-five years old. Its activities consisted of leadership training, sports, and religious programs such as organizing Majlis Ta'lim (the NU term for *pengajian,* or preaching gatherings), recitation of the Qur'an, praises of the Prophet (*berzanji*), and Arabic poetry (*qasida*). *Qasida* were often organized on the occasion of feasts, the birth of a child, or the death of a parent.[12] They were called "cultural" (*kebudayaan*) or "Islamic art" (*kesenian*) programs and not only strengthened NU religiously but also provided a powerful tool to promote its political agenda. The goal of the Fatayat was to educate young, devout Muslim women of high morality who were knowledgeable, responsible, and charitable and wanted to spend their energy in service of their religion and nation. Reinforcing NU religious values and interpretations, Fatayat vowed to strive for social justice and prosperity as desired by God.[13]

By the end of the 1970s, the religious programs continued, but the concentration shifted to mother and child care. During gatherings for young women, the Fatayat provided advice and information about birth control, breastfeeding, and health care for babies and toddlers. In 1986 they joined a national UNICEF drive for immunization and diarrhea prevention in young children, training thousands of "motivators" and assisting local religious leaders in raising awareness about measures that could prevent hundreds of infants from dying.[14] It was the first project that used a religious approach to educate mothers about health issues. When the number of Fatayat leaders with a college education increased in the 1980s, the organization started to use strategies for community development, taking as its point of departure the condition of mothers and children.

The organization estimates that its network now comprises around five million women between fifteen and forty years old. Its largest program aims at improving women's health through research, education, counseling, and the establishment of consultation bureaus. Information is still provided through the Majlis Ta'lim. The goal is to create awareness among women about their health and rights and to empower them to take charge of their own bodies.[15] Teachings about nutrition, pregnancy, birth, and hygiene are presented in religious language and include the "modern" topics of reproductive rights and domestic violence. Two verses from the Qur'an inspire the Fatayat to do their work. The first is the verse made especially famous by Muhammadiyah, Surah Ali Imran (3:104): "Let there arise out of you a band of people inviting to all that is good, enjoining what is right, and forbidding what is wrong: they are the ones to attain felicity." The second verse from Surah Luqman (31:14) concerns parents, in particular mentioning the mother: "And We have enjoined on man [to be good] to his parents: in travail upon travail did his mother bear him, and in years twain [two years] was his weaning: [hear the command], Show gratitude to Me and to thy parents: to Me is [thy final] Goal."

Following the 1994 Cairo International Conference of Population and Development and encouraged by the results of the P3M programs, the Fatayat designed active strategies to advocate for women's reproductive rights.[16] They were the first NU women to adopt this focus. What started as a movement from the top in Jakarta slowly transformed into regional action groups that included local physicians, health centers, midwives, village heads, and *kiai*. In combination with several government-driven initiatives, the Fatayat programs were successful in lowering the infant mortality rate. Yet the news from the field did not show the same progress in lowering the rate of women dying in childbirth. Women in rural areas lacked access to basic medical care or did not find transportation to the nearest clinic in emergencies.[17] According to Fatayat leaders, Islamic religion also played a role in the mortality rate. Sometimes women postponed seeking medical assistance, believing that a woman who dies in childbirth meets the same fate as a martyr (*shahid*). In many poor areas the prospect of Paradise seemed more attractive than the daily grind of life. Fatayat leaders found the high maternal mortality rate disturbing, but the organization's mandate did not provide for the building of clinics. Women dying in childbirth seemed particularly unacceptable on the densely populated island of Java that had more health-care facilities than the remote islands. The Fatayat in Yogyakarta had the poverty-stricken area of Gunung Kidul in their backyard and decided that to alleviate this lack of health facilities, building a clinic would fit their foundational beliefs in social justice and human rights. Since this activity had to take place outside the Fatayat organization, YKF was born on December 9, 1991, and the first stone was laid for the clinic.

Creating Justice

The Process

After the birthing clinic was in operation and a center for birth control was added, YKF turned to what its members considered the roots of women's suffering: the fundamental inequality between men and women instilled by religion and culture. The formative event for their activities was the 1997 advice of the NU national conference about the status of women. Based on Surah Al-Ahzab 33:35, the majority of NU leaders pronounced that "women's rights within Islam are equal to men's and that women are not subordinated."[18] With this advice in hand, YKF could aim at reeducating the heart of the NU community, the *pesantren,* where many still studied texts laden with biases against women. YKF set up a system that focused on young *kiai* and *nyai,* addressing the themes of women's reproductive rights and women's political rights. These two themes were considered foundational by YKF; combined, they covered the lack of power for women in the private and public spheres. The rubric of "reproductive rights" covered the issues of early and forced marriage, gender sensitivity, sexuality, family planning, abortion, HIV/AIDS, and violence against women. Following in the footsteps of P3M, the key activity remained the reinterpretation of Fiqh texts.

The inspiration for the workshops came from the P3M model that utilized a variety of educational methods, including academic presentations and role-playing sessions. The goal was to include young men as well as women teachers from the *pesantren* who would address the intellectual formation of the new generation. According to YKF, it was critical that both sexes be involved from the beginning. This approach was new: the P3M meetings had mainly addressed the women leaders from the *pesantren,* and apart from the male presenters, few men were involved in the discussions.

YKF also broadened the context of women's rights and did not shy away from themes that were considered sensitive, even taboo, but fundamental to the human experience, especially those related to women.[19] They stressed that prejudices are deeply rooted within society and do not arise from texts only. The issues were not studied in isolation; rather, the consequences of certain behavior were contextualized. Studying sexual relationships between men and women was not limited to the conventional model of what happens between spouses but also included the topics of abortion and forced child marriage. The discussion about HIV/AIDS and venereal diseases (Penyakit Pemulut Seksual; PMS) could not ignore the issue of prostitution, as both subjects had as a logical point of consideration the dehumanization of those suffering from AIDS or those forced to sell their body for a living. YKF also pointed out that discrimination stemming from religious teachings and societal bias often influences laws produced by the state, harming those who are most in need of protection—women applying for a divorce, for instance, and prostitutes.

Noteworthy in the YKF approach was that the network to broadcast these ideas went far beyond the *pesantren.* Young *kiai* and *nyai* reread religious texts during intensive study sessions under the guidance of established authorities such as Kiai Husein Muhammad and Dr. Nasaruddin Umar. The results of these sessions were then published in YKF's journal *Mitra,* which is sent mainly to *pesantren.* YKF summarized the essential points of their discussions in handy booklets for *kiai* and *nyai* to carry around when giving talks or sermons.[20] Eventually these new findings can gain the status of reinterpreted Fiqh. To underscore their authoritative position within that body of jurisprudence, YKF plans to translate its publications about the "new Fiqh" into Arabic. Mbak Masruchah and her colleagues also reflected on possible ways to spread their ideas and reinterpretations beyond the world of the *pesantren*. As a way to transform the new interpretations on gender into experiments in civil reflection, they arrived at the idea of commissioning the writing of a novel and the production of a radio show.

Nyai and Kiai in Conversation

The reinterpretation of texts in the YKF workshops follows the conventional method of NU scholars: *ijtihad* via *ijma'*; that is, exercising one's own judgment within the frame of communal consensus. The opinions of respected scholars of Islam throughout the ages form the basis for reinterpretations. As usual, NU deliberations take into consideration both the negative and positive arguments. Moreover, in this new format building opinion is no longer the privilege of the *kiai* only, but the *nyai* are involved from the beginning. After the first step of deciding what topic to discuss and how to subdivide it, women and men have their own meetings, so as not to hold each other back when discussing issues that are sensitive and specific to gender. A plenary session held after several weeks of further study provides the platform for women and men to form a communal opinion together. Discussion starts with two or three presentations prepared in advance, after which the main issues are discussed in detail. The proceedings are carefully recorded and made available in published reports. The most influential presentations, with relevant remarks from the participants, make their way into the pocket booklets. To set the stage for other topics, the discussion series started with analysis of the teachings in the *pesantren* about gender and sexuality.

The presentations try to touch on the heart of gender discrimination in Java. For example, for his presentation about gender equality in Islam, the young Kiai Edy Musoffa Izzudin researched the frame of reference in ultraconservative *pesantren* where, in his view, discrimination against women is the norm.[21] After a short introduction about the understanding of gender, he investigates the custom of genital mutilation of women (female circumcision), which does occur in Indonesia, although rarely in an excessively invasive manner. He then discusses the issues of women leading mixed prayers and women in public positions of leadership.

Female circumcision is an interesting issue through which to understand YKF's methodologies, since it is not widely practiced in Indonesia and is almost entirely based on Middle Eastern and African cultural conventions. Kiai Edy begins his analysis with a Hadith that states, "Circumcision is normative [*sunnah*] for men and honorable for women." He describes the difference in procedure between men and women, concluding, "For men it is positive to have their foreskin cut, because apart from diminishing the risk of venereal diseases . . . it increases the man's pleasure and prolongs sexual intercourse. Circumcision for a woman, on the contrary, is extremely negative. It decreases her pleasure, and for some women it can even result in severe psychological trauma."[22] He bases most of his arguments against the practice on the physical and psychological suffering it can entail for women and on the fact that circumcision in men is ultimately beneficial, while for women it has only negative consequences: "It prevents them from having an orgasm and thus should be forbidden." Kiai Edy points out straightforwardly that it not only degrades women but also dehumanizes them by taking away potential pleasure. As he knows that female circumcision is customarily practiced in countries such as Egypt, his argument contains veiled criticism of Middle Eastern influence. He concludes his presentation with a suggestion for a way out: to reread the Fiqh texts that allow the practice, following the NU teachings that discern two value levels in the text of the Qur'an:

> When discussing the religion, there are two levels of values, the fundamental values [*qath'i*] and the instrumental values [*dhanni*]. The fundamental values are universal, for example, that men and women are equal and of the same rank. On that level there is no problem. The problems emerge on the level of instrumental values because of social and cultural differences. . . . This is the level where we have to reinterpret the teachings of Islam, including those concerning women.[23]

He refers to the *dhanni* values as "instrumental," while NU explains them as "contingent upon time and place."[24] The group sees confusion between the two levels as most detrimental to women's issues and appeals to the *pesantren* to reconsider their interpretations that perpetuate bias against women, by men and by society: "The intentions of the Shari'ah are for justice and benefit, but in its technical implementation male bias appears."[25]

The group stressed scrutiny of the concept of *fitnah*, the perceived threat that women are pure temptation. Fear of *fitnah*, in their opinion, is one of the fundamental reasons that women are kept out of positions of leadership. Finally, the team members suggest counteracting biases in the *pesantren* world by training more women specialists of Qur'an interpretation (*tafsir*) and Tradition (Hadith).

The next step in this process is to discuss sexuality and to accept that it not only encompasses the relationship between spouses but also includes other types of relationships, such as homosexual ones. To gain clear understanding of the Islamic concept of the marriage bond, the team led by Nyai Hindun Annisa analyzed the conventional Islamic marriage contract and concluded that, based mostly on teachings of the Hanafi school, the majority of Indonesian Muslim men consider it a contract of ownership (*'aqd al-Tamlik*), similar to that of the possession of slaves, rather than a contract of worship (*'aqd al-Ibadah*) that allows both partners to fulfill their religious obligations while sharing the bond of marriage. When the husband views his wife as his possession, says Nyai Hindun, he sees sexual intercourse as his sole privilege.[26] As we saw in the teachings of the *Kitab 'Uqud,* he expects his wife to be ready for him at all times, while it is frowned upon if she shows her desires. More egalitarian teachings that contradict this view about how to treat one's wife are available, but according to Nyai Hindun, Javanese society has adopted those that assert the man's right while ignoring Traditions that allow equal status to women. Among others, preferred Traditions teach that a woman who does not immediately satisfy her husband's desires but delays them by one hour ends up in the lowest hell.[27] By highlighting alternative interpretations, the team tried to reassess the essence of marriage.

After pointing out the influence of culture on opinions about marital relationships, the team moved on to reconsider human sexual inclination. The presenters quoted studies that show sexual identities to be the product of complex intersections of genetic makeup and social surroundings. Taking this point of view allowed the topic of homosexuality to be included. Sexuality already is among the most contentious topics within NU (and, for that matter, in Indonesian Islamic circles more generally), and mentioning same-sex relationships adds fuel to the fire. Yet taking this step allows for the deconstruction of deep-rooted ideas about a woman's *kodrat* (inborn nature), the content of which is defined by local cultures. The team focused instead on the Qur'an verse that considers men and women as each other's garments (Q. 2:187). Moving away from the concept of a woman's *kodrat* opened up space for the inclusion of the taboo topic of homosexuality. Apart from the ideological aspects, YKF's emphasis on what conventionally has remained unmentioned is urgent in view of the increasing number of AIDS victims.

The issue of abortion is related to ideas about marriage and violence against women. The team's point of departure on this matter is, foremost, sympathy with the victims. Although abortion is a contested topic, the team has adopted the opinions of Islamic scholars, who in principle allow abortion before the fetus is 120 days old. What matters most to the team, however, is not the surgical procedure but the reasons that force women to turn to abortion, especially in cases of rape. The rules of the state here clash with those of the religion, since Indonesian law considers abortion a crime, regardless of the circumstances, while several scholars of Islam cautiously allow it. Denying a woman the option of abortion, to the team, is a great injustice that puts victims of rape in double jeopardy: the rape brings great shame on the victim, and being forced to give birth to the child results in an even more severe stigma. The team has recommended lobbying government agencies to have this part of the law changed.[28]

Another pressing issue of women's reproductive rights is the free choice of one's partner. This concerns both women and men, but for a woman, being forced to marry against her will can ruin her future life, since the man has more freedom to file for divorce or to marry other women. Especially in conservative *pesantren* circles, the right of individual choice is easily disregarded, and many *kiai* give their daughters in marriage to the sons of other *kiai* at the onset of their menstruation. Women who were wedded in this manner told me that they were barely aware of the negotiations going on around them. When girls are told about the upcoming wedding event, their baffled silence is interpreted as acceptance. The marriage law forbids the practice and has set the minimum age at sixteen for women. But since there is no age limit in Islamic law (the Prophet married 'Aisyah when she was only nine), conservative *kiai* choose to ignore the state law. Forcing children to marry partners not of their own choice especially occurs in NU circles as a way to conserve and strengthen bonds between families. Activists consider it a serious breach of a girl's basic human rights—and, for that matter, of a man's as well. A young girl's health is endangered by early childbirth, often she cannot finish her education, and many face early divorce or polygyny.

To YKF, forced and early marriage, divorce, prostitution, HIV/AIDS, and polygyny are interrelated from a woman's point of view. They add to a woman's suffering, and the last three practices make her subject to prejudice and discrimination within society. Their culture stigmatizes divorced women, prostitutes, and those who are HIV-positive, although the situation is seldom the result of their own choice. Divorce and polygyny are not only socially problematic, the team says, but the Islamic law and the Fiqh are entirely on the man's side. Any effort to strengthen the rights of the woman in cases of divorce or polygyny runs the risk of being interpreted as an outright assault on the Fiqh and the Shari'ah. Yet YKF aims to increase awareness and open the discussion, showing how the institutions of state and religion reinforce each other in supporting men over women. To deepen the impact of their findings, YKF teams go beyond theoretical study and humanize the victims of these attitudes. Giving a human face to those stigmatized is part of YKF's mission in creating a community that provides justice not only for the successful. *Mitra* regularly speaks for those who are downtrodden.

In the process of rereading texts and contexts, YKF moves from textual theory to uncovering what has become hidden under Islamic jurisprudence and state law. For example, it stresses that the marital bond is not a contract of possession that grants a man superiority over a woman but a bond that encourages both to be strong believers. YKF reconsiders fixed patterns of thought, such as those concerning sexual orientation, and tries to underscore justice over law by showing the influence of culture and state on what seem to be objective laws. Following the work of NU women for half a century, YKF then introduces the findings to a wider audience, partly through preaching, with the help of the small booklets. But it also thinks carefully about which groups to target and packages the messages accordingly. Apart from publishing its findings, YKF has held writing contests about the issue of gender for high school students, formulated public statements, organized public rallies, and designed a radio show. The following are some examples of how the findings from reinterpreting the Fiqh texts and reunderstanding concepts such as gender are translated into everyday language and activities for a wider audience.

Justice in Print

YKF's journal *Mitra* is the platform that presents the discussions of *nyai* and *kiai* to a larger audience and highlights societal ills that are hard to tackle through the Fiqh. *Mitra* spells out the Qur'anic injunctions, teachings from other sources, and laws of the land, placing them within the context of everyday human suffering. For example, its issue about divorce starts with the stories of two women whose husbands simply vanished one day and the next communication from them was an official letter of divorce.[29] Some women never hear officially that they are divorced. Experts agree that although Indonesian family law allows a woman to ask for divorce, it is strongly influenced by the teachings of Fiqh, and de facto the woman is treated unfairly.[30] *Mitra* shows that if the woman makes it to court at all, she often takes the blame, even if she did not initiate the divorce. For that reason, many women do not dare ask for a divorce, since they know society

will stigmatize them.[31] The state-related agency Badan Penasihat Perkawinan, Perselisihan, dan Perceraian (Body for Counseling [with regards to]
Marriage, Disagreement, and Divorce; BP4) provides the counseling mandatory for couples. It is the same agency where the 'Aisyiyah leader Ibu Uswatun provided her premarital counseling. BP4 has a history of siding with
the husband in divorce cases, especially when the wife initiates the process.
This was the experience of Sulis, a woman who worked at a bank. During her discussion—or altercation, actually—with a BP4 counselor, she was
told: "'A woman is a mother and a Muslim. As a Muslim woman she has to
protect her status and her innate womanly nature [*kodrat*].'" With this "nature" the counselor implied that Sulis should not work outside the house
because it is her natural disposition to raise her children and attend to her
husband. She was stunned and answered: "'But I earned the family income
long before my husband started to work, and now I get the blame!'"[32] The
family law dovetails with religious teachings and local culture, as it basically
continues to see a woman only in her capacity as a housewife. From the
religious point of view, YKF cannot change the principles of Islamic law,
but it can link up with those who advocate that the civil law be changed in
favor of women.

In fact, unofficial revision of the marriage law started shortly after YFK
and other activist groups started to dissect the parts of the law that are unfa-
vorable to women. Musdah Mulia, the former Fatayat leader who moved to
the position of Muslimat NU secretary, has a high position in the Ministry
of Religion. With ten scholars of Islam, she made a draft revision that has
new wordings such as: "Monogamy is the basis of marriage," and, "The status, rights, and duties of husband and wife are equal, both within the household and in society." About the concept of disobedience (*nuzyuz*), which
normally in Islamic law only women can commit, the draft says: "Both husband and wife are disobedient if they do not fulfill their duties."[33]

This draft stresses the equality of women and men. If even half of it is accepted as law, it will be a showcase scenario of bringing a topic up from the
grassroots level. Using the rereadings of the holy texts as practiced by the
Fatayat, YKF, and other activist groups such as Rahima and Rifka Annisa,
the team could make a new draft that stresses equality between men and
women and protects the rights and well-being of both.

While most aspects of the marriage procedure are enshrined in national
law, oddly there are no official laws concerning prostitution. The law only
provides for trading of women.[34] Yet prostitutes are regularly rounded up by
the police and put in jail for several days. Activists argue that prostitution is
actually an economic problem. Poverty forces parents in the large metropol-

itan centers to send their daughters to the streets. Prostitution, says Wardah Hafidz, an activist for street children and the poorest of the poor, is often the last resort for a divorcee to feed her children; women who are destitute with little education have few other options.[35] With the threat of AIDS their predicament has doubled, since many clients refuse to use condoms.

Discussion of prostitution, homosexuality, and HIV/AIDS creates moral panic in society as it calls up the deep-rooted fear of *zina* (fornication) that inspires the defense of early marriage and polygyny. According to the judgment of society, these aberrations embody all the evils and excesses of sexual debauchery and fallen morality that marriage safeguards a man against. YKF shows that prostitution is the flipside of the same morality. Men can vanish and get a divorce, but that leaves their wives and children destitute, perhaps with few alternatives to prostitution. With growing urbanization, family networks have weakened and can no longer absorb those left behind. Society's judgment is swift and harsh as it denies its own role and responsibility in the plight of women. The activists hold up a mirror that reveals an ugly picture, warning: "The government should provide for more alternatives such as work opportunities and education." They point out that no educated, skilled person will choose the alternative of prostitution lightly. "Only those who have no choice become prostitutes," repeats Wardah Hafidz.[36]

Women Wearing the Turban

Mitra has a limited but carefully targeted audience. Its factual language attracts those interested in the specific issues it discusses. To attract other readers, YKF decided that ideas about women's reproductive rights needed to be publicized through fiction and poetry, as, according to Mbak Masruchah, they can help "bring about change in our times."[37] They found the ideal collaborator in Abidah el Khalieqy, who offered the rare combination of being *pesantren*-educated and a woman poet. After carefully studying the ideas advocated by YKF, she wrote the novel *Perempuan Berkalung Sorban* (Women wearing the turban).[38] The turban in Indonesia symbolizes male Islamic knowledge, leadership, and charisma. The novel is not a masterpiece of prose, but the presentation of its subject from the woman's point of view makes it a unique work. It documents all forms of bias and prejudice a woman can experience, starting from the time she is a small girl.

The story opens with Nisa (Arabic for "woman"), the eight-year-old daughter of a conservative *kiai*, playing with her brother Rizal near the pond behind their *pesantren*. While trying to disturb a bird that is laying eggs, Rizal falls into the water. His soaking-wet appearance does not please the father, who questions the children about what they have been up to. When they reply that they were looking for Lek Khudhori, who could teach them horse riding, the father chastises Nisa: "'Did your mother never tell you that only your brothers can teach you how to ride horses? And you know why? Because you are a girl, Nisa. It is not proper for a girl to ride on a horse, [going to] remote places, loafing around the field, even as far as the pond. Shameful! You are already that big and still so stupid!!'" (6). Since the brothers don't ride horses, and Lek Khudhori is not allowed to teach her, Nisa will not be able to learn that skill.

This incident sets the stage for Nisa's future. Throughout the book she questions her position as a woman. Why can't she ride a horse without her brothers, when several heroines from Islamic history rode into battle on horseback? Why must she get up early to cook breakfast while her brothers can sleep late? Why do her father and brothers have "men's" discussions and fall silent when she enters the room? "'You make me think I am a ghost,'" she complains (9). The Indonesian language teacher drills the class: "'Father goes to the office. Mother cooks in the kitchen. Budi plays in the courtyard. Ani washes the dishes'" (10). Nisa disturbs him with her questions: "'But what about mothers who go to the office?'" All he can answer is that those working mothers might be widowed or divorced. Wherever Nisa turns she is confronted with fixed ideas about her *kodrat;* it seems that her inborn nature entails certain well-defined duties. Her father, mother, and teacher all confirm that men and women have their own specific responsibilities. Nisa must learn how to run the household so her future will be secure. When she asks her mother if that means that her brothers' future is not secure because they stay in bed, her mother answers, "They have to study" (21). But Nisa wants to study too!

Her mother also teaches Nisa that a woman represents a seduction (*godaan*) "like a watermelon or a pear in the desert," and "[w]hen she steps out of the house, seventy devils march in line to accompany her." She can trick the devils by covering her body so that they think she is a pillow and not a human being (45). Ustadz Ali, the Qur'an teacher, tells the girls in her class, "'The Qur'an mentions that a woman is a human being, but that her brain and religion are not perfect [*kurang sempurna*]'" (70). He asserts, "'It is proven that men have more brain than women'" (71). For the Ustadz, the proof lies in the many teachings of the Shari'ah and Fiqh that give women only half a share of the inheritance, do not grant her the right to divorce or to practice polygyny, and render her impure several days of the month (72).

Lek Khudhori, who studies in the progressive *pesantren* of Gontor, is the only one who provides a counterpoint. He teaches Nisa about the many women heroes in Indonesian history and takes her questions seriously. With him she discusses the many inconsistent views about women she finds in the Tradition and the Fiqh. "For women everything is the opposite of men," Nisa concludes (75). She observes that the entire *Kitab 'Uqud* not once mentions a woman's rights, only her duties (80). Lek Khudhori teaches her that Fiqh is created by man, not by God (169).

When Nisa gets her first period, her life darkens: now she will regularly be impure, and during that time she cannot pray or fulfill other religious duties. Around the same time, Lek Khudhori leaves to do his graduate studies in Egypt, and Samsudin comes on the scene. The son of a respected *kiai*, he is considered the perfect match for Nisa. She suddenly learns that she will have to live with him. Since she was not present when the wedding contract was signed, she does not understand that he now is her husband (161). He is a brute who beats her and plays violent sex games. When he gets bored he takes a second wife, whose presence jeopardizes Nisa's education, since the lazy and irresponsible Samsudin does not have a job (his family helps out) and now stops giving her money for tuition. He breaks all the Islamic laws that prescribe providing for a woman and a strict division of means in case of multiple wives. Nisa reveals none of this to her parents because of the deep shame she would bring on them. All along, Nisa's heart longs for Lek Khudhori, who writes her poetic letters but has neither a prestigious *kiai* for a father nor any wealth.

When Lek Khudhori finally returns from Cairo, Nisa confides in him and with his help tells her parents about the violent character of her husband. The family decides to demand a divorce, and after the obligatory waiting period (*'idda*) has passed, Nisa is allowed to marry Lek Khudhori. Here the picture turns. He does all the right things; he knows the Qur'anic teachings and their interpretation. The author does not miss a chance to describe explicitly how the relationship between husband and wife ought to be. She discusses the issues of birth control and how to have good sex that pleases the woman. She implies that a good husband encourages his wife to go to college. In the end, the reinterpretation of the Fiqh is complete; all the traditionally sanctioned actions that suppressed women in the beginning of the story get turned around. The reader's sympathy is drawn to Nisa and Lek Khudhori, while Samsudin personifies mindless and brutal male dominance, a sinner who habitually trespasses the laws of Islam. At the end of the book, he even intentionally crashes his car into Lek Khudhori (305). At the university, Nisa gets acquainted with a center for battered women and realizes that she used to be one of them without knowing it. Now the harsh facts of wrongdoing and prejudice against women have a human face. Readers of this novel must become aware of these kinds of domestic and institutional violence; no longer can women or men invoke the excuse of ignorance when they are maltreated or when they maltreat others.

This novel is a powerful tool to build awareness about the universal human rights of women and the rights granted to them by the Qur'an. Books, however, are still relatively expensive for many Indonesians, and in rural areas, where ideas are often transmitted orally, there is not yet a strong reading culture. To reach that important segment of Indonesia's population, YKF created a radio show that serialized the novel's plot in 100 fifteen-minute segments. To get feedback and to learn what listeners thought of the program, YKF sent free t-shirts to all who provided their opinion. The reactions were overwhelmingly positive. Listeners expressed their sense of enlightenment about these issues, some even suggesting that YKF rewrite the material into children's books. But occasional voices complained that "the man is too much ignored in these plays."[39]

Overall, women and men were generally pleased and eager to learn about the new ideas they listened to weekly. Especially when they realized the heavy influence of men on the jurisprudence about women, listeners could accept that certain changes were necessary in understanding these texts. What was most important to them was that through the division of the Qur'anic teachings into fundamental values (*qath'i*) and instrumental values (*dhanni*), the core of the Islamic faith and rules remained unquestioned.

This division, however, left the discussion of polygyny in limbo. Because it was considered to belong to the fundamental values described in the Qur'an, the Muslimat NU refrained from challenging the practice openly. After the fall of the Suharto regime, the climate has changed. Suddenly, extremist groups are competing for headlines to spread an Arab-inspired brand of Islam. As in other parts of the Muslim world, Indonesian activists could observe that the symbols and values concerning women are often at the center of the battle over who interprets Islam.[40] For some it seems that the introduction of Shari'ah law is equivalent to women veiling and promoting the practice of polygyny. Discussing polygyny was on YKF's agenda, but following the old pattern, they moved cautiously. This changed when a staunch defender with four wives, Puspo Wardoyo, chose Yogyakarta as the base to promote his ideas. His intense lobbying became the proverbial last straw. It was perceived as so offensive that Mbak Masruchah, as the local chair of a national interreligious women's network called the Pro-Women Alliance, unleashed a countermovement. She chose April 21, 2002, as the day to launch the offensive. That was the Day of Kartini, the Javanese princess who inspired the emancipation of millions of Indonesian women yet herself had been a victim of polygyny.

Polygyny

The Last Taboo

In a 2002 issue of *Mitra*, the contentious topic of polygyny is raised in the gentlest and most careful of ways: "Not all the women's movements take a serious interest in the issue of polygyny," the YKF staff writes, but "when the Pro-Women Alliance in Yogyakarta questioned the matter within the framework of justice, many aspects of this issue came up that need attention. The bottom line is that polygyny is justified with arguments from culture and religion, thus it needs to be reinvestigated."[41] Carefully stepping where few have dared to go, the YKF article set up the intellectual framework to guide the discussions.

The opening article of *Mitra*'s special issue compares the views on polygyny within various religions, especially referring to the other religions of Abraham—Judaism and Christianity—since, according to the author of the article, "There is not one verse in the New Testament that forbids the practice of polygyny."[42] Through reference to the other religions, the article forwards the claim that local culture, more than religion, has contributed to this practice. *Mitra* then presents a long list of arguments that build a case against polygyny. At the time of the Prophet Muhammad, polygyny as taught in the Qur'an (Surah al-Nisa' 4:3, 129) was an improvement, since it reduced the number of women to four rather than dozens and gave the women in such an arrangement the protection of law. While in its own cultural moment the practice of polygyny benefited women, throughout its long history and even today examples of excesses and negative influences abound. But, the YKF writer insists, "a woman's fate will not change as long as the issue of polygyny is not immediately tackled with deep knowledge concerning every aspect."[43] The author points out that many other countries have been forced to come to terms with the issue. For example, he states that even though their holy scriptures allowed the practice, in 1950 the national conference of Jewish rabbis in Israel issued a decree that forbade polygyny.

After citing examples from other religions, the argument turns to Islam. Great religious scholars like Muhammad Abduh (d. 1905) preached that Islam only reluctantly allows polygyny. Others teach that, with changes, over time it has become an obsolete custom: widows and orphans who were desolate in the early days of Islam now are cared for differently. Having said this, YKF stresses that the practice of polygyny concerns a moral dilemma related to justice as ordained by the Qur'an.[44] Although the Qur'an allows a man to marry more than one wife, Surah al-Nisa' 4:129 states: "You are never able to do justice between wives, even if it is your ardent desire."

Then *Mitra* provides the example of Ibu Shinto Nabila, a *nyai* from Magelang, who provides a view from the inner world of those who lived in a marriage with more than one wife. When her own mother grew older, her father married a second wife. This brought her great heartache. On his deathbed, however, he confessed his regret and urged his children never to enter a polygynous marriage: "Copy all of my good works and deeds, but don't follow my example in marrying more than one wife."[45] Polygyny, activists agree, often brings families to financial ruin and renders all the offspring dissatisfied.

In the new, more open social climate, however, the proponents of polygyny have become fierce and persistent. They argue that it prevents *zina* (fornication) and that it helps solve the demographic problem of imbalance between men and women. YKF activists wonder if it will become polyandry, if the balance shifts and men outnumber women.[46] Defenders of polygyny flood the market with booklets bearing titles such as *Guidance to Polygyny and Its Superiority, Why Does Islam Allow Polygyny? The Wisdom of the Prophet's Marriages, Polygyny, Not for Kiai and the Rich Only,* and *The Secret of Muslim Polygyny: The Experience of Puspo Wardoyo and His Four Wives.*[47] These booklets argue that the first wife does not need to give her permission, that a good wife cannot but accept her husband's desire to take another spouse, that it helps all those involved—first wife, husband, second, third, and perhaps fourth wife—to grow in their faith, and that, of course, the husband will be fair and just to all of his wives.

The Wardoyo case reflects how the Islamic scene has changed since the demise of the Suharto regime, as it provides real-life examples of extremists' reasoning and shows a great disregard of the marriage law. Wardoyo's monograph recounts that he married his second wife without consent of the first and that the union with the fourth wife initially was an illegal *kawin sirri* (secret marriage).[48] From the Islamic point of view, Wardoyo considers his marital state "a challenge" that should not be "feared" but "answered." "This is *jihad*," he explains.[49] When his wives vie for his attention, he calls it a "competition in goodness" (*fastabiqul khairat*). But by the third and fourth marriages, he has botched the Qur'anic injunction to treat them all the same, meaning that they should all have a house of the same size. The fact that some of his wives have smaller dwellings than the others he explains as a good deed, "guiding them away from a materialist orientation in life."[50] Hidden in this lofty, religious language is the real reason for having four wives: "It is not that I no longer loved my wife, but after gaining wealth my desire to have another woman became increasingly stronger."[51]

Wardoyo's case serves as an example of the second agenda many of the proponents of polygyny hold: they compete for the power to dominate the Indonesian Islamic teachings and discourse. This quest for power can be economic or political. Wardoyo's two published testimonies about the superiority of marrying more than one wife both open with a description of his restaurants that specialize in chicken and serve dishes such as "es poligami" (polygyny ice cream), a combination of different flavors. When interviewed in the press, he does not miss an opportunity to advertise not only his business but that his wives are co-workers in the various restaurants he runs in several Indonesian cities. He does not eat the chicken himself but follows a special diet of "fish, vegetables, and several kilos of fresh fruit to guard his vitality."[52]

The antagonists to polygyny could not detect the Islamic injunction of justice in Wardoyo's self-aggrandizement and felt moved to bring their struggle out in the open: "Nobody ever contended with him. He paid the media to put him on the front page and he made us angry with his TV appearances, calling upon the youth to take more than one wife not to fall into *zina*."[53] The activists decided to hold a media rally against polygyny. A petition against it, signed by thousands of dignitaries and public figures, was brought to the local Parliament on April 21, 2002. This was followed by daily communications to the press, resulting in two weeks' media coverage of antipolygyny opinions. At the same time, the activists wrote Friday sermons explaining their ideas about Islam, justice, and polygyny, sending these all around Java so that the message would resound in mosques every Friday.

Amid the cacophony of arguments thrown around in this arena, the activists' message remained clear and simple: How can you pretend to treat all of your wives with justice, while only God can practice true justice? Justice in such a marriage is only measured in the material aspects, not in terms of love and affection. Spiritual life cannot be seen apart from the material side, since humans consist of both. Because feelings are so difficult to measure, the activists say, the scholars of Islam limited their discussions about polygyny to the material side and left out the crucial aspect of emotions and psychological suffering.

YKF does not really bring a new message, for the groundwork has already been laid by others. Few activists, however, have dared to come out into the open and face the opponent head-on. The effect was immediate; the discussion about polygyny was out in the open, and the taboo factor weakened. Awareness is a powerful tool, and many activists realized that the strong lobby for polygyny did not emerge out of religious sentiments only but that many nonreligious factors played even greater roles. The activists faced the confrontation and gave Wardoyo a chance to defend himself during a public seminar.

He appeared in the company of his religious guides, who had condoned his desire for multiple wives. The activists were impressed neither by them nor by their opinions. Coming out of the meeting, they concluded: "Those leaders provided weak explanations, were very conservative, and lacked a sound methodology."[54] This occasion also indicates how the social and political climate has changed since the Suharto regime suppressed extremist and activist voices. Activists all over Indonesia have been transformed on the inside as well. They have become more confident of the importance of their message and no longer shy away from spreading it. After all, the welfare of women is at stake.

Boldness to Reinterpret Islam for Women

YKF and similar initiatives started penniless and grew on the enthusiasm for change, the desire to rid society of some of its evils. The lack of money was never considered an obstacle. Most leaders came from families where the parents had to scrape to get by. For them, as for all other leaders in this book, *ikhlas* was more valuable than the quest for material wealth. When YKF needed new office space, the absence of funds was so dire that the staff held a special prayer marathon that lasted throughout the night until the call for morning prayers. No immediate result was visible. Several months later, YKF's initiatives caught the attention of the Ford Foundation in Jakarta. Realizing the potential of this group, the foundation has endowed its activities ever since. The Ford money has been put to good use; small but irreversible changes are becoming visible in society. During a YKF meeting on August 7, 2002, Nyai Hibatun Wafira, from a rural *pesantren* near the town of Magelang, reported: "The *kiai* in Magelang are not yet on the academic level [to study the new discourse and reinterpret the texts]. But we organize meetings to familiarize them with the books published by YKF. Now we notice that in Magelang the discourse about gender is spreading. The local Department for Religious Affairs [Depag] already has adopted the YKF books to inform the Muslims there."

The sociologist Manuel Castells considers groups like YKF as operating from an "identity for resistance." According to him, it forms the basis from which to build new communes or communities and leads to true change in society.[55] In Melucci's view, these groups are "conflict oriented"; they want change and nothing less. YKF activists and those engaged in other groups all over Indonesia started their resistance on a personal level, working against the manifold forces in their social and religious environment that obstructed them from finding their full potential. In the process of developing methods and strategies that aimed for changes acceptable to the NU establishment, they broadened their vision to society at large. They perceived the NU hierarchy to be suffocating progress by denying women religious power and perpetuating archaic teachings from the *pesantren*. They saw the NU situation reflected in a society where negative views on women dominated the media, and stifling hierarchies of power allowed only those with the right connections to climb socially. They also took issue with the destructive corruption found in all layers of economic life. NU had been a community of resistance during most of the Suharto era. It officially withdrew from politics in 1984 and had been one of the few organizations the regime had failed to control. Now, resisting the undesirable in society, including some NU attitudes, the new activists take inspiration from this original model in reconstructing identities, focusing on shared humanity, and promoting fundamental justice as taught by the Qur'an.

In their quest for what they see to be human nature, they do not mince words. Instead of imagining how the harmonious marriage should be or how a bond with more than one spouse can fare, they look at reality. In journals such as *Syir'ah,* initiated by NU followers to counter extremist discourse, they tell it as it is: many young people, including those from the *pesantren,* have sex before marriage.[56] To the new activists, coming to terms with that reality is more important than chasing idealistic discourses that are unrealizable for average Indonesians.

YKF and similar initiatives, such as LKiS, Rahima, and LKPSM, have become the new face of Indonesia's Islamic and social structure. Ingrained hierarchical patterns of age and position are disregarded by this generation; they give preference instead to creativity, vision, capacity, and talent. YKF, for example, tries to find the truly talented by giving them a day-long test that shows their skills and vision for the work. Those who excel are hired. In the Indonesian context, this can lead to awkward situations. For example, once the selection included a young teacher at the *pesantren* and her student. Both women were extremely bright, but the student had the better vision for future developments and won the job. The teacher had equally great potential and was offered a job of lower rank. The fact that the older woman was willing to accept the lesser job illustrates true generosity and dedication and a flexible sense of hierarchy that will be necessary in the new social context.

The discussions about gender and human rights challenge *kiai* and extremists alike. *Kiai* are challenged to contribute to these discussions, and even those holding ultraconservative opinions are compelled to write and disseminate them. The result is a flood of Indonesian literature about Islam and gender. The ultimate challenge in the hierarchy of knowledge is that now the new Fiqh advices are formed by men *and* women. In fact, they bring Fiqh back to its original level of fallible human interpretation. To strengthen the validity of their opinions, the activists plan to translate them into sacrosanct Arabic. Reflecting on the reasons projects of legal reform have failed, for example in the Middle East, John Bowen concludes on a positive note: "Changing fiqh through fiqh may hold out the greatest promise."[57]

A new religious discourse is developing within Indonesian traditionalist Islam that is concerned with the plight of "little" people, those who conventionally lack real power or are rendered powerless by religion, culture, or society. Many of Indonesia's women belong in this category, finding themselves crushed between biased interpretations of Islamic law, governmental rules, and societal prejudices. Within this context, the adage "knowledge is power" is pregnant with true meaning: Islamic learning raised up advocates for women's rights, advocates who have needed to develop a new discourse. That discourse, solidly rooted within the Islamic tradition, not only promotes real justice for women but encourages them to raise their own voices in achieving it.

Conclusion

> What is needed now is to apply to society and disseminate Islamic teachings that advocate emancipation, without causing anxiety among men that their dominance might be threatened or that these new applications will lead to moral decadence in the society. The concrete solution we offer is to embark on theologically grounded deconstruction of the Islamic teachings, especially of those that pertain to the relationship between men and women.
> —Siti Musdah Mulia

The women introduced in this book have to be extraordinarily creative in juggling the many demands emerging from their families, careers, society, and the Muslim organizations they belong to. I came to know them at a time when the Suharto regime was still firmly in power. Indonesian society and trends in Islamic discourse have since undergone seismic changes. The Islamic resurgence has resulted in increased awareness of religious identity. For some Muslims this means increased practices of personal piety. For others it means an emphasis on the rules of the Islamic law: they may wish to follow the law more closely, or in some cases to enforce it more rigorously. The Islamization of Indonesian society also led to competition in and thus fragmentation of religious authority.[1] Some follow the leader of their small extremist group; others listen to the opinions of religious authorities on TV; and many others try to escape confusion by staying within the framework of organizations such as Muhammadiyah and NU.

The newly opened climate led to the rise of Islamist groups of young, aggressive, well-organized men whose mindset was not necessarily friendly to women. They had been around before 1998, but most women regarded them with mild amusement for their sometimes exotic outfits of turbans and long tunics. Some of their ideas they found irritating and some entertaining, or both. For example, the brother of a female professor at IAIN one day, upon destroying his drum set after the leader of his sect made him aware of its inherent evil, announced to his sister that she was on her way to hell because she was teaching Islamic studies to mixed audiences. These groups also influenced setbacks in the ranks of even the most progressive activists. Now some practiced polygyny more openly, and a leading male authority who had paved the way for the reinterpretation of women's Fiqh took a second wife.

As these Arab/Wahhabi-influenced groups clamored to introduce the holy law of Shari'ah, their ideas resonated among a disillusioned people suffering from economic crisis. In a 2002 survey, 71 percent of Indonesians supported the application of Shari'ah in some form or another.[2] Many thought that there was no other remedy for the ills of society but a law directly revealed by God. Certain districts have begun to experiment with its implementation; for example, in Padang Panjang a rule was issued requiring women to be indoors after 10:00 P.M. Few knew what applying the Shari'ah would mean in real life, so women and minorities became the first subjects of its application.

As this change began, women leaders all over Indonesia refocused and increased their workload once again. They had to study how the introduction of these laws affected women's real lives and to deal with the repercussions of certain practices that increased under the umbrella of extremist trends, especially secret and temporary marriages. This was a new form of globalization, brought in not on the winds from the West but by pervasive forces from the worldwide Muslim community that benefited from Saudi affluence.

Fragmentation of opinion was also the result of a new political climate. Democracy, a word that used to be whispered in fear, is now in active progress. People can freely elect parties, leaders and, since 2004, even the president. For women leaders, free elections meant a tidal wave of new work. NU and Muhammadiyah women plunged into programs to create awareness among women voters who, influenced by patterns long established by religion and the Suharto regime, had habitually followed their husband's choice.

From the other side of the globe came forces challenging the economic, moral, and social order. Indonesia's Muslims felt besieged by materialism and sensed the beginning of the corruption of their values and morals. The specter of *zina* especially frightened Muslims, as it eroded not only their morality but also the fabric of their religious lives. *Zina*, as they saw it, was the source of pornography and increased prostitution. In a moral panic, some Muslims took refuge in what they considered a safeguard from *zina*: polygyny, illegal temporary marriages (*mut'a*), and secret marriages (*kawin sirri*). Needless to say, none of these practices boded well for women.

Not all these winds of change brought disruptive elements; they also carried new ideas about gender, human rights, and democratic rights. Women leaders joined international networks focusing on these benefits; they also learned about innovative economic models that could help overcome poverty.

The women's organizations had to negotiate and bring together layers of complex realities to achieve their ultimate goal of making Islam a vital and empowering force for women. While the women had gained higher public profiles with a woman president and female politicians, professors, and judges, in the personal sphere they still had to insist on their liberties, in some instances even defending them from pointed attack. This shifting paradox of public and private acceptance pairs with another: inconsistencies about women's role and position within their own organizations and among the women themselves. At the same NU meeting in Lombok (1997) where the *kiai* agreed that there was no limit to women's sphere or scope of work, they discussed the question of whether a woman has the right to refuse her husband, even if she is tired or sick. This discussion was inspired by the issues of domestic violence and marital rape, which young activists had started to bring up. While the activists wanted to move violations against women into the area of detestable or punishable acts, the *kiai* firmly stayed within the frame of the four schools that consider a woman's refusal to be grounds for punishment or divorce. Their prevailing opinion was that a woman can never refuse. Ibu Fatma, in her unique way, expressed the reality that a man comes first:

> If a *kiai* dies, his wife receives guests for three days and offers up to 450 dishes with food to the guests. She will repeat this to commemorate his passing after forty, one hundred, and one thousand days. Then she will organize a *khaul* every year. She will probably never remarry and will continue to devote her life to him. When she dies, he probably will remarry within one week.[3]

Even though the picture clearly has two sides, women themselves see dramatic improvements in their condition. When I asked what were the most significant changes the organizations had helped bring about, many answered that women gained the right to learn, they have the right to work, and they enjoy more protection in case of a divorce. Together, these rights have strengthened the position of women, not only in the public but also in the private sphere.

Through their example, the women leaders have brought home the point that participation in religious discourse can change women's destiny. The teachings from the Qur'an in combination with the jurisprudence are at the heart of women's issues. The jurisprudence consists of rules of law that do not change; what changes is the interpretation and application of these rules. It is the responsibility of religious leaders to adapt the jurisprudence to the needs of society and guard it from becoming a tool for certain causes or interests.[4] This is what Khaled Abu Fadl refers to when he warns against the danger of authority becoming authoritarian. Women can greatly benefit from fragmentation of authority, especially if they manage to appropriate a share of their own. Indonesian women leaders of Islam have developed a range of methodologies to participate in the process of interpretation. Often, before women brought the issues that needed to be changed to the attention of the religious leaders—the *kiai* in NU and the Majlis Tarjih in Muhammadiyah—they had started to apply their own reinterpretations of texts in their daily work. From this experience, they learned the importance of informal and formal participation in the process of shaping religious discourse. Abdurrahman Wahid confirms that this sometimes means facing disagreements or upsetting the social order:

> Women have to be part of shaping attitudes within society. In my opinion, this depends on the women themselves. Do they just want to go with the flow or make their own decisions?[5]

To help women "make their own decisions" was among the first ideals of the women's organizations: to make every woman a leader who could empower other women to be self-sufficient and independent. "Women should respect themselves," repeated Ibu Asmah Sjachruni.[6] This study has only begun to open the many rich and diverse understandings of that concept: respect.

For several decades, the organizations worked to empower women while operating through layers of discourse and activities, always stressing women's potential as agents of change who deserve respect. Focusing on religious discourse, the women created what Leila Ahmed has described as an understanding and application of Islam that is congenial to women.[7] As members of Muhammadiyah and NU, the women leaders worked to convert the unofficial discourse into official interpretations of the Islamic sources.

Miriam Cooke has pointed out that "[w]omen's protest against male hegemony in the production of official Islamic knowledge is not new. Already at the end of the nineteenth century, women like the Lebanese Zaynab al-Fawwaz were framing feminist demands and arguments within Islamic norms and values in order to deflect criticism that their inspirations and goals were Western."[8] Middle Eastern writer-activists from the past include

Huda Sha'rawi from Egypt and Zaynab al-Fawwaz from Lebanon. In the present, the writings of Fatima Mernissi from Morocco and the Egyptian Nawal el-Sa'adawi have gained worldwide fame. But we are hard-pressed to cite such examples in Indonesia, where the exercise of reinterpretation was written in the Indonesian language, undertaken communally, and cannot be found in a single book. We can find the results of these efforts in journals such as *Suara Aisyiyah,* in reports of conferences, and in individual articles. The production of Indonesian books about the status of women in Islam and the reconstruction of the gender discourse began only with the rise of NGOs. Other Muslim countries can claim a few women writers and name their books, but often these writers meet with great resistance in their own countries. In fact, most are "secular feminists" in the sense that they fight against injustices arising from Islamic teachings. Islam serves them as a tool to justify their work; however, Islam is not the soul of their work. In quite a different dynamic, Indonesia has produced thousands of anonymous women whose rereadings of Islamic discourse emerged from their deep commitment to Islam. They applied these readings within their sphere of society, guaranteeing that the thinking transcended academic discourse alone.

Ultimately, this reality identifies the goal of the women leaders and believers: to translate Islam into a vital force for women and to create awareness of the power of the individual. Their entire way of life testifies to the sincerity of their commitment to achieving this goal. While working as professionals, wives, and mothers, they frame the rhythms of their desires and work, spiritual, economic, and social needs within the structures of the Islamic holy scriptures.

To translate Islam into a vital force for women, the women leaders use methods that depend on NU or Muhammadiyah interpretations of Islam and agree with their organization's level of progressiveness. The result is an evolving reconstruction of the role of women in Islam. Clearly, women participate in this process. That they do not yet take this participation for granted was apparent in the question of a participant from Sumatra during a 1997 meeting about Islam and women's reproductive rights:

> Does a woman have the right to interpret the revelation of God? I ask this because especially in the IAIN in North Sumatra, many female professors exercise *ijtihad* by themselves. As a result, sometimes they even reject the advances of their husbands when they don't want them.[9]

Her question refers to the opinion that women must be available for their husbands at all times. What if reading the holy texts while using their own judgment (*ijtihad*) results in an opposite conclusion to that of the men? At the same time, the women referred to are professors at the Islamic State Institute for Higher Learning, the highest body in their field. This clash of opinion can indeed result in an "authority panic" in the minds of their hearers.

The women leaders are most deeply connected by their absolute dedication (*ikhlas*) and their desire to reinvent society by modeling the right morals and values (*akhlak*). The interpretation of these morals and values is always evolving. We should not forget the past: during the 1960s, "right morals and values" meant eliminating women whose views about emancipation were not framed within the Islamic teachings. As the great majority of Indonesian Muslims now takes the injunctions of Islam more seriously than ever before, the interpretation ranges much more widely, touching on issues such as obedience to one's husband and compassion for homosexuals. The bottom line is that these women want to be virtuous in creative ways. They use the media to rebuke Puspo Wardoyo on TV; they air radio shows that explain complex matters of Islamic law tailored to the audience; and, inspired by the Grameen bank, they give women loans to advance small businesses.

Reinterpretative discourses have thus become the driving power to improve women's lives on the local level in situations where not all have entered the era of globalization. True to the character of the organizations, the types of activities continually have evolved in reply to grassroots needs, emerging like a colorful garden filled with varieties of plants and flowers. The neverending debates about polygyny reflect this diversity. 'Aisyiyah has never advocated its prohibition but tries to prevent it by convincing men and women to apply the guidelines of their harmonious family program. NA women's opinions range from those who would accept such a marriage (for example, young women in some of the reformist *pesantren*) to those who reject it outright. Muslimat NU has almost said that they would favor abolishing it, while the majority of the Fatayat decidedly reject it. It remains an acceptable practice in *pesantren* circles, but Siti Musdah Mulia, now a Muslimat NU leader but recently a Fatayat leader, led a team that produced a draft revision of the marriage law that declares the bond of marriage to be monogamous, period.

The women leaders, each according to her own philosophies, continue to create new discourses and methodologies to bring home their message. These processes encompass strengthening the traditional clinics as well as pursuing wild ideas that sometimes fall flat. Here are some of the most recent examples:

Observing a trend of booming national tourism, 'Aisyiyah tried to in-fuse Islamic religion into the program of those visiting Buddhist shrines such as Borobudur and came up with a program called "'Aisyiyah Religious Tourism" (Wisata Religius 'Aisyiyah). A colorful flyer announces that apart from visits to the tourist sites, visitors can add to the value of their stay by learning the Qur'an and the basics of the Islamic faith. NA is organizing discussions about women and the media aiming to counter the portrayal of women as sex objects in the media and to prevent women from imitating these stereotypes.[10] In the *pesantren,* Ibu Fatma tried to set a new trend at the wedding of her daughter by suggesting a women-only reception so that they could "relax and enjoy the occasion." The idea was shot down by the extended family. Lily Zakiyah Munir is trying to bring the work of the Muslimat NU Women's Study Center into the public discourse by joining the new forum of the Liberal Islam group. By 2000, she had earned a graduate degree in medical anthropology from the University of Amsterdam, and since then she has started to discuss Muslimat ideas about women and Islam more publicly in her writing and through the forum. Mbak Masrucha moved to Jakarta, where the ideas developed in YKF are reaching a wider national audience. When Ibu Fatma finally gave in to her family's pressure to remarry, she chose a husband twenty years her junior because "his head would not be stuffed with old-fashioned ideas about women."

Although they were more successful at the level of textual interpretations and local activities, the women leaders also made inroads on the third level of national and local politics. Since Indonesia's independence they had been active as politicians, but in the Suharto era they again faced repression. While working on laws to improve the conditions for female workers, they could do little about the prevailing government discourse about women as appendages of the husbands. With husbands in civil service, they also could not avoid being co-opted into Dharma Wanita, the organization designed to keep civil servants in line by controlling their wives. Yet their exclusion from the larger voice was not entirely negative. By mere participation, women prepared themselves for the post-Suharto era. Also, they polished political skills appropriate not only for public politics but any type of leadership position.

All the women in Muhammadiyah and NU work toward an Indonesian society where justice for all will be the reality. They know that immense progress toward their goal has already been made, but many challenges remain. They are confident that, although God allows those challenges they face, He wants justice to be accomplished. The women accept the fact that often human beings complicate acts of justice, but this knowledge will not deter them from acting to bring about change in a communal way. The road

Notes

Introduction

1. Chapter 2 provides an extensive discussion of the teachings of Muhammadiyah and NU and how their characteristics have shaped their views about the position and rights of women in Islam.

2. The four schools are Shafi'ite, Maliki, Hanafi, and Hanbali. These schools were formed to systematize the various local interpretations of the legal teachings of the Qur'an and Sunnah. The schools reflect opinions from the geographical regions where they developed (such as Medinah and Iraq). The Shafi'ite school is predominant in Indonesia. The schools vary in their understanding of details of the law. For example, in a divorce, custody of young children belongs to the mother. Schools differ concerning the duration of the mother's custody in the case of girls: Shafi'i until the age of seven, Hanafi until puberty, while the Maliki school teaches that a girl can remain in her mother's custody until she marries. Although the outcomes differ, these opinions nearly overlap, as girls married much younger at the time these decisions were made than they do today.

3. See the introduction to Ong and Peletz, *Bewitching Women;* and Mohanty, Russo, and Torres, *Third World Women.*

4. Abou El Fadl, *Speaking in God's Name,* 18. Abou El Fadl bases his distinction between "an authority" and "in authority" on Friedman, "On the Concept."

5. See "Leader," *American Heritage College Dictionary,* 4th ed. (Boston: Houghton Mifflin, 2002).

6. For how much input reformist women were allowed in the early discussions about gender and marriage, see White, "Reformist Islam."

7. Other verses in the Qur'an that explicitly or implicitly mention equality between men and women include: Q. 9:71,72, Q. 3:195, Q. 4:124, Q. 16:97, Q. 40:40 and Q. 48:5–6. All quotations from and references to the Qur'an are from Abdullah, *Meanings of the Illustrious Qur'an.*

8. See Badran, "Islamic Feminism"; Badran, "Feminism and the Qur'an"; and van Doorn-Harder, "Gender and Islam."

9. Karam, *Women, Islamisms, and the State.*

10. See Webb, *Windows of Faith,* for writings by Hasan, al-Hibri, and Wadud. Amina Wadud's *Qur'an and Woman* was among the first systematic studies by a woman that offered rereadings of Qur'anic teachings on women. For a similar study, see Barlas, *"Believing Women."*

11. Mir-Hosseini, *Islam and Gender.*

12. Abou El Fadl, *Speaking in God's Name.*

13. See Wheeler, *Applying the Canon,* 9.

14. Ali, "Progressive Muslims," 169.

15. Wahid, "Principles of Pesantren Education," 202.

16. Mahfudh, *Nuansa Fiqh Sosial.*

17. Masud, Messick, and Powers, "Muftis, Fatwas, and Islamic Legal Interpretation," 4.

18. Author's interview with Amin Abdullah, Yogyakarta, June 11, 2004.

19. Susan Blackburn points out the importance of the term *kemadjoean* in "Why Send Girls to School?"

20. See also the essays in Jeffrey and Basu, *Girls' Schooling.*

21. Gaffney, *Prophet's Pulpit,* 34–36.

22. Mir-Hosseini, *Islam and Gender,* 87.

23. Mir-Hosseini, "Debating Women."

24. I rely here on the theories of Antonio Gramsci about the interplay of coercion and consent in relations and struggles of power, and on the observations of Michel Foucault about power, the production of knowledge, and the roles of individuals in resisting structures of power and constructing discourses about contested issues. See Gramsci, *Selections;* Foucault, *Power/Knowledge;* Foucault, *History of Sexuality;* and Foucault, *Discipline and Punish.*

25. Abou El Fadl, *Speaking in God's Name,* chap. 2.

26. White, "Reformist Islam," 4.

27. "Congresnummer: Congres Perompoean Indonesia jang Pertama," Report of the First Indonesian Women's Congress, December 22–25, 1929.

28. See, for example, Vreede de Stuers, *Indonesian Woman,* 91, 104–8.

29. Saskia Wieringa has done extensive work on Gerwani, addressing the question of how this large movement could have been wiped away, not only from earth but also from Indonesian memory. See Wieringa, *Sexual Politics;* and Wieringa, "Perfumed Nightmare."

30. White, "Reformist Islam," 365.

31. Pimpinan Pusat 'Aisyiyah, *Kepemimpinan Wanita.* For the 1998 discussion about whether or not a woman could be allowed to be president according to Islamic teachings, see van Doorn-Harder, "Indonesian Islamic Debate."

32. Shahidian, *Women in Iran,* 13.

33. Melluci, *Challenging Codes,* 22–23.

34. The title of the forum was "Membuka Cakrawala Baru Peran Perempuan NU" (Opening new horizons concerning the role of NU women). It was held on November 10, 1999.

35. The references to each of these topics are myriad. For a good overview of such issues in Egypt, see Zuhur, "Mixed Impact."

36. For an excellent summary of how the Indonesian marriage law affects the legal position of women, see Bowen, *Islam, Law, and Equality,* 200–24.

37. Robinson, "Women," 238–39.

38. Mulia, *Keadilan dan Kesetaraan,* 111.

39. Ibid., 115.

40. Hasyim, *Menakar "Harga" Perempuan,* 82. See also Katjasungkana, "Kedudukan Wanita."

41. There are too many books about these topics to list. Examples produced by IAIN Yogyakarta include PSW IAIN Yogyakarta, *Islam dan Konstruksi Seksualitas;* and Sodik, *Teelah Ulang Wacana Seksualitas.* For a useful bibliography, see YKF, *Anotasi 50 Buku.* Homosexuality is discussed in articles in *Musāwa. Jurnal Studi Gender dan Islam* (Musawa, the journal for studies about gender and Islam).

42. YKF in Yogyakarta, for example, published small booklets about gender and issues specific to NU. All are edited by Mukhotib MD and were published by YKF in 2002: *KB dan Aborsi* (Birth control and abortion); *Ketika Pesantren Membincang Gender* (When the pesantren discusses gender); *Menghapus Poligami, Mewujudkan Keadilan* (Doing away with polygyny, generating justice); *Seksualitas: Menggugat Konstruksi Islam* (Sexuality: Criticizing the construction of Islam); *Menghapus Perkawinan Anak; Menolak Ijbar* (Abolishing child marriage; rejecting forced marriage); *Menolak Mut'ah dan Sirri; Memberdayakan Perempuan* (Rejecting the temporary and [illegal] secret marriage; empowering women); *HIV/AIDS: Pesantren Bilang Bukan Kutukan* (HIV/AIDS: *Pesantren* say it is not a curse).

43. See, for example, Feillard and Marcoes, "Female Circumcision"; Office of the Senior Coordinator for International Women's Issues, "Indonesia"; and "In the Cut."

44. See, for example, Mukhotib MD, *Menolak Mut'ah.* Nancy Smith-Hefner has done extensive research about sexual behavior among young adults. See Smith-Hefner, "New Romance"; and Smith-Hefner, "More Sex in the City."

45. Mir-Hosseini proposes this model in *Islam and Gender,* 3. The second level she discerns is produced by local and national political ideologies. Examples for Indonesia in this context are the influence of Dutch colonialism on gender issues and, more recently, the power exercised by the Indonesian state under the governance of Suharto as it tried to "domesticate" women's activities.

46. Hefner and Horvatich, *Islam in an Era of Nation-States;* Hefner, *Civil Islam;* Bowen, *Muslims through Discourse;* and Bowen, *Islam, Law, and Equality.*

47. White, "Reformist Islam," is a notable exception. Nancy Smith-Hefner has recently addressed how a stronger commitment to Islam is influencing patterns of dating and sexuality among Indonesian Muslim university students.

48. Blackwood, *Webs of Power;* Hadler, "Places Like Home"; Whalley, "Virtuous Women."

49. Brenner, *Domestication of Desire;* Jellinek, *Life of a Jakarta Street Trader;* Jellinek, *Wheel of Fortune;* Murray, *No Money, No Honey;* Sullivan, *Masters and Managers;* Wolf, *Factory Daughter.*

50. Ibu Asmah Sjachruni, the former Muslimat NU chair, was raised in Kalimantan and moved to Java in her early twenties. Ibu Elyda Djazman, the former chair of 'Aisyiyah, was born and raised in Sumatra and came to Java as the young bride of a prominent Muhammadiyah official.

51. These works helped me understand how ideas about "modernity" and "feminism" were shaped within the competing forces of the colonial period. Many studies focused on education, labor practices, polygyny, suffrage, and dress. See, for example, Taylor, *Women Creating Indonesia;* Locher-Scholten and Niehof, *Indonesian Women in Focus;* and Locher-Scholten, *Women and the Colonial State.*

52. Bunnell, "Community Participation," 191.

53. Sears, *Fantasizing the Feminine;* Wieringa, *Sexual Politics.*

54. Lies Marcoes-Natsir and Andree Feillard have written most about women and Islam in Indonesia. See Feillard, "Indonesia's Emerging Muslim Feminism"; Marcoes-Natsir, "Female Preacher as Mediator"; Marcoes-Natsir, "Antara Amal dan Tuntunan"; and Marcoes-Natsir, "Muslim Female Preacher." The only two articles about 'Aisyiyah before those by Marcoes-Natsir were by Ibu Baroroh Baried, national chair of 'Aisyiyah from 1965 through 1985. See Baried, "Islam and the Modernization"; and Baried, "Konsep Wanita dalam Islam." In 2000, Ro'fah wrote a master's thesis on 'Aisyiyah at McGill University. The Muslimat NU leader Lily Zakiyah Munir published an article on marital sexuality, and several of her respondents were Muslimat NU leaders from the older generation. See Munir, "'He Is Your Garment.'" Blackburn, *Love, Sex, and Power,* includes two essays addressing women, Islam, and power: Machali, "Women and the Concept of Power," and Robinson, "Gender, Islam, and Culture."

55. See Sears, "Fragile Identities."

56. This overview is partly based on Ricklefs, *History of Modern Indonesia.*

57. For the role of Islam in developing early Indonesian nationalism, see Laffan, *Islamic Nationhood.*

58. Vreede de Stuers, *Indonesian Woman,* 67.

59. The original Presidential Decision (no. 1) in 1965 recognized Confucianism as well. During the Orde Baru it lost this position, but in 1999, President Abdurrahman Wahid granted it its original status again.

60. Ricklefs, *History of Modern Indonesia,* 197. For an extensive discussion of this topic, see Boland, *Struggle of Islam.*

Chapter 1: Discussing Islam, Discussing Gender

1. Five-yearly meeting of the Muslimat NU, Jakarta, June 26, 1998.

2. Featherstone and Lash, *Global Modernities,* 3. See also Osborne, *Politics of Time,* 13–14.

3. Robert W. Hefner gives the numbers of mosques for East Java as 15,574 in 1973 and 25,655 in 1990, and for Central Java as 15,685 in 1980 and 28,748 in 1992 (*Civil Islam,* 121).

4. Opening speech at the five-yearly meeting of the Muslimat NU, Jakarta, June 24, 1998.

5. Coté, *Letters from Kartini.*

6. Shiraishi, *Age in Motion.*

7. Blackburn, "Why Send Girls to School?" In 1904, Dewi Sartica (1884–1947) opened the first school for girls in Bandung.

8. For the other national and local associations, see Vreede de Stuers, *Indonesian Woman,* 61–65.

9. Blumberger, *Nationalistische Beweging,* 377.

10. See, for example, *Soeara 'Aisjijah* 12 (December 1932): 328; and Pimpinan Pusat 'Aisyiyah, *Sikap terhadap Loearan,* 4–6.

11. Blumberger, *Nationalistische Beweging,* 376–77.

12. For more about Indonesian women during this period, see Lucas and Cribb, "Women's Roles."

13. Nakamura, *Crescent Arises,* 103–5.

14. Religious movements in particular felt threatened by the Communist party, especially when it was at the height of its power by 1965. 'Aisyiyah and Muslimat NU, together with Christian women's groups, actively worked to eradicate Gerwani. At the time it was brought down, it was Indonesia's largest women's movement with around 1.5 million members drawn from the lower middle classes and the working classes. See Wieringa, "Perfumed Nightmare."

15. Marcoes-Natsir, "Antara Amal dan Tuntunan," 154.

16. Ibid., 158.

17. Van Bruinesssen, *Kitab Kuning,* 178. See chapter 5 of this book for more information about the *pesantren.*

18. This position is similar to Miriam Cooke's definition of Islamic feminism. See Cooke, *Women Claim Islam,* 59–62.

19. Van Doorn-Harder, "Muslim Feminist."

20. Kuntowijoyo, *Muslim Tanpa Masjid,* 127–34.

21. Among others, the NGO Rahima has started to research this trend, and the Ford Foundation sponsors a report written by authors such as the Muslimat NU leader Lily Munir.

22. See Atkinson and Errington, *Power and Difference.* Barbara Ramusack makes the same observation in an article that surveys the writing about women in Southeast Asia. She especially compares the position of women in Southeast Asia to that of women in South Asia. Ramusack, "Women in Southeast Asia," 99.

23. Ong and Peletz, *Bewitching Women, Pious Men,* 1.

24. Ramusack, "Women in Southeast Asia," 88.

25. See Van Bruinessen, *Kitab Kuning,* 179–81.

26. Abdel-Fattah, "Besieged Rights," 34. The term "classic patriarchy" is from Kandiyoti, "Islam and Patriarchy," 31.

27. Ahmed, *Women and Gender in Islam,* 174.

28. Badran, "Islamic Feminism"; Karam, "Women, Islamisms, and State."

29. Karam, *Women, Islamisms and the State.*

30. Ibid., 12.

31. Author's interview with Professor Amna Nosseir, Cairo, May 25, 2003.

32. Hafez, *Terms of Empowerment,* 99.

33. Magnis-Suseno, *Javanese Ethics and World-view,* 68. Robert R. Jay made the same observation in the 1950s. See Jay, *Javanese Villagers.* Andrew Beatty discusses "an egali-

tarian ethos and customary rules limiting status competition." Beatty, *Varieties of Java-nese Religion,* 149.

34. Munir, "'He Is Your Garment,'" 196.

35. Magnis-Suseno, *Javanese Ethics and World-view,* 67–68.

36. Keeler, "Speaking of Gender in Java," 131.

37. See, for example, Sen, *Indonesian Cinema;* Hellwig, *In the Shadow of Change;* and Berman, *Speaking through the Silence.*

38. Hatley, "Nation, 'Tradition,' and Constructions of the Feminine," 91.

39. Several authors have commented on this reality. For a summary of the different arguments, see Berman, *Speaking through the Silence,* chap. 2.

40. *Nafsu* derives from the Arabic *nafs,* which has a wide meaning ranging from "soul" or "personal identity" to "desire" or even "appetite." In the Javanese and Malay context *nafsu* is identified with "passion," "desire," or "lust." *Akal* comes for the Arabic *'aql* (reason, rationality, intelligence). See Mernissi, *Women's Rebellion and Islamic Memory,* 118; Brenner, "Why Women Rule the Roost"; and Peletz, "Neither Reasonable nor Responsible," 88–95.

41. Mernissi, *Women's Rebellion and Islamic Memory,* 118.

42. Brenner, "Why Women Rule the Roost."

43. Ibid., 33–37; Berman, *Speaking through the Silence,* 42; and Peletz, "Neither Reasonable nor Responsible," 95–100.

44. Author's interview with Bapak Djili, brother of Ibu Badilah Zuber, first chair of 'Aisyiyah, Yogyakarta, July 1, 1997.

45. *Java Pos,* October 21, 1998.

46. Hefner, "Muslim Civil Society?" 310.

47. Lev, "On the Other Hand?" 198.

48. Suryakusuma, "State and Sexuality," 98.

49. Brenner, *Domestication of Desire,* 227.

50. Foucault calls these techniques of resistance and adaptation to reach one's goal "technologies of the self." See Foucault, "Technologies of the Self."

51. Mohanty, "Cartographies of Struggle," 38–39.

52. Robinson, "Women," 247.

53. Ibid., 238.

54. Sears, *Fantasizing the Feminine.*

55. Quoted in Hooker, "Expression," 264.

56. Researchers of development issues consider the word "empowerment" to be problematic and ambiguous, as it is based on western ideas of individualism. It would take half a chapter to properly describe what the notion means in Indonesia. I have adopted the word, since many Indonesian activists use it frequently. See Oxaal and Baden, "Gender and Empowerment."

57. Author's interview with Bapak Hendro, Muhammadiyah headquarters, Yogyakarta, May 22, 1998.

58. Author's interview with Bakhtiar Effendi, Jakarta, June 9, 2004.

59. See, for example Ro'fah, "Study of 'Aisyiyah," esp. the section entitled "The Birth of Indonesian Feminism: Another Challenge for 'Aisyiyah?"

60. Quoted in Feillard, "Emerging Muslim Feminism," 103.
61. Author's interview with Franz Magnis Suseno, Jakarta, August 1, 2002.

Chapter 2: Competing in Goodness

1. See Liddle, "Media Dakwah Scripturalism," 332; and Suryadinata, *Elections and Politics in Indonesia.*
2. The terms *santri* and *abangan* were first used by Dutch colonial observers of Indonesian Islam and became famous through Geertz's *Religion of Java.* He discerned three religious modes among Javanese Muslims: *santri* (who tried to follow the teachings of normative Islam), *priyayi* (upper-class aristocracy and bureaucrats), and *abangan* (who were oriented towards pre-Islamic indigenous beliefs and practices). This model was useful to start the discussion about the various groups, but the model has shifted towards a division between those who take the Islamic faith seriously and try to practice it daily and those who practice summarily, incorporating local beliefs and practices. This model is based on Koentjaraningrat, *Javanese Culture.*
3. Hamka, *Tasauf Moderen,* 2–7. For background and contemporary movements within Tasawwuf in Indonesia, see Howel, "Sufism and the Indonesian Islamic Revival."
4. The Egyptian Heba Raouf is a widely known representative of Muslims who want to establish a Shariʿah-run state but believe that women's public roles are as important as men's. For more information about Heba Raouf and similar women, see Karam, *Women, Islamisms, and the State.*
5. There are several publications about the topic. To get an impression of the scholars and Islamic leaders involved in this network, see Assyaukanie, *Wajah Liberal Islam di Indonesia.*
6. *Abangan* means "red" and was also used to identify Communists.
7. See Hefner, "Islamization and Democratization"; Hefner, *Civil Islam;* and Liddle, "Islamic Turn in Indonesia."
8. Feillard, "Indonesia's Emerging Muslim Feminism," 95–98.
9. For example, the NU vision for the 1999–2004 period was "Creating a just and democratic society on the basis of the Islamic doctrine" (Nadhlatul Ulama brochure, undated, 28). Robert W. Hefner's book *Civil Islam* has illustrated how Indonesian Muslims are creating a civil and democratic society based on religion.
10. Since 2000, several articles have tried to explain the advent and background of the Islamist groups in Indonesia: see Van Bruinessen, "Genealogies of Islamic Radicalism"; and Hasan, "Faith and Politics." Elizabeth Collins traces the lineages of the different groups. The following section is based on Collins, "*Dakwah* and Democracy."
11. Hefner, "Islamization and Democratization," 90.
12. Hefner, "Indonesian Islam at the Crossroads," 17–18.
13. See, for example, the research done by the NU-related NGO Rahima in its publication *Swara Rahima: Media Islam untuk Hak-Hak Perempuan.* The Ford Foundation has commissioned a report by several Muslim intellectuals to research the Islamist trends within Indonesian society.
14. Karam, *Women, Islamisms, and the State,* 203–4.
15. Ibid., 204.

16. The other votes went to the parties set up by NU (PKB: 12.6 percent in 1999; 7.3 percent in 2004) and Muhammadiyah's former chair, Amien Rais (PAN: 7.4 percent in 1999; 6.4 percent in 2004). These are open parties, which means that they have Muslim and non-Muslim members. Only three parties were solely based on Islamic ideology: PPP (11.7 percent in 1999; 8.1 percent in 2004), Development Unity party (PBB), the Crescent Star party (1.9 percent in 1999; 2.6 percent in 2004), and PK, the Justice party (1.7 percent in 1999; 7.3 percent as the Prosperous Justice Party [PKS] in 2004). Combined, they received over 15 percent. PBB and PK are the most conservative or extremist of the three; together they gained 3.6 percent in 1999 and 9.9 percent in 2004.

17. Author's interview with Agus Purnomo, Yogyakarta, June 12, 2004.

18. Qodir, "Wacana Keagamaan Generasi Muda," 116.

19. See, for example, *Jakarta Post*, January 22, 2003, where Amien Rais, the former national chair of Muhammadiyah, declares that the discussion about whether or not to implement Shari'ah is over.

20. Suryadinata, *Elections and Politics,* 173.

21. See Feillard, "Potensi Perubahan Relasi Gender."

22. "Selama ini kita berdakwa dengan politik, sekarang ini kita berpolitik dengan dakwah." See also Van Bruinessen, "New Perspectives on Southeast Asian Islam?" 531.

23. Hefner, "Islamizing Java?" 533–34.

24. This section is based on an official interview I had with Dr. Yati, September 2, 1998, and from social and professional encounters with her when she was our pediatrician. I met Ibu Utaryo several times during 1998–99; I recorded an extensive interview with her on August 6, 1999.

25. Muhammadiyah and NU are not the only traditionalist or modernist organizations in Indonesia; there are several similar local groupings spread out over the archipelago.

26. Alfian, *Muhammadiyah;* Federspiel, "Muhammadijah"; Nakamura, *Crescent Arises;* Peacock, *Purifying the Faith.* Indonesian studies by Muhammadiyah members are too numerous to mention. Some are repetitive, and few actually analyze the organization. One of the best is Jainuri, "Formation of the Muhammadiyah Ideology." Several studies address the character of Muhammadiyah. See, for example, Rais, *Pendidikan Muhammadiyah dan Perubahan Sosial;* and Rais, *Visi dan Misi Muhammadiyah.* Examples from the younger generation include Nashir, "Perilaku Politik Elit Muhammadiyah"; and Saleh, *Modern Trends in Islamic Theological Discourses.*

27. Sally Jane White's thesis represents a refreshing new start of studies on Muhammadiyah. See White, "Reformist Islam." For an example of Indonesian work on Muhammadiyah, see Jainuri, "Formation of the Muhammadiyah Ideology."

28. Barton and Fealy, *Nahdlatul Ulama.* See also Van Bruinessen, *Kitab Kuning;* Van Bruinessen, *NU;* Fealy, "Ulama and Politics"; and Feillard, *Islam et l'armée.*

29. These titles are too numerous to mention. Some examples include Haidar, *Nahdlatul Ulama dan Islam;* Amin, *NU dan Ijtihad Politik Kenegaraannya;* and Wahid et al., *Dinamika NU.*

30. Armstrong, *Battle for God,* xvi.

31. Stowasser, "Women's Issues in Modern Islamic Thought," 8.

32. Van Bruinessen, "Traditions for the Future," 165. The observations in this paragraph are based on Van Bruinessen's brilliant analysis of "tradition" in NU contexts.

33. Ibid., 166.

34. Ibid., 167.

35. NU does accept the schools of Hanafi, Maliki, and Hanbali as well, yet its theological concepts are mostly based on the Al-Shafi'i school.

36. Rofiq et al., *Pelajaran KeNuan,* 4.

37. Ibid., 6

38. Van Bruinessen, *NU,* 212.

39. Author's interview with Chamamah Suratno, vice president of 'Aisyiyah, Yogyakarta, June 24, 1998.

40. See Murata and Chittick, *Vision of Islam,* 30–34.

41. See Hobsbawm and Ranger, *Invention of Tradition.*

42. For more about this practice, see Van Doorn-Harder and de Jong, "Pilgrimage to Tembayat"; and Fox, "Ziarah Visits to the Tombs."

43. For an extensive description of Javanese rituals surrounding death, see Geertz, *Religion of Java,* chap. 6. For Gayo, see Bowen, *Muslims through Discourse,* esp. chap. 11.

44. See Bowen, *Muslims through Discourse,* 262–72.

45. Pijper, *Fragmenta Islamica,* 178–80.

46. My understanding of the Muhammadiyah ideology has benefitted immensely from Jainuri, "Formation of the Muhammadiyah Ideology."

47. Qur'an study led by Ibu Broto Mulyono, June 19, 1998.

48. Beatty, *Varieties of Javanese Religion,* 178.

49. See also Jainuri, "Formation of the Muhammadiyah Ideology," 127.

50. Rais, *Visi dan Misi Muhammadiyah,* 47.

51. Jainuri, "Formation of Muhammadiyah Ideology," 79.

52. Pimpinan Pusat 'Aisyiyah, 12.

53. Ozment, *Protestants,* 6. See also Wertheim, *Indonesian Society in Transition,* 209–12.

54. The concept of *tauhid sosial* is especially prevalent in the teachings of Amien Rais and derives from the Marxist-Islamist theories of the Iranian intellectual Ali Shari'ati (1933–77). See Kepel, *Jihad,* 52–60.

55. Jainuri, "Formation of Muhammadiyah Ideology," 175.

56. Ibid., 112, 146.

57. Soebardi and Woodcroft-Lee, "Islam in Indonesia," 185.

58. Pimpinan Pusat 'Aisyiyah, *Sejarah pertumbuhan,* 17–24.

59. Mansoer, *12 Tafsir Langkah.*

60. Jainuri, "Formation of Muhammadiyah Ideology," 88–89.

61. Mansoer, *12 Tafsir Langkah,* 32.

62. Ibid., 34.

63. Magnis-Suseno, *Javanese Ethics and World-view,* 57.

64. Ibid., 42. See also Mulder, *Mysticism in Java.*

65. Slamet, "Priyayi Value Conflict," 26.

66. Magnis-Suseno, *Javanese Ethics and World-view,* 62–71.

67. Ibid., 153.

68. Mansoer, 12 *Tafsir Langkah*, 25–27.

69. Ibid., 24.

70. Ibid., 34–35. In 1925, R. Kern observed: "The words of the [Muhammadiyah] speaker show that the unity of Islam (that to the Javanese stands out when seen opposite the diversity within Christianity) fascinates him, it satisfies his Javanese longing for synthesis and respect for humanity that in fact is not Islamic but Javanese." R. Kern, "Verslag van het kongres der vereeniging *Moehammadijah* gehouden te Jogjakarta van 12 tot 17 maart 1925" (Report of the Muhammadiyah Congress, held in Yogyakarta, March 12–17, 1925), 22–23.

71. Jainuri, "Formation of Muhammadiyah Ideology," 198.

72. Hobsbawm and Ranger, *Invention of Tradition*, 1.

73. Ibid., 4.

74. See, for example, Pimpinan Pusat Muhammadiyah, *Pedoman Hidup Islami Warga*.

75. Wahid, "Perkembangan Teologi Islam," 55.

76. Van Bruinessen, "Traditions for the Future," 169.

77. Rais, "Muhammadiyah dan Pembaharuan," 65.

78. The definition continues: "having no organizational ties and being nonaffiliated with any political party or any other organization whatsoever." *Muhammadiyah Movement in Indonesia*, 11.

79. Quoted in Wieringa, "Politization of Gender Relations," 154.

80. Jainuri, "Formation of Muhammadiyah Ideology," 102. The Majlis Tarjih produces two types of decisions: *tarjih* are binding for all the members and become the formal position of Muhammadiyah, and *fatwas* are less binding.

81. Nashir, "Perilaku Politik Elit Muhammadiyah," 108.

82. Peacock, *Purifying the Faith*, 46.

83. Another reason for banding together of the *ulama* was that they needed an official body to send a representative to a congress in Mecca concerning the question of the caliphate. Muhammadiyah and SI had chosen their delegates, ignoring NU. When NU was initiated, Muhammadiyah was in a process of rapid growth from four thousand members in fifty-one groups and branches in 1926 to 44,879 members in 283 groups and branches in 1932. See Alfian, *Muhammadiyah*, 186–87.

84. Barton, "Liberal, Progressive Roots," 216; Wahid, *Kiai Nyentrik Membela Pemerintah*.

85. For further elaboration about the Qur'anic teachings of *akhlak* and *ikhlas*, see Murata and Chittick, *Vision of Islam*, 277–82, 304–5.

86. For a discussion of the process of finding truth and meaning in the holy texts of Islam, see Abou El Fadl, *Speaking in God's Name*, 30–69.

87. Van Bruinessen, *NU*, 3.

88. Nakamura, "Radical Traditionalism," 80.

89. Ibid., 80–81.

90. Barton and Fealy, *Nahdlatul Ulama*, xxi.

91. Pijper, *Fragmenta Islamica*, 14–15.

92. *Suara 'Aisyiyah* 7 (July 1932): 145.

93. "Kepoetoesan Madjlis Tardjih," *Suara 'Aisyiyah* 12 (December 1932): 306–8. Sally Jane White explains that the justification came from the fact that the Prophet's wife 'Aisyah was known to have related many of the traditions. One of these says, "Take half of your religion from her." White, "Reformist Islam," 106.

94. *Suara 'Aisyiyah* 2 (February 1932): 30–32.

95. *Suara 'Aisyiyah* 9 (September 1933): 283–86; *Suara 'Aisyiyah* 10 (December 1933): 305–7.

96. Pimpinin Pusat Muhammadiyah, *Adabul Marah fil Islam,* elaborates on this decision.

97. Ahmed, *Women and Gender in Islam,* 194–95.

98. Quoted in ibid., 195.

99. Pimpinan Pusat 'Aisyiyah, *Kepemimpinan Wanita.*

100. See, for example, Surat 5:51, 9:71–71, 33:35, 39:17–18. 'Aisyiyah's website quotes from Surat 16:97.

101. "Muhammadiyah di Kata Kaum Muda" (Muhammadiyah in young peoples' words), *Media Inovasi, Muhammadiyah menyongsong Abad XXI* 11 (December 1994): 56–57.

102. Hamid Baidlowi, "Perempuan NU Dewasa Ini," 8.

103. Feillard, "Potensi Perubahan Relasi Gender," 225.

104. Bush, "Wacana Perempuan," 32.

105. Machali, "Women and the Concept of Power," 7.

Chapter 3: 'Aisyiyah's Jihad

1. Author's interview with Professor Chamamah Suratno, member of the 'Aisyiyah Central Board, Yogyakarta, June 24, 1998.

2. Suratmin, *Nyai Ahmad Dahlan,* 70.

3. Niehof, "Changing Lives of Indonesian Women," 239.

4. According to the 2000 census, 16,806 inhabitants of the Kraton area are Muslim, and 2,932 are Christian. Badan Pusat Statistik Propinsi D.I. Yogyakarta, *Penduduk Kota Yogyakarta Hasil Sensus 2000.*

5. Pimpinan Pusat 'Aisyiyah, *Peringatan Congres Moehammadiyah,* 219.

6. Author's interview with Ibu Broto Mulyono, Yogyakarta, June 11, 1998.

7. Medan branch of 'Aisyiyah, August 11, 1998.

8. Interview with Ibu Barorah Baried, October 21, 1995 (by Andree Feillard).

9. Pimpinan Pusat 'Aisyiyah, *Pedoman Kepribadian Muslimah,* 6.

10. Pimpinan Pusat 'Aisyiyah, *Peringatan Congres Moehammadiyah,* 195.

11. *Suara 'Aisyiyah* 12.1 (October–November 1952): 195.

12. See Hefner, *Hindu Javanese,* 143–44.

13. Federspiel, "Muhammadijah," 66.

14. "Hidup-hiduplah Muhammadiyah, dan jangan sekali-kali mencari hidup dalam Muhammadiyah." Pimpinan Pusat Muhammadiyah, *Membina Keluarga Sejahtera,* 1.

15. Author's interview with Ibu Uswatun, Yogyakarta, January 29, 1998.

16. For calculations of blessings, see, for example, Zaini, *Bimbingan Praktis Tentang Puasa.*

17. Pimpinan Pusat 'Aisyiyah, *Peringatan Congres Moehammadiyah,* 211.

18. White, "Reformist Islam," 87–94.

19. During an interview on October 21, 1995, Ibu Baroroh Baried, 'Aisyiyah's chairperson from 1965 to 1985, told Andree Feillard that since childhood she would always wear this dress, often being the only one.

20. Author's interview with Ibu Alfiyah Muhadi, Yogyakarta, April 30, 1997.

21. Poesposuwarno and Siradj, *Beberapa Soal Jawab Kemuhammadiyahan*, 42.

22. "Muhammadiyah Youth Wing to Elect New Leader," *Jakarta Post,* July 9, 2002.

23. Muhammadiyah Report of the Meeting of the Council for Higher Education, Period 1995–2000 (held in Semarang, July 5–7, 1998).

24. Fachruddin, *Memelihara Ruh Muhammadiyah*, 53–54.

25. Boland, *Struggle of Islam*, 191.

26. On the power of discourse, see Northup, *Ritualizing Women*, 88–89.

27. Fachruddin, *Memelihara Ruh Muhammadiyah*, 54.

28. The Javanese language has three levels of speech. Depending on a person's rank in societal hierarchy, a high or low level is used. Women use the low level with their children. When addressing men, even their own husbands, they use a higher level. Women preachers speaking to women mix the low and high levels; female preachers addressing an audience with men switch to the higher level; while men tend to address women in low Javanese. When using the Indonesian language, this code switching does not occur. Weix, "Islamic Prayer Groups," 411.

29. *Pengajian* led by Ibu Uswatun, January 11, 1998.

30. January 11, 1998, 4:00 a.m., in the prayer house for women in the Kauman; 8:00 a.m. in a community hall in Kota Gede.

31. Blumberger, *Nationalistische Beweging*, 345.

32. Pimpinan Pusat 'Aisyiyah, *Sikap terhadap Loearan*, 4–6.

33. Stivens, "Theorizing Gender," 3.

34. Foucault, *Archeology of Knowledge*, 152.

35. Qur'an study in the Shuhada Mosque, Yogyakarta, September 28, 1998. I attended the study three times (September 14, 28, and October 12). All quotes and observations are taken from these visits.

36. Ibu Elyda Djazman, national chair of 'Aisyiyah, in her speech to celebrate 'Aisyiyah's anniversary, Yogyakarta, November 28, 1997.

37. Smith-Hefner, "New Romance."

38. Faiz Manshur, Annuri F. Hadi, Fathuri SR, Agus Salim, and Yenni HN, "Terpuruknya Iman di Lubang Hasrat" (Faith drowning in an abyss of desire), *Syir'ah* 30.4 (May 2004): 19.

39. Fathuri SR, "Antara Akad dan Bersetubuh" (Between marriage contract and intercourse), *Syri'ah* 30.4 (May 2004): 32.

40. Manshur, Hadi, Fathuri SR, Salim, and Yenni HN, "Terpuruknya Iman" (Faith pushed aside), 22.

41. Author's interview with Ibu Uswatun, May 29, 1998.

42. Fathuri SR, "Niat Terbebas Dosa, Keluarga Menghujat" (A Promise free of sin, a family blames), *Syir'ah* 30.4 (May 2004): 28.

43. Fathuri SR, "Antara Akad," 33.

44. Pimpinan Wilayah 'Aisyiyah, *Kumpulan Syair,* 19.

45. Author's interview with Ibu Lies Sulistyowati, Yogyakarta, August 7, 1999.

46. Author's interview with Ibu Nibras Salim, Jakarta, August 3, 1999.

47. Pimpinan Pusat 'Aisyiyah, *Buku Tuntunan Taman Kanak-kanak.*

48. Author's interview with Ibu Nibras Salim, Jakarta, August 3, 1999.

49. Interview with Ibu Baroroh Baried, October 21, 1995 (by Andree Feillard).

50. Author's interview with Ibu Kholifah, director of Mu'allimat, Yogyakarta, November 13, 1998.

51. Discussion with the students of Pesantren Niyai Ahmad Dahlan, October 29, 1998, and written essays that were kindly passed on to me on November 16, 1998, by Mbak Ida, supervisor at the *pesantren.*

52. Berit Tjorbjornsrud comments on the fact that Foucault sees body control as entirely negative while ignoring religious contexts, where women can see it as positive and ultimately liberating. See Tjorbjornsrud, *Controlling the Body.*

53. Murata and Chittick, *Vision of Islam,* 279.

54. Ibid., 282.

55. Author's interview with Ibu Uswatun, October 1, 1998.

56. Murata and Chittick, *Vision of Islam,* 278–79.

57. The first quote is from Malik Fadjar, Minister for Religious Affairs, October 24, 1998 (during an 'Aisyiyah congress); the second quote is from a sermon by Ibu Uswatun, Yogyakarta, December 1, 1998.

58. "Mereka bekerdja dengan ichlas hati, / Ta'memikir lain jang mereka tjari / Ja'ni merdeka dan ketinggian boedi / Jang mendjoendjoeng deradjat iboe kini." *Suara 'Aisyiyah* 7 (December 1929): 88.

59. Ozment, *Protestants,* 6.

60. For example, see Pimpinin Pusat Muhammadiyah, *Jati Diri dan Akhlak Muhammadiyah,* 29.

61. Author's interview with Mbak Terias, Yogyakarta, July 18, 2001.

62. Dzuhayatin, "Women in Muhammadiyah," 7.

63. Ibid.

64. See Pimpinan Pusat 'Aisyiyah, *Tuntunan menuju Keluarga Sakinah.*

65. See Foucault, *Power/Knowledge.*

66. See Q. 2:248, Q. 9:26, and Q. 48:4, 18, and 26. In Q. 2:248, *sakinah* is used in its original Old Testament meaning, referring to God's continual presence in the Ark that guarantees tranquility and security: "A Sign of his authority is that there shall come to you the Ark of the Covenant, with [an assurance] therein of security [*sakinah*] from your Lord."

67. Author's interview with Ibu Baroroh Baried, Yogyakarta, October 31, 1997.

68. See Pimpinan Pusat 'Aisyiyah, *Indikator Keluarga Sakinah.* This is a checklist to help 'Aisyiyah preachers identify families that have not yet reached all the elements of the harmonious family.

69. Pimpinan Pusat 'Aisyiyah, *Pedoman Kepribadian Muslimah,* 3.

70. Pimpinan Pusat 'Aisyiyah, *Tuntunan menuju Keluarga Sakinah,* 19.

71. Pimpinan Pusat 'Aisyiyah, *Indikator Keluarga Sakinah,* 10.

72. Author's interview with Ibu Wardanah Muhadi, Yogyakarta, June 10, 1998.

73. Author's interview with Ibu Uswatun, April 24, 1998.

74. Badan Penasihat Perkawinan, Perselisihan, dan Perceraian (Body for Counseling [with regards to] Marriage, Disagreement, and Divorce).

75. See the official brochure of the BP4 office in Yogyakarta: *Membina Keluarga Bahagia Sejahtera* (1998).

76. As Sachiko Murata and William Chittick explain, the Qur'an frequently summons people to have *taqwa* (for example, 4:128, 2:233, 5:7, and 49:13). It is translated as: "Be wary of God, be dutiful toward God, be conscious of God, be pious toward God, be god-fearing." Murata and Chittick, *Vision of Islam,* 282.

77. Pimpinan Pusat 'Aisyiyah, *Sikap terhadap Loearan,* 8.

78. *Suara 'Aisyiyah* 2 (February 1932): 33.

79. Author's interview with Ibu Wardanah Muhadi, June 10, 1998. Muhadi is a judge in the Shari'ah court for family affairs. According to her, she spends a large part of her time teaching couples that women are not their husbands' slaves.

80. Interview with Ibu Baroroh Baried, October 21, 1995 (by Andree Feillard).

81. Pimpinan Pusat 'Aisyiyah, *Pedoman Kepribadian Muslimah,* 3.

82. Mir-Hosseini, *Islam and Gender,* 246.

83. Siti Ruhaini Dzuhayatin, during the discussion of her paper, "Women in Muhammadiyah."

84. Pimpinan Pusat 'Aisyiyah, *Pedoman Kepribadian Muslimah,* 9.

85. Pimpinan Pusat 'Aisyiyah, *Bidang Agama dan Ke-'Aisyiah-an,* 73.

86. Author's interview with Ibu Uswatan, April 24, 1998.

87. Author's interview with Ibu Alfiyah Muhadi, April 30, 1997.

88. Marcoes, "Female Preacher as Mediator," 225. Usury in Indonesia can be outrageous, especially in times of need. Most often the poor fall into an endless cycle of borrowing and reborrowing from ruthless lenders who charge up to 100 percent interest.

89. Author's interview with Ibu Alfiyah Muhadi, April 30, 1997.

90. Author's interview with Ibu Broto Mulyono, Yogyakarta, June 10, 1998.

91. Pimpinan Pusat 'Aisyiyah, *Technical and Organizational Guideline,* 3–4.

92. Author's interview with Ibu Istiqoma, Potorno, June 10, 1998.

93. Data conveyed during author's interview with Ibu Istiqoma, June 10, 1998.

94. Abdi Tauhid quotes AR Fakhruddin, a longtime Muhammadiyah chair: "'Muhammadiyah is based on Pancasila, but only in politics, government, and society, not in matters of Muhammadiyah teachings.'" Tauhid, "Masih ada Islam."

95. Terias Setiyawati, "Hubungan antara Program Desa Sejahtera dan Dinamika Kelompok Pengajian 'Aisyiyah."

96. Interview with Ibu Baroroh Barid, Yogyakarta, October 21, 1995 (by Andree Feillard).

97. Author's interview with Ibu Djazman, Yogyakarta, July 7, 1998.

98. Author's interviews with Siti Ruhaini, Yogyakarta, January 9 and October 2, 1998.

99. For example, the handful of women preachers active in Egypt meet great resistance from the male religious establishment. See Hafez, *Terms of Empowerment.*

100. According to the president of IAIN Sunan Kalijaga in Yogyakarta, students are losing interest in detailed study of the Fiqh and no longer focus on one *madhhab* only. The trend is towards comparing the *madhahib.* Author's interview with Amin Abdullah,

Yogyakarta, June 11, 2004. For the new changes in Indonesian society, see Hill, *Indonesia's New Order.*

Chapter 4: Nurturing the Future

1. Stivens, "Theorising Gender," 2.

2. Pimpinan Pusat Nasyiatul 'Aisyiyah, *Riwayat Singkat,* 29–30.

3. Ibid., 31.

4. This short history is based on an internal, undated, and unpublished NA document, "Riwayat Singkat Nasyiatul 'Aisyiyah." Unless otherwise indicated, all quotes in this section are taken from this document.

5. Hoesnij, "Asas dan toedjoean Nasjiatoel 'Aisijijah."

6. *Suara 'Aisyiyah* 2 (February 1941): 86.

7. Author's interview with Mbak Terias, Yogyakarta, May 8, 1998.

8. "Wees Hulpvaardig" (Offer help), in *Lima belas* Tahoenan Soeara 'Aisjijah, 9–12.

9. During his survey research between 1969 and 1972, James Peacock found that reformist Muslims ranked "building society" as the second most important priority (following the five prayers) in moral action. Peacock, *Muslim Puritans,* 112.

10. For example, students at the reformist *pesantren* Shobron in Solo annually perform a so-called *dakwah safari,* during which they preach and meet with local Muhammadiyah leaders. Author's interview in *pesantren* Shobron, October 10, 1998. Muhammadiyah schools of Mu'allimin and Mu'allimat follow the same system.

11. Author's interview with Mbak Ama, Yogyakarta, May 8, 1998.

12. Author's interview with Ibu Baroroh Baried, October 31, 1997.

13. Author's interview with Mbak Ama, Yogyakarta, May 26, 1999.

14. Author's interview with Mbak Ama, Yogyakarta, July 25, 1999.

15. Mbak Ama, speech to SMA Muhammadiyah II in Yogyakarta, July 26, 1998.

16. Author's interview with Mbak Terias, Yogyakarta, May 8, 1998.

17. Author's interview with Mbak Terias, May 8, 1998.

18. The rest of this section is based on my long interview about extremist groups with Mbak Ama, July 18, 2001.

19. For the diversity of opinions among Javanese women concerning Islamic teachings that influence women's lives such as covering the head, women's share of inheritance, and polygyny, see Feillard, "Indonesia's Emerging Muslim Feminism."

20. Author's interviews with Mbak Ama, Yogyakarta, May 8 and 26, 1998.

21. Pimpinan Pusat Nasyiatul 'Aisyiyah, *Matan Kepribadian Nasyiatul 'Aisyiyah* (Text and explanation of the NA personality; unpublished internal document, 1996).

22. Author's interview with Mbak Terias and Mbak Ama, Yogyakarta, May 26, 1998.

23. Author's interview with Ibu Sulistyowati, Yogyakarta, August 7, 1999.

24. Author's interview with Mbak Nurdjannah, Yogyakarta, July 14, 1998.

25. Author's interview with Mbak Ama, May 26, 1998.

26. Author's interview with Ibu Nur'aini, Surakarta, October 31, 1998.

27. Baitul Mal wal Tanwil (BMT) and Lembaga Keuangan Masyarakat Nasyiatul 'Aisyiyah (LKM).

28. Author's interview with Mbak Terias and Mbak Ama, May 8, 1998.

29. Author's interview with Ibu Sulistyiowati, August 7, 1999.

30. Author's interview with Mbak Ama, August 5, 2000. The head of Pemuda Muhammadiyah, Joko Susilo, made this remark during the national meeting in Jakarta in 2000.

31. Author's interview with Mbak Ama, August 5, 2000.

32. Pimpinan Ranting NA, *Laporan Pertanggungjawaban* (Accountability report, 1995–98). The information that follows is also from this report.

33. Author's interview with Mbak Ama, August 5, 2000.

34. Author's interview with Mbak Terias, August 8, 2000.

35. Author's interview with Mbak Terias, August 8, 2000.

36. Author's interview with Mbak Ama, July 28, 1999.

37. Author's interview with Mbak Ama, May 8, 1998.

38. Author's interview with Mbak Terias, May 8, 1998.

39. Author's interview with Ibu Nur'aini, October 31, 1998.

40. Author's interview with Mbak Terias, May 8, 1998.

41. Author's interview with Ibu Siti Ruhaini, Yogyakarta, January 11, 1998.

42. Author's interview with Ibu Siti Ruhaini and one of the directors of Rifka Annisa, Mbak Ida, Yogyakarta, January 8, 1998.

43. Author's interview with Mbak Ama, September 2, 1998.

44. Rais, *Visi dan Misi Muhammadiyah,* 42–43.

45. Pimpinan Pusat Nasyiatul 'Aisyiyah, *Matan Kepribadian Nasyiatul'Aisyiyah,* 16.

46. Ibu Siti Ruhaini refers to the influential book about Third World feminism by Kumari Jayawardena, *Feminism and Nationalism.*

47. Author's interviews with Ibu Siti Ruhaini, January 8, 1998, and July 30, 1999.

48. Author's interview with Mbak Terias, May 8, 1998.

49. Author's interview with the staff of Pesantren Shobron, Solo, October 10, 1998.

50. Author's interview with Ibu Siti Ruhaini, January 8, 1998.

51. Author's interview with Ibu Siti Ruhaini, July 28, 1999. The collection of essays about gender Ibu Siti Ruhaini refers to is in the journal of the Majlis Tarjih, *Tarjih* (1996).

52. Author's interview with Ibu Siti Ruhaini, July 18, 2001.

53. Pimpinan Pusat Muhammadiyah, *Himpunan Putusan Majelis Tarjih Muhammadiyah.*

54. Ibid., 285.

55. Pimpinan Pusat 'Aisyiyah, *Tuntunan menuju Keluarga Sakinah,* 40.

56. Author's interview with Amien Abdullah, August 7, 2002.

57. Author's interview with Mbak Terias and Ibu Siti Ruhaini, July 29, 1999.

58. Author's interview with Mbak Terias, July 29, 1999.

59. Author's interview with Ibu Siti Ruhaini, July 29, 1999.

60. Pimpinan Pusat Nasyiatul 'Aisyiyah, *Agama dan Harmoni.*

61. During its national conference in January 2002, one of Muhammadiyah's decisions was to reconsider its relation to local cultures and become more sensitive about including them in its Islamic teachings. See Effendy, "Di Muhammadiyah Juga ada "Munu" dan "Marmud.""

62. Pimpinan Pusat Nasyiatul 'Aisyiyah, *Riwayat Singkat.*

63. Author's interview with Mbak Ama, July 18, 2001.

Chapter 5: Tradition Revisited

1. For a brilliant analysis of Qur'an memorization in Indonesia, see Gade, *Perfection Makes Practice.*

2. Barton and Fealy, *Nahdlatul Ulama,* xiv.

3. Mas'udi, "Perempuan dalam Wacana Keislaman," 61.

4. Author's interview with Ibu Murshida Thahir, Jakarta, August 3, 2002.

5. Author's interview with an anonymous *santri,* Yogyakarta, August 15, 2000.

6. In 1978 there were 4,195 pesantren in Java, with a total of 677,384 students. Dhofier, *Pesantren Tradition,* 21. In 1997 the number had grown to 9,388, with 906,341 male students and 725,089 female students. Ministry for Religious Affairs, *Data Potensi Pondok Pesantren Seluruh Indonesia.*

7. Dhofier, *Pesantren Tradition,* xxiv.

8. See Wahid, "Principles of Pesantren Education."

9. Speech by Kiai Abd el Aziz Maskuri, Malang, October 5, 1998.

10. The information about the *kiai* is partly based on Wahid, "Principles of Pesantren Education."

11. Author's interview with Ibu Fatma, Yogyakarta, June 23, 1998.

12. Wahid, "Principles of Pesantren Education," 200.

13. Ibid., 198.

14. See Van Bruinessen, *Kitab Kuning,* 177–78.

15. Dhofier, *Pesantren Tradition,* 30. Some *pesantren* do not fit the traditionalist category, as they do not teach the traditional books but focus on modern topics. An example of this type is the Gontor *pesantren,* where students learn modern, spoken Arabic and English. There are also *pesantren* affiliated with Muhammadiyah.

16. For the books taught at *pesantren,* see Van Bruinessen, "Kitab Kuning." Van Bruinessen found around nine hundred different titles that were used as textbooks in the *pesantren.*

17. Ibid., 234.

18. Author's interview with Ibu Fatma, Yogyakarta, August 26, 2000.

19. Mahali and Mahali, *Kode Etik Kaum Santri,* 94–95.

20. Wahid, *Menggerakkan Tradisi,* 6.

21. Wahid, "Principles of Pesantren Education," 199.

22. Quoted in Dhofier, *Pesantren Tradition,* 147.

23. The information about the first female *santri* is based on the author's interviews with Abd el Aziz Maskuri and Ibu Iskandar, December 12, 1997, at the Denanyar *pesantren* in Jombang. Quotes in this section derive from this interview.

24. Author's interview with Ibu Enda Nizar, Jombang, June 27, 1998.

25. Lembaga Studi Pengembangan Perempuan and Anak (LSPPA), Mbak Ida, November 11, 1997.

26. The author's interviews with Ibu Fatma took place between 1999 and 2002. I met her through some IAIN students who were active in NU, and over the years I visited her regularly. During this period certain topics recurred regularly. When quoting some of these topics, I will omit reference to a particular interview.

27. Author's interview with Ibu Fatma, August 15, 2000.

28. Author's interview with Ibu Fatma, August 9, 1999.

29. Author's interview with Ibu Fatma, August 9, 1999.

30. Brenner, "Why Women Rule the Roost," 31.

31. Author's interview with Ibu Fatma, August 9, 1999.

32. Author's interview with Ibu Fatma, August 9, 1999.

33. Author's interview with Ibu Fatma, June 23, 1998.

34. The large Tebuireng Pesantren in Jombang has introduced co-education in the face of large protests. See Dhofier, *Pesantren Tradition.*

35. Author's interview with Ibu Fatma, August 26, 2000.

36. Author's interview with Maria Ulfa, Jakarta, August 3, 2002.

37. Pesantren Al Badriyah Al Hikmah, Kediri, December 27, 1997.

38. Author's interview with Nyai Nafisa Sahal, regional head of the Muslimat NU in Middle Java and wife of Kiai Sahal Mahfudh, Pati, September 19, 1997.

39. "Kajian Pleno Kiai dan Nyai Kualitas dan Hubungan Seks Sehat," workshop for senior *santri* and young *kiai* and *nyai,* organized by Yayasan Kesejahteraen Fatayat (YKF) and the Ford Foundation, Yogyakarta, August 20, 2000.

40. Information given by Mbak Masrucha at YKF, August 7, 2002.

41. What follows I learned from Ibu Siti during the course of three years but taped most of it during a visit to her *pesantren* on August 14, 2000.

42. Author's interview with Ibu Elli and Ibu Siti Ruhaini, Yogyakarta, January 8, 1998.

43. Masruhan al-Maghfuri, *Al-Mar'a al-Saliha.* I thank Mbak Masrucha for helping me with the translation of this text and look forward to the day that YKF will initiate a project for its reinterpretation.

44. Author's interview with Ibu Siti, August 14, 2000.

45. *Dialog dengan KH MA Sahal Mahfudh,* 102–3.

46. Author's interview with Ibu Siti, August 14, 2000.

47. Author's interview with Ibu Endah Nizar, June 27, 1998.

48. Author's interview with Ibu Siti, August 14, 2000.

49. Perhimpunan Pengembangan Pesantren dan Masyarakat.

50. For examples of essays and presentations from the 1970s, see Wahid, *Menggerakkan Tradisi.*

51. Wahid, "Principles of Pesantren Education," 202.

52. Mahfudh, *Nuansa Fiqh Sosial.*

53. Ibid., vii.

54. Ibid., viii.

55. Ibid.

56. The name "Lakpesdam" represents "Pusat Dokumentasi dan informasi NU: Lajnah Kajian dan Pengembangan Sumberdaya Manusia." The center's main areas of activity are: 1) to research and study dialogues about developments within society; 2) to provide courses for NU leaders about issues such as local democracy and civil society; 3) the publication of the journal *Tashwirul Afkar* with interpretations and reflections about intellectual and religious developments within society; and 4) publication of books. Author's interview with the staff, Lakpesdam, July 31, 2002.

57. Forum Kajian Kitab Kuning (FK3), *Wajah Baru Relasi Suami-Istri.* The members of the forum include: Ibu Sinta Nuriyah Abdurrahman Wahid, Kiai Husein Muhammad, Lies Marcoes-Natsir, Attashendartini Habsjah, Ahmad Lutfi Fathullah, Syafiq

Hasyim, Badriyah Fayyumi, Arifah Choiri Fauzi, Juju Juhairiyyah, Djudju Zubaedah, Farhah Ciciek, and Faqihuddin Abdul Kodir.

58. For a short biography of Nawawi, see Riddell, *Islam and the Malay-Indonesian World,* 193–97. See also FK3, *Wajah Baru Relasi Suami-Istri,* 207–9.

59. FK3, *Wajah Baru Relasi Suami-Istri,* 208.

60. Abou El Fadl, *Speaking in God's Name,* discusses many of the teachings found in *Kitab 'Uqud.* Abou El Fadl bases his analysis on other Arabic sources.

61. FK3, *Wajah Baru Relasi Suami-Istri,* x.

62. Masdar Mas'udi, during a P3M seminar on women's jurisprudence at the Krapyak Pesantren, Yogyakarta, September 27, 1997.

63. An-Na'im, *Toward an Islamic Reformation.* The following information is based on an article published by the P3M staff (Sciortino, Marcoes-Natsir, and Mas'udi, "Learning from Islam"), the transcripts P3M makes of all its meetings, and my own observations when attending some of workshops and seminars in Yogyakarta and Jakarta in 1997 and 1998. Masdar Mas'udi explained the basic human rights, among others, at a workshop about provisions for the wife and the dilemma of woman's work, Tasikmalaya, July 17–19, 1997.

64. See Riddell, *Islam and the Malay-Indonesian World,* 252.

65. See Mas'udi, *Islam dan Hak-Hak Reproduksi Perempuan.*

66. Report of the meeting in Tasikmalaya, July 17–19, 1997, 30–31.

67. Ibid., 91–92.

68. Ibid., 71.

69. Author's interview with Ibu Djudju Zubaidah, Pesantren Cipasung, Tasikmalaya, August 4, 1999.

70. Mas'udi, "Perempuan di antara Lembaran Kitab Kuning," 162.

71. Quoted in Van Bruinessen, *Kitab Kuning,* 172. See also Mas'udi, "Perempuan di antara Lembaran Kitab Kuning," 156–60.

72. Van Bruinessen, *Kitab Kuning,* 182.

73. FK3, *Wajah Baru Relasi Suami-Istri.*

74. Mas'udi, "Perempuan dalam Wacana Keislaman," 61.

75. Rofiq et al., *Pelajaran KeNUan,* 7.

76. Mas'udi, "Perempuan dalam Wacana Keislaman," 61–63.

77. FK3, *Wajah Baru Relasi Suami-Istri,* p. 61.

78. Ibid., 61–62.

79. Ibid., 158–59.

80. Author's interview with Kiai Husein Muhammad and Kiai Khozin Nasuchah, May 25, 1998.

81. Author's interview with Kiai Husein Muhammad and Kiai Khozin Nasuchah, May 25, 1998.

82. Speech by Kiai Muhyiddin Sofyan, July 12, 1998.

83. Author's interview with Ibu Enda Nizar, June 21, 1998.

84. Author's interview with Kiai Husein Muhammad and Kiai Khozin Nasuchah, May 25, 1998.

85. Author's interview with Kiai Husein Muhammad, May 25, 1998.

86. Author's interview with Ibu Enda Nizar, June 21, 1998.

87. For this aspect of Javanese ethics, see Magnis-Suseno, *Javanese Ethics and Worldview,* chap. 3.

Chapter 6: Tradition in Action

1. Fealy, "Wahab Chasbullah," 16.

2. Ibid., 16 and 27.

3. Aboebakar, *Wahid Hasjim,* 533.

4. Pimpinan Pusat Muslimat NU, *Sejarah Muslimat Nahdlatul Ulama,* 42.

5. Author's interview with Ibu Asmah Sjachruni, Jakarta, June 26, 1998.

6. Dachlan, *Keharibaan Kebangunan,* 34.

7. Pimpinan Pusat Muslimat NU, *Sejarah Muslimat,* 46. See also Aboebakar, *Wahid Hasjim,* 533.

8. Dachlan, *Keharibaan Kebangunan,* 31–33.

9. Ibid., 30–31.

10. Pimpinan Pusat Muslimat NU, *50 Tahun Muslimat NU,* 84.

11. Author's interview with Ibu Asmah Sjachruni, August 23, 2000.

12. Pimpinan Pusat Muslimat NU, *Sejarah Muslimat,* 76.

13. Ibid., 166.

14. Lucas and Cribb, "Women's Roles in the Indonesian Revolution," 93.

15. Fealy, "Islamic Politics."

16. Author's interview with Ibu Asmah Sjachruni, June 26, 1998.

17. See Soelarto, *Garebeg di Kesultanan Yogyakarta,* 68–72.

18. Author's interview with Ibu Asmah Sjachruni, June 26, 1998.

19. Author's interview with Ibu Asmah Sjachruni, August 23, 2000.

20. Author's interview Ibu Asmah Sjachruni, June 26, 1998.

21. Pimpinan Pusat Muslimat NU, *50 Tahun Muslimat NU,* 23.

22. See Bell, *Ritual,* 171.

23. Beatty, *Varieties of Javanese Religion,* 27.

24. Ibid., 26–27.

25. Ibid., 26

26. For details about the *slametan,* see Geertz, *Religion of Java,* chaps. 1–7.

27. Author's interview with Ibu Siti, August 2, 2000.

28. Oral communication by Kees de Jong, who frequently witnessed that the priority of his Indonesian in-laws is to visit the grave of the son who died at the age of five rather than attend the prayers for the feast. Author's interview with Ibu Ismawati, July 27, 1998.

29. Author's interview with Ibu Ismawati, July 27, 1998.

30. Pimpinan Pusat Muslimat NU, *Sejarah Muslimat,* 76.

31. Author's interview with Ibu Muhammad Baidawi, head of the Muslimat NU chapter in Jombang, December 27, 1997.

32. Author's interview with Mbak Dede Mardliyah, Ibu Chunainah's daughter, Jakarta, August 6, 1998.

33. Author's interview with Mbak Masruchah, Yogyakarta, January 22, 1998.

34. Author's interview with Ibu Aisyah Hamid, national chair of Muslimat, 1995–2000, Jakarta, August 8, 1998.

35. Author's interview with Ibu Asmah Sjachruni, June 26, 1998.

36. Author's interview with Ibu Asmah Sjachruni, August 26, 2000.

37. Author's interview with Ibu Siti Maryam, October 3, 1997.

38. Author's interview with Mr. and Mrs. Muhammad Baidawi, Jombang, December 27, 1997.

39. Dachlan, *Keharibaan Kebangunan*, 11.

40. Wahid, "Merumuskan kembali agenda," 18.

41. Ibid.; Author's interview with Ibu Umroh Mahfudzoh, Yogyakarta, August 1, 1999.

42. Author's interview with Ibu Umroh Mahfuzdoh, August 1, 1999.

43. Lucas and Cribb, "Women's Roles in the Indonesian Revolution," 75. Lucas and Cribb point out that the special connotation of the term *pemuda* had been pointed out first by Anderson, *Java in a Time of Revolution.*

44. Observations about the struggle with the Communist groups are mostly based on my interview with Ibu Asmah Sjachruni, June 26, 1998. See also Sjachruni, "Bersatulah Muslimat NU!"

45. Author's interview with Ibu Aisyah Hamid Baidlowi, August 8, 1998.

46. Boland, *Struggle of Islam*, 167.

47. These recommendations can be found in the report of the special PKB committee for women's issues: *Hasil Semiloka Pemberdayaan Perempuan DPP PKB Rekomendasi* (August 1, 1999).

48. Hamid Baidlowi, "Perempuan NU Dewasa Ini: Mereka yang Tak Ingin Terus di Balik Layar" (Contemporary NU women: They no longer want to stay behind the screen).

49. Author's interview with Ibu Mahmudah Mawardi, Jakarta, June 26, 1998.

50. Author's interview with Ibu Aisyah Hamid Baidlowi, August 8, 1998.

51. Author's interview with the presenter of the results, Maria Ulfah, national chair of Fatayat NU, Jakarta, August 22, 2000. See also Hamid Baidlowi, "Perempuan NU Dewasa Ini."

52. Quoted in Feillard, "Potensi Perubahan Relasi Gender," 224–25.

53. See Van Doorn-Harder, "Indonesian Islamic Debate."

54. Author's interview with Ibu Khofifah Paraningsih, Jakarta, June 27, 1998. For more on *kualat,* see Van Doorn-Harder and de Jong, "Ziarah to Tembayat."

55. Author's interview with Ibu Aisyah Hamid Baidlowi, August 23, 2000.

56. Author's interview with Ibu Asmah Sjachruni, June 26, 1998.

57. Author's interview with Ibu Umroh, June 13, 1998.

58. See Van Bruinessen, "Traditions for the Future."

59. Author's interview with Kiai Abd el-Aziz Maskuri, Jombang, December 27, 1997.

60. Author's interview with Malik Madani, professor at IAIN Yogyakarta, December 5, 1998.

61. Author's interview with Ibu Nafisa Sahal, September 19, 1997.

62. *Kitab 'Uqud al-Lujjain,* 24.

63. Forum Kajian Kitab Kuning (FK3), *Wajah Baru Relasi Suami-Istri.*

64. *Kitab 'Uqud al-Lujjain,* 246.

65. Van Doorn-Harder, "Muslim Feminist."

66. Author's interview with Ibu Ismawati, Kaliurang, July 24, 1998.

67. Author's interview with Ibu Abidah about her experience as a judge in the Shari'ah court, July 19, 1998.

68. Katjasungkana, "Kedudukan Wanita dalam Perspektif Islam," 62–63.

69. See also Greg Fealy's explanation of these concepts. Fealy, "Wahab Chasbullah."

70. Author's interview with Ibu Aisyah Hamid Baidlowi, August 23, 2000.

71. Author's interview with Professor Afif Rifa'i, Yogyakarta, October 23, 1998.

72. Author's interview with Ibu Nuriyah Abdurrahman Wahid, August 1, 2002.

73. Author's interview with Ibu Nuriyah Abdurrahman Wahid, August 1, 2002.

74. See, for example, Ulfa Anshori, "Jika Rasul Hidup Sekarang"; and Van Doorn-Harder, "Muslim Feminist."

75. Author's interview with Ibu Nuriyah Abdurrahman Wahid, August 24, 2000.

76. Author's interview with Ibu Noer Cholidah Badrus, December 29, 1997.

77. Author's interview with Ibu Asmah Sjachruni, August 23, 2000.

78. Katjasungkana, "Kedudukan Wanita dalam Perspektif Islam," 62.

79. Author's interview with Ibu Iskandar, December 28, 1997.

80. Author's interview with Ibu Zaini, Bantul, July 15, 1998.

81. Author's interview with Ibu Umroh, June 13, 1998.

82. Author's interview with Ibu Asmah Sjachruni, August 23, 2000.

83. Author's interview with Ibu Maryam, October 3, 1997.

84. Author's interview with Ibu Asmah Sjachruni, August 23, 2000.

85. Author's interview with Ibu Aisyah Hamid, August 23, 2000.

86. Katjasungkana, "Perempuan dalam Peta Hukum Negara di Indonesia," 82.

Chapter 7: Post-Tradition

Parts of this chapter have been previously published in "Indonesian Women Creating Justice," *Nordic Journal of Human Rights* 21.1 (Spring 2003): 46–66.

1. For extensive information about LKiS and LKPSM, see their Web pages: <http://www.lkis.or.id> and <http://www.lp3es.or.id/direktori/data/yogya/yogya_006.htm>.

2. For more information about this project, see its Web page: <http://islamlib.com>. Also see one of their first edited volumes: Assyaukanie, *Wajah Liberal Islam di Indonesia.*

3. Husaini and Hidayat, *Islam Liberal.*

4. Husaini, "Krislib Yes, Islib No!"

5. Mas'udi, *Islam dan Hak-Hak Reproduksi Perempuan.*

6. Remark by Kiai Ihsan u-Din at a YKF meeting, August 7, 2002.

7. Wahid, "Post-Traditionalisme Islam," 17.

8. Author's interview with Mbak Masruchah, Yogyakarta, July 16, 2001.

9. Author's interview with Mbak Masruchah, Yogyakarta, September 10, 1998.

10. "Pemudi NU siaplah kamu diwaktu, / Membela negeri dan igamamu. / Karena kamulah tulang punggung orang tua. / Yang telah payah memikirkannya kita. / Tegak senantiasa di waktunyalah yang tepat. / Karena bangsa, nusa butuh tenaga yang sehat." Pimpinan Pusat Fatayat NU, *Sejarah Fatayat NU,* 50.

11. Mawardi, "Kebangkitan Generasi," 107.

12. Pimpinan Pusat Fatayat NU, *Sejarah Fatayat,* 57 and 66.

13. Prasetyo and Ulfah, "Community Development Activities," 3.

14. Author's interview with Ibu Lily Zakiyah Munir, Jombang, July 21, 1998. See also Pimpinan Pusat Fatayat NU, *Sejarah Fatayat,* 76, 79, 85.

15. For the larger program, see Pimpinan Pusat Fatayat NU, "Garis Besar." For the mother and child program, see Ulfa Anshori, "Promosi Kesehatan."

16. For the P3M programs, see chapter 5 of this book.

17. The infant mortality rate dropped from 142 per thousand births in 1971 to 52.2 per thousand in 2000. The maternal mortality rate is estimated at 390 per hundred thousand births. See Maternal Neonatal Health Program in Indonesia: <http://www.jhuccp. org/asia/indonesia/neonatal.shtml>.

18. YKF, *Agenda 1998–2002,* 3.

19. YKF, *Laporan Program Penguatan Hak-Hak Reproduksi,* 3.

20. To date, seven booklets have been published in this series. All are edited by Mukhotib MD and were published by YKF in 2002: 1) *KB dan Aborsi* (Birth control and abortion); 2) *Ketika Pesantren Membincang Gender* (When the *pesantren* discusses gender); 3) *Menghapus Poligami, Mewujudkan Keadilan* (Doing away with polygyny, generating justice); 4) *Seksualitas: Menggugat Konstruksi Islam* (Sexuality: Criticizing the construction of Islam); 5) *Menghapus Perkawinan Anak; Menolak Ijbar* (Abolishing child marriage; Rejecting forced marriage); 6) *Menolak Mut'ah dan Sirri; Memberdayakan Perempuan* (Rejecting the temporary and [illegal] secret marriage; Empowering women); and 7) *HIV/AIDS: Pesantren Bilang Bukan Kutukan* (HIV/AIDS: *Pesantren* say it is not a curse).

21. The following section is based on Musoffa, "Kesetaraan Jender dalam Islam."

22. Ibid., 8.

23. Ibid., 13.

24. See "Reconsidering the Texts" in chapter 5 of this book.

25. Mukhotib MD, *Ketika Pesantren Membincang Jender,* 27. All the following recommendations can be found on this page.

26. Annisa, "Islam dan Hubungan Seksual yang Sehat," 2.

27. Ibid., 3–4.

28. YKF, *Laporan Program Penguatan Hak-Hak Reproduksi,* 3.

29. Mukhotib MD, Nor Ismah, and Triwahyuni, "Perceraian."

30. Ibid., 3.

31. Ibid., 9.

32. Quoted in ibid., 6.

33. Tim Pemberdayaan Perempuan Departemen Agama, "Draft Kompilasi Hukum Islam," 2, 15, and 16.

34. Mukhotib MD and Nor Ismah, "Pekerja Seks," 3.

35. Hafidz, "Prostitusi Bukan Persoalan Norma," 12.

36. Ibid., 12.

37. Masruchah, Preface, v.

38. El Khalieqy, *Perempuan Berkalung Sorban.* For further references to this novel, page numbers will be given in parentheses in the text.

39. "Daftar Pengirim Kuis Sandiwara Radio Bahasa Jawa untuk Kampanye Hak-Hak Reproduksi Perempuan" (List of those sent a t-shirt from the radio plays in Javanese for the campaign for women's reproductive rights) (Yogyakarta: n.d.), entry no. 9.

40. Gole, *Forbidden Modern,* 29.

41. Mukhotib MD, "Perempuan Menolak Poligami," 5.

42. Mukhotib MD, "Merunut Praktek Poligami," 3.

43. Ibid., 4.

44. Mukhotib MD, "Perempuan Menolak Poligami," 5–8.

45. Ibid., 5.

46. Mukhotib MD, *Menghapus Poligami,* viii.

47. Thalib, *Tuntunan Poligami dan Keutamaannya;* Kisyik, *Mengapa Islam Membolehkan Poligami?;* Suryono, *Poligami.* This is only a fraction of the booklets promoting polygyny in Islam.

48. Nurbowo and Mulyono, *Indahnya Poligami,* 56 and 102.

49. Ibid., 53.

50. Ibid., 57 and 62.

51. Ibid., 52.

52. Ibid., 67.

53. Author's interview with Mbak Masruchah, August 10, 2002.

54. Author's interview with Mbak Masruchah, August 10, 2002.

55. Castells discerns three forms of identity building that contribute to the development of societies: the identity for resistance, the legitimizing identity that generates civil society and in due time takes over the state without a direct assault, and the "project identity" that is formed when social actors build a new identity that redefines their position in society. Castells, *Power of Identity,* 8–10.

56. *Syir'ah* 30.4 (May 2004): 19.

57. Bowen, *Islam, Law, and Equality in Indonesia,* 169.

Conclusion

1. See, for example, Van Dijk, "Religious Authority."

2. The survey was carried out by the Center for the Study of Islam and Society of the State Islamic University in Jakarta. See *Tempo,* December 24, 2002, for a series of articles concerning this survey.

3. Author's interview with Ibu Fatma, July 20, 2001.

4. Wahid, "Refleksi Teologis Perkawinan dalam Islam," 173.

5. Ibid., 181.

6. Author's interview with Ibu Asmah Sjachruni, August 23, 2000.

7. See Ahmed, *Border Passage,* 123–25. See also the introduction to Cooke, *Women Claim Islam.*

8. Cooke, *Women Claim Islam,* xiv.

9. Discussion transcript in Hasyim, *Menakar "Harga" Perempuan,* 177.

10. Author's interview with Mbak Ama, July 18, 2001.

11. El Khalieqy, *Perempuan Berkalung Sorban,* 305–6.

Glossary

Adat: Local customary law.

Ahl as-Sunnah wa al-Jama'a: People of the Prophet's Sunnah and the Islamic community; name used for NU followers.

'Aisyiyah: Reformist or modernist organization for Muslim women founded in 1917, related to the Muhammadiyah organization. Also written as 'Aisjijah.

Akal (Ar.: Aql): Brain or mind, the capacity for logical thought.

Akhlak (Ar.: akhlaq): Morals and ethics.

Daerah: District level of NU or Muhammadiyah.

Dakwah (Ar.: Da'wah): Islamic propagation.

Dharma Wanita: Organization for wives of civil servants, set up by the Suharto government to control civil servants and to espouse the particular gender philosophy of the government.

Extremism: Interpretation of Islam that wants to return to the unadulterated teachings of the time of the Prophet Muhammad and demands that society is under Muslim rule and law (also called radicalism or Islamism).

Fatayat NU: Traditionalist organization founded in 1950 for women between twenty and forty, related to the NU organization.

Fatwa: Legal opinion given by a scholar or group of scholars of Islam.

Fiqh: Islamic jurisprudence.

Hadis (Ar.: Hadith): The tradition that reports the words and actions of the Prophet Muhammad and some of his companions. When only referring to the words and actions of the Prophet, the word *Sunnah* is used.

IAIN: Institut Agama Islam Negeri (the Islamic State Institute for Higher Learning).

Ibadah: Worship.

Ijma': The community of Muslim scholars who gather to reach agreement concerning the interpretation of an Islamic holy text.

Ijtihad: Independent reasoning in the interpretation of an Islamic holy text (the opposite of *ijma'*).

Ikhlas: Pure devotion to one's work; work done for the sake of God only.

Islam Baru: Islamist trend that started in university circles.

Jihad: Commonly translated as "holy war," it can mean physical struggle but is more commonly understood by Muslims as the spiritual struggle against sinful inclinations.

Jilbab: Veil that fully covers the hair.

Keluarga Sakinah: Harmonious family program designed by 'Aisyiyah.

Kembali ke khittah: 1984 decision by NU to move away from politics and focus on social and religious development.

Kerudung: Veil that is worn as a scarf loosely draped over the head.

Kerukunan: Harmony.

Khaul: Feast to commemorate the passing away of a *kiai*.

Kiai: Scholar of Islam who owns and/or teaches in a *pesantren*.

Kodrat: An elusive concept signifying a woman's innate or essential nature.

Majlis Tarjih: Muhammadiyah board that issues religious/legal advice (*fatwa*) and gives direction to the Muhammadiyah philosophy.

Mazhab/Madzhab (Ar.: madhab): One of the four legal schools accepted in Islam: Shafi'ite, Maliki, Hanafi, and Hanbali. These schools came into existence to systematize the various local interpretations of the legal teachings of the Qur'an and the Sunnah. The schools reflect opinions from the geographical regions where they developed (such as Medinah and Iraq). The Shafi'ite school is predominant in Indonesia.

Mu'allimat: First Muhammadiyah school to train female teachers, founded in 1923.

Muballighat (masculine: *muballigh*): Preacher.

Muhammadiyah: Reformist or modernist Muslim organization, founded in 1912, with twenty to twenty-five million followers.

Muslimat NU: NU-related organization for married women, founded in 1946.

Mut'a: Shi'ite temporary marriage that is not legal according to Sunnite law.

Nahdlatul Ulama (NU): Traditionalist Muslim organization, founded in 1926, with thirty to thirty-five million followers.

Nasyiat ul-'Aisyiyah: Muhammadiyah-related branch for young women, founded in 1919.

NGO: Nongovernmental Organization; see *Ormas* below for an explanation of the difference between Ormas and NGOs.

Nikah sirri: Secret marriage that is conducted without the obligatory presence of the woman's guardian.

Nyai: Wife of a *kiai*, or female teacher in the *pesantren*.

Orde Baru: "New Order," name of the Suharto regime (1966–98).

Ormas (Organisasi Masa): Mass-based organization such as Muhammadiyah and NU. An Ormas is independent from the government and strictly speaking an NGO. In Indonesia, Ormas differ from NGOs in that an Ormas is homegrown, mass-based, and focuses on a variety of causes. For Muhammadiyah and NU, these causes are inspired by Islam. An Ormas does not rely on foreign money; often its members sacrifice part of their salaries and work as volunteers. NGOs are small organizations with salaried staff that advocate a particular cause; they lack mass followings and are often funded by money from the West.

Pancasila ideology: The ideology of Indonesia's constitution that is based on five principles: belief in God, nationalism, humanitarianism, social justice, and democracy. It professes freedom of religion for Muslims, Catholics, Protestants, Hindus, and Buddhists.

Perhimpunan Pengembangan Pesantren dan Masyarakat (P3M): Center for the Development of *Pesantren* and Society.

Pesantren: Rural Islamic boarding schools where students focus on memorizing the Qur'an, the holy texts of the Islamic Tradition, while rigorously following the rules of Islam in daily life.

Pimpinan Pusat (PP): The Central Board of a Muhammadiyah organization.

Qoryah Thoyyibah: The "good village," where, according to Muhammadiyah philosophy, all inhabitants follow and practice the rules of reformist Islam.

Ranting: Local level of NU or Muhammadiyah.

Reformasi: "Reformation," the name for the post-Suharto era.

Reformists: Muslims who promote the direct, independent reading of the holy texts of Qur'an and Hadith. They do not tolerate indigenous beliefs and practices in combination with Islam.

Santri: Male or female student at *pesantren.*

Shari'ah: The Islamic law as revealed in the holy texts of Islam.

Slametan: A ritual meal of reconciliation.

Suara 'Aisyiyah: "Voice of 'Aisyiyah"; journal published by 'Aisyiyah.

Suara Muhammadiyah: "Voice of Muhammadiyah"; journal published by Muhammadiyah.

Sumpa Pemuda: The Youth Pledge, taken during a Youth Congress in 1928, which for the first time expressed Indonesian ideals of independence from Dutch colonial rule as one fatherland, one nation, and one language, Indonesian.

Sunan Kalijaga: The most famous of the nine saints who are credited with bringing Islam to Indonesia. According to the Tradition, he used Javanese art forms such as the shadow play and the gamelan in spreading Islam.

Sunnah: The words and deeds of the Prophet Muhammad.

Syuriah: Religious council of NU that issues religious/legal advice (*fatwa*).

Talqin: "Prompting of the dead," NU custom to prepare the deceased for interrogation by angels concerning the correctness of their faith.

Tandfidziah: The executive council of NU.

Taqlid: "Imitation," following the authority of the *madzhab.*

Tasawwuf: Islamic mysticism (also called Sufism).

Tauhid: The Oneness of God. Used also in Tauhid Sosial: applying the doctrine of the Oneness of God in society, striving for a just society.

Traditionalists: Original Indonesian Muslims who accept expressions of local culture as long as they do not contradict Islam.

Ulama (Ar.: 'Ulama'): Scholars of Islam (in Arabic the singular is *'alim,* but in Indonesia *ulama* is used for both the plural and the singular).

Wali songgo: Nine saints who are credited with bringing Islam to Indonesia.

Wilaya: Provincial level of NU or Muhammadiyah.

Yayasan Kesejahteraan Fatayat (YKF): Fatayat Welfare Foundation, an NGO related to the NU branch for young women called Fatayat NU.

Zina: Adultery or fornication.

Bibliography

Journals, Newspapers, and Web Sites

Archipel

Bijdragen Koninklijk Instituut voor de Tropen (Contributions from the Royal Tropical Institute)

Bijdragen tot de Taal-, Land- en Volkenkunde (Contributions to the knowledge of languages, countries, and peoples)

Christian Science Monitor

Critique of Anthropology

Indonesia

Islam21

Jakarta Post

Journal of Asian Studies

Jurnal Pemikiran Islam tentang Pemberdayaan Perempuan (Journal for Islamic thought about women's empowerment; Jakarta: PP Muslimat NU and Penerbit Logos Wacana Ilmu).

Middle East Review of International Affairs

Muslim World

Mitra

Musawa: Jurnal Studi Gender dan Islam (Musawa: The journal for studies about gender and Islam; published by PSW IAIN Sunan Kalijaga, Yogykarta).

Soeara 'Aisjijah (Voice of 'Aisyiyah)

Sojourn

South East Asia Research

Studia Islamika

Suara 'Aisyiyah

Suara Muhammadiyah (Voice of Muhammadiyah)

Swara Rahima: Media Islam untuk Hak-Hak Perempuan (Voice of Rahima: Islamic press for women's rights)

Sydney Morning Herald
Syir'ah (Law)
Tashwirul Afkar: Jurnal Refleksi Pemikiran Keagamaan dan Kebudayaan (Exchange of thoughts: Journal for reflection on religion and culture; published by Lakpesdam, Jakarta).
Tempo
Van Zorge Report
http://www.islamlib.com (Liberal Islam Group)
http://www.lkis.or.id (Institute for Islamic Research)

Indonesian Titles

Aboebakar, H. *Wahid Hasjim dan Nahdlatul Ulama* (Biography of Wahid Hasjim and the history of NU). Jakarta: NU, 1957.

Al-Barbasy, Ma'mun Murod, Faozan Amar, Imam Santoso, and Khoirul Ikhwan, eds. *Muhammadiyah-NU: Mendayung Ukhuwah di Tengah Perbedaan* (Muhammadiyah NU: To peddle brotherhood in the midst of difference). Malang: UMM Press, 2004.

Amin, M. Masyhur. *NU dan Ijtihad Politik Kenegaraannya* (NU and the *ijtihad* of state politics). Yogyakarta: Al-Amin, 1996.

Annisa, Hindun. "Islam dan Hubungan Seksual yang Sehat" (Islam and healthy sexual relationships). In *Seksualitas: Menggugat Konstruksi Islam* (Sexuality: Criticizing the construction of Islam). Ed. Mukhotib MD. Yogyakarta: YKF, 2002.

Assyaukanie, Luthfi, *Wajah Liberal Islam di Indonesia* (The Face of liberal Islam in Indonesia). Jakarta: Jaringan Islam Liberal, 2002.

Azalmanij, Hoesnij, "Asas dan toedjoean Nasjiatoel 'Aisjijah" (Foundation and goal of NA), *Suara 'Aisyiyah* 8 (August 1941) 419–22.

Badan Pusat Statistik Propinsi D.I. Yogyakarta. *Penduduk Kota Yogyakarta Hasil Sensus 2000.* Yogyakarta: N.p., 2000.

Badan Pusat Statistik Propinsi D.I. Yogyakarta. *Penduduk Kota Yogyakarta Hasil Sensus 2000.* Yogyakarta: N.p., 2000.

Baried, Baroroh. "Konsep Wanita dalam Islam" (The Islamic view on women). In *Wanita Islam Indonesia dalam Kajian Tekstual dan Konstekstual* (The Indonesian woman in textual and contextual research). Ed. Lies M. Marcoes-Natsir and Johan H. Meuleman. Jakarta: INIS, 1993. 35–44.

Bush, Robin L. "Wacana Perempuan di Lingkungan NU" (Discourse about women in the NU environment). *Tashwirul Afkar* 5 (1999): 24–33.

Dachlan, Nj. Aisjah. *Keharibaan Kebangunan Muslimaat Nahdlatul 'Ulama di Indonesia* (In the presence of the development of the Muslimat NU in Indonesia). Jakarta: Muslimat NU: 1968.

Dahlan, Muhammad, Rofiqul-Umam Ahmad, and Ali Zawawi, eds. *Solichah A. Wahid Hasyim: Muslimah di Garis Depan.* (Solichah A. Wahid Hasyim: A Muslim woman at the frontline). Jakarta: Yayasan K. H. A. Wahid Hasyim, 2001.

Effendy, Bahtiar. "Di Muhammadiyah Juga ada 'Munu' dan 'Marmud.'" Radio interview, March 7, 2002.

El Khalieqy, Abidah. *Perempuan Berkalung Sorban* (Women wearing the turban). Yogyakarta: YKF and the Ford Foundation, 2001.

Fachruddin, Kiai Hajji, AR. *Memelihara Ruh Muhammadiyah* (Protecting the Muhammadiyah spirit). Yogyakarta: Muhammadiyah Library, 1996.

Feillard, Andree. "Potensi Perubahan Relasi Gender di Lingkungan Umat Islam: Sebuah Proyeksi dan Pemaparan Data" (Potential changes in gender relations within the Muslim community: A prediction and explanation of data). In *Menakar "Harga" Perempuan Eksplorasi Lanjut atas Hak-Hak Reproduksi Perempuan dalam Islam* (Measuring the "value" of women: A further exploration of women's reproductive rights in Islam.) Ed. Syafiq Hasyim. Bandung: Penerbit Mizan, 1999. 221–41.

Forum Kajian Kitab Kuning (FK3), ed. *Wajah Baru Relasi Suami-Istri: Telaah Kitab 'Uqud al-Lujjayn* (The new face of the relation between man and wife: About the *Kitab 'Uqud*. Yogyakarta: LKiS, 2001.

Hafidz, Wardah. "Prostitusi Bukan Persoalan Norma" (Prostitution is not a matter of values). *Mitra* (January-April 2001): 12–14.

Haidar, M. Ali. *Nahdlatul Ulama dan Islam di Indonesia: Pendekatan Fikih dalam Politik Jakarta* (NU and Islam in Indonesia: Using Fiqh in Jakarta politics). Jakarta: Gramedia Pustaka Utama, 1994.

Hamid Baidlowi, Hj. Aisyah. "Perempuan NU Dewasa Ini: Mereka yang Tak Ingin Terus di Balik Layar" (Contemporary NU women: They no longer wish to stay behind the screen). Unpublished manuscript in author's possession, 2000.

Hamka. *Tasauf Moderen* (Modern Islamic mysticism). 3d ed. Jakarta: Penerbit Pustaka Panjimas, 1994.

Hasyim, Syafiq, ed. *Menakar "Harga" Perempuan: Eksplorasi Lanjut atas Hak-Hak Reproduksi Perempuan dalam Islam* (Measuring the "value" of women: A Further exploration of women's reporoductive rights in Islam). Bandung: Penerbit Mizan, 1999.

Hoesnij, Azalmanij. "Asas dan Toedjoean Nasjiatoel 'Aisjijah" (Foundation and goal of NA). *Suara 'Aisyiyah* 8 (August 1941): 419–22.

Husaini, Adian, and Nuim Hidayat. *Islam Liberal: Sejarah, Konsepsi, Penyimpangan, dan Jawabannya* (Liberal Islam: Its history, ideas, misconception, and answer). Jakarta: Gema Insani, 2002.

———. "Krislib Yes, Islib No!" (Liberation of crisis yes, liberal Islam no!). In *Membedah Islam Liberal: Memahami dan Menyikapi Manuver Islam Liberal di Indonesia* (To discern Liberal Islam: Understanding and taking a stand against the maneuvers of liberal Islam in Indonesia). Ed. Adian Husaini, Husin M. Al-Banjari, M. Syamsi Ali, and Santi W. E. Soekanto. Bandung: PT Syaamil Cipta Media, 2003. 57–87.

Katjasungkana, Nursyahbani. "Kedudukan Wanita dalam Perspektif Islam" (Woman's position from the Islamic perspective). In *Wanita Islam dalam Kajian Tekstual dan Konstekstual* (The Indonesian woman in textual and contextual research). Ed. Lies M. Marcoes-Natsir and Johan H. Meuleman. Jakarta: INIS, 1993. 57–68.

———. "Perempuan dalam Peta Hukum Negara di Indonesia" (Women in the map of national law in Indonesia). In *Menakar "Harga" Perempuan: Eksplorasi Lanjut atas Hak-Hak Reproduksi Perempuan dalam Islam* (Measuring the "value" of women: A Further exploration of women's reporoductive rights in Islam). Ed. Haysim Syafiq. Bandung, Penerbit Mizan, 1999. 69–82.

Kisyik, Abd Hamid. *Mengapa Islam Membolehkan Poligami? Hikmah Pernikahan Rasulullah Saw* (Why does Islam allow polygyny? The wisdom of the Prophet). 2d ed. Jakarta: Penerbit Hikmah, 2000.

Kuntowijoyo. *Muslim Tanpa Masjid* (Muslims without a mosque). Bandung: Mizan, 2001.

Mahali, Mudjab A., and Umi Mujawazah Mahali. *Kode Etik Kaum Santri* (Ethical code for *santri*). Bandung: al-Bayan, 1988.

Mahfudh, Kiai Sahal. *Nuansa Fiqh Sosial* (The Nuances of social jurisprudence). Yogyakarta: LKiS, 1994.

Mansoer, K. H. M. *12 Tafsir Langkah Muhammadiyah* (Twelve interpretations of Muhammadiyah steps). Yogyakarta: PP Muhammadiyah Majlis Tabligh, N.d.

Masruchah, Mbak. Preface to *Perempuan Berkalung Sorban* (Women wearing the turban), by Abidah el Khalieqy. Yogyakarta: YKF and the Ford Foundation, 2001. v–vii

Mas'udi, F. Masdar. *Islam dan Hak-Hak Reproduksi Perempuan: Dialog Fiqih Pemberdayaan* (Islam and women's reproductive rights: A dialogue of empowering jurisprudence). Rev. ed. Bandung: Penerbit Mizan, 2000.

———. "Perempuan dalam Wacana Keislaman" (Women in Islamic discourse). In *Perempuan dan Pemberdayaan* (Women and development). Ed. Smita Notosusanto and E. Kristi Poerwandari. Jakarta: Program Studi Kajian Wanita Universitas Indonesia, 1997. 53–64.

———. "Perempuan di antara Lembaran Kitab Kuning" (Women in the yellow books). In *Wanita Islam Indonesia dalam Kajian Tekstual dan Konstekstual* (The Indonesian woman in textual and contextual research). Ed. Lies M. Marcoes-Natsir and Johan H. Meuleman. Jakarta: INIS, 1993. 155–64.

Marcoes-Natsir, Lies. "Antara Amal dan Tuntunan Profesional di 'Aisyiyah" (Between charity and professional persistence in 'Aisyiyah). In *Perempuan Indonesia: Dulu dan Kini* (Women of Indonesia: Then and now). Ed. Mayling Oey-Gardiner, Mildred Wagemann, Evelyn Suleeman, and Sualstri. Jakarta: Gramedia Publishers, 1996. 148–71.

Marcoes-Natsir, Lies M., and Johan H. Meuleman, eds. *Wanita Islam Indonesia dalam Kajian Tekstual dan Konstekstual* (The Indonesian woman in textual and contextual research). Jakarta: INIS, 1993.

Masruhan al-Maghfuri, Kiai. *Al-Mar'a al-Saliha* (The Virtuous woman.) Surabaya: Toko Kitab al-Hikma, n.d.

Masyhur, M. Amin. *NU dan Ijtihad Politik Kenegaraannya* (NU and the *ijtihad* of state politics). Yogyakarta: Al-Amin, 1996.

Mawardi, H. A. Chalid. "Kebangkitan Generasi Muda NU dan Perspektifnya" (Awareness building among the young NU generation and its perspectives). In *Sejarah Fatayat NU* (History of the Fatayat NU). Ed. Pimpinan Pusat Fatayat NU. Jakarta: PP Fatayat NU, 1984. 95–110.

Ministry for Religious Affairs. *Data Potensi Pondok Pesantren Seluruh Indonesia.* Jakarta: Ministry for Religious Affairs, 1997.

Mukhotib MD. "Merunut Praktek Poligami: Dari Budaya ke Agama?" (Tracing the practice of polygyny: From culture to religion?). *Mitra* (January-July 2002): 3–4.

———. "Perempuan Menolak Poligami, Ada Apa?" (Women reject polygyny, what is the matter?). *Mitra* (January-July 2002): 5–8.

———, ed. *HIV/AIDS: Pesantren Bilang Bukan Kutukan* (HIV/AIDS: *Pesantren* say it is not a curse). Yogyakarta: YKF, 2002.

———, ed. *KB dan Aborsi* (Birth control and abortion). Yogyakarta: YKF, 2002.

————, ed. *Ketika Pesantren Membincang Gender* (When the *pesantren* discusses gender). Yogyakarta: YKF, 2002.

————, ed. *Menghapus Perkawinan Anak; Menolak Ijbar* (Abolishing child marriage; Rejecting forced marriage). Yogyakarta: YKF, 2002.

————, ed. *Menghapus Poligami, Mewujudkan Keadilan* (Doing away with polygyny, generating justice). Yogyakarta: YKF, 2002.

————, ed. *Menolak Mut'ah dan Sirri; Memberdayakan Perempuan* (Rejecting temporary and secret marriage; Empowering women). Yogyakarta: YKF, 2002.

————, ed. *Seksualitas: Menggugat Konstruksi Islam* (Sexuality: Criticizing the construction of Islam). Yogyakarta: YKF, 2002.

Mukhotib MD and Nor Ismah. "Pekerja Seks: Meggugat Keadilan Hukum" (Prostitution: Criticizing the justice of law). *Mitra* (January-April 2001): 2–5.

Mukhotib MD, Nor Ismah, and Triwahyuni. "Perceraian: Perempuan Mempertanyakan Haknya" (Divorce: Women question their rights). *Mitra* (September-December 2000): 3–9.

Mulia, Siti Musdah, ed. *Keadilan dan Kesetaraan Gender: Perspektif Islam* (Justice and gender equality: The Islamic perspective). Jakarta: Lembaga Kajian Agama dan Jender, 2003.

Musoffa, Kiai Edy. "Kesetaraan Jender dalam Islam" (Gender equality in Islam). In *Ketika Pesantren Membincang Jender* (When the *pesantren* discusses gender). Ed. Mukhotib MD. Yogyakarta: YKF, 2002.

Nashir, Haedar. "Perilaku Politik Elit Muhammadiyah di Pekanjangan" (The political behavior of the Muhammadiyah elite in Pekanjangan). Master's thesis, Gadjah Mada University, 1998.

Nawawi al-Jawi al-Bantani al-Shafi'i, Muhammad bin 'Umar. *Kitab Syarh 'Uqud Al-Lujjain fi Bayan Huquq Al-Zaujain* (Notes on the mutual responsibility concerning the clarification of the rights of spouses). Surabaya: Bintang Terang, 1985.

Nurbowo and Apiko Joko Mulyono. *Indahnya Poligami: Pengalaman Keluarga Sakinah Puspo Wardoyo* (The Beauty of polygyny: Experiences from the harmonious family of Puspo Wardoyo). 2d ed. Jakarta: Senayan Abadi Publishing, 2003.

Oey-Gardiner, Mayling, Mildred Wagemann, Evelyn Suleeman, and Sulastri. *Perempuan Indonesia: Dulu dan Kini* (Women of Indonesia: Then and now). Jakarta: Gramedia Publishers, 1996.

Pimpinan Pusat 'Aisyiyah, ed. *Bidang Agama dan Ke-'Aisyiah-an* (On the topic of religion and information about 'Aisyiyah). Yogyakarta: PP 'Aisyiyah, 1982.

————, ed. *Buku Tuntunan Taman Kanak-kanak 'Aisyiyah Bustanul Athfal* (Guidelines for the Bustanul Athfal 'Aisyiyah kindergartens). Jakarta: PP 'Aisyiyah, 1974.

————, ed. *Indikator Keluarga Sakinah* (A Checklist for the harmonious family). Yogyakarta: PP 'Aisyiyah, n.d.

————, ed. *Kepemimpinan Wanita Menurut Ajaran Islam* (Women's leadership according to Islamic teachings). Yogyakarta: PP 'Aisyiyah, 1999.

————, ed. *Lima belas Tahoenan* Soeara 'Aisyiyah (Fifteen years of *Voice of 'Aisyiyah*). Yogyakarta: PP 'Aisyiyah, 1940.

————, ed. *Pedoman Kepribadian Muslimah* (Guideline for the personality of a Muslim woman). Yogyakarta: PP 'Aisyiyah, 1995.

————, ed. *Peringatan Congres Moehammadiyah Bahagian 'Aisjijah ke 21* (Report of the 'Aisyiyah meeting during the twenty-first Muhammadiyah congress). Yogyakarta: PP 'Aisyiyah, 1932.

————, ed. *Sejarah pertumbuhan dan Perkembangan 'Aisyiyah* (The History of 'Aisyiyah's growth and development). Yogyakarta: PP 'Aisyiyah, n.d.

————, ed. *Sikap terhadap Loearan* ('Aisyiyah's attitude towards the outside world). Yogyakarta: PP 'Aisyiyah, 1940.

————, ed. *Pedoman teknis dan operasional "Qoryah Thoyyiba"* (Technical and organizational guideline for the Qoryah Thoyyibah project). Yogyakarta: PP 'Aisyiyah, 1992.

————, ed. *Tuntunan menuju Keluarga Sakinah* (Guidelines for the harmonious family). Yogyakarta: PP 'Aisyiyah, 1994.

Pimpinan Pusat Fatayat NU. *Garis Besar: Program-program Fatayat Nahdlatul Ulama Tahun 1996–2000* (Outline: Fatayat NU programs for the years 1996–2000). (Jakarta: Unpublished, 1996.

————. *Sejarah Fatayat NU* (History of the Fatayat NU). Jakarta: PP Fatayat NU, 1984.

Pimpinan Pusat Muhammadiyah, ed. *Adabul Marah fil Islam, Keputusan Muktamar Tarjih ke XVII* (Rules of conduct for women in Islam: Decisions of the Seventeenth Tarjih Conference). Yogyakarta: PP Muhammadiyah, 1982.

————, ed. *Himpunan Putusan Majelis Tarjih Muhammadiyah* (Collection of Majelis Tarjih decisions). Yogyakarta: PP Muhammadiyah, 1974.

————, ed. *Jati Diri dan Akhlak Muhammadiyah* (Muhammadiyah identity and ethics). Jakarta: PP Muhammadiyah, 1994.

————, ed. *Membina Keluarga Sejahtera* (Formation of the wholesome family). 5th ed. Yogyakarta: Persatuan Publishers, 1972.

————, ed. "Muhammadiyah di Kata Kaum Muda" (Muhammadiyah in young peoples' words). *Muhammadiyah menyongsong Abad XXI. Media Inovasi* 11 (December 1994): 56–57.

————, ed. *Pedoman Hidup Islami Warga Muhammadiyah: Keputusan Muktamar Muhammadiyah Ke-44 Tangal 8 s.d. 11 Juli Tahun 2000 di Jakarta* (Guidelines for the Islamic way of life for the Muhammadiyah family: Decisions made by the forty-fourth Muhammadiyah conference, July 8–11, 2000, in Jakarta). Yogyakarta: PP Muhammadiyah, 2001.

————, ed. *Tarjih: Jurnal Tarjih dan Pengembangan Pemikriran Islam* (Tarjih: The Journal for religious consideration and Islamic thinking). Special issue: "Wanita dalam Perspektif Islam" (Women according to the Islamic perspective). December 1996.

Pimpinan Pusat Muslimat NU, ed. *Sejarah Muslimat Nahdlatul Ulama* (The History of the Muslimat NU). Jakarta: PP Muslimat NU, 1979.

————, ed. *Lima puluh Tahun Muslimat NU: Berkhidmat untuk Agama, Negara dan Bangsa* (Fifty years of Muslimat NU: Serving religion, country, and people). Jakarta: PP Muslimat NU, 1996.

Pimpinan Pusat Nasyiatul 'Aisyiyah, ed. *Agama dan Harmoni Kebangsaan dalam Perspektif Islam, Kristen-Katolik, Hindu, Buddha, Khonghuchu* (Religion and national harmony from the Islamic perspective: Catholicism, Hinduism, Buddhism, Confucianism). Yogyakarta: PP NA, 2000.

————, ed. *Riwayat Singkat, Khittah Perjuangan, Kepribadian* (NA's short history, guiding principles for the struggle, personality). Yogyakarta: Departemen Dokin PP NA, 1999–2000.

Pimpinan Wilayah 'Aisyiyah, ed. *Kumpulan Syair untuk Taman Kanak-Kanak 'Aisyiyah Bustanul Athfaal* (Collections of songs for the 'Aisyiyah Bustanul Athfaal kindergartens). Yogyakarta: Pimpinan Wilayah 'Aisyiyah, 1997.

Poesposuwarno, M. Margono, and Solihin M. Siradj. *Beberapa Soal Jawab Kemuhammadiyahan.* (Some questions and answers concerning Muhammadiyah). Yogyakarta, PP Muhammadiyah, 1976.

Puset Studi Wanita IAIN Yogyakarta, ed. *Islam dan Konstruksi Seksualitas* (Islam and the construction of sexuality). Yogyakarta: Pustaka Pelajar, 2002.

Qodir, Zuli. "Wacana Keagamaan Generasi Muda Muhammadiyah-NU" (The Religious discourse of the young Muhammadiyan-NU generation). In *Muhammadiyah-NU: Mendayung Ukhuwah di Tengah Perbedaan* (Muhammadiyah-NU: To peddle brotherhood in the midst of difference). Ed. Ma'mun Murod Al-Barbasy, Faozan Amar, Imam Santoso, and Khoirul Ikhwan. Malang: Universitas Muhammadiyah Malang Press, 2004. 111–19.

Rais, M. Amien. "Muhammadiyah dan Pembaharuan" (Muhammadiyah and renewal). In *Pendidikan Muhammadiyah dan Perubahan Sosial* (Muhammadiyah education and social change). Ed. M. Amien Rais. Yogyakarta: Pusat Latihan dan Pemgembangan Masyarakat, 1985. 62–76.

Rais, M. Amien, ed. *Pendidikan Muhammadiyah dan Perubahan Sosial* (Muhammadiyah education and social change). Yogyakarta: Pusat Latihan dan Pemgembangan Masyarakat, 1985.

————, ed. *Visi dan Misi Muhammadiyah* (The Muhammadiyah vision and mission). Yogyakarta: Pustaka Suara Muhammadiyah, 1997.

Rofiq et al., eds. *Pelajaran KeNuan Ahlussunnah walJama'ah* (Lessons in NU knowledge: People of the Sunnah and the community). 3 vols. Yogyakarta: Lajnah Ta'lif wa Nasyr-NU, 1995.

Setiyawati, Terias. "Hubungan antara Program Desa Sejahtera dan Dinamika Kelompok Pengajian 'Aisyiyah (Studi Kasus di Kabupaten Bantul, Propinsi Daerah Istemewa Yogyakarta)" (The relationship between the wholesome *desa* project and the dynamics of the 'Aisyiyah *pengajian* group [Case study in the district of Bantul, province of Yogyakarta]). Master's thesis, Institute Pertanian, 1994.

Sjachruni, Asmah. "Bersatulah Muslimat NU!" (Muslimat NU unite!). In *Solichah A. Wahid Hasyim: Muslimah di Garis Depan* (Solichah A. Wahid Hasyim: A Muslim woman at the frontline). Ed. Muhammad Dahlan, Rofiqul-Umam Ahmad, and Ali Zawawi. Jakarta: Yayasan K. H. A. Wahid Hasyim, 2001. 143–62.

Sodik, Mochamad, ed. *Teelah Ulang Wacana Seksualitas* (Reinvestigating the discourse about sexuality). Yogyakarta: PSW IAIN Sunan Kalijaga and Canadian International Development Agency, 2004.

Soelarto, B. *Garebeg di Kesultanan Yogyakarta* (The Garebeg festivity in the sultanate of Yogyakarta). Yogyakarta: Kanisius, 1993.

Suratmin, S. F. *Nyai Ahmad Dahlan, Pahlawan Nasional: Amal dan Perjuangannya* (Nyai Ahmad Dahlan, national hero: Her works and struggle). Yogyakarta: PP 'Aisyiyah, 1990.

Suryono, Eko, ed. *Poligami Bukan Hanya Milik Kyai dan Orang Kaya: Kiat Sukses Polig-ami Islami: Pengalaman Puspo Wardoyo dan Empat Istrinya* (Polygyny does not to belong to the *kiai* only: The secret of the success of polygyny according to Islam: The experience of Puspo Wardoyo and his four wives). N.p.: Published by the author, n.d.

Syahminan, Zaini. *Bimbingan Praktis Tentang Puasa* (A Practical guide for fasting). Surabaya: Al-Ikhlas, n.d.

Tauhid, Abdi. "Masih ada Islam yang anti-Pancasila" (Anti-Pancasila Islam still exists). *Istiqlal* online. June 15, 2000. www.listserv.dfn.de/cgi_bin/wa?A2=indo006C&L=indo news&O=D&F=&S=&P=1492.

Tedjo, Sasongko, ed. *Dialog dengan Kiai Hajji MA Sahal Mahfudh Telaah Fikih Sosial* (A dialogue with Kiai Hajji MA Sahal Mahfudh about the social application of Fiqh teachings). Semarang: Yayasan Karyawan Suara Merdeka, 1997.

Thalib, Muhammad. *Tuntunan Poligami dan Keutamaannya* (Guideline for polygyny and its good qualities). Bandung: Irsyad Baitus Salam, 2001.

Tim Pemberdayaan Perempuan Departemen Agama, ed. "Draft Kompilasi Hukum Islam" (Draft Islamic law compendium). Jakarta: Unpublished, 2004.

Ulfa Anshori, Maria. "Jika Rasul Hidup Sekarang, Tak akan Poligami" (If the Prophet would live today, he would not practice polygyny). April 28, 2002. www.islamlib.com/id/index.php?page=article&id=216.

———. "Promosi Kesehatan dengan bahasa Agama: Sebuah Pengalaman Fatayat dalam Mensukseskan Program Kelangsungan Hidup, Pemgembangan, Perlindungan Ibu dan Anak (KHPPIA) di Indonesia" (Promoting health from a religious approach: The Experience of the Fatayat NU in designing programs that extend life and develop and protect Indonesian mothers and children successfully [KHPPIA]). Paper presented at the Conference on Population and Reproductive Health in the Muslim World, Cairo, February 21–24, 1998.

Van Bruinessen, Martin. *Kitab Kuning, Pesantren dan Tarekat: Tradisi-Tradisi Islam di Indonesia* (The Yellow Books, *Pesantren* and Sufi Orders: Islamic Traditions in Indonesia). Bandung, Mizan Publishers, 1995.

———. *NU: Tradisi, Relasi-Relasi Kuasa, Pencarian Wacana Baru* (NU: Tradition, power relations, and the search for a new discourse). Yogyakarta: LkiS, 1994.

Wahid, K. H. Abdurrahman. *Kiai Nyentrik Membela Pemerintah* (Eccentric *kiai* defend the government). Yogyakarta: LkiS, 1997.

———. *Menggerakkan Tradisi: Esai-Esai Pesantren* (Setting tradition in motion: Essays about the *pesantren*). Yogyakarta: LKiS, 2001.

———. "Refleksi Teologis Perkawinan dalam Islam" (A Theological reflection about marriage in Islam). In *Menakar "Harga" Perempuan: Eksplorasi Lanjut atas Hak-Hak Reproduksi Perempuan dalam Islam* (Measuring the "value" of women: A Further exploration of women's reproductive rights in Islam). Ed. Syafiq Hasyim. Bandung, Penerbit Mizan, 1999. 170–75.

Wahid, Marzuki, et al. *Dinamika NU: Perjalanan Sosial dari Muktamar Cipasung (1994) ke Muktamar Kediri (1999)* (NU dynamics: The social journey from the 1994 Cipasung Conference to the 1999 Kediri Conference). Jakarta: Kompas and Lakpesdam NU, 1999.

————. "Post-Traditionalisme Islam: Gairah Baru Pemikiran Islam di Indonesia" (Islamic post-traditionalism: A New stimulus in Indonesian Islamic thinking). *Tashwirul Afkar: Jurnal Refleksi Pemikiran Keagamaan & Kebudayaan* 10 (2001): 2–24.

Wahid, Marzuki, Suwendi, and Saefuddin Zuhri. *Pesantren Masa Depan: Wacana Pemberdayaan dan Transformasi Pesantren.* (The Future of the *pesantren:* A Discourse on developing and transforming the *pesantren*). Bandung: Pustaka Hidaya, 1999.

Wahid, Sinta Nuriyah Abdurrahman. "Merumuskan kembali agenda perjuangan perempuan dalam konteks perubahan social budaya Islam di Indonesia" (Reflections on the struggle of women in the context of social change within Indonesia's Islamic culture). In *Jurnal Pemikiran Islam tentang Pemberdayaan Perempuan* (Journal for Islamic thought about women's empowerment). Jakarta: PP Muslimat NU and Penerbit Logos Wacana Ilmu, 2000. 13–20.

YKF. *Anotasi Lima puluh Buku Penguatan Hak Reproduksi Perempuan* (Annotation of fifty books about strengthening women's reproductive rights). Yogyakarta: Yayasan Kesejahteraan Fatayat, 2002.

————. *Laporan Program Penguatan Hak-Hak Reproduksi Perempuan di Pesantren* (Report of the program to strengthen women's reproductive rights in the *pesantren*). Yogyakarta: YKF and the Ford Foundation, 2000–2001.

Zuhri, Saefuddin. *Pesantren Masa Depan: Wacana Pemberdayaan dan Transformasi Pesantren* (The Future of the *pesantren:* A Discourse on developing and transforming the *pesantren*). Bandung: Pustaka Hidaya, 1999.

Non-Indonesian Titles

Abdel-Fattah, Nabil. "Besieged Rights: An Overall View of the Conditions of Women in Some Arab Countries." In *The Role of Islamic Women's Organizations in Advocacy and the Elimination of Discrimination: A Comparative Study between the Middle East and Southeast Asia.* Ed. Nelly van Doorn-Harder, Mbak Masrucha, and Brigit Keenan. Yogyakarta: YKF, 2002. 34–35.

Abdullah, Taufik, ed. *The Heartbeat of Indonesian Revolution.* Jakarta: PT Gramedia Pustaka Utama, 1997.

Abdullah, Taufik, and Sharon Siddique, eds. *Islam and Society in Southeast Asia.* Singapore: Institute of Southeast Asian Studies, 1986.

Abdullah, Yusuf Ali, trans. *The Meanings of the Illustrious Qur'an.* New Dehli: Kitab Bhavan, 1997.

Abou El Fadl, Khaled. *Speaking in God's Name: Islamic Law, Authority, and Women.* Oxford: Oneworld Publications, 2001.

Afkhami, Mahnaz, and Erika Friedl. *Muslim Women and the Politics of Participation: Implementing the Beijing Platform.* Syracuse, N.Y.: Syracuse University Press, 1997.

Ahmed, Leila. *Women and Gender in Islam: Historical Roots of a Modern Debate.* New Haven, Conn.: Yale University Press, 1992.

Alfian. *Muhammadiyah: The Political Behavior of a Muslim Modernist Organization under Dutch Colonialism.* Yogyakarta: Gadjah Mada University Press, 1989.

Ali, Kecia. "Progressive Muslims and Islamic Jurisprudence: The Necessity for Critical Engagement with Marriage and Divorce Law." In *Progressive Muslims: On Justice, Gender, and Pluralism.* Ed. Omid Safi. Oxford, England: Oneworld Publications, 2003. 163–89.

Anderson, Benedict R. O'G. *Java in a Time of Revolution: Occupation and Resistance, 1944–1946.* Ithaca N.Y.: Cornell University Press, 1972.

Anderson, Benedict R. O'G, Mitsuo Nakamura, and Mohammad Slammet, eds. *Religion and Social Ethos in Indonesia.* 1975; reprint, Clayton, Victoria: Monash University, Centre for Southeast Asian Studies, 1995.

An-Na'im, Ahmed Abdullahi. *Towards an Islamic Reform: Civil Liberties, Human Rights, and International Law.* Syracuse, N.Y.: Syracuse University Press, 1990.

Armstrong, Karen. *The Battle for God: A History of Fundamentalism.* New York: Ballantine Books, 2001.

Atkinson, Jane Monnig, and Shelley Errington, eds. *Power and Difference: Gender in Island Southeast Asia.* Stanford, Calif.: Stanford University Press, 1990.

Badran, Margot. "Feminism and the Qur'an." In *Encyclopeadia of the Qur'an.* Leiden: Brill, 2002 199–203.

———. "Islamic Feminism: What's in a Name?" *Al-Ahram Weekly Online.* January 17–23, 2002. www.weekly.ahram.org.eg2002/56q/cu1.htm.

Baried, Baroroh. "Islam and the Modernization of Indonesian Women." In *Islam and Society in Southeast Asia.* Ed. Taufik Abdullah and Sharon Siddique. Singapore: Institute of Southeast Asian Studies, 1986. 139–54.

Barlas, Asma. *"Believing Women" in Islam: Unreading Patriarchal Interpretations of the Qur'an.* Austin: University of Texas Press, 2002.

Barton, Greg. "The Liberal, Progressive Roots of Abdurrahman Wahid's Thought." In *Nahdlatul Ulama: Traditional Islam and Modernity in Indonesia.* Clayton, Victoria: Monash Asia Institute, 1996. 190–226.

———. "Neo-Modernism: A Vital Synthesis of Traditionalist and Modernist Islamic Thought in Indonesia" *Studia Islamika* 2.3 (1995): 1–75.

Barton, Greg, and Greg Fealy, eds. *Nahdlatul Ulama: Traditional Islam and Modernity in Indonesia.* Clayton, Victoria: Monash Asia Institute, 1996.

Beatty, Andrew. *Varieties of Javanese Religion: An Anthropological Account.* Cambridge, Mass.: Cambridge University Press, 1999.

Bell, Catherine. *Ritual: Perspectives and Dimensions.* New York: Oxford University Press, 1997.

Berman, Laine. *Speaking through the Silence: Narratives, Social Conventions, and Power in Java.* New York: Oxford University Press, 1998.

Blackburn, Susan. *Love, Sex, and Power: Women in Southeast Asia.* Clayton, Victoria: Monash Asia Institute, 2001.

———. "Why Send Girls to School? Debates about Education of Indonesian Girls in the Colonial Period." Paper presented at the Conference on Asian Women, University of New South Wales, October 1–3, 1997.

Blackwood, Evelyn. *Webs of Power: Women, Kin, and Community in a Sumatran Village.* Lanham, Md.: Rowman and Littlefield, 2000.

Blumberger, J. Th. Petrus. *De Nationalistische Beweging in Nederlandsch-Indie* (The Nationalist movement in the Dutch-Indies). Haarlem: H. D. Tjeenk Willink and Sons, 1931.

Boland, B. J. *The Struggle of Islam in Modern Indonesia.* The Hague: Martinus Nijhof, 1971.

Bowen, John R. *Islam, Law, and Equality in Indonesia.* Cambridge: Cambridge University Press, 2003.

———. *Muslims through Discourse: Religion and Ritual in Gayo Society.* Princeton, N.J.: Princeton University Press, 1993.

Brenner, Susanne A. *The Domestication of Desire.* Princeton, N.J.: Princeton University Press, 1998.

———. "Why Women Rule the Roost: Rethinking Javanese Ideologies of Gender and Self-Control." In *Bewitching Women, Pious Men: Gender and Body Politics in Southeast Asia.* Ed. Aihwa Ong and Michael G. Peletz. Berkeley: University of California Press, 1995. 19–50.

Bunnell, Frederick. "Community Participation, Indigenous Ideology, Activist Politics: Indonesian NGOs in the 1990s." In *Making Indonesia: Essays on Modern Indonesia in Honor of George MCT Kahin.* Ed. Daniel S. Lev and Ruth McVey. Ithaca, N.Y.: Cornell University Press, 1996. 180–201.

Castells, Manuel. *The Power of Identity.* Vol. 2 of *The Information Age: Economy, Society, and Culture.* Malden, Mass.: Blackwell, 1997.

Collins, Elizabeth. "*Dakwah* and Democracy: The Significance of Partai Keadilan and Hizbut Tahrir." Paper presented at the annual meeting of the Asian Studies Association. New York, March 29, 2003.

Cooke, Miriam. *Women Claim Islam: Creating Islamic Feminism through Literature.* New York: Routledge, 2001.

Coté, Joost, trans. *Letters from Kartini: An Indonesian Feminist, 1900–1904.* Clayton, Victoria: Monash Asian Institute, 1992.

Dhofier, Zamakhsyari. *The Pesantren Tradition: The Role of the Kiai in the Maintenance of Traditional Islam in Java.* 1982; reprint, Tempe: Arizona State University Program for Southeast Asian Studies, 1999.

Dzuhayatin, Siti Ruhaini. "Women in Muhammadiyah: The Shifting Paradigm on Women's Issues in Indonesia." Paper presented at the International Workshop on the Role of Islamic Women's Organizations. Yogyakarta, July 27–31, 1999.

Emmerson, Donald K., ed. *Indonesia Beyond Suharto: Polity, Economy, Society, Transition.* Armonk, N.Y.: M. E. Sharpe, 1999.

Fealy, Greg. "Islamic Politics: A Rising or Declining Force?" In *Indonesia: The Uncertain Transition.* Ed. Damien Kingsbury and Arief Budiman. Adelaide: Crawford House, 2001. 119–36.

———. "Ulama and Politics in Indonesia: A History of Nahdlatul Ulama, 1952–1967." Ph.D. dissertation, Monash University, 1998.

———. "Wahab Chasbullah, Traditionalism, and the Political Development of Nahdlatul Ulama." In *Nahdlatul Ulama, Traditional Islam, and Modernity in Indonesia.* Ed. Greg Barton and Greg Fealy. Clayton, Victoria: Monash Asia Institute, 1996. 1–41.

Featherstone, Mike, and Scott Lash. *Global Modernities.* Cambridge, Mass.: Harvard University Press, 1995.

Federspiel, Howard. "The Muhammadijah: A Study of an Orthodox Islamic Movement in Indonesia." *Indonesia* 10 (1970): 57–79.

Feillard, Andree. "Indonesia's Emerging Muslim Feminism." *Studia Islamika* 4.1 (1997): 83–108.

————. *Islam et l'armée dans l'Indonésie contemporaine: les pionniers de la traditions.* Paris: Association Archipel, 1995.

Feillard, Andree, and Lies Marcoes. "Female Circumcision in Indonesia: To 'Islamize' in Ceremony or Secrecy." *Archipel* 56 (1998): 337–68.

Foucault, Michel. *Discipline and Punish: The Birth of the Prison.* Trans. A. Sheridan. London: Penguin Books, 1977.

————. *The History of Sexuality.* Vol. 1. Trans. R. Hurley. New York: Pantheon, 1978.

————. *Power/Knowledge: Selected Interviews and Other Writings, 1972–1977.* Ed. Colin Gordon. Trans. Colin Gordon et al. New York: Pantheon Books 1980.

————. "Technologies of the Self." In *Technologies of the Self: A Seminar with Michel Foucault.* Ed. Martin Luther, Hugh Gutman, and Patrick H. Hutton. Amherst: University of Massachusetts Press, 1988. 10–49.

Fox, James J. "Ziarah Visits to the Tombs of the Walis, the Founders of Islam on Java." In *Islam in the Indonesian Social Context.* Ed. M. C. Ricklefs. Clayton, Victoria: Centre for Southeast Asian Studies, Monash University, 1991. 19–38.

Friedman, B. D. "On the Concept of Authority in Political Philosophy." In *Authority: Readings in Social and Political Theory.* Ed. Joseph Raz. Albany: New York University Press, 1990. 56–92.

Gade, Anna M. *Perfection Makes Practice: Learning, Emotion, and the Recited Qur'an in Indonesia.* Honolulu: University of Hawaii Press, 2004.

Gaffney, Patrick D. *The Prophet's Pulpit: Islamic Preaching in Contemporary Egypt.* Berkeley: University of California Press, 1994.

Geertz, Clifford. *The Religion of Java.* London: The Free Press of Glencoe, 1960.

Gole, Nilofer. *The Forbidden Modern: Civilization and Veiling.* Ann Arbor: University of Michigan Press, 1996.

Gramsci, Antonio. *Selections from the Prison Notebooks.* Trans. Quintin Hoare and Geoffrey Nowell Smith. London: Lawrence and Wishart, 1971.

Hadler, Jeffrey Alan. "Places Like Home: Islam, Matriliny, and the History of the Family in Minangkabau." Ph.D. dissertation, Cornell University, 2000.

Hafez, Sherine. *The Terms of Empowerment: Islamic Women Activists in Egypt.* Cairo: American University in Cairo Press, 2001.

Hasan, Noorhaidi. "Faith and Politics: The Rise of the Laskar Jihad in the Era of Transition in Indonesia." *Indonesia* 73 (2002): 145–69.

Hatley, Barbara. "Nation, 'Tradition,' and Constructions of the Feminine in Modern Indonesian Literature." In *Cultural Politics and the Politics of Culture.* Ed. James William Schiller and Barbara Martin-Schiller. Athens: Center for International Studies, University of Ohio, 1997. 90–120.

Hefner, Robert W. *Civil Islam: Muslims and Democratization in Indonesia.* Princeton, N.J.: Princeton University Press, 2000.

————. *Hindu Javanese: Tengger Tradition and Islam.* Princeton, N.J.: Princeton University Press, 1985.

————. "Indonesian Islam at the Crossroads." *Van Zorge Report on Indonesia* 4.3 (February 19, 2002): 12–20.

————. "Islamizing Java? Religion and Politics in Rural East Java." *Journal of Asian Studies* 46.3 (August 1987): 533–34.

————. "Islamization and Democratization in Indonesia." In *Islam in an Era of Nation-States.* Ed. Robert W. Hefner and Patricia Horvatich. Honolulu: University of Hawaii Press, 1997. 75–128.

————. "A Muslim Civil Society? Indonesian Reflections on the Conditions of Its Possibility." In *Democratic Civility: The History and Cross-Cultural Possibility of a Modern Political Idea.* Ed. Robert W. Hefner. New Brunswick, N.J.: Transaction Publishers, 1998. 285–327.

————, ed. *Democratic Civility: The History and Cross-Cultural Possibility of a Modern Political Idea.* New Brunswick, N.J.: Transaction Publishers, 1998.

Hefner, Robert W., and Patricia Horvatich, eds. *Islam in an Era of Nation-States.* Honolulu: University of Hawaii Press, 1997.

Hellwig, Tineke. *In the Shadow of Change: Women in Indonesian Literature.* Berkeley: Centers for South and Southeast Asian Studies, 1994.

Hill, Hal, ed. *Indonesia's New Order: The Dynamics of Socio-Economic Transformation.* Sydney: Allen and Unwin, 1994.

Hobsbawm, Eric, and Terence Ranger, eds. *The Invention of Tradition.* Cambridge: Cambridge University Press, 1983.

Hooker, Virginia Matheson. "Expression: Creativity Despite Constraint." In *Indonesia Beyond Suharto: Polity, Economy, Society, Transition.* Ed. Donald K. Emmerson. Armonk, N.Y.: M. E. Sharpe, 1999. 262–94.

Howel, Julia Day. "Sufism and the Indonesian Islamic Revival." *Journal of Asian Studies* 60.3 (2001): 701–29.

Israeli, Raphael. *The Crescent in the East: Islam in Asia Minor.* London: Curzon Press, 1989.

Jainuri, Achmad. "The Formation of the Muhammadiyah Ideology, 1912–1942." Ph.D. dissertation, McGill University, 1997.

Jay, Robert R. *Javanese Villagers: Social Relations in Rural Modjokuto.* Cambridge: Massachusetts Institute of Technology Press, 1969.

Jayawardena, Kumari. *Feminism and Nationalism in the Third World.* London: Zed Books, 1986.

Jeffrey, Roger, and Alaha M. Basu, eds. *Girls' Schooling, Women's Autonomy, and Fertility Change in South Asia.* New Dehli: Sage, 1996.

Jellinek, L. *The Life of a Jakarta Street Trader.* Melbourne: Monash University, Centre for Southeast Asian Studies, 1974.

————. *The Wheel of Fortune: The History of a Poor Community in Jakarta.* Sydney: Allen and Unwin, 1990.

Kandiyoti, Deniz. "Islam and Patriarchy: A Comparative Perspective." In *Women in Middle Eastern History: Shifting Boundaries in Sex and Gender.* New Haven, Conn.: Yale University Press, 1991. 23–42.

Karam, Azza. "Women, Islamisms, and the State: Dynamics of Power and Contemporary Feminisms in Egypt." In *Muslim Women and the Politics of Participation: Implementing the Beijing Platform.* Ed. Mahnaz Afkhami and Erika Friedl. Syracuse, N.Y.: Syracuse University Press, 1997. 18–28.

————. *Women, Islamisms, and the State: Contemporary Feminism in Egypt.* New York: St. Martin's, 1998.

Keddie, Nikki R., and Beth Baron, eds. *Women in Middle Eastern History: Shifting Boundaries in Sex and Gender.* New Haven, Conn.: Yale University Press, 1991.

Keeler, Ward. "Speaking of Gender in Java." In *Power and Difference: Gender in Island Southeast Asia.* Ed. Jane Monnig Atkinson and Shelly Errington. Stanford, Calif.: Stanford University Press, 1990. 127–52.

Kepel, Gilles. *Jihad: The Trail of Political Islam.* Cambridge, Mass.: Harvard University Press, 2002.

Kingsbury, Damien, and Arief Budiman, eds. *Indonesia: The Uncertain Transition.* Adelaide: Crawford House, 2001.

Koentjaraningrat, R. N. *Javanese Culture.* Singapore: Oxford University Press, 1985.

Lev, Daniel. "On the Other Hand?" In *Fantasizing the Feminine in Indonesia.* Ed. Laurie J. Sears. Durham, N.C.: Duke University Press, 1996. 191–202.

Lev, Daniel, and Ruth McVey, eds. *Making Indonesia.* Ithaca, N.Y.: Cornell University Press, 1996.

Liddle, William R. "The Islamic Turn in Indonesia: A Political Explanation." *Journal of Asian Studies* 55.3 (1996): 613–34.

———. "Media Dakwah Scripturalism: One Form of Islamic Political Thought and Action in New Order Indonesia." In *Toward a New Paradigm: Recent Developments in Indonesian Islamic Thought.* Ed. Mark Woodward. Tempe: Arizona State University Press, 1996. 323–56.

Locher-Scholten, Elsbeth. *Women and the Colonial State: Essays on Gender and Modernity.* Amsterdam: Amsterdam University Press, 2000.

Locher-Scholten, Elsbeth, and Anke Niehof, eds. *Indonesian Women in Focus.* Leiden: KITLV Press, 1992.

Lucas, Anton, and Robert Cribb. "Women's Roles in the Indonesian Revolution: Some Historical Reflections." In *The Heartbeat of Indonesian Revolution.* Ed. Taufik Abdullah. Jakarta: PT Gramedia Pustaka Utama, 1997. 70–93.

Machali, Rochayah. "Women and the Concept of Power in Indonesia." In *Love, Sex, and Power: Women in Southeast Asia.* Ed. Susan Blackburn. Clayton, Victoria: Monash Asia Institute, 2001. 1–15.

Magnis-Suseno, Franz. *Javanese Ethics and World-view: The Javanese Idea of the Good Life.* Jakarta: PT Gramedia Pustaka Utama, 1997.

Marcoes-Natsir, Lies. "The Female Preacher as Mediator in Religion: A Case Study in Jakarta and West Java." In *Women and Mediation in Indonesia.* Ed. Sita van Bemmelen, Madelon Djajadiningrat-Nieuwenhuis, and Elsbeth Locher-Scholten. Leiden: KITLV Press, 1992. 203–28.

———. "Muslim Female Preacher and Feminist Movement." In *Muslim Feminism and Feminist Movement: Southeast Asia.* Ed. Abida Samiuddin and R. Khanam. Dehli: Global Vision Publishing House, 2002. 253–89.

Masud, Muhammad Khalid, Brinkley Messick, and David S. Powers. "Muftis, Fatwas, and Islamic Legal Interpretation." In *Islamic Legal Interpretation: Muftis and Their Fatwas.* Ed. Muhammad Khalid Masud, Brinkley Messick, and David S. Powers. Cambridge, Mass.: Harvard University Press, 1996. 3–32.

Melluci, Alberto. *Challenging Codes: Collective Action in the Information Age.* New York: Cambridge University Press, 1996.

Mernissi, Fatima. *Women's Rebellion and Islamic Memory.* London: Zed Books, 1996.

Mir-Hosseini, Ziba. "Debating Women: Gender and the Public Sphere in Post-revolutionary Iran." In *Civil Society in Comparative Muslim Contexts.* Ed. Amyn Sajoo. London: I. B. Tauris and the Institute for Ismaili Studies, 2002. 95–122.

———. *Islam and Gender: The Religious Debate in Contemporary Iran.* London: I. B. Tauris, 2000.

———. "The Quest for Gender Justice: Emerging Feminist Voice in Islam." *Islam21* 36 (May 2004): 6–8.

Mohanty, Chandra Talpade. "Cartographies of Struggle: Third World Women and the Politics of Feminism." In *Third World Women and the Politics of Feminism.* Ed. Chandra Talpade Mohanty, Ann Russo, and Lourdes Torres. Bloomington: Indiana University Press, 1991. 1–41.

Mohanty, Chandra Talpade, Ann Russo, and Lourdes Torres, eds. *Third World Women and the Politics of Feminism.* Bloomington: Indiana University Press, 1991.

Muhammadiyah Movement in Indonesia. Bande Aceh: Central Board of Muhammadiyah, 1995.

Mulder, Niels. *Mysticism in Java: Ideology in Indonesia.* Amsterdam: Pepin Press, 1998.

Munir, Lily Zakiyah. "'He Is Your Garment and You Are His . . .': Religious Precepts, Interpretations, and Power Relations in Marital Sexuality among Javanese Muslim Women." *Sojourn* 12.2 (October 2002): 191–220.

Murata, Sachiko, and William C. Chittick. *The Vision of Islam.* New York: Paragon House, 1994.

Murray, Alison F. *No Money, No Honey: A Study of Street Traders and Prostitutes in Jakarta.* Singapore: Oxford University Press, 1991.

Nakamura, Mitsuo, *The Crescent Arises over the Banyan Tree: A Study of the Muhammadiyah Movement in a Central Javanese Town.* Yogyakarta: Gadjah Mada University Press, 1993.

———. "The Radical Traditionalism of the Nahdlatul Ulama in Indonesia: A Personal Account of the Twenty-sixth National Congress, June 1979, Semarang." In *Nahdlatul Ulama: Traditional Islam and Modernity in Indonesia.* Ed. Greg Barton and Greg Fealy. Clayton, Victoria: Monash Asia Institute, 1996. 68–93.

Niehof, Anke. "The Changing Lives of Indonesian Women: Contained Emancipation under Pressure." *Bijdragen tot de Taal-, Land- en Volkenkunde* 154.2 (1998): 236–58.

Northup, Lesley A. *Ritualizing Women.* Cleveland: Pilgrim Press, 1997.

Nussbaum, Martha C. *Women and Human Development: The Capabilities Approach.* Cambridge: Cambridge University Press, 2001.

Oepen, Manfred, and Wolfgang Karcher, eds. *The Impact of Pesantren in Education and Community Development in Indonesia.* Jakarta: P3M, 1988.

Office of the Senior Coordinator for International Women's Issues. "Indonesia: Report on Female Genital Mutilation (FGM) or Female Genital Cutting (FGC)." Washington, D.C.: Department of State, 2001.

Ong, Aihwa, and Michael G. Peletz, eds. *Bewitching Women, Pious Men: Gender and Body Politics in Southeast Asia.* Berkeley: University of California Press, 1995.

Oxaal, Zoë, with Sally Baden. "Gender and Empowerment: Definitions, Approaches, and Implications for Policy (report 40)." Report for the Swedish International Development Cooperation Agency (SIDA), 1997. www.bridge.ids.uk/reports/R40%20Gen %20Emp%20Policy%202C.doc.

Ozment, Steven. *Protestants: The Birth of a Revolution.* New York: Doubleday, 1993.

Peacock, James L. *Muslim Puritans: Reformist Psychology in Southeast Asian Islam.* Berke-
. ley: University of California Press, 1978.

———. *Purifying the Faith: The Muhammadijah Movement in Indonesian Islam.* Menlo Park, Calif.: Benjamin/Cumming Publishing Co., 1978.

Peletz, Michael. "Neither Reasonable nor Responsible: Contrasting Representations of Masculinity in a Malay Society." In *Bewitching Women, Pious Men: Gender and Body Politics in Southeast Asia.* Ed. Aihwa Ong and Michael G. Peletz. Berkeley: University of California Press, 1995. 76–123.

Pijper, G. F. *Fragmenta Islamica: Studien over het Islamisme in Nederlandsch-Indie* (Studies about Islam in the Dutch Indies). Leiden: E. J. Brill, 1934.

Prasetyo, Sabarinah, and Maria Ulfah. "Community Development Activities of Women's Organizations in Indonesia." Paper presented at a meeting about the involvement of women organizations in family planning and community development, Seoul, Korea, June 13, 1996.

Ramusack, Barbara N., and Sharon Sievers. *Women in Asia: Restoring Women to History.* Bloomington: Indiana University Press, 1999.

Ricklefs, M. C. *A History of Modern Indonesia c. 1300 to the Present.* London: Macmillan, 1981.

———, ed. *Islam in the Indonesian Social Context.* Clayton, Victoria: Monash University, 1991.

Riddell, Peter. *Islam and the Malay-Indonesian World: Transmission and Responses.* Honolulu: University of Hawaii Press, 2001.

Robinson, Kathryn. "Gender, Islam, and Culture in Indonesia." In *Love, Sex, and Power: Women in Southeast Asia.* Ed. Susan Blackburn. Clayton, Victoria: Monash Asia Institute, 2001. 17–30.

———. "Women: Difference versus Diversity." In *Indonesia beyond Suharto: Polity, Economy, Society, Transition.* Armonk, N.Y.: M. E. Sharpe, 1999. 237–61.

Ro'fah. "A Study of 'Aisyiyah: An Indonesian Women's Organization (1917–1998)." Master's thesis, McGill University, 2000.

Safi, Omid, ed. *Progressive Muslims: On Justice, Gender, and Pluralism.* Oxford: Oneworld Publications, 2003.

Saleh, Fauzan. *Modern Trends in Islamic Theological Discourses in Twentieth-Century Indonesia.* Leiden: Brill Publishers, 2001.

Schiller, James William, and Barbara Martin-Schiller, eds. *Imagining Indonesia: Cultural Politics and the Politics of Culture.* Athens: Center for International Studies, University of Ohio, 1997.

Sciortino, Rosalia, Lies Marcoes-Natsir, and Masdar Mas'udi. "Learning from Islam: Advocacy of Reproductive Rights in Indonesian Pesantren." *Reproductive Health Matters* 8 (November 1996): 86–93.

Sears, Laurie J. "Fragile Identities: Deconstructing Women and Indonesia." In *Fantasizing the Feminine in Indonesia.* Ed. Laurie J. Sears. Durham, N.C.: Duke University Press, 1996. 3–22.

————, ed. *Fantasizing the Feminine in Indonesia*. Durham, N.C.: Duke University Press, 1996.

Sen, Krishna. *Indonesian Cinema: Framing the New Order*. London: Zed Books, 1994.

Sen, Krishna, and Maila Stivens, eds. *Gender and Power in Affluent Asia*. London: Routledge, 1998.

Shahidian, Hammed. *Women in Iran: Emerging Voices in the Women's Movement*. Westport, Conn.: Greenwood Press, 2002.

Shiraishi, Takashi. *An Age in Motion: Popular Radicalism in Java, 1912–1926*. Ithaca, N.Y.: Cornell University Press, 1990.

Slamet, Mohammad. "Priyayi Value Conflict." In *Religion and Social Ethos in Indonesia*. Ed. Benedict R. O'G Anderson, Mitsuo Nakamura, and Mohammad Slammet. 1975; reprint, Clayton, Victoria: Monash University, Centre of Southeast Asian Studies, 1995.

Smith-Hefner, Nancy. "More Sex in the City: Muslim Youth, Sexuality, and Moral Panic in Yogyakarta." Paper presented at the Annual Meeting of the Association for Asian Studies, San Diego, March 5, 2004.

————. "The New Romance: Courtship and Marriage among Muslim Javanese." Paper presented at the Annual Meeting of the Association for Asian Studies, New York, March 27, 2003.

Soebardi, S., and C. P. Woodcroft-Lee. "Islam in Indonesia." In *The Crescent in the East: Islam in Asia Minor*. Ed. Raphael Israeli. London: Curzon Press, 1989. 180–210.

Stivens, Maila. "Theorizing Gender, Power, and Modernity in Affluent Asia." In *Gender and Power in Affluent Asia*. Ed. Krishna Sen and Maila Stivens. London: Routledge, 1998. 1–24.

Stowasser, Barbara F. "Women's Issues in Modern Islamic Thought." In *Arab Women: Old Boundaries, New Frontiers*. Ed. Judith Tucker. Bloomington: Indiana University Press, 1993. 3–28.

Sullivan, N. *Masters and Managers: A Study of Gender Relations in Urban Java*. St. Leonards, New South Wales: Allen and Unwin, 1994.

Suryadinata, Leo. *Elections and Politics in Indonesia*. Singapore: Institute of Southeast Asian Studies, 2002.

Suryakusuma, Julia I. "The State and Sexuality in New Order Indonesia." In *Fantasizing the Feminine in Indonesia*. Ed. Laurie J. Sears. Durham, N.C.: Duke University Press, 1996. 92–119.

Taylor, Jean Gelman, ed. *Women Creating Indonesia: The First Fifty Years*. Clayton, Victoria: Monash Asia Institute, 1997.

Tjorbjornsrud, Berit. *Controlling the Body to Liberate the Soul: Towards an Analysis of the Coptic Orthodox Concept of the Body*. Oslo: Faculty of Arts, 1999.

Tucker, Judith, ed. *Arab Women: Old Boundaries, New Frontiers*. Bloomington: Indiana University Press, 1993.

Van Bemmelen, Sita, Madelon Djajadiningrat-Nieuwenhuis, Elsbeth Locher-Scholten, and Elly Touwen-Bouwsma, eds. *Women and Mediation in Indonesia*. Leiden: KITLV Press, 1992.

Van Bruinessen, Martin. "Genealogies of Islamic Radicalism in Indonesia." *South East Asia Research* 10.2 (2002): 117–54.

————. "Kitab Kuning: Books in Arabic Script Used in the Pesantren Milieu." *Bijdragen Koninklijk Instituut voor de Tropen* 146 (1990): 226–69.

————. "New Perspectives on Southeast Asian Islam?" *Bijdragen tot de Taal- Land- en Volkenkunde* 143 (1987): 519–38.

————. "Traditions for the Future: the Reconstruction of Traditionalist Discourse within NU." In *Nahdlatul Ulama: Traditional Islam and Modernity in Indonesia.* Ed. Greg Barton and Greg Fealy. Clayton, Victoria: Monash Asia Institute, 1996. 163–89.

————, trans. "Traditionalist Muslims in a Modernizing World: The Nahdlatul Ulama and Indonesia's New Order: Politics, Factional Conflict, and The Search for a New Discourse." Unpublished manuscript in the author's possession.

Van Doorn-Harder, Nelly. "Gender and Religion: Gender and Islam." In *Encyclopedia of Religion.* 2d ed. Vol. 5. Ed. Lindsay Jones. Detroit: Macmillan Reference, 2005. 3364–71.

————. "The Indonesian Islamic Debate on a Woman President." *Sojourn* 17.2 (October 2002): 164–90.

————. "Indonesian Women Creating Justice." *Nordic Journal of Human Rights* 21.1 (Spring 2003).

————. "A Muslim Feminist Stirs Indonesia's Waters." *Christian Science Monitor,* May 17, 2001.

Van Doorn-Harder, Nelly, Mbak Masrucha, and Bridget Keenan. *The Role of Islamic Women's Organizations in Advocacy and the Elimination of Discrimination: A Comparative Study between the Middle East and Southeast Asia.* Yogyakarta: YKF, 2002.

Van Doorn-Harder, Nelly, and Kees de Jong. "The Pilgrimage to Tembayat: Tradition and Revival in Indonesian Islam." *Muslim World* 91.3–4 (Fall 2001): 325–54.

Van Dijk, Kees. "Religious Authority, Politics, and Fatwa in Contemporary Indonesia." Paper presented at the Islamic Law in Modern Indonesia Conference, Harvard Law School, Cambridge, Mass., April 17, 2004.

Vreede de Stuers, Cora. *The Indonesian Woman: Struggles and Achievements.* The Hague: Mouton, 1960.

Wadud, Amina. *Qur'an and Woman: Rereading the Sacred Text from a Woman's Perspective.* New York: Oxford University Press, 1999.

Wahid, K. H. Abdurrahman. "Principles of Pesantren Education." In *The Impact of Pesantren in Education and Community Development in Indonesia.* Ed. Manfred Oepen and Wolfgang Karcher. Jakarta: P3M, 1988. 197–203.

Webb, Gisela, ed. *Windows of Faith: Muslim Women Scholar-Activists in North America.* Syracuse, N.Y.: Syracuse University Press, 2000.

Weix, Gretchen G. "Islamic Prayer Groups in Indonesia: Local Forums and Gendered Responses," *Critique of Anthropology* 18.4 (1998): 405–21.

Wertheim, W. F. *Indonesian Society in Transition.* The Hague: W. van Hoeve, 1956.

Whalley, Lucy. "Virtuous Women, Productive Citizens: Negotiating Tradition, Islam, and Modernity in Minangkabau, Indonesia." Ph.D. dissertation, University of Illinois at Urbana-Champaign, 1993.

Wheeler, Brannon. *Applying the Canon in Islam: The Authorization and Maintenance of Interpretive Reasoning in Hanafi Scholarship.* Albany: State University of New York Press, 1996.

White, Sally Jane. "Reformist Islam, Gender, and Marriage in Late Colonial Dutch East Indies, 1900–1942." Ph.D. dissertation, Australian National University, 2004.

Wieringa, Saskia. "The Perfumed Nightmare: Indonesian Woman's Organizations after 1950." In *Pramoedya Ananta Toer 70 Tahun* (Essays to honor Pramoedya Ananta Toer's seventieth birthday). Ed. Bob Hering. Edisi Sastra Kabar Seberang, Sulating Maphilindo 24/25, 1995. 265–75.

———. "The Politization of Gender Relations in Indonesia: The Indonesian Women's Movement and Gerwani until the New Order State." Ph.D. dissertation, University of Amsterdam, 1995.

———. *Sexual Politics in Indonesia*. New York: Palgrave Macmillan, 2002.

Wolf, Diane. *Factory Daughters: Gender, Household Dynamics, and Rural Industrialization in Java*. Berkeley: University of California Press, 1992.

Woodward, Mark, ed. *Toward a New Paradigm: Recent Developments in Indonesian Islamic Thought*. Tempe: Arizona State University, 1996.

Zuhur, Sherifa. "The Mixed Impact of Feminist Struggles in Egypt During the 1990s." *Middle East Review of International Affairs Journal* 5.1 (March 2001): 78–89.

Index

Abangan, 50, 52, 65, 66, 70
Abdallah, Ulil Abshar, 52
Abdel-Fattah, Nabil, 39
'Abduh, Muhammad, 9, 51, 255
Abdullah, Amin, 12, 72, 152, 157, 158
abortion, 17, 244, 247, 248
Abou El-Fadl, Khaled, 4, 9, 12, 264
Abu Zayd, Nasr Hamid, 238
Aceh, kindom of, 21, 38
activist. *See* feminist
adat (local customary law), 22, 61
adultery. *See zina*
Ahmed, Leila, 264
'Aisyiyah, 1, 3, 5, 6, 8, 11, 13, 20, 32, 33, 46, 66,
    72, 73, 78, 80–81, 108–10, 131, 139, 152, 160,
    206, 209, 250; education, 42, 93, 95, 104–9,
    128; family model, 45, 104, 108, 114–24,
    230; headquarters (central office, PP), 90,
    98, 100, 149; ideology, 34, 36; leaders, 112,
    124, 125; preacher, 87, 94–104; prophet's
    wife, 89, 248; religious tourism, 268;
    women, 47, 111, 132, 148, 208; work, 27,
    90–92
akhlak. See moral values
Al-Afghani, Jamal al-Din, 51
Al-Banna, Hasan, 51
Al-Fawwaz, Zaynab, 264, 265
Alfian (author), 59
Al-Ghazali, 197
Al-Hibri, Aziza, 9, 10
Ali, Kecia, 9, 10
Al-Jabiri, Muhammad Abid, 238

Al-Nawawi, Shaykh, 191, 197, 228, 229
Al-Shatibi, Abu Ishaq, 192
An-Na'im, Abdullahi Ahmed, 192, 238
Annisa, Hindun, 247
Arab, 21, 36, 39, 42, 175, 262
Arabic, 30; as language, 5, 36, 56, 58, 64, 67,
    68, 89, 96, 108, 116, 133, 134, 140, 236, 245,
    260; in *pesantren,* 123, 168, 171, 174, 181, 242
arisan (savings and loan club), 96
Arkoun, Muhammad, 238
Armstrong, Karen, 60
Asia Foundation, 145
Assegaf, Ciciek Farha, 35
Aswaja (Ahl al-Sunnah wa al-Jama'ah;
    People of the Tradition and Commu-
    nity), 168, 210
Asy'ari, Hasyim, 74, 77, 173, 174, 201, 203,
    222, 223
authority, 18, 147, 198, 201, 261; men over
    women, 7, 109, 116, 158, 262; religious, 4, 5,
    9, 11, 12, 21, 41, 61, 62, 89, 166, 168, 190, 202,
    229, 235, 264; women's, 97, 167, 208

Badawi, Muhammad Ibu, 216, 218
Baidlowi, Aisyah Hamid, 203, 222
Baried, Baroroh, 72, 92, 107, 115, 119, 125, 138,
    272n54
Barlas, Asma, 9, 10
Barton, Greg, 59
batik: production, sales of, 43, 93, 155, 215
bid'ah (innovations), 65, 66, 102
birth control, 12, 13, 17, 33, 44, 115; 'Aisyiyah

and, 96; Fatayat NU on, 242, 243, 253; Muslimat NU on, 209, 216–18, 225, 235
Borobudur Temple, 183, 266
Bowen, John, 19, 260
BP4 (governmental marriage counseling office), 117, 250
Brenner, Suzanne, 43
Bruinessen, Martin van, 59, 61, 71, 285n16
Budihargo, Umar, 142

Castells, Manuel, 258, 292n55
Centers for Women's Studies. *See* PSW
Chasbullah, Abdul Wahab, 74, 77, 203, 206, 207
child marriage, 14, 31, 33, 203, 239, 244
Chittick, William, 110
Christian/Christianity, 2, 3, 22, 23, 58, 65, 67, 90, 102, 103, 169, 238, 255; women organizations, 13, 14
communist, 219; party, 23, 204, 208, 220; women, 33
Cooke, Miriam, 264

Dachlan, Aisjah, 208, 218
Dachlan, Mohamad, 208
daerah (district), 72, 105; NA and, 146
Dahlan, Ahmad, 65, 67–70, 89, 92, 112, 134, 151, 152, 154, 160 Niyai Ahmad Dahlan dorm, 108
d'ai (missionaries). *See* mission/missionary
dakwah (religious propagation), 57, 65, 67, 146, 153, 155; Muslimat NU, 210–16; NU, 75, 211, 212
dhanni (time and place), 196, 198, 246, 254
Dharma Pertiwi (women's organization), 33
Dharma Wanita (women's organization), 33, 44, 45, 155, 267
Diniyyah Puteri Pesantren. *See pesantren*
divorce, 6, 9, 16, 22, 48, 117, 145, 179, 239, 248, 263; right to, 33, 208, 230, 244, 249–53, 269n2
Djazman, Elyda, 126, 149
dukun (Javanese shaman), 58, 93
the Dutch, 32, 65, 67, 216; colonial government of, 4, 22, 31, 45, 74, 75, 155, 156, 169, 191, 208, 209, 218, 239, 250; language, 23, 134, 135
duty, 51, 52, 140, 148, 175, 193, 197, 199, 217; women and, 7, 27, 35, 56, 150, 151, 154, 175, 186–88, 200, 252; Panca Dharma Wanita ("five duties of women"), 44
Dzuhayatin, Siti Ruhaini, 130, 153, 155–57

economic crisis, 98, 99
education, 5, 29, 32, 33, 47, 48, 56, 60, 80, 110, 127; 'Aisyiyah and, 93, 95, 104–9, 128, 158; Islamic, 132, 145; Muhammadiyah, 65–67, 88; Muslimat NU, 213, 215, 220, 234; NA, 147, 159; NU, 75, 198; in *pesantren*, 168–73; Qur'an and, 3, 30, 52, 143, 240; women and, 31, 150, 174, 195, 201, 203, 208, 227, 229, 233, 242, 248, 250, 253, 268
Effendi, Bakhtiar, 48
Egypt, 9, 16, 22, 39, 40, 51, 55, 246, 253
El-Khalieqy, Abidah, 251, 268
El-Sa'adawi, Nawal, 265
El-Yunusiyah, Rahmah, 173
Engineer, Ali Asghar, 35, 238
Esack, Farid, 238
Ethical Policy (program), 22, 31
extremist groups: Islamic, 1, 53, 125, 128, 132, 160, 210, 238, 258; other groups, 2, 3, 29, 38, 100, 142, 144, 161, 254, 260–62

Fadjar, Malik, 27, 28, 29, 64, 138
family, 28, 29, 33, 44, 92, 102, 114, 133. 143, 150, 184, 229, 230, 232, 233, 261; *keluarga sakinah, see* harmonious family; *keluarga sejahtera* (comfortable family), 115, 116; NA and, 132; nuclear, 37, 114, 121, 222, 227; *keluarga maslaha* (wholesome family) of NU, 187, 225–28
Fatayat NU, 3, 8, 14–16, 74, 166, 184, 186, 187, 199, 206, 220, 236, 237, 241–43, 266
fatwa (legal opionion), 11, 13, 30, 62, 71, 174, 218; women's issues and, 56, 81, 82, 83, 119, 157
Fealy, Greg, 59
Federspiel, Howard, 59
Feillard, Andree, 53, 59, 272n54
female genital mutilation (FGM), 15, 18, 245, 246
feminism, 41; Islamic, 7, 8, 35, 40, 48, 49, 176, 201; western, 37, 152, 192
feminist, 1, 6, 7, 9, 35, 69, 207; Islamic, 15, 37, 129, 167; feminist-activist, 33, 34, 36, 38, 40, 55, 58, 126, 166, 175, 176, 238, 239, 251, 258, 259, 263; western, 7, 35, 40, 264, 265
Fiqh (Islamic jurisprudence), 2, 9, 10, 11, 17, 31, 51, 61, 62, 101, 142, 193, 202, 212, 227, 228, 235; 264; reinterpretation of, 167, 195–201, 245–49, 260, 262; social, 10, 190; women's issues and, 34, 42, 94, 99, 120, 153, 170, 175, 183, 192, 207, 225, 231, 252–54, 263
FK3 (Forum Kajian Kitab Kuning; Forum

for the Research of Yellow Books), 196, 197, 228, 286n57

Ford Foundation, 39, 40, 145, 192, 258

Foucault, Michel, 101, 109, 114, 238

gamelan, 143, 210, 211

Geertz, Clifford, 50, 275n2

gender, 19, 37, 46, 47, 72, 81–83, 108, 112, 129, 198, 202, 204, 228, 244; awareness, 36, 46, 101, 152, 183; discussions/ discourse, 14, 15, 17,18, 31, 33–35, 38, 132, 148, 157, 195, 200, 201, 260, 265; differences in, 20, 41, 43, 78, 167, 245; equality, 8, 16, 39, 40, 42, 51, 55, 79, 158, 250; ideology, 108, 118, 120, 263; issues, 180, 182, 186, 188, 227, 238, 249; roles, 30, 105; segregation, 106, 159, 173, 181; studies, 135, 153, 155, 225

Gerakan Pemuda Ansor (NU branch for young men), 74, 219, 237, 241

Gerwani (movement for communist women), 14, 33, 220, 273n14

globalization, 4, 29, 88, 97, 98, 100, 182, 262, 266; NA, 132. 141, 161

Grameen Bank, 147, 266

Gramsci, Antonio, 114

graves: of *kiai* (leaders of *pesantren*), 62, 170, 171, 240; visits to, 58, 60, 89, 214, 215

guardian. *See mahram; wali*

guidance. *See pembinaan*

Gunung Kidul (area), 243

Habermas, Jurgen, 238

Habibie, Bacaruddin Jusuf, 24

Hadith, 2, 3, 10, 51, 193, 196–98, 232, 253; in Muhammadiyah, 63, 151, 152; in NU, 61, 62, 169, 170, 171, 227, 228; rereading, 9, 142, 246, 247

hafidz (person who has memorized the Qur'an), 165

Hafidz, Wardah, 27, 251

halal (permissible according to Shari'ah law), 99, 218; *halal bi-halal* tours, 138

Hanafi, Hasan, 238

harmonious family (*keluarga sakinah*), 42, 88, 93, 95, 104, 108, 114–24, 129, 226, 229, 266; NA and, 138, 142, 146, 148, 152–60

harmony: Javanese concept of, 58, 59, 70, 75, 122, 124, 200

Hasan, Tolhah, 197

Hassan, Riffat, 9, 10, 35

Hasyim, Nyai Choiriyah, 77, 81, 174, 203, 204, 223

Hasyim, Solichah, Wahid, 174, 203, 234

Hasyim, Wahid, 174, 207, 225, 234

Haz, Hamzah, 207

Hefner, Robert, W., 19, 54

hierarchy: Javanese, 46, 48, 61, 187, 200, 235; organization, 132, 148, 159, 191, 259; religious, 166, 236, 260

Hindu, 41, 185; Hindu-Buddhist, 21, 23, 39

HIV/AIDS, 126, 146, 239, 244, 247, 248, 251

Hizbu-ut Tahrir (radical group), 53

Hobsbawm, Eric, 71

homosexuality, 17, 83, 247, 251, 266, 271n41

honor killings, 15

"housewifezation program," 44, 155

human rights. *See* rights

Husaini, Adian, 238

IAIN (Institut Agama Islam Negeri; Islamic State Institute for Higher Learning), 3, 12, 20, 35, 76, 175, 199, 201, 206, 223, 225, 227, 261, 265, 266

Ibu Chunainah, 216

Ibu Djunaisih, 207

Ibu Fatma, 165, 166, 175–80, 187, 189, 191, 200, 201, 213, 214, 263, 267

Ibu Iskander, 175

Ibu Ismawati, 214, 215, 228, 229

Ibu Ismiyatun, 99, 100

Ibu Istiqoma, 122, 123

Ibu Kholifa, 107

Ibu Maryam, 217

Ibu Muhadi, Alfiyah, 122

Ibu Muhadi, Wardanah, 117, 282n79

Ibu Mulyono, Broto, 122

Ibu Murshida Thahir, 166

Ibu Nur'aini, 146

Ibu Salim, Nibras, 106

Ibu Siti, 166, 167, 175, 183–87, 189, 191, 199–201

Ibu Sulistyowati, 87 (quoted), 105, 145

Ibu Uswatun, 87, 88–92, 94, 97–103, 108, 110, 112, 115, 117–21, 124–26, 131, 250

Ibu Utaryo, 58–59

Ibu Zaini, 234

ICMI (Muslim think tank), 147

ijama' (consensus among Muslim scholars), 62, 245

ijtihad (independent reasoning among reformists): Muhammadiyah, 2, 8, 9, 41, 51, 62, 73, 83; NU and, 3, 61, 196, 197, 245; women and, 101, 153, 265

ikhlas (dedication to God), 266; 'Aisyiyah

and, 109–14, 129; Muhammadiyah, 59, 65, 66, 69, 70, 72, 88; Muslimat NU, 232–35; NA, 135, 142, 148, 150; in *pesantren*, 76, 172, 179, 180, 185, 258
illiteracy, 31, 89
Indonesian Women's Congress (1928), 13, 32
inheritance: Islamic, 16, 22, 53, 54, 144, 195, 225, 252
IPNU (NU branch for male students), 74, 206
IPPNU (NU branch for female students), 74, 206, 219, 236
Iran: religious debates in, 9, 12, 15; revolution in, 52
Islam Baru (radical group)s, 52, 53, 58, 82, 127, 132
Islamic boarding school. *See pesantren*
Islamic law. *See shari'ah*
Islamist, 50, 51, 207
Izzudin, Kiai Edy Musoffa, 245, 246

Jakarta, 34, 35, 48, 52, 54, 58, 74, 98, 100, 106, 126, 127, 133, 148, 174, 176, 203–5, 216, 217, 241, 243, 258, 267; Jatinegara, 212
Jakarta Charter, 23
Japanese occupation, 23, 32, 75, 208
Java, 18–20, 39, 41, 46, 90, 114, 123, 144, 145, 153, 155, 174, 200, 204, 210, 258; East, 176, 177, 183, 205, 206, 215, 216, 239; *pesentren* and, 168, 169, 179
Javanese, 21, 67, 71, 110, 127, 129, 155, 171, 200, 211, 214, 245; beliefs of, 59, 90, 213; context, 111, 198, 234; culture, 20, 27, 36, 38, 41, 43, 46, 65, 69, 70, 118, 161, 182, 186, 211; Islam and, 19, 39, 61, 87, 92; language, 97, 174, 178; Muslims, 50, 88, 185; society, 48, 58, 78, 111, 120, 247; women, 32, 42, 89, 187
jihad (struggle), 54, 256; 'Aisyiyah and, 87, 91, 107; Muslimat NU and, 208
jilbab (full veil), 28, 53, 133; *jilbabisasi* (veiled women), 142–45
Jombang, 173, 206, 218
judges: women as, 43, 46, 80, 109, 117, 201, 204, 225–27
jurisprudence. *See Fiqh*

kajian (study, research), 149–52
Kalyanamitra, 34, 35
Kantor Urusan Agama (KUA). *See* Office for Religious Affairs
Karam, Azza, 40, 55
Kartini, Raden Ajeng, 31, 255

Katjasungkana, Nursyabani, 17
Kauman, 43, 65, 68, 79, 88–90, 93, 98, 124, 127
kawin sirri/nikah sirri (secret marriage), 18, 54, 103, 104, 107, 262
keluarga sakinah. *See* harmonious family
kemuhammadiyaan (facts about Muhammadiyah), 71, 105
"KeNUan" (facts about NU), 71
kerudung (loose scarf), 28, 125, 134
khaul (memorial ceremony), 171, 212, 240, 263
khul' (consensual divorce), 16
kiai (religious leader), 17, 60, 62, 74, 75, 81–83, 165, 188, 191, 193, 198, 199, 201; 207, 208, 221, 225, 227, 233–35, 243, 244, 248, 251, 258, 260, 263, 264; charismatic, 75, 76, 213, 229; and *pesantren*, 167–84, 218; reinterpretations of, 245–49; woman as, 203, 232
Kiai Sholeh, 239
kindergarten: 'Aisyiyah and, 92, 95, 117; Muslimat NU and, 209, 212, 217, 221; in *pesantren*, 75
Kitab Uqud(-ulligain) (text), 167, 191, 193, 195, 197–99, 201, 202, 207, 228, 229, 247
Koalisi Perempuan Indonesia (Indonesian Women's Coalition), 241
kodrat (God-given innate nature), 20, 42, 105, 111, 120, 154, 247, 250, 252
Kowani (Indonesian Women's Congress), 44, 220
the Kraton (sulton's palace), 58, 87–90, 117, 211
Kudus (town), 239, 240
Kuntowijoyo (sociologist), 38

Lakpesdam (Center for NU Documentation, Information, Research and Human Development), 190, 237, 286n56
Lashkar Jihad, 1, 54
Lek Khudhori (character), 252, 253
lesbianism, 17
liberal Islam, 52, 238, 267
Lirboyo: 1999 NU national meeting in, 223, 224
literacy, 6, 33
LKiS (Lembaga Kajian Islam dan Sosial; Institute for Islamic and Social Research), 237, 238, 259, 290n1
LKKNU (NU program for family welfare), 230, 240
LKPSM (Lembaga Kajian dan Pemgembangan Sumberdaya Manusia; Institute for

Research and Development of Human Resources), 237, 240, 259, 290n1

Lombok: 1997 NU national meeting in, 81, 224, 263

Madiun, 209, 223

Madjid, Nurcholish, 19

Magelang (town), 258

magic/magical powers, 169, 180

Magnis-Suseno, Franz, 49, 70

Mahfudh, Kiai Sahal, 10, 188, 190

Mahfudzoh, Umroh, 77, 205–7, 220, 222, 226, 227, 234

mahram, 16, 157, 180

Majlis Mujahidin Indonesia (group), 38

Majlis Tabligh (department), 72

Majlis Ta'lim (religious gatherings), 215–18, 236, 242

Majlis Tarjih (Muhammadiyah), 11, 72, 73, 78, 79, 113, 115, 123, 127, 157, 264; women and, 129, 130, 151, 157

Majlis Ulama Indonesia (group), 188

Malaysia, 15, 16, 35, 39, 100, 142, 209, 220, 226

Mansoer, Haji Mas, 69

Marcoes-Natsir, Lies, 20, 33, 34, 35, 272n54

marriage, 19, 22, 32, 39, 47, 55, 79, 104, 108, 114, 117, 121, 128, 153, 180, 201, 203, 225, 226, 251; contract, 9, 10, 183, 247; Islamic, 167, 175, 192, 197, 231, 256, 257; law, 13, 16, 17, 18, 33, 204, 221, 230, 232, 233, 248, 250, 266; mixed, 102, 103

————, secret. *See kawin sirri/nikah sirri*

————, temporary. *See mut'a*

Mashkuri, Kiai Abd el-Aziz, 227

Mas'udi, Masdar, 191, 195–97, 201, 238

Masud, Muhammad, Khalid, 10

Masyumi party, 56, 74, 75, 209, 241

Mawardi, Mahmudah, 81, 208, 215, 222, 223, 232

mazhab/mazhab (the four legal schools accepted by Sunni Islam), 3, 9, 62, 181, 190, 198, 269n2

Mbah Liem, Kiai, 75, 76

Mbak Ama, 109, 131, 138–40, 143, 144, 146, 150, 151

Mbak Masrucha, 239–41, 254, 267

Mbak Nurdjannah, 145

Mbak Rini, 143

Mecca, 22, 28, 39, 57, 58, 76, 89, 111, 125, 174, 176, 180, 184, 191, 192, 204

Medinah, 89, 192

Melucci, Albert, 15, 259

merit. *See pahala*

Mernissi, Fatima, 35, 238, 265

Messick, Brinkley, 10

Middle East, 8, 22, 29, 30, 51, 55, 83, 89, 92, 106; influences from, 38, 39, 100, 125, 142, 195, 246; ideas/intellectuals, 35, 171, 264

Middle Eastern culture, 27, 42, 49, 78

Mir-Hosseini, Ziba, 1, 9, 12, 120

mission/missionary, 92, 95, 104, 107, 143, 216

Mitra (journal), 244, 249, 251, 255

MMI (youth organization for students), 72

morals/ethical values (*akhlak*), 28, 65, 69, 70, 76, 143, 189, 251, 266; 'Aisyiyah on, 97, 105, 108, 109, 124, 219; Muslimat NU, 212; NA, 137, 139, 150, 151; *pesantren*, 172, 180–83

Mu'allimat School, 24, 68, 88, 90, 95, 105, 107, 108, 139

Mu'amalat Bank, 147

muballighat. See preachers

Muhammad, Hussein, Kiai, 193, 199, 244

Muhammadiyah, 2–6, 9,10, 19, 22, 30, 32, 44, 45, 50, 59, 66, 74, 145, 151, 157, 158, 171, 207, 238, 267; central board (PP), 72; gender roles, 61, 62, 119–21; interpretation of texts, 57, 265; journals, 68, 112; members, 13, 15, 28, 43, 82, 88, 108, 120, 159; ideology, 64, 65–72, 114, 115, 121, 136; organization, 72–74, 81, 110, 127, 145, 147; schools, 96, 106, 135, 137–39; spirit, 96, 100, 105; values, 140; women and, 7, 8, 14, 19, 20, 34, 48, 54, 56, 78–81, 132, 153, 210, 261, 262

Mulia, Siti Musdah, 16, 250, 261, 266

Munir, Lily Zakiyah, 203, 224, 267, 272n54

Murata, Sachiko, 110

musholla (prayer house for women), 68, 79, 91

Muslimat NU, 3, 8, 14–16, 30, 36, 45–47, 74, 77, 167, 177, 241, 250, 254, 266; activism, 12, 166, 203–5; clinics and hospitals, 225; *dakwah*, 210–15; family, 225–28; history, 207–10; polygyny, 229–33; politics, 204, 218–22; preaching, 215–18; women's position in, 222–25

Muslim Brotherhood, 52, 56, 79, 80, 114, 126

Mustofa, Bisri, 191

mut'ah (temporary marriage), 18, 54, 103, 104, 226, 262

Muzadi, Kiai Hajji Hasyim, 50, 82

mysticism: Islamic (Tasawwuf, Sufism), 50, 51, 52, 60, 65, 127, 128, 212, 235; Javanese, 42; in *pesantren*, 169, 170, 171, 175, 184–87

NA. *See* Nasyiatul 'Aisyiyah

Nabila, Shinto, 256

Nahdlatul Ulama (NU), 2–5, 9, 10, 18, 22, 24, 44, 45, 50, 59, 63, 68, 123, 200, 211, 215, 224, 238, 240, 241, 267; Forum for Religious Matters (Bahs ul-Masa'il), 226, 227; ideology, 74–76, 170; interpretive texts of, 11, 57, 173, 237, 265; leaders of, 109, 166, 189, 190, 216, 239; members of, 13, 63, 103, 184, 207, 213, 217, 223, 259; milieu, 30, 204; national meeting in Lirboyo (1999), 223, 224, national meeting in Lombok (1997), 81, 224, 263; political party, 219; 220; women and, 7, 8, 14, 19, 20, 34, 48, 56, 61, 78, 81–82, 185, 203, 205, 206, 209, 222, 227, 233, 241, 249, 261, 262

Nakamura, Mitsuo, 59

Nasyiatal 'Aisyiyah (NA), 3, 8, 14, 54, 72, 83, 90, 107, 118, 122, 166, 169, 267; central office, 133, 136, 147; future generation, 131–33, 138–42; history, 134–35; leaders, 109, 113, 124, 145–49; members, 127; role of women in, 152–59

New Order (*Orde Baru*), 24

NGO, 3, 20, 35, 36, 123, 126; NA involvement with, 145–47, 153; NU-related, 34, 166, 225, 236, 241

nikah sirri (secret marriage). *See kawin sirri*

Nisa (character), 251–55

Nosseir, Amna, 40

NU. *See* Nahdlatul Ulama

NU Party. *See* Nahdlatul Ulama

nyai (spouse of male scholar of Islam), 81, 108, 167, 168, 176–87, 199–201, 244–49

Nyai Fatimah, 81

obedience: in *pesantren*, 169, 180, 182, 240; in women, 16, 54, 116, 187, 188, 206, 207, 226, 227, 230, 232, 266

Office for Religious Affairs (KUA), 90, 91, 103

Ong, Aihwa, 39

ormas (grassroots organizations), 3, 6, 20, 36, 38, 75, 241

P3M (NGO), 34, 189, 190–94, 200, 227, 237–40, 244

pahala (religious merit), 94, 95, 98, 106, 111, 119, 179

Pancasila (Indonesian state ideology), 23, 37, 75, 124

Paraningsih, Khofifa, 204, 222, 224

parliament, 203–5, 209, 220–22, 227, 233, 257

Peacock, James, 59

Peletz, Michael, 39

pembinaan desa (village guidance, formation), 121, 158

Pemuda Muhammadiyah, 72, 113, 137, 148

permuda/pemudi (male adolescent/female adolescent), 219

pengajian. See Qur'anic study groups; sermon

Personal Status Law (Islamic), 16

pesantren (Islamic boarding school), 2, 5, 8, 9, 17, 20, 22, 27–29, 50, 57, 65, 74–77, 83, 103, 122, 171, 207, 210, 224, 232, 234, 239, 240, 248; Denanyar, 173, 175; Diniyyah Puteri, 68, 173; domestic violence, 223; education, 128, 135, 168–73, 198, 227; Gontor, 253, 285n15; Nyai Ahmad Dahlan, 108; Nyai Ibu Fatma, 176–83; Nyai Ibu Siti, 183–87, 199; reformist, 138, 142, 266; Sobron, 156, 283n10; Tambakberas, 206; transmission of NU Islam, 42, 61, 165–67, 212; women and, 36, 173–75, 222, 232, 266–68; YKF, 244, 245, 251–55, 258, 259

PKB (Partai Kebangkitan Bangsa; National Awakening party), 204, 205, 221, 222

PKK (Pembinaan Kesejahteraan Keluarga; Family Guidance Welfare Program), 44, 45

polygyny, 6, 9, 13, 16, 17, 18, 31, 32, 55, 80, 262, 266; 'Aisyiyah on, 13, 33, 116, 129; NA and, 142, 153, 160; Muslimat NU and, 179, 203, 204, 207, 221, 222, 225, 229–33; YKF and, 240, 248, 251, 252, 254–58

Powers, David S., 10

preachers/preaching, 50, 211. 213, 229, 234; female (*muballighat*), 2, 5, 6, 13, 35, 79, 114, 119–20; 'Aisyiyah and, 45, 94–104; missionary, 5; Muslimat NU, 206, 207, 220. 223; NA, 146, 149–52, 157; NU, 168, 249; *penantren*, 185, 189

preschool: 'Aisyiyah and, 95, 104–7

priyayi (Javanese intellectual class of officials), 42, 155

Prophet Muhammed, 2, 51, 76, 77, 100, 102, 153, 187, 196, 199, 214, 255; praise, 211, 212, 216; role model, 118, 120, 122, 169, 177

prostitute, 17

prostitution, 32, 96, 125, 244, 248, 250, 251, 262

Pro-Women Alliance, 255

PSW (Pusat Studi Wanita; Women's Studies

Center), 12, 34, 35, 148; Muslimat NU and, 203, 224, 226, 267
Putri Mardika (Independent Women Association), 32

qath'i (fundamental values), 196, 198, 246, 254
Qodir, Zuli, 56
qoryah thoyyibah (the good village), 88, 121–24, 155, 156
Qur'an(ic), 227, 230, 238, exegesis, 57; interpretations, 8, 61, 65, 150, 178, 200, 247; memorization, 177, 178; reciting/recital; 68, 76, 88, 133, 171, 174, 175,185, 201, 211, 212, 216, 236; study groups, 67, 91, 123, 143, 196, 215, 217; studies, 116, 142, 149, 170, 179, 184, 185, 231; teachings/injunctions, 60, 79, 156, 166, 240, 249, 252, 253, 254, 256; verses, 186, 193
Qutb, Sayyid, 56

radio show, 249, 254, 266
Rahima (activist group), 35, 250, 259
Rais, Amien, 19, 45, 56, 74, 113, 127, 154
Ramadan (fasting month), 64, 89, 93, 98, 137, 138, 214, 216, 240
ranting, 72, 96, 117, 149, 216
rape, marital, 17, 263
reformist, 2, 3, 9, 51, 59, 62, 63, 76–78, 81, 102, 160, 210, 213; Islam and, 8, 54, 70, 71, 88, 114, 132, 139, 150, 161; interpretation method, 9, 11, 52, 65, 119; model, 108, 124, 125, 142, 210; movement, 22, 83, 128, 219; teaching, 69, 100, 156
reinterpretation: *pesantren* and, 175, 181, 182, 189, 190; religious texts for, 9, 40, 151, 153, 195–200, 225, 228–33, 262, 264; YKF and, 245–50
Rendra, W. S., 47
renewalist, 51
Rida, Rashid, 9
Rifa'i, Afif, 230, 231
Rifka Annisa (activist group), 34, 153, 186, 250
rights: human, 3, 36, 37, 48, 120, 152, 154, 159, 160, 186, 192, 231, 238, 243; men's, 182, 193, 233, 247; women's, 8, 18, 31, 35, 102, 103, 119, 126, 150, 152, 191, 195, 200, 201, 203, 208, 222, 254, 260, 263; women's reproductive, 6, 17, 34, 114, 127, 146, 158, 190, 226, 236, 239, 242, 244, 248, 251, 265
ritual: indigenous/Javanese, 29, 60, 64, 93.

97, 144, 123, 127, 199, 213, 214; for the dead, 215; Muslim, 59, 60, 63, 75, 93, 128, 137, 139, 148, 151, 169, 172, 173, 188, 210; women's, 152, 211
RMI (youth organization for young males), 72

sabar (patience): 'Aisyiyah and, 98; in *pesantren*, 180
Sadli, Saparina, 35
saint. *See wali*
salafiyya pesantren (conservative Islamic boarding school), 171, 176
Samsudin, 253, 254
santri (students at *pesantren*), 50, 51, 62, 65, 168, 170–72, 195, 240; female, 173–87, 190, 199, 202
Sarikat Islam, 32, 74
Saudi Arabia, 16, 53, 142, 226, 262
secularization, 97, 100
sekaten (confession of faith), 211
sermon (*pengajian*), 5, 29, 67, 87, 211; and 'Aisyiyah, 96–104, 108, 143; NA, 132, 149; NU, 75, 183, 198, 257
Setiawati, Terias, 49, 124, 131–38, 147, 149, 150, 152, 159
sexuality, 1, 117, 225, 244, 245
Shafi'ite (*madhhab*), 3, 61, 104; Fiqh, 62, 198; menstruation and, 181
Shahidian, Hammed, 15
Sha'rawi, Huda, 265
shari'ah (Islamic law), 2, 3, 8, 22, 31, 38, 50, 52, 53, 218, 223, 246, 248, 249; adoption, 35, 55, 56, 124, 241, 262; interpretation, 168, 260; women's position in, 34, 197, 225, 226, 233, 250, 252, 254, 266
Sharia'ati, 120
Shihab, Quraish, 197
Shi'ism, 3
Shi'ite (Islam), 18, 54
shirk (polytheism), 94
Sholeh, Ibu Noer Cholida Badrus, 232, 233
sholehah. See virtuous
Sisters in Islam, 35
Siswa Praja, 134
Siti Moendjiah, 13, 32
Sjachruni, Asmah, 30, 46, 203, 204, 208, 210–12, 217, 220–23, 264
slametan (meal of reconciliation), 58, 60, 63, 70, 185, 213–15
slave/slavery, 10, 119, 196, 197, 247
Smith-Hefner, Nancy, 103

Sofyan, Kiai Muhyiddin, 199
Solo, 206, 222
Soroush (reformist thinker), 120
Stivens, Maila, 101, 132
Stowasser, Barbara, 60
Suara 'Aisyiyah, 73, 78, 79, 91, 93, 119, 126, 265
Suara Muhammadiyah, 73
Sufism. *See* mysticism
Suharto, President, 1, 14, 23, 24, 30, 53, 128, 142, 207, 235; daughter Tutut, 224; government, 29, 32, 43, 45, 52, 155, 160, 259; post-Suharto, 17, 74, 113, 204, 267; regime, 20, 27, 38, 44, 47, 48, 75, 78, 87, 95, 98, 151, 202, 221, 239, 254, 256, 258, 261, 262
Sukarno, 23
Sukarnoputri, Megawati, 24, 43, 82, 207
Sultan Agung, 211
Sumatra, 19, 21, 22, 68, 89, 173, 213, 265
Sumpah Pemuda, 22
Sunan Kalijaga, 21, 185, 214
Sunnah: Prophet, 61
Sunni (Islam), 3, 18, 55
Surabaya, 110, 241
Suratno, Chamama, 1, 43, 126
Suryakusuma, Julia, 44
Syamsuri, Bisri, 173, 174, 201
Syir'ah (journal), 103, 259
Syuriah (NU), 11, 77, 82, 188, 204, 218, 223

Tahlil(an), 63, 211, 212
taman kanak-kanak. See kindergarten
Tanfidziah (NU), 77, 206, 218, 223, 224
Taqlid, 61, 62, 66
taraweh prayers, 64, 137
tasawwuf. See mysticism
tauhid/tawhid ("Oneness of God"), 66, 67, 110, 137, 139; NU, 170; social, 154
Thahir, Mursyidah, 81, 223
Tiga Serangkai, 241
tradition. *See* Hadith
traditionalist, 51, 59, 83, 102, 127, 128, 171, 181, 204, 210; in Islam, 2, 3, 8, 10, 54, 68, 74, 76, 125, 165, 166, 168, 171, 201, 236, 238, 260; scholars, 60, 69, 71

Uhud, battle of, 231
Ulama, 50, 60, 62, 74, 77, 81–82, 168, 169; female, 108, 191, 223
Ulfah, Maria, 174
Umar, Nasaruddin, 244
UNICEF, 235, 242

United Nations, 217, 221, 239
unity: of being, 59, Muhammadiyah, 70, 71

values, 193; among *pesantren* women, 187–89; community, 10, 16, 17, 71, 141; Muhammadiyah, 109, 140, 142; religious, 132, 190
veil, 9, 13, 54, 107, 137, 195, 220, 254
violence: domestic/against women, 17, 36, 160, 185, 186, 223, 224, 231, 239, 242, 244, 247, 254, 263
virtue(s), 69, 70, 80, 101, 109
virtuous: Muslim woman as, 45, 69, 70, 92, 94, 167, 181, 194, 22–31, 266
vision (and mission): Muhammadiyah, 71, 72, 73, 91, 105, 108, 147, 152; NU, 76, 77, 81, 204, 259

Wadud, Amina, 9, 10
Wafira, Nyai Hibatun, 258
Wahid, Abdurrahman, 10, 19, 24, 45, 74, 75, 165, 167, 172, 174, 203–5, 219, 222, 231–33; reinterpretation texts, 189, 192, 239, 264
Wahid, Sinta Nuriyah Abdurrahman, 37, 196, 203, 219, 231–33
wali: as guardian, 18, 54, 105, 178; *wali songgo* (nine saints), 21, 176, 210, 211
Wali Yulloh Simbah, 185, 186
Wardoyo, Puspo, 254–58, 266
Wheeler, Brannon, 9
White, Sally, Jane, 13, 94
Wieringa, Saskia, 270n29, 273n. 14
wilayah (province), 72, 217; NA, 146
Women's Study Center. *See* PSW

Yanggo, Huzaemah, 81, 223
Yasanti, 145, 146
Yati, Dr., 57–58
yellow books, 170, 182, 195
Yogyakarta area, 19, 34, 35, 38, 58, 68, 72, 211; 'Aisyiyah in, 88, 108, 119, 123, 126, 127; Muslimat NU, 205, 210, 217, 234; NA, 133, 136, 142, 146, 160; YKF, 237, 239, 240, 255
Yudhoyono, Susilo, Bambang (president), 24
YKF (Yayasan Kesejahteraan Fatayat; Fatayat Welfare Foundation), 20, 37, 200, 237, 239–43; reinterpretation of *Fiqh*, 245–51, 254–60

zina (fornication), 18, 37, 55, 103, 106, 125, 126, 231, 233, 251, 256, 257, 262

PIETERNELLA VAN DOORN-HARDER is an associate professor of Islam and world religions at Valparaiso University. She is the author of *Contemporary Coptic Nuns*, editor of *Lima Titik Temu*, and coeditor of *Between Desert and City: The Coptic Orthodox Church Today*. She has published articles in Dutch, English, French, and Indonesian, and contributed to the *Encyclopedia of Islam* and the *Encyclopedia of Islam and the Qur'an*.

The University of Illinois Press
is a founding member of the
Association of American University Presses.

Composed in 10.5/13 Adobe Minion
by Jim Proefrock
at the University of Illinois Press
Manufactured by Thomson-Shore, Inc.

University of Illinois Press
1325 South Oak Street
Champaign, IL 61820-6903
www.press.uillinois.edu